# Victory at Sea

## Tales of His Majesty's Coastal Forces

Hal Lawrence

**Canadian Cataloguing in Publication Data**

Lawrence, Hal, 1920–
    Victory at sea; tales of His Majesty's coastal forces

Bibliography: p.
Includes index.
ISBN 0-7710-4727-4

1. World War, 1939-1945 – Naval operations, Canadian. 2. World War, 1939-1945 – Personal narratives, Canadian. 3. World War, 1939-1945 – Biography. 4. Canada. Royal Canadian Navy – History – World War, 1939-1945. I. Title.

D779.C2L39 1989        940.54'5971        C89-094205-6

Printed and bound in Canada

McClelland & Stewart Inc.
*The Canadian Publishers*
481 University Avenue
Toronto, Ontario
M5G 2E9

# Contents

# Foreword

I am grateful to my old friend Hal Lawrence for the invitation to write the foreword to his latest book because my links with and admiration for the Royal Canadian Navy stretch back many years. In August, 1938, a schoolboy on an expedition to Newfoundland, I saw my first Canadian warship, a smart destroyer at anchor in the harbour of St. John's, HMCS *Restigouche* perhaps? I studied her with more than passing interest because I had it in my mind to join the Royal Navy. Within months I was a cadet in HMS *Frobisher*, a training ship based at Portsmouth.

In those days before the war, the Commonwealth navies were too small to justify their own officer training establishments, and young men came from Australia, Canada, India, and New Zealand to join with the cadets of the Royal Navy to learn the first rudiments of their profession. Here were made friendships that have lasted a lifetime, although in our case our training was cut short. In August, 1939, we were sent off to join ships of the fleet and were soon to be at war.

Serving in the battleship *Valiant* I was in Halifax early in 1940 – "26th January 1940" inside a favourite volume of Masefield's *Salt Water Ballads* recalls a shopping run ashore and fixes the date exactly. We came to join the escort of the first large troop convoy, which included some fine Canadian Pacific liners. *Valiant* was one of the earliest ships to be fitted with air warning radar and the expert in charge of this technical miracle was a Canadian, Lieutenant Apps. He and many others like him, scientists trained in Canadian universities, were soon to be found throughout the fleet. Later, when I had graduated to the tribal class destroyer HMS *Ashanti*, a Canadian boffin dressed in the uniform of a sub-lieutenant, RCNVR, installed and operated a high-frequency direction finding set which gave us new and unforeseen opportunities to seek out the enemy.

It was while in *Ashanti* that I enjoyed the closest association with the RCN. By 1943 Canadian warships were ubiquitous. Part of the escort of a convoy returning from North Russia toward the end of that year, *Huron* and ourselves were detached to the Shetlands to fuel from an oiler at anchor in Sullom Voe. The pumping rate was slow; topping up would take all night. Christmas had been spent at sea in cruel weather and it was spontaneously decided by both ships' companies that this was the opportunity to celebrate the missed festive occasion. For some reason which now escapes me, *Huron* had beer on board, which was generously shared with their mates in the next door ship. You will find in any good dictionary of naval terms a definition: "Chummy Ships (slang) – pairs of ships working together on especially friendly terms, thus to be relied on to assist at times of trial." From that night on *Huron* and *Ashanti* were chummy ships.

A few weeks later four British and four Canadian tribals, *Huron* and *Ashanti* among them, were grouped together to form the Tenth Destroyer Flotilla and detached from the Home Fleet at Scapa Flow to be based at Plymouth. The activities of this fine flotilla are well described in this book, sufficient for me to say that they were an outstanding example of the close, happy, efficient, and successful co-operation between the two navies. For me the strongest recollection of that time is the kind companionship of Lieutenant, now Rear Admiral, Patrick Budge, who I am honoured to call my friend. Pat was the First Lieutenant of *Huron* and my opposite number. He had joined the navy as a boy seaman in 1923, when I was three years old. It had been my good fortune that the concurrent replacement of the Captain of *Ashanti* and my predecessor had elevated me to First Lieutenant at the early age of twenty-two in the interests of continuity. Jimmy Green would have been a very apt description, and it was to Pat that I turned for advice based on the wisdom and experience of a really fine seaman. He saw me through some difficult times and our friendship even survived a collision between our ships in the mêlée of a night action. The bond between the two ships was well known and it was usually arranged that when in harbour we berthed alongside each other. *Huron* had a piano, *Ashanti* had a pianist, and many good evenings were spent round the instrument in *Huron*'s wardroom. When, as the war advanced into Europe, the time came for the Tenth Flotilla to disperse, an hour before *Ashanti* was to sail for refit that piano was carried across the gangway between the ships as a parting gift. Harmony to the end!

Sadly, the young officers of our two navies no longer meet and get to know one another as early as they did. The Royal Canadian Navy now has its own training establishment. I had the pleasure of meeting the graduating class of sub-lieutenants when I visited Esquimalt in 1981. I bored them with my memories of working with the RCN in the war, but I hope they got the message – we share a common heritage and need to keep in touch. Other opportunities to meet do occur: our submarines work closely together, we meet in NATO, and our ships serve together in the Standing Naval Force, Atlantic. On such co-operation our common security depends.

The fifty-fold expansion of the Royal Canadian Navy during the war can only be described as explosive. Contrary to pre-war thinking, which envisaged the Canadian navy as a coast protection force, its ships operated in almost every ocean, but in the vital battle for the control of the Atlantic, where the weather was almost as dangerous an enemy as the U-boat, the Canadian contribution was crucial and decisive. Those many, many thousands of men who fought and won that war understand the importance of the free use of the sea and are the founders of a Canadian maritime tradition. They must pass on their experience to new generations, for with its long coastline, longer still now that ice is no longer an impenetrable barrier, Canada is a maritime nation.

Lower Ufford, Suffolk

Admiral of the Fleet Lord Lewin, KG, GCB, LVO, DSC, RN

# Abbreviations

| | |
|---|---|
| A/A | Anti-Aircraft |
| AB | Able Seaman |
| A/S | Anti-Submarine |
| asdic | Underwater sound-ranging device (acronym for Allied Submarine Detection & Investigation Committee. Developed by the RN in the 1930s; adopted by the USN and named "sonar.") |
| ATS | Auxiliary Territorial Service (army version of WRNS) |
| BLO | Bombardment Liaison Officer (an RA Officer) |
| CAP | Combat Air Patrol; fighter aircraft over the ships |
| C-in-C | Commander-in-Chief |
| CPO | Chief Petty Officer |
| DEMS | Defensively Equipped Merchant Ship |
| D/F | Direction Finding (from radio signals) |
| DR | Dead (Deduced) Reckoning (navigation position) |
| ERA | Engine Room Artificer |
| FOO | Forward Observation Officer (an RA Officer) |
| GMT | Greenwich Mean Time |
| HF | High Frequency |
| HF/DF | High Frequency Direction Finding ("Huff Duff") |
| HMAS | His Majesty's Australian Ship |
| HMCS | His Majesty's Canadian Ship |
| HMS | His Majesty's Ship (British Navy) |
| HMNZS | His Majesty's New Zealand Ship |
| IFF | Identification Friend or Foe |
| LS | Leading Seaman |
| NOIC | Naval Officer in Charge |
| NSHQ | Naval Service Headquarters |
| PO | Petty Officer |
| RA | Royal Artillery |
| RAF | Royal Air Force |
| RCAF | Royal Canadian Air Force |
| RCN | Royal Canadian Navy (Permanent navy) |
| RCNVR | Royal Canadian Naval Volunteer Reserve ("Wavy Navy." Yachtsmen and others recruited "off the beach," i.e., little sea training.) |
| RCNR | Royal Canadian Naval Reserve (professional seamen recruited from the merchant service) |
| RM | Royal Marine |
| RN | Royal (British) Navy (RNR and RNVR; see above) |
| r/t | radio telephone (voice) |
| SO | Senior Officer |
| sonar | See asdic |
| USS | United States Ship |
| VHF | Very High Frequency |
| WRCNS | Women's Royal Canadian Naval Service ("Wrens") |
| WRNS | Women's Royal Naval Service ("Wrens") |
| w/t | wireless telegraphy (key) |

# Acknowledgements

I must acknowledge the help I received in 1978 from my first editor, Jan Walter, then working with Doug Gibson at Macmillan of Canada. She analysed my manuscript with precision, tact, and a sympathy for inchoate thoughts I was trying to give form to, so much so that she became part of the creative process. The book that came out of her hands was better than the manuscript that went in; it is ten years since *A Bloody War* came out, and, largely due to her, it won the Best Non-Fiction Award of the Canadian Authors Association in 1979 and in 1980 an award from the Foundation for the Advancement of Canadian Letters in conjunction with the Periodical Distributors of Canada; it is still selling in hardcover and soft in Canada and the United States.

My wife, Alma, typed that book through six drafts; after draft number three she started making suggestions as to the propriety of certain passages, pointing out clumsy sentences that could be better presented, and more. This advice increased when in 1985 I did *Tales of the North Atlantic*. In this 1989 book she has been more active than ever in its formation, so much so that she gets the same laurels as Jan. In Alma I got a bargain. I married a sweetheart, got a good wife and mother as well, and now a researcher, a substantive-editor/copy-editor/computer-operator – and sweetheart still.

Commander Alec Douglas, CD, Ph.D., Royal Canadian Navy (retired) is the Historian of the Armed Forces of Canada. I could not have done this book without his support and that of others in the Directorate of History: Elsie Roberts, Ed Ramsey, Dr. Norman Hillmer. This applies also to Vice-Admiral Nigel Brodeur and Anne, and Rear-Admiral Bob Yanow and Val. These last nine years I have derived much from the nourishing friendships of three colleagues – and authors of many books – at the University of Victoria: Dr. John Jackson, a reserve sailor and now a vice-president of the university; Dr. Michael Hadley, a reserve sailor now teaching German language and literature; and Dr. Reg Roy, a professor of military history and strategic studies. Reg has an advantage which is now disappearing with the passing years: he was a professional soldier who fought the battles he writes of as a professional historian.

No writer works in a vacuum; rather, he creates inside an existing corpus, and so I owe an immeasurable debt to writers shown in the Bibliography, in particular, Tony Law, Mack Lynch, and Jim Lamb.

Jerene Lane is a cartographer on the staff of the Naval Hydrographer, and, as you can readily discern from her charts, is a true professional; I am grateful for her patience and diligence as much as for her professional skill. Craig W. Finn and Norman J. Wilson of the Tandy Computer Centre have kept me operational through two books now. Their skill is comparable to that of Jerene and their patience to that of Job.

I thank Ginny Sumodi, Eleanor McEachren, Karen O'Reilly, and Fred Kerner for helping me preserve free time to write while they did tasks that were properly mine.

The inspiration of this book is the work done by the men and women of coastal forces. I thank for their help and patience the twenty-four I have interviewed. They have taught me something of humility, never my strong suit. I always rather fancied myself as something of a salt horse and a warrior. They saw more action in a month than I saw in the whole war.

# Dedication

This book is dedicated to all those in Canada who learned – in our navy, army, and air force – the basic tenets of good citizenship: that submission to lawful authority is essential, that self-discipline is the highest form of freedom, and that you sometimes have to fight to keep that which you have and which you hold to be true and good.

In particular it is dedicated to those men whose yarns are told here. When talking to them I find myself in awe of what they have done. I find myself looking at them with some incredulity because, after the gales and the fog that put them at hazard, the dangers of night fighting at close quarters in a mêlée, the thousands of rounds of smaller shells – the 20mm and the 40mm and the 88mm – and the fewer rounds of the larger 6-inch and 8-inch that had been fired at them, I am amazed they are alive and that I am actually talking to them. And the mines they missed and the torpedoes that missed them and the bombs . . .

# Prologue

## A Good War

*The world is passing through troubled times. The young people of today think of nothing but themselves. They have no reverence for parents or old people. They are impatient of all restraint. They talk as if they alone knew anything, and what passes with us as wisdom is foolishness to them. As for girls, they are forward, immodest, and unwomanly in speech, behaviour, and dress . . .*

*– Peter the Hermit, d. 1151*

Only ignorance of historical fact allows people to assert that moral standards have declined. I'm sure that in the late 1930s my father and the fathers of others of my generation must have been thinking along the lines of Peter the Hermit, when, just emerging from the grinding poverty of the Great Depression, we youngsters seemed to think that making the rugger team and getting a date with this girl or that girl (it varied monthly) was the summit of our ambition; that and establishing new records for the number of live goldfish swallowed, how many we could crowd into a telephone booth, and chanting the words of the latest song at the head of the hit parade:

> Marzy doats an dozy doats and liddle lamsze divy
> A kiddle eetivy two, wouldn't you?

When Hitler invaded Poland in August, 1939, one of his premises must have been that the youth of the British Isles would not fight. Well, if they were acting in the United Kingdom as we were in Canada, then there was reason to form such a premise. But the youth of all the countries in the British Empire flocked to the colours, as did the older

men, those in their thirties, their forties, and those who had served in
the Great War, 1914 to 1918, the "War To End Wars." Why was there
this willingness to take up arms?

The standard answer is we did it to preserve democracy. Perhaps
some did; most I know, however, didn't give such political abstractions
a thought. Or we did it to protect our country. Yet Canada had not been
invaded since the Americans were thrown back in 1814, and that was
a minor skirmish in the history of invasions. To protect our wives and
children, then? Ninety-nine per cent of the men I write about in this
book had neither wives nor children and intended to keep it that way.
War produces, among other things, propaganda in exceedingly bad
taste, which perhaps reached its peak when the United States entered
the war two years later. Then men joined to protect "the Amurrican
Way of Life and Mom's Apple Pie." Remember?

Men joined for several reasons and always a combination of them.
Some joined to *get away* from their wives and children and a dreary
clerk's job where life was uniformly a monotonous round of mortgage
payments, snotty noses, and smelly diapers. Some were still out of work,
and $45 a month plus room and board was freedom. But most joined
because everybody else was joining. It was a great adventure, Kipling's
"the Great Game." It was infinitely better than sitting in a classroom or
an office. It was glamorous: we would wear the uniform of an elite
corps; we would see distant parts of the world, meet foreign peoples;
we would be fighting men! We had heard the stories our fathers and
uncles told and old sweats always talk of the good times, the adventures,
the fun. (The knowledge of the monotony, the misery, the pain, the
maiming, and the death came later; and now, we, too, in our turn forty
years later, talk of the adventure and the fun.) When you are young you
feel immortal. You know some will be killed. Of course. But not you.
You can see that your friends *might*, but not you. This is one of the
blessings God gives fighting men; the main emotion of men I have seen
die is one of surprise.

So most men volunteer for a war to seek adventure – that and the
certainty that the cause is just. That the enemy is equally certain that *his*
cause is just is merely a point for piddling philosophers who theorize.
Normal Canadian boys could hate the enemy with intensity and, at the
same time, respect him for his qualities as a fighting man doing his duty
as he sees it – and doing it well, doing it so well, in fact, that he has
caused a wrenching in our bowels many a time. An adventurous youth,
we had.

Is there such a thing as a *good* war? We in the Royal Canadian Navy think so, as do those in the Royal Navy and the Royal Australian and the Royal New Zealand and the Royal Indian . . . We had a hammock or a bunk to sleep in; hot food, usually; the man directing the battle was, if not onboard, at least within a mile and not in a headquarters behind the lines – he *led* us, he didn't merely direct. We had fewer maimed than the pongos, and if our small ship was hit and we were hurt we usually sank, drowned – a "clean" death – and as a consequence we were not sweating out the soldier's prayer going into a battle, "Not in the gut, please Lord."

That war is a ridiculous waste of money and is immoral and repugnant is not the point here. Wars are a continuation of politics by other means. Wars are started for unsavoury causes by unscrupulous men for selfish reasons. Patriotism can be a cruel delusion. Pain wracks us and the innocent are not spared. We shudder at the thought of the millions who were torn apart in battle, who died in the gas ovens . . . and the children in cellars during an air raid when the ceiling collapsed.

But there is something admirable about the individual doing his duty as he sees it without thought of his personal safety, about putting the safety of the ship and the welfare of shipmates before his own. There is more.

In the 1960s Rear-Admiral William M. Landymore, OBE, CD, Royal Canadian Navy, was asked to attend a reunion of Korean War veterans. In 1952 he had commanded HMCS *Iroquois* on one of her tours of duty in Korea. The mayor of Ottawa was also invited but refused on the grounds that she would not participate in a function that glorified war.

Quite right! Who would? It is un-Canadian. No sane woman or man would glorify war – particularly a woman who has had a loved one killed or wounded; particularly a man who had seen the shooting from the receiving end. And yet . . . And yet . . . Is there *nothing* good that can be said about war?

Yes, there is.

In 1986, the Admiral, who now lives on his farm at the head of Chezzetcook in Halifax County, Nova Scotia, visited Victoria, British Columbia, to open a naval hospital named after Surgeon Rear-Admiral Blair McClean. A deceased shipmate of his from his days in HMCS *Fraser* in 1941, McLean had been a surgeon lieutenant then, the ship's doctor. With the public side of Landymore's visit over, about thirty men and women who had served with him during his years in the navy had him to lunch. He told us that story about the reunion of the Korean War sailors in Ottawa and said:

"Do we then glorify war when we remember the exploits of our fighting men? No, not at all. We remember those who did their duty to their country. The House of Commons decided that Canada should fight aggression when North Korea invaded South Korea. Professional sailors do not ask the political why or wherefore. The navy was told to send ships to police the area and fight if need be. Sixty days after being ordered, we had three destroyers patrolling in Korean waters; we had fulfilled our peacetime duty of being prepared for any emergency our civilian masters ordered us to deal with and we sailed 6,000 miles to the scene of the trouble.

"On a July day in Sasebo I was invited to a civic luncheon. *Iroquois* was having a boiler-clean and maintenance period and the hands were getting a few days of badly needed rest and recreation – R&R. On my left was a local lady, a Korean, but by her dress, deportment, and speech obviously used to the international scene. She commented on my being Canadian and asked if I had been to her country before.

" 'No, I regret to say I'd hardly heard of Korea until this war.'

" 'But didn't you serve in the Pacific in the Second World War?'

" 'Yes, in 1945 I was with the British Pacific Fleet; I was the gunnery officer of our cruiser . . . when we bombarded Truk; we were around Sakishima Gunto a while. Later just about seventy miles off the south coast of Japan – not that far from here.'

" 'I suppose you have compulsory military service in your country?'

" 'No, Madam. The Canadian navy has always been a volunteer force.'

" 'And you and your sailors volunteered to come out to Korea and help us?'

" 'Well . . . not exactly. We volunteered to join the navy and we were *told* to come. But my men and I are glad to be here and hope we can help.'

" 'I suppose you've been in the fighting. Have you had any men hurt?'

" 'Yes, we were hit by a shore battery a few months ago and three of my men were killed, several wounded.'

"The lady averted her head and I caught a glimpse of tears in her eyes. There was silence for a few minutes and then she turned to me again and said, 'And your sailors came 6,000 miles to help a country they had never heard of – until they came here?'

"What could I say? I just said, 'Yes, Madam.' ' "

The Admiral looked out the window across the rain-swept harbour, and we who knew him sensed that he was not in that room but back in his ship of thirty years ago.

He then spoke of ancient Korean civilization, of their subjugation for hundreds of years by the Chinese and then by the Japanese, of how the Japanese had even taken away their language, their Korean names, and used them as a virtual under-class in slavery. And he spoke again of the charming Korean woman with tears in her eyes.

"I think she must have sacrificed one of her own sons. But when she thought of a Canadian mother who lost a boy out there, she just couldn't believe that there was *anyone* in the world who would do what we were doing. And when I told her, she was so emotionally conscious of this that her eyes filled with tears and they trickled down her cheeks. I can understand that feeling. Of course, we as sailors wouldn't look at it that way but some women who thought of their children in that light most certainly would. And that's what happened. To me it brought home that our sacrifices were appreciated. This was the kind of thanks that no one would ever *say* to you. But those tears were the thanks that told me that my three sailors who were killed had not died in vain. This is not glorifying war; but the overall concept that gave so many people peace and freedom, well, that is wonderful."

Admiral Landymore concluded, "I suppose we did some good. . . . We kept the South Koreans free to determine their own future. From 1939 to 1945 we had done the same thing for most of the world against the Germans, the Italians, and the Japanese. I suppose we did some good. We believed in what we were fighting for; we put our lives on the line to back up our beliefs. And a lot of our friends lie buried in foreign lands and under distant waters. So no, I don't glorify war. But I do honour those of our generation who did what had to be done to preserve what we have today."

And this book honours the men in the small ships in British coastal waters and in the Mediterranean who fought long and hard to ensure that a war we didn't start came to a successful end. Some of these men were from our coastal towns but most came from inland, from the yacht clubs and from sailing the family dinghy at the summer cottage. They graduated to motor torpedo boats and motor gun boats. Some got command as sub-lieutenants at age twenty. An adventurous youth, indeed; and a good war to fight.

As a naval officer for thirty years – and one who followed an interest in the sea through another career as a lecturer at the University of Ottawa and the University of Victoria and yet another as a civil servant in international development – sea warfare has been my abiding interest for over sixty years. The most striking feature of fighting men is devotion to their profession, their ship (regiment, squadron), and their shipmates. And their pride in doing their job well. They neither cause the occasions for war nor declare war; this authority is vested in the civil government. Yet when war is declared, the nation's men-at-arms must fight it. It is not for us to question the justice or the wisdom or the propriety of the government's declaration. But naturally, professional seamen favour preparedness so they *can* do as ordered.

The vital part sea power has played in the development of the nations of the world has been recognized from earliest times. A letter from Cicero to Atticus written in 49 B.C. is often cited as an example. But Cicero quoted Themistocles who, nearly four hundred years before, had said, "Who so can hold the sea has command of the situation." The particularity of naval warfare is that it is directed to the seizure of property rather than the mastery of people (which is the job of the army). Maritime war is secondary to that on land. Man lives off the land's bounty, calls this place home, the resting place of his folkways, mores, history, and visions of the future. War at sea has the objective of controlling sea-borne commerce. Attacks on property are indirect ways of striking at the national life of the enemy. Battles won by large fleets are not profitable unless they alter the conditions of the moving of men and materials in favour of the victor.

The best example I know is what the Royal Navy refers to as "The Battle of the Glorious First of June." This was the first naval encounter of the French Revolutionary Wars (1792 to 1799) and was fought in 1794. The Royal Navy was carrying out a traditional role by blockading the ports of France. A convoy of grain was on the way to France from America, probably due to the influence of America's representative in Paris, Benjamin Franklin. Admiral Villaret de Joyeuse commanded the French fleet covering the convoy of merchant ships carrying grain. Admiral Lord Howe intercepted this covering force and scored a resounding victory, taking six prizes and sinking a French ship of the line without the loss of a single ship. A glorious victory? Not at all. A tactical victory, certainly, but a strategic defeat. After four days' fighting it was still possible to locate and destroy the convoy as well. But Admiral Howe was age sixty-eight and was exhausted. The grain convoy got through to starving France.

There are parallels between the naval battles of the French Revolution and the battles of the motor torpedo boats (MTBs) and motor gun boats (MGBs) of the 1940s in the English Channel, the Straits of Dover, and the North Sea. The object of the German E-boats was the destruction of our coastal convoys, who bore in their holds the sinews of war imported into Britain from Canada, the U.S.A., and the rest of the world. The task of our coastal craft was (1) to protect our convoy and (2) to attack enemy convoys bringing iron ore, tungsten, and other war materials from occupied Norway, Denmark, Holland, and France to German garrisons. The German E-boats consistently refused to do battle with our MTBS, and rightly so, for their job was to sink our merchant ships. Yet, how does one then explain the consistency with which our coastal craft sought out the enemy warships? (This was only done when no merchant-ship targets were available.)

There is a fascinating feature to notice when comparing Allied and Axis naval traditions, that is, the willingness and even eagerness of the Royal Navies to do battle, every time, no matter what the cost. The only way to explain it is to say that it has always been so. This eagerness to do battle is due in no small measure to what I call "the habit of success." It really didn't matter if, over those centuries, Britannia ruled the waves or not. The British were sure that this was so. And it became so. The habit of success certainly was part of this attitude, as was the fact that we did not particularly try to build better or larger ships than a putative opponent, we just built more, and so, I suppose, could afford to lose more. (When I was a sub-lieutenant in two corvettes, once in 1941 in *Moose Jaw* and again in 1942 in *Oakville*, I found distressing my captains' pugnacity to make the U-boats' demise more certain than gunfire and depth-charging had been able to guarantee. We rammed them without a thought, it would seem, to the notion that we might sink, too – and in *Oakville* we nearly did.)

In our Canadian coastal craft there were no warriors of sixty-eight. Twenty-eight was considered ancient. Tom Fuller of Ottawa was thirty-two when he was Senior Officer of an MGB flotilla and he was known as "Gramps." But all those who fought those battles in Canadian MTBS and MGBS and motor launches (MLS) and who read this narrative will remember how tired they were after four days of fighting – they would understand and feel sympathy for poor old Admiral Howe.

So it is really only a tactical victory when we sink an enemy warship; it is a strategic victory when we sink one of his merchant ships. You will notice this time and again in the small-ship actions, sometimes to the point of absurdity when a flotilla of our MGBS is crossing to attack a convoy off the Dutch coast and it passes, without a gun being fired, a flotilla of E-boats on their way to attack one of our convoys. Strategic victories are better than tactical, which brings us to the Battle of Jutland in May, 1916, between the main German and British fleets.

The battle cruisers and cruisers were commanded by Vice-Admiral Sir David Beatty and Vice-Admiral Franz von Hipper, respectively; the battleships and their attendant cruisers and destroyers by Admiral Sir John Jellico and Admiral Reinhard Scheer. The series of ballzups by the professional officers of the world's largest navies far exceeded the ballzups you will read of in the stories of the Canadian naval reserves of World War Two; the result was that Jellico lost his chance to bring the German main fleet into a decisive action. But the Brits were going for the Germans all out, at any cost. The Germans' main aim was to return to harbour. In this battle we lost more ships than did the Germans. *But we could afford the losses.* The German fleet remained in harbour the rest of the war. This encounter can be termed a tactical defeat for us, for we lost more ships and could not force the action to its deadliest conclusion. But it was a strategic victory in that we blockaded the enemy ports. Nothing moving on their coastline was secure from our attacks. In November, 1918, Scheer ordered his fleet to sea "to break the block-ade." The crews refused to weigh anchor. So, the Battle of Jutland was a tactical defeat but a major strategic victory.

Some may have wondered how it is that the Royal Navy, historically, has so many glorious victories to her credit. Now you know; she claims both types.

This book is about both tactical and strategic victories at sea during World War Two. Its focus is the Coastal Forces – the small craft, the motor gun boats and the motor torpedo boats – of the Royal Navy and the Royal Canadian Navy and their valiant and ultimately successful efforts to open the seaways for Allied shipping, to close those same seaways against German and Italian transport of men and materials, and to assist in the historic invasions of North Africa, Sicily and Italy, and Normandy. It is a book about the Canadian and British men who overcame fear to fight these small-craft battles in the larger theatre of total war. It is a book of their experiences, their stories – those who lived to tell; those who died.

Finally, one must remember that for every victory there is defeat as well. The Allied Forces won the war, but there were many defeats, millions of deaths, before final victory. And at sea, our small boats faced a brave, formidable, and worthy foe. Indeed, many of the British small-craft captains, who were yachtsmen before the hostilities, knew the German E-boat commanders, also yachtsmen, from international com-petitions in more peaceful times and places. Mutual respect and a chivalric sense of honour imbued their deadly battles, and when a ship was sunk on either side the "enemy" became the "survivor" to be rescued. It was not a good war – no war is. But at sea, for these men, there was a rightness to it, a knowing that duty to one's country was being done – time and again. So it was a *good* war, at least for those who lived to tell.

# 1  Early Patrols

"There are E-boats in your sector attacking convoy NB 121. Sail units of the 6th Flotilla chop-chop."

"Right. I have the convoy on our plot; they're just entering our bailiwick. I'll sail the second division. Hichens has it tonight."

An autumn night in Felixstowe, Suffolk, England; the water flat and black, the air still and silent except for tinny music of the BBC light program coming from one of the looming hulls of three squat silhouettes at an MGB jetty; a low gibbous moon in the southern sky throws long shadows from cranes at the dockside. Outside the harbour a convoy of merchant ships is ghosting along, one in the endless chain carrying war materials from the north of Scotland to the south of England. On this night in 1941 Holland is occupied by the Germans; indeed, since May, 1940, enemy *Schnellboote* (we called them E-boats) have sunk several destroyers and many merchantmen. Tonight would tempt any E-boat flotilla: the North Sea calm ruffled only by light airs, with good visibility. Against a westering moon our convoys will stand out nicely – a night for E-boats to hunt. Those from the Hook of Holland and the Scheldt estuary sailed after sunset; at eleven p.m. they attack. Our convoy escort swings out to intercept and bleats the warning to the Commander-in-Chief of the English Channel and the North Sea area – C-in-C the Nore – Admiral Commanding, Dover. His operations room telephones the warning to Staff Officer Operations (SOO) at HMS *Beehive*.

The alarm sounds; three boats are on immediate notice; captains rush to the operations room for a quick briefing by SOO; an engine coughs into life; pounding feet, slamming hatch covers, first lieutenant barking:

"Let go head and stern lines; let go after spring; hold forrard spring."

The first engine roars to a crescendo, shattering the silence of the village. The second and third destroy all talk unless yelled in your ear. Acrid fumes and blue smoke curl upward. The captains run back, charts and notes in hand, and leap on board.

"Slow ahead starboard."

Three boats surge ahead, sterns angling out.

"Slip. Slow ahead port. Port wheel. Slow ahead starboard."

The boats move into the harbour.

"Midships. You see the harbour entrance, cox'n?"

"Aye, sir."

"Steer for that."

"Steer for the entrance, sir."

In column they steam to the gate vessels. The net swings open. They pass.

"What's the first course to intercept, pilot?"

"North-48-East, sir," replies the navigator.

"Steer that, cox'n."

"North-48-East, sir."

"Revolutions for thirty knots."

Throttles are lifted, the roar of the engines deepens, spray flies from the bow, the fore-foot lifts, and the boats begin to plane. Over the wireless telegraph (w/t) is babble and chatter of attacking E-boats and defending escort.

"Sounds as though there's a lot of them out tonight, pilot."

"Yes, there should be plenty for us."

"How far to go, pilot?"

The navigator replies, "Forty-two miles, sir, sixty-nine minutes."

The moon sinks, mist is forming, the boats are in three-quarter line, each off the starboard quarter of her next ahead. Three white wakes plume astern pointing back to home and going on to battle. The senior officer of the half-flotilla is Lieutenant-Commander Robert Peverell Hichens, RNVR, until recently a country solicitor; he has a few months' more experience than the rest. Hitch leads his boats across the North Sea to the fray a few miles ahead. The hands are at action stations, tactics agreed on, battle plans rehearsed time and again over the past months. The stage is set. In command of the two following boats are RNVR Lieutenants L.G.R. Campbell, known as "Boffin," and G.E. Bailey, known as "George." Both have over a year in coastal forces and before the war were a tea planter and an insurance agent. Now Hitch settles down to a blank state of watchfulness, the least tiring way of passing long hours under way. It is midnight; his mind drifts.

". . . moon still up, sea flat calm. Like this, motor gunboating is sheer joy; station-keeping is easy; boats fly along with a powerful sense of speed . . . very beautiful . . . one of the most lovely sights . . . setting moon showing orange . . . a gun boat unit at speed in moonlight, with white pluming wakes, cascading bow waves, the thin black outline of guns starkly silhouetted, figures of gunners motionless at their positions . . . carved out of black rock, and all against the beautiful setting of a sparkling moon-path on the water . . . between moving billows of mist . . . fog bank ahead . . ."

The smell of rubber burning breaks his reverie. The motor mechanic sticks his head up the hatch, "Will you stop, sir, please; a pendulastic is going." (This fantastic name is for a piece of equipment between the engine and the gearbox – unreliable and temperamental.) Engines cut; a deafening silence descends on the moonlit sea. The dilemma now is that there is a certain chance of action ahead, yet if he goes on it will have to be at reduced speed, and he is needed next night for an important job. It is a difficult decision the kind captains are paid to make.

"There are lots of E-boats ahead. Do you think those damn pendulastics will hang on for eight hours if we don't exceed eighteen knots?"

"I'll keep an eye on them, sir, let you know if trouble gets worse. Probably all right. Let's give it a go."

The peace of the night is rent again as the boats slide off. Hitch's engine-room troubles are not over; George Bailey signals he has an excessive quantity of water in the carburetor and filters of his starboard engine. He can't clear it and will have to return to harbour. He peels off at reduced speed and fades into the mist. Boffin and Hitch continue on North-48-East.

"How far to go now, pilot?"

"Thirty-six miles, sir."

Mist is forming low on the water, a common occurrence in quiet weather. The moon sinks, and from the sound of the radio chatter there are lots of E-boats ahead, probably two groups out tonight, six to a group – plenty of targets. We're the only British unit clear of convoy routes, so anything we see will be enemy and we can fire on sight, and this course should intercept them as they head home. Visibility is getting worse, making it hard to see them over a hundred yards, but it's a good night to hear them.

"How much longer to go, pilot?"

"Fifteen and a half minutes, sir."

All on the bridge peer anxiously.

"Two minutes, sir."

"Let me know at thirty seconds."

The guns swing to a forward bearing; the ammunition-supply hands follow.

"Thirty seconds, sir."

A lamp flashes to Boffin astern; the two boats slow.

"Cut engines."

Silence. The bows sink, the rush of water fades. What a relief after hours of noise! The exquisite absence of noise. Homey sounds, the clink of a cocoa mug, a muffled laugh. It's now two a.m. From the silence of the convoy and escort w/t it would seem the attack is over. The E-boats are returning but won't be here until about four. The MGB crews settle down to a listening vigil. Hitch goes below for a doze. At a quarter to five he is called.

"Distant sound of engines, sir, bearing about west."

At last, the murmur of engines, growing louder, louder. Music to their ears. Have they not flogged these waters for nearly a year without being able to meet E-boats head on, fairly and squarely, see their bows and not only their arse, and that through the smoke made to cover their retreat. Yes, the boats making that noise are approaching, heading home to Holland. Can we intercept and cut them off? If only we had more than eighteen knots. The rumble is increasing.

"The bearing is west-southwest now, sir."

"E-boats all right, moving east; they've moved from west to west-southwest. I'll plot them for a while and get a course and speed. With luck we'll head them off. *Damn* this eighteen knots and damn all pendulastics to hell!"

The North Sea is wide; the moon has set and the night has grown dark and misty. The rumble grows to a full-throated growl. All hands peer into the dark as the growling, thudding mutter grows and grows; but even as close as 200 yards they could pass unseen. Should we edge forward a bit? No, better to stay silent.

"Bearing is south 50 west now, sir; time 0553."

"Then we've heard them now for eight minutes, say twenty-seven knots, four miles; in another six minutes we'll be on the beam of their line of advance."

Captains can't keep from theorizing, yet so much was a matter of estimate, of chance. One last look at the rough plot.

"Start up. Steer south 25 east, cox'n."

But now you can't hear them; where *are* they now? The boats go on a few minutes. He *has* to get another sound bearing; but if he stops to get one they might pass ahead and draw away. He flashes Boffin; the throttles are slammed down; Boffin, caught short by the suddenness of the order, surges up on the beam. Silence, only silence; then the louder rumble of enemy engines to the south'ard. If the bearing is the same as before, then the intercept course is okay. No, it has drawn a little eastward, we are falling astern, slightly; we must alter:

"Start up, steer south 50 east, cox'n."

Seconds go by; then a minute.

"Flashing light to port, at red three oh, sir."

Yes, there it is, a little blue light winking, then the blur of a low hull, a faintly darker shape in the mist. The challenge flashes out; the reply is garbled; then all doubt is removed. There they *are* – five low, white hulls nuzzled together, stopped. A rendezvous? Why? Never mind – there they *are*! Four are off to port, the fifth dead ahead.

"Sparks, send a w/t report giving our position and that we're engaging the enemy."

"Open fire. Hard a-port."

Guns crash out toward an E-boat, now drawing aft to starboard. Boffin's guns are firing, too. The range is fifty yards and hits are steady, a constant red flicker as our shells explode. The E-boat to port is at the same range and now both MGBs are pumping a steady hail of shot into her as well. Neither E-boat replies; they are dead before they know we're there. Hitch and Boffin pass the port E-boat at twenty yards, pouring fire into her.

By now the other three E-boats are wide awake and firing vigorously, some rounds zipping overhead, some tracing small spouts of water across the bow, some hitting. The vivid streams of tracer arch between the British and German boats, and the fourth E-boat is getting good. Hitch's forward gun is smashed and its stand shot from beneath the gunner's feet. The scene is confused – "the fog of battle." Hitch weaves this way and that; Boffin stays faithfully on his stern. The sounds and sights of the mêlée suffuse us – a constant roar of our own and the enemy engines; the spitting of the small, chatter of larger, and thudding of the largest guns; creaming, crisscrossing white wakes; flames from barrels, arcs of amber and green tracer; the red wink of hits. The enemy skims along at thirty knots, we at our more sedate eighteen. The after gun jams, but the fourth E-boat is on fire aft. And then they're scattering! Which to follow? There's one to starboard, same course as ourselves, about sixty yards.

"Open fire, clear that damn after gun, the forrard one is finished. *Must* I fight an E-boat with only a Lewis gun? Firing .303 bullets? Damn *rifle* bullets?"

This E-boat is strangely silent. The Lewis gun opens up; her tracer points out the target to Boffin, who opens up with larger guns. The silent E-boat is stung into activity and chatters back with commendable dexterity and accuracy. Then she peels off, heads for Holland, making smoke, still firing her after gun, which falls silent as she works up to thirty-five knots. She is gone. Nothing is now in sight – time to stop again and listen.

"Stop engines."

Silence is complete and nothing is near; 5:45 a.m., still dark.

"Sparks, crank up your w/t again and tell the Admiral our position and that we've been in contact with five, three damaged."

Sparks jumps to it. As with all other wireless telegraphists, it is his greatest pleasure to send an enemy report like this. While he is sending it all tels in the area must listen; the repeated prefix – ER ER ER: Enemy Report – silences all others and while transmitting it *he* is the star of the airwaves; his chums in other ships will recognize his "hand" on the key.

On the bridge the vigil goes on.

"I think I hear something, sir, over there," pointing.

"Quiet everyone. Do you hear anything, Boffin?"

"Yes, in the southwest, I think."

"Let's go and see. Start up. Steer southwest."

It is not nautical twilight but it now somehow seems less dark, the mist thinning. They steam in for ten, fifteen minutes. Then, following the proper naval procedure, a lookout reports:

"Vessel bearing green four five, sir," followed by the unorthodox but heartfelt, "It's one of them bloody bastards!"

She is lying black and still about 200 yards away; what can this mean? Is she abandoned? Is it a trap? Will she open fire any minute? Slow speed. She is obviously badly beaten up but is she crippled? Boffin appears out of the dark from astern, introduced by a burst of Lewis gunfire. Boffin roars, "Cease fire!" and the cease-fire bell is heard shrilling out. Some bloody-fool gunner too worked up!

"I'm going to send a boarding party over. Stand off a bit so we don't get in each other's crossfire if we have to open up. When we get close put your searchlight on her. If she opens up, plaster her."

So, in a glimmering dawn, they approach.

"Snottie, you speak the lingo. Ask if they surrender."

"Gelben Sie auf? Gelben Sie auf?"

No answer.

"Gelben Sie auf? Do you surrender?"

Silence.

Boffin's light blazes on the E-boat. Nobody appears on deck, and the swastika flag droops from the yard arm. The boarding officer jumps over, and a burst of a 20mm gun breaks the silence. Christ, they *are* there. *No*. That's our own after gun that was jammed; it's now cleared. The silly bugger must have pulled the trigger. The gunfire ceases, and the boarding officer ruefully looks at the line of holes just ahead of him that his own gunner has put there. Then the looting starts – everything that's not fastened down. Yes, the E-boat *is* empty; the crew must have been taken off by another E-boat. Nearly all hands swarm onboard. Their boarding stations ("looting stations") have been detailed from the day they joined the boat. The motor mechanic heads to shut off the sea valves, which will certainly have been opened by the Germans before they abandoned ship. The German-speaking midshipman looks for demolition charges – and finds one, a fuse leading down the ladder. Follow it.

"Where does it go?

"Wait a minute . . . here . . . there's a wooden handle at the bottom, sir"

"Is the fuse lit?"

"If it is, sir, then it's a long fuse. How long have they been gone? Fifteen minutes? Twenty?"

"About."

"Wait, here's the plunger, the detonator; it says, 'Remove handle to fire.' "

"I presume the handle is still in place."

"Yes, of *course!*"

"Then leave the handle in."

"*Naturally*. Do you think I'm a . . . I'm chucking the *whole lot* overboard."

The engine room is flooded with water and diesel oil and it is impossible for the motor mechanic to get at the sea cocks; other compartments are filling, and she rolls sluggishly. "Bring them back alive," Admiralty had said, but perhaps not this one. She is too deep and heavy to take in tow. It would only ruin our engines, and without a power pump we cannot empty her. Still, we'll try and save her. I'll ask that a power pump be sent by motor launch; an ML can get here in time. Meanwhile, let's see what we can get; charts, books, logs, revolvers, ammunition, pictures (one of Hitler). Sparks takes all the w/t equipment he can move; the gunners take all the small guns they can lift; others grab a compass, a searchlight, a long sausage, black bread, sauerkraut, binoculars. The stern is lower. Jot down all the external features of the E-boat we can see; we must give Their Lordships as much as possible.

But it doesn't look as though they're going to get *this* boat. No, she's lower in the water; her smoke-making gear is fizzling and emitting tentative whisps. She is going under.

"Abandon the E-boat. Get back to your own boats."

Her bows lift high, higher, as she slips back, bows pointing to the sky as if in supplication. She is gone. All hands watch, silent. It's a sad thing to see a ship die – her crew have lavished her with as much care as we give this old girl.

"Oh Lord, our boats are so small and Your sea is so large."

The ML bringing the power pump is turned back. It would have been nice to bring in a prize of war but we didn't do too badly. A victory, certainly. And in this case there are no deaths to mar our victory, only four wounded, none seriously.

The two MGBs head for home and make a triumphal entry into harbour. The sun is high and it's nearly time for up-spirits. The swastika flag is flying inferior to the white ensign. As we reach the convoy route we pass the destroyers who had engaged our friends the night before and had listened with rapt interest to our signals. The crews of the destroyers and trawlers cheer as we steam through the gate and up to the base. The word is out: the dockside is crowded with enthusiastic mateys, sailors, Wrens from the maintenance shops, the transport pool, and the offices; white handkerchiefs flutter. The Captain of the base, who is always there to see us off, stands out in front to see us safely in. He looks pleased.

"I've got to go and make a preliminary report, pilot; you start writing the final. I'll check it when I get back. Number One, get tingles *only* on the lower holes; no time for bloody refit, we've got to get out again. And get that sodding gun replaced; and see if you can finish ammunitioning early so the hands can get their heads down for a few hours. The other boats will help with ammunition and stores. We have to sail again at sunset."

## II  In the Beginning . . .

**M**otor torpedo boats and motor gun boats are practically interchangeable; at least at the start of the war they each had both guns and torpedoes. Depending on the tactics they are used as one or the other. The Vosper Company of Portsmouth, England, built what are called the Vospers. They are seventy-three feet long, with two 18-inch torpedo tubes; usually a 20mm was her heaviest gun, and this boat would carry perhaps two 20mm and four .303 automatic guns. Three Packard engines of 4,500 bhp drove her at forty-two knots. These were also called "the Shorts." Because of their small size the ship's company of about eighteen hands slept ashore.

Those built by the British Power Boat Company were shorter – 71' 6", with two torpedo tubes; a 6-pounder gun forward with two 20mm and four machine guns artistically spaced elsewhere; four Packard engines of 4,050 bhp gave a speed of thirty-nine knots; later they got 4,500 bhp and forty knots.

The Electric Boat Company of New York built many PCs (patrol craft) and MTBs of both British and their own design. They were called the ELCOS.

The Fairmile Company built the D-class MTB, which was most frequently used as an MGB, called the "Dog" boat: 115 feet long with a beam of twenty feet; four 18- or 21-inch torpedoes; a 6-pounder gun forward and aft with several 20mm. They had Packard engines and a speed of thirty to thirty-five knots. There was also the Fairmile motor launch – the ML: 112 x 17 $\frac{3}{4}$ x 4 feet, four 20mm and four machine guns, and twelve depth charges. Two Hall-Scott engines of 1120 bhp drove her at eighteen knots. The ship's company would number twenty. In the Fairmiles the crews slept onboard.

The MTB's main task is to sink enemy merchant ships. MGBs do the same thing but guns are not as lethal as torpedoes. They all bristle with .303 machine guns, .5 automatic, 20mm, 40mm, 3-pounder, 6-pounder – anything the captain or the gunnery officer can scrounge or loot. These boats are jammed with weapons and engines and gas tanks, but the early boats had no radar and little in the way of navigation equipment. The navigator relied on dead reckoning (DR). He plotted his course and speed and time in this direction or that, allowed as instinct and sea sense demanded for wind and tide, and, after a confused battle, took an educated guess as to where he had ended up since his last DR position.

Thus it was tempting when escorting a convoy to rely on a merchant ship's more sophisticated equipment and just tag along with her in sight. The trouble is that if the merchant ship on which you are keeping station strays off course, the dawn finds you two alone on an empty sea; or worse, aground. On one occasion an ML was escorting a southbound convoy from Edinburgh to Plymouth and the merchant ship chosen as guide ran ashore on the Goodwin Sands between Ramsgate and Dover. So did the ML.

"What is your estimated position?" the ML Captain asked the merchant-ship Captain.

"The Goodwins. I'm here to pick up sand. What are you here for?"

In 1878 Thornycrofts had built a sixty-foot steam torpedo boat for the Admiralty, and, for Russia during the Russian-Japanese war, a fifty-foot MTB carrying guns and a 14-inch torpedo. In July, 1915, the Admiralty ordered from America fifty motor launches; these were eighty-foot boats with two 250-horsepower engines giving a speed of twenty knots. They were so successful that 500 more were ordered. They attacked U-boats and enemy coastal craft; they escorted our convoys and attacked the enemy's; they swept for mines; and, finally, they earned immortality in the folklore of small craft by the blocking of Zeebrugge and Ostend. At the same time the MLs were arriving Thornycrofts designed a forty-foot motor torpedo boat; twelve were built in the first lot. All these were designated coastal motor boats – CMBs. Successive designs of CMBs were larger, faster, and carried two torpedoes. They, like the protagonists of these yarns, fought in the North Sea, along the Belgium and Dutch coasts, and finally in Russia. In the oral history of the navies of the world and at defence colleges of many countries there is still told the tale of how eight CMBs forced an entry into Kronstadt harbour on the night of

17-18 August 1919 and torpedoed two battleships and one submarine depot ship, thus altering the balance of power in the Baltic.

Small coastal craft are subject to the same immutable laws of power-weight ratios as a battleship. If you want armour you sacrifice speed. And there is no use increasing the power beyond a certain point. For instance, if a destroyer of a certain weight is powered by 40,000 hp and gets a speed of thirty knots, it will not get sixty knots by an increase of power to 80,000 hp. So it was that the CMB of 1917 with two 270-hp engines made good speed of thirty-five knots; yet some modern MTBS with four 1,250-hp engines can only do the same. They are larger, heavier, and more suited to rough seas, but even our fastest could only get about forty knots.

The Germans were ahead of us in producing their *Schnellboote*. Firstly, they were powered by diesel engines and thus were not subject to the fire hazard we constantly worried about because our boats were powered by high-octane gasoline. When you have 5,000 gallons onboard and tracer is buzzing past your ears it is hard to decide if you are fretting about having your head knocked off or blowing up should a gas tank be hit. Secondly, diesel engines and the German power-weight ratio allowed an E-boat to show a clean set of heels to any of our ships in a pursuit. Time and again the E-boats cranked on their maximum speed and steamed safely back to harbour when we were trying to bring them into a gunfight. As the war went on from 1940 to 1941 our coastal mariners were constantly entreated by Admiralty to send in reports on the performance of E-boats; this intelligence was vital, Their Lordships assured us.

Hichens comments on this. "Hitch" was certainly the most intrepid of all up to the time he was killed on 13 April 1943 (by a stray bullet after breaking off an action). He had by then the Distinguished Service Order and bar, the Distinguished Service Cross and two bars, and was three times Mentioned In Despatches. He had captured an E-boat and brought her in. She had a raised foredeck, bridge, four torpedoes (two of them reloads), the inset torpedo tubes, a large compass aft, smoke-making apparatus ... One day he had been discussing tactics in the office of the shore-based staff officer (operations) and was then waiting to see the Commander-in-Chief. He idly flipped over the pages of a 1938 edition of *Jane's Fighting Ships*. Suddenly he stared in disbelief at a photo of an E-boat exactly like the one he had captured. He said, "It was the advertisement of a German shipbuilding yard, proclaiming their wares and inviting all and sundry to come and buy ... The whole thing seemed too fantastic. The reiterated instructions to bring one back alive at all costs; the intense interest in all the details we could guess at or find out; the continual bombardment of questions on every point, even as to whether the engines were diesel, carried on for weeks over Admiralty telephone lines; the tremendous discussions and controversies as to maximum speeds. And here it was all laid out for us in *Jane's*. Come see. Come buy!"

German naval strategy in the 1930s has been discussed for forty years and the consensus is that Hitler, the soldier, didn't understand sea power and ignored the advice of his admirals. Grossadmiral Erich Raeder had wanted to build a balanced fleet before war was declared, and the year 1942 was his choice. Kommodore Karl Dönitz wanted to wait until he had 300 submarines but had to start the war with twenty-five, this because of Hitler's "intuition" that September, 1939, was the time to strike against Poland. Until 1943, whether we would win or not was in doubt. Had Hitler waited the world order might have been quite different today. The policy forced on both Raeder and Dönitz was not to engage even an equal force. The small Kreigsmarine must be conserved. Our policy was the reverse. Attack anything. Attack everything. Well, *almost* anything.

If we are to judge this policy by reason alone, we were often in error. For instance, one night in 1943 one of our flotillas was off Cherbourg to intercept a large merchant ship we thought would pass. We met a German force of three times our number. Even though the main target – the merchant ship – was not there, the Senior Officer immediately attacked. Several of his ships were damaged and during the time they were undergoing repairs the German merchant ship made a safe passage. From a materiél point of view the Senior Officer was wrong. But from every other point of view he was right. A chance to engage the enemy outside his own harbour should not be passed up. It was because of this truculence that the initiative in the battles never passed from us. Similarly, in 1942 when Vice-Admiral Kummitz led the pocket battleship *Lützow* (11-inch guns), the heavy crusier *Hipper* (8-inch), and six destroyers against one of our Murmansk convoys. Captain Sherbrooke, VC, in HMS *Onslow*, with *Orwell*, *Obedient*, *Obdurate*, and *Achates*, held them at bay during the twilight – about ten a.m. to three p.m. – of that New Year's Eve in the High Arctic until our light cruisers *Jamaica* and *Sheffield* (6-inch) finally hove into view out of the northern gloom. Kummitz fled. He had been told to sink merchant ships, not warships. Time and again German commanders snatched defeat from the jaws of victory.

And none of the above detracts one iota from the reputation of the

German sailor as a fighting man. It is a case of racial temperament and the balance of forces. It is neither just nor wise to belittle the E-boat crews. Many were led by commanders quite equal in skill to ours and they inflicted grievous damage upon us. But the E-boats carried torpedoes and mines for use against merchant ships. Those were their instructions and if they met anything else they retired at speed behind a smoke screen. Exasperating! In spite of inferior weapons and boats and numbers, this was never our mind set. In his Trafalgar memorandum of 9 October 1805 Admiral Nelson said, ". . . no Captain can do very wrong if he places his ship alongside that of the enemy."

But the training of German sailors since the 1800s has been to make a foray and return to harbour. To us the sea is our home, where we live and where we have kept open for 300 years the flow of trade to a worldwide Empire. Although not a maritime country, Germans were always in the forefront of ocean racing before the war and thus the E-boat commanders had competed before against those of our commanders who raced their yachts in the 1930s.

In September, 1939, our small, fast motor anti-submarine boat – MA/SB, the "Masby" – carried out anti U-boat patrols. The enemy's small boats were too far away to attack our convoys. But with the fall of France, Belgium, Denmark, and Holland, E-boats could now attack our east coast convoys. The Masbys were refitted with automatic quick-firing guns, and hence was the motor gun boat born; later types were designed this way.

The crews of the smaller boats numbered perhaps nine or ten; the larger carried thirty or more: a captain, a first lieutenant, a navigator, a coxswain, an engine-room artificer, and various stokers and seamen. These crews were mostly – later exclusively – "Hostilities Only." They joined for the war and went gratefully back to civvy street when it ended. The temporal nature of our officers' appointments could be seen in their rank upon entering the Royal Canadian Navy; they came in as probationary acting sub-lieutenants, Royal Canadian Naval Volunteer Reserve (Temporary)! Most went to sea; some, like Sub-Lieutenant Jack Breadner, who was radar and wireless officer, and Leading Motor Mechanic Tom Forrester in HMS *Beehive* at Felixstowe, served ashore maintaining equipment. But they got to sea when an emergency called a boat out before repairs were completed and sailed with her to get her in fighting trim before action was joined. This was welcomed. One gets weary of repair work day after day, night after night, week after week, for years, all the while having to listen to the death-or-glory boys talk of their battles; it didn't seem fair that they had all the fun. On one occasion the shore-based flotilla engineer officer had to sail to nurse a temperamental gearbox. The enemy was encountered and there was the usual hail of shot and shell. It was the engineer's first battle and he stuck his head out of the engine room to see the crisscrossing red, green, and amber tracer and hear the thud-thud of the 3-pounders and the chatter of the smaller guns: "Oh, I say – madly war, isn't it?"

✳   ✳   ✳

In February, 1942, Vice-Admiral Ciliax made his famous dash up the Channel from Brest with *Scharnhorst*, *Gneisneau*, and *Prinz Eugen*. He caught us with our pants down and was through the Straits of Dover (at high noon; he had sailed the previous night) before we sounded the tocsin. Ciliax was escorted by just about every destroyer available and most of the E-boat fleet. General Galland's Luftwaffe were overhead with scores of planes. Admiralty belatedly threw everything we had against the German fleet. The RAF flew off Spitfires and Hurricanes and just about anything else that would fly; the Fleet Air Arm flew off Swordfish and Ansons; C-in-C the Nore sailed every ship that had steam up and could hope to intercept, and our MTBs and MGBs – Lieutenant Anthony Law, RCNVR, of Halifax was Captain of one. Leading Telegraphist Fred Langford came to the bridge with a message and viewed the fearful and awesome scene.

"Roll, bowl, pitch, every time a coconut!"

By the 1st of January 1940 the 1st Flotilla was ready to operate from Felixstowe; by March 4, the 10th Flotilla was ready also. The enemy E-boats were still distant and work consisted of a miscellany of air-sea rescue, aimless patrols, and even acting as bum boats taking provisions to large ships lying off the harbour. But when the Wehrmacht invaded Holland the 4th Flotilla was sent to Ijmuiden where one of her functions would be to prevent enemy seaplanes from landing on the Zuider Zee (they never tried). But during the evacuation of France, Holland, and Belgium – June and July of 1940, the time of Dunkirk – they were busy enough taking their share of the 300,000-odd who were plucked from the shoreline.

About the year 1436, in *The Libel of English Policie*, Bishop Adam de Moleyns wrote:

> The true processe of English policie . . .
> Is this, that who saileth South, North, East and West,
> Cherish Merchandise, keepe the Admiraltie;
> That we bee Masters of the narrowe see.

\* \* \*

The English policy the good Bishop talked of 500 years earlier had not much changed by the summer of 1941. The merchandise we cherished had to be defended up and down the east coast of England. All the North Sea ports had to be kept working as close to full capacity as possible, particularly the port of London. In just one product, coal, the south coast ports needed 40,000 tons a week. The enemy now had the advantage of the French Channel and Bay of Biscay ports and the very favourably placed bases at Den Helder, the Hook, and Ijmuiden in Holland. By coastal guns, aircraft, mines, submarines, and surface craft he challenged our admiralty of the narrow seas. Convoys passing through the Straits of Dover were shelled from German shore batteries at Cape Griz Nez. In July of 1940 a convoy of twenty-one ships was passing westward through the Straits escorted by two destroyers and an air CAP (Combat Air Patrol) of RAF Hurricanes. But the enemy threw so many fighters and dive-bombers against it that the defence was swamped. On the 25th five merchant ships were sunk by bombs and the two destroyers and five merchant ships damaged. E-boats entered the fray and on the 26th of July sank three more, for a total of fourteen losses out of twenty-five.

But nine days later, the 4th of August, the Mobile Balloon Barrage Flotilla was the extemporized solution by this innovative island race whose pelagic past urges them to ad-lib, ad-hoc, pro-tem, and Harry-Tate solutions. Seamen of a dozen countries sailed for the first time in small ships with a balloon billowing serenely astern and thus vexed the dive-bombers no end. The balloons forced them to pull out of their dives much higher than they wanted to. But despite the fact that from June, 1940, to April, 1941, one ship in three was sunk or damaged when the attacks were at their peak, nevertheless, four million tons of coastal shipping entered or left our harbours. Besides the balloon ships, to stiffen the merchant ships' defence, teams of light machine-gunners were formed and two or three teams would be sent to each ship; these were suitably named "The Channel Guard." They joined a westbound convoy before it sailed from the Thames and returned on an eastbound convoy.

Still there were the omnipresent mines: contact mines, acoustic mines, time-delay mines, moored mines, floating mines, magnetic mines. The peak of the enemy's mine-laying period saw some eighty of his aircraft employed on mine-laying as well as some twenty-nine E-boats; on the night of 12–13 December 1940, for instance, over fifty mines were dumped in the Thames estuary. Our mine sweepers sailed at once and sweeping went on for four days without result. Then mines started going off all over the place; they had been fitted with a four-day delay mechanism. During the whole of 1940 we lost 201 merchant ships to mines.

With this background in mind we have a better picture of the significance of our MGB and enemy E-boat strategy and tactics.

We both had the problem of keeping our coastal shipping moving, we from the north of Scotland to the south of England, they from Norway to France. But the main battle area was in the North Sea and the English Channel. On the European coast the enemy convoys passed south from the Texal (opposite Yarmouth and Lowestoft – 100 miles across), to the Hook (opposite Felixstowe – ninety miles across), down to Ostend, Dunkirk, and Calais (opposite Ramsgate and Dover – twenty to fifty miles across), to Le Havre and Cherbourg (opposite Weymouth – seventy miles across). By September of 1941 the enemy had about fifteen E-boats suitable to cross these stretches of water and attack our convoys. We had a lesser number of MTBS and MGBS suitable to attack German convoys.

Attack and defence were uniquely mixed. We sailed MGBS on a defensive patrol for one of our convoys, and one MGB tactic was to lie in wait for marauding E-boats. This was called a "Z" patrol; when the night was quiet the crew could sleep ("zizz"), hence the name. Sometimes the E-boats would get through undetected, fire their torpedoes, and head for home. We pursued but invariably fell astern and lost them. So the next time we would go further out and then if we missed the E-boats on the way in we could intercept them on the way out, on their run home. This led to both interception and hot pursuit. Maybe battle would be joined and maybe not. But in any event, what had started out as defence of a British convoy off the coast of England ended up off the coast of Holland. If we then sighted a German convoy hugging the Dutch coast, what did we do? Go home? Not bloody likely!

And so we were back to doing what had worked so well in the Napoleonic wars and before, and in the Great War of only twenty years earlier: deny the enemy the free use of his harbours and protect our own harbours. Had not Admiral Nelson said that our first line of defence was off the enemy's coast? It was working out that way. Further, in this war the German nation that had complained for so many years that it was geographically shut in, that it needed *liebensraum*, now found that it had perhaps too much living space. German garrisons now had to guard from the southernmost part of France, on the border with Spain, in latitude 44° North, north through the Low Countries and Norway to North Cape in latitude 72° North. That is a coastline of about 2,000 miles measured from cape to cape; if we measure the coastline counting the inlets and the rivers and fiords, it is about 3,600 nautical miles. So the Germans had an obvious problem in defending such an extensive coast, and our policy was to spread alarm and despondency as widely as possible. So it was that no German garrison from Cherbourg to Texel ever knew when our coastal craft would appear at their harbour gates and shoot them up. Indeed, some of our lads were positively insulting, as you will see presently.

So, we must harass the enemy in all theatres, forcing him to extend his garrisons, increasing his anxiety. We had the maritime power to land a small body of men for a limited time – a hit-and-run raid. The successes achieved were not of great importance but the mere threat of our raids could lock up a disproportionate number of enemy troops. When Vice-Admiral Lord Louis Mountbatten took over combined operations from Admiral Lord Keyes he said to his men, "Your job is to be offensive." And indeed they were in scores of raids. On a 3,600-mile coastline no German sentry going on night guard could be sure that he wouldn't have his throat cut. It was for this reason in March, 1941, that it was expedient to raid the Lofoton Islands; they are near Narvik, above the Arctic Circle. The Norwegian government in exile helped choose the targets – fish-oil factories.

Two cross-channel steamers had been fitted out as landing craft and they embarked 500 Commandos, fifty Royal Engineers especially trained in demolitions, and about 500 Norwegian troops. Captain C. Caslin, RN, in *Somali* and four other destroyers were the escort on the Scotland-to-Norway voyage, about 1,000 miles. Admiral Tovey sailed with the main body of the Home Fleet as a covering force staying about 200 miles to seaward. As they neared the target he detached two cruisers as close support. A submarine was on station at Vestfiord to give a navigational beacon. At five a.m. on the 4th of March the landings were made. Surprise was complete: all the objectives on shore were found and destroyed, and a fish factory-ship of 9,780 tons and some smaller craft were sunk. The landing parties were greeted with enthusiasm by the locals, shared a dram or two of aquavit, took 200 prisoners, and were on the way home by one p.m. This minor operation showed again one of the greatest benefits conferred by maritime power – the capacity to land troops on an enemy-held coast. From North Cape to St. Jean de Luz, all enemy coastal garrisons feared surprise and no enemy coastal shipping could sail with certainty that our coastal forces would not descend upon them, guns blazing and torpedoes hissing and bubbling toward them.

It was at this March, 1941, stage of the build-up, which would reach its zenith on our return to the continent in June, 1944, that Robert Hichens took over the converted Masbys, the first MGBs, to do battle with the E-boats that had sunk twenty-three of our ships in 1940. Several of our Canadian MGB officers were to serve with him.

# III   The Coastal Forces Navy

*It is upon the Navy, wherein, under the good Provi-
dence of God, the Wealth, Safety, and Strength of This
Realm Do Chiefly Attend.*
  – Preamble to the *Articles of War*, Charles II, 1661

In 1914 the German army, against all the predictions
of our military strategists, reached the Channel coast, and such a small-
ship hustle and bustle there was then! Minelayers, minesweepers, trawlers, and fast torpedo boats had precedence over all else. These were
clearly disapproved of by blue-water, deep-sea admirals as not the
authentic navy, and the small ships disappeared without a trace in 1918.
In 1940 the German army reached the Channel coast again and the
whole wretched business had to start over. In February, 1941, Robert
Hichens had been the first RNVR officer to be appointed in command;
his flotilla leader was Lieutenant Peter Howes, RN. Until then all the
boats had been commanded by permanent force lieutenants and sub-
lieutenants, although many RNVRs were first lieutenants. Another senior
officer was Lieutenant Peter Dickens, RN. These two were well out of
the mainstream for career officers. But if the RN admirals thought thus,
the young RN officers did not – here was fun and excitement such as
did not exist in cruisers and battleships, as well as the opportunity to
command as a sub-lieutenant. A lieutenant could even be a senior
officer, command a flotilla of eight boats, and be a mini admiral! And
the design of new boats was coming on apace.

Hubert Scott-Payne of the British Power Boat Company and Peter
Du Cane of Vosper were the chief designers and builders of small, fast

boats. Vospers were built around the best engine then designed, the Italian Issota-Frascini, and Admiralty was asked to negotiate a contract with Italy to build these in England. Admiralty said no, on the dubious grounds that we could always get them because we were unlikely to fight Italy. Besides, so they claimed, if we did we could use Rolls-Royce Merlins. Scott-Payne became disenchanted and took his business to America and so it came about that the U.S. Navy's patrol craft, with a Packard engine, was primarily of British design. Du Cane struggled on in England and produced his beautiful seventy-foot hull, but the Issota-Frascini engines were now denied him by a belligerent Italy. And in 1941 the RAF could spare no Rolls-Royce Merlins.

Now, it is axiomatic in shipbuilding and design that the marriage of hull and engine must be one of compatibility and love, not a marriage of convenience, but time did not permit the redesign of the Vosper hull around the Packard engine. By 1942 enemy raids strongly advocated to their Lordships that MTBs and MGBs must be produced in large numbers. Vosper's seventy-foot existed in large numbers and the Packard engine was available from the United States under lend-lease. Then let us wed the two. The marriage was a failure from the start; bride and groom did not belong together. The beautiful Packard had to lie on a wrong-size bed at an uncomfortable angle, anxious to use her passionate power but uncertain, hard to please, and, despite unceasing attention lavished on her by her motor mechanic, the pouting cause of repeated frustration.

And then there was the matter of "boost." A good thing for a marriage, one might say: "Good oh, boost! That's what we need more of, the more the better."

Not so. These Packards had a supercharger that contained this boost, and how much there was could be seen on a small dial. At +1 it was watched closely (+1 *what* was never explained) and at +2 you got agitated and made sure the motor mechanic was doing something (what to do was seldom explained); at +3 the trouble began – things flew off, there was a loud crunch.

There was another reason Their Big-Ship Lordships disapproved. The large ships were a *career* with a past that went back with previous ships of the same name to the Spanish Armada and before. They were *pusser*; they were a *home*, and one dressed for dinner; a post captain commanded, a commander was second in command, heads of departments were commanders, the first lieutenant was a career lieutenant-commander; officers were properly divided according to accepted social strata between wardroom, gun room, and warrant officer's mess. Who were these unruly youngsters careening over the ocean at forty knots in hare-brained actions fought at ranges that had gone out with the age of sail – fifty yards, twenty yards, *even less*! And where did they come from, these civilian sailors? And how did they comport themselves away from the hand of properly ordained authority? And who could tell what abhorrent deviations of discipline were perpetrated?

Few could tell and they didn't.

But a case can be made for unorthodox behaviour, that is, when old methods do not work in new situations. The tried-and-true methods of a century ago did not work in small boats in 1941.* For instance, most of the Canadian small-boat officers came by way of a training period in an armed merchant cruiser. It was sea time, yes, and it started them on the long road to get their official Bridge Watchkeeping Certificate. But many never got it; they were in command before they got it. Tommy Fuller of Ottawa, for one, was in command of a flotilla in the Mediterranean without a Bridge Watchkeeping Certificate. And there is little else besides sea time in common between an eighteen-knot, 18,000-ton, 500-foot luxury liner with 6-inch guns and a forty-knot, forty-five ton, seventy-foot motor boat with 6-pounder guns and smaller. But they learned celestial navigation! They didn't use it, of course, because they were always just off shore and pilotage was quite enough, and besides, who can hold a sextant steady to take a sunsight on a bobbing cork. In the matter of formation they solemnly were taught the red, white, and blue turns and wheels that the battle fleets used at Jutland: the yardarms were too short and too low for flag hoists; there was no voice radio and w/t was ponderous; even though only fifty feet apart you couldn't shout because of the noise of the engines. The small light was the best, these young officers decided. That and hand signals when you could see. Tony Law showed me in Halifax a couple of years ago how he pumped his hand up and down to increase speed, lowered his palm to decrease, pushed away to open up, beckoned to close in.

Admiral Nelson had discussed tactics with his captains at every opportunity. After the regular-force officers left to further their careers in large ships, Hichens had his RNVR officers in his small wardroom night after night. Over a bottle of port they would plan tactics.

"Now, what if . . ."

---

*There are exceptions. Crossing the enemy's T, used with such success in the Napoleonic wars, never has gone out of style in gun battles. It simply means that you steer across the bow of your enemy, so you can fire with all your guns and he can only use his forward guns. You are the top part of the T, the horizontal part; the enemy is the bottom, the vertical part of the T.

"Suppose that . . ."

With him were RCNVR officers. Lieutenant George Duncan, "Fearless and Resolute George," was among the first. Tommy Ladner, RCNVR, and other Canadians joined later. From these "tactical talks," as Hichens called them, came the new methods of attack to be developed by such Canadians as Tony Law, Jim Kirkpatrick, Jack McClelland, Douglas Maitland, Tommy Fuller, Bones Burk, Corny Burke . . .

Flat-out pursuit was the first feature – maximum speed to get as close as possible as soon as possible, but then slow down; the large bow wave is easily seen and on phosphorescent nights you might as well show a searchlight as approach at high speed. The stealthy approach was best. And when challenged, answer immediately with the same challenge, letter by letter as he sends it if that can be done. Then he should be confused; who is challenging whom? He might even give you the reply, and then you know it for the rest of the night. In any case you are now closer, much closer. Keep your boats astern tight up on your arse as if held there by a steel bar. This way you know where others are. Turn together when you are close – under 100 yards if possible, closer is better. Then you have four boats acting as one gun boat with eight 6-pounders, eight 20mm, four pom-poms, and four Lewis .303s. Devastating firepower! Use more tracer than normal, for while MTBs can sink the largest ships with their torpedoes, gun boats can only set them on fire. Thus, the essence of our tactics was a combination of stealth and the intent to hit the enemy with everything before he knew we were there.

Alas, how times have changed. Where has gone the chivalry of old? Admiral Nelson recounted the story of how he had hailed a Spaniard at the start of a fight with the challenge, "This is an English frigate. Lower your colours, turn into the wind, and surrender or I will open fire."

And how he had been delighted by the "noble" reply: "This is a Spanish frigate, and you may begin as soon as please."

By 1942 our torpedo boats and gun boats were proving a solace to our friends and a trial to our enemies. One evening at dusk Hichens sailed with three other boats to lie off the convoy route and intercept E-boats. One boat had an engine defect and had to return. The other two reached their station, cut engines, and wallowed in silence. The wind was westerly, force four and freshening; silence reigned except for the thudding, swishing, whooshing of a boat lifting and dipping and rolling through sixty degrees. By two a.m. the wind was gusting to force five; it was not the sort of night that E-boats came across. Orders allowed Hichens to return to base at two a.m. if all was quiet but something impelled him to have a look-see over the other side. A sense of adventure.

"Start up."

Muttering engines rose to a growl, then to a roar, as they set off to the southeast. A light was sighted to starboard.

"Enemy in sight" was signalled to the boats astern.

They slid from three-quarter line to line ahead. The hands donned steel helmets and anti-flash gear and closed up at action stations. The wind was from ahead and they would not be heard until they were right on them. They approached slowly, just enough speed to overtake. Luckily, the enemy was steaming *away*, so they crept up astern of him (and after lookouts are always the most lax). The targets were two large trawlers heading west at about eight knots. Should they creep up further or increase speed now to hit the trawlers before being seen? The danger of being heard was weighed against the danger of being caught without speed – a real and present danger against trawlers with 88mm. They were now abeam the aftermost trawler at one hundred yards. She was challenging.

"Revs for forty knots. Open fire."

A crescendo of noise and light, flashes from gun barrels and streaks of tracer, dazzling and bewildering. The target never replied. Hose her decks and make sure her gun crews are dead; she is on fire. Now surge ahead and get across her bow at the other trawler. But now they saw a small tanker ahead; the trawlers must have been her stern escort. They headed for the tanker, to depth charge her.

This tactic had been rehearsed time and again, as recently as the previous week. (On that last practice the target had been a friendly trawler, horrified by what she was being used for. They had cleared the target's bows *by two feet*. They creamed in, got halfway across the stem, and the coxswain cranked his helm over and flicked the gun boat's stern clear as the depth charge was dropped. But that was too close – ten or twenty feet was all right.) A stream of shells now poured into the tanker as the gun boat overtook her and swung to cross her bow. The tanker's bow wave piled up as she sped away at full speed – "a bone in her teeth." Hichens made the approach and conned the coxswain by constant helm orders. But as they had found out in the practices, for the last few yards control passed from the captain to the coxswain.

They were nearly up to the tanker and altered to cross her bow. But now the second trawler was fully awake and had a clear field of fire.

She hit Hichens with a withering blast; his boat shuddered from hit after hit; everybody ducked – it doesn't do any good but it's instinctive. The tanker's stem loomed over them now; they were ten feet off, at the foot of the curling bow wave and *underneath* the bullring on the tanker's forecastle. The depth charge splashed in; the coxswain whirled the helm over and they were clear. The depth charge exploded at fifty feet under the tanker.

But they were on fire, in the wheelhouse and below toward where ammunition was stored. Shells kept thumping and exploding in the hull from the second trawler, who now had her blood up. Smoke and flames and bangs and crashes: a proper "panic station."

> The lights went out! The windows broke!
> The room was filled with reeking smoke.
> And in the darkness shrieks and yells
> Were mingled with electric bells.

Beat the fire down and stamp it out! Where's the fire extinguisher?

They were now low on fuel and ammunition and, consequently, their weight was much reduced. The effect was that the hull, thrust forward by the upward drive of the propellers, could plane. The constant stern wave – a cascading plume that normally hangs a few feet astern – was gone, and the boat, with throttles hard up, was skimming straight as an arrow, the wake hard, flat, clean.

They pulled in a long circle ahead of the astonished forward escorts and were gone before fire was opened. Hichens's boat was badly damaged, the engine room the only part unscathed. Half the crew were casualties: one dead, one seriously wounded, five slightly wounded.

In one stretch of good weather that spring they had done nineteen operations in six weeks and casualties had been high. Hitch's policy was attack, attack, get in close, now get in closer; let the E-boats know that we will *always* go for them. For this policy a price was paid. Hitch had lost the equivalent of a whole crew – dead and wounded – in two successive actions. But always awaiting them at the base was their Canadian doctor, Surgeon Lieutenant Bob Swan, RCNVR.

Hichens said of Doctor Swan that he was early called upon to show his worth. "And what a showing he made! He was tireless in his efforts on our behalf. He concerned himself not only with the wounded, but with the active sea-going personnel. He studied our problems and produced valuable suggestions. Nothing was too much trouble for him. He noticed that we came in with red, sore eyes after a rough night, and produced eye shields and eye lotions. He saw that several men and one officer were beginning to suffer from a bout of hay fever, and he produced the necessary preventative before they were fully aware of their trouble. He saw we were working night after night and produced benzedrine and vitamin pills. At one time I went out on ten successive nights, and at another, eight nights running. There were occasions when I was considerably exhausted, but I was determined to deal faithfully with the E-boats and I knew that opportunities for rest would come when the weather broke. Swan's concern on my behalf, however, was often quite embarrassing. He would shake his head over me and utter the direst warnings if I continued. I was not used to such attention. Tall and rather thin, with a pale face, he did not look strong himself. Whether this was so or not, he did not spare himself, and the whole flotilla appreciated his efforts greatly. Aside from these professional activities he was the pleasantest of companions, and did much to make our life easier and more amusing."

Two days later Hitch was again at sea with Fearless and Resolute George Duncan and Tommy Ladner (Ladner's first trip in command). Orders were to sweep down the convoy route and look for wreckage. There was often quite a lot of this; some of the north-south convoys numbered up to forty ships, and twenty convoys were at sea on any given day. George signalled he had found a survivor; it was a young naval officer, barely conscious, who had been in the water about twenty-two hours. No, he didn't think there were any more alive. George headed back to Doctor Swan at maximum speed.

On the night of 1–2 August 1943 came another chance to wish confusion to the King's enemies. As they cleared the harbour they shot off the guns in the routine test, then headed for the patrol area. It was a rotten night, with fog and visibility of only sixty yards. Hitch was thinking of returning when he got a signal that E-boats were on their way across to the English coast. That was more like it! He altered course to intercept. Boffin was with him, and George Duncan and Tommy Ladner, each thirty yards on his port quarter – not more, not less. Here was where the training and experience paid off: full speed in poor visibility and a rising sea ahead.

Reports continued to pour in, and then one said the E-boats had turned back, probably because they had run into the fog. There was only one thing to do. Crank on the absolute maximum speed and try and reach them before they entered their harbours; they had twenty miles to go. Hitch had sixty miles to go to catch them. The enemy would not be in a hurry and would approach his base at low speed, so it was worth a try. They thundered on. Time passed; the E-boat reports ceased;

the fog cleared. The night was still and cool, and soon they arrived at the interception point.

"Stop engines."

The boats slumped, immobile, silent. All hands listened. To the east was a subdued growl, indicating it was too late, they were entering harbour. But weren't there two groups? Where then was the other? Hitch studied the plot. Reports showed another group of E-boats further to the west; they must be still out there.

A minute dragged by, then another, then three more.

"Do you hear anything from the southwest?" This from Boffin.

"No. Wait. Yes, about west-southwest. Louder now, I think."

A rhythmic thudding could be heard, muffled but recognizable. E-boats!

"Start up. Steer south-fifteen-east."

The enemy could not be more than two miles outside their harbour. This would have to be swift. Form line ahead; maximum speed. The dark line of the breakwater showed now, just a half-mile ahead. There was a German torpedo boat at rest, unsuspecting. What a chance! But E-boats were the quarry, and there they were! In line ahead, just stooging along at four knots. The British boats swept past the stern of the after-most E-boat; each in turn raking her with fire. Then they moved up to each of the others.

No gun fired back. What German would expect to be attacked here, a half-mile outside his own harbour. The enemy's guns were secured for the night, the hands preparing ropes and fenders for coming alongside, looking forward to a few hours' sleep. The British continued to circle, raking the silent E-boats with concentrated fire. This went on for *eight minutes*! Ashore they thought their boats had gone mad.

Then the enemy realized what was happening and a fine pyrotechnic display followed. The shore batteries opened up, with star shells fired by the score. Two German torpedo boats cautiously approached, as the sky was lit by the eerie greenish-yellow light of the descending star shell and the red, green, and yellow interlacing tracer, the silent dark hulks of the E-boats suspended on the water. The British gun boats changed target to the two torpedo boats, and their crews watched the red splotches as the torpedo boats were hit. They watched, too, the shell splash from the enemy guns. The German torpedo boats were as big as our small destroyers and had heavy guns. Hichens knew his boats would have to get out of it soon. The shell splashes were getting closer – too close! He broke off the action. Throttles were lifted and the British boats sped away.

But the fight continued astern. To the huge delight of the Allied crews the picture was now so blurred to the German torpedo boats, E-boats, shore batteries, and rapidly arriving reinforcements that they were firing at each other. Some boats, pounded steadily from shore, fired back. The battle continued to rage for ten minutes, while our boats by now were five miles away and headed for home.

Hitch had had reservations about Tommy Ladner in his first command; after all, Ladner had had no time at sea with gun boats as watchkeeper or Number One, no sea time in the navy at all – except a bloody big-armed merchant cruiser. He had not proved himself yet in command.

Now Hitch could say, "He did magnificently."

Almost a year earlier, on the evening of 2 October 1942, Hichens's unit of four boats set out on another patrol; the old moon rose at 1:30 a.m. It was a clear, cool night with a gentle southwest wind. The white-grey hulls glimmered and their stems threw up feathers of spray at the creeping, stalking speed at which they sought their prey. There should be trawlers to the northeast, they figured, and on that course the rising hump-backed moon would be on the starboard bow. But should they engage trawlers that had superior armament? To destroy E-boats that sought out our convoys was their proper function. And yet, was it not our duty, if no E-boats presented themselves, to harry the enemy? Certainly so, if we could achieve complete tactical surprise. That was the *sine qua non*: surprise. Hichens had had a run of successes without serious loss but surprise had been the key – approach undetected; when challenged, reply and try to bluff your way closer; if close enough, reply to the challenge with a continual hail of fire. The sudden overwhelming attack was absolutely necessary in this type of warfare, particularly when they fought a more powerfully armed opponent. Go for him balls out, hit him hard, and then get out. Stab the Germans again and again with rapier thrusts. It now seemed passing strange that only two years ago they had tentatively skirmished with nothing but .303 automatic guns; the new boats coming out had 6-pounders fore and aft, two twin .5 machine guns in power mounts, and 20mm here and there midships. But the thrusts must become harder and harder and more and more frequent. Germans must learn to dread going to sea. But tonight he would not attack unless he could surprise the trawlers. Yet, his troops would not like to see the enemy unfired upon. This crew was a gung-ho lot. Well, let's give 'em a treat!

There they were! A black smudge in the moon's path, another, then two more. The enemy approached slowly in line abreast at about four knots; they would pass less than a half-mile to starboard. They could be given a good dose of gunfire but that would not be decisive. It would not be possible to cut one out from the others in the close formation they were maintaining. What about a depth-charge attack? Hichens had carried one out successfully only five weeks previously and Boffin only three. But the ideal for that was darkness and poor visibility; tonight the depth-charging boat might be sighted not at one hundred yards but at a half-mile and to have to run the gauntlet of gunfire before dropping a depth charge. Still, down-moon the low motor gun boat hull was vague in that toneless obscurity. A good diversionary gun attack by three boats might let a fourth put down a depth-charge.

Hichens knew he was the most experienced and the best boat for the job, but his captains were good and they all longed for an opportunity to have a go. Hichens was piling up medals and mentioned-in-despatches at a great rate; it was getting to be the flotilla joke how often he was at Buckingham Palace to collect another gong from the King. He wanted very much for his officers to share to the full the flotilla's success. George Duncan in particular had been pining for another chance; he had missed one recently when, being the last in the line, he could have peeled off on his own initiative and carried out such a run.

"Would you like to carry out a depth-charge attack, George?"

"Yes, please."

"Then we'll open fire on his beam, work up-moon and draw his fire. This will leave the down-moon side clear for you to attack from."

George faded into the down-moon side to start his approach; three boats continued to close. At 400 yards the trawlers flashed the challenge. A blast of gunfire into the closest answered. The trawlers replied hesitantly at first, then with mounting conviction they increased the fusillade. Hichens slid around their stern and into the path of the moon, where his boats made a good silhouette. All three blazed away as the range opened. Tracer flared out toward them and the shot whistled shrilly by; but a lot of German shells were hitting. All four trawlers now were firing steadily at the British gun boats steaming so conveniently in the moon path; all enemy tracer converged on them.

But the shot of the port-hand trawler suddenly veered aft and concentrated on the down-moon side; then tracer was coming the other way – George firing back. They obviously had seen him coming in for his attack. There was little time to think about it, but George's attack, it seemed, should have been over, and shell was arriving inboard with alarming frequency.

"Let's get out of it. Full speed. Steer west."

From a half-mile away out of the moon's path the trawlers could safely be watched. They were stopped with a cloud of black smoke hanging over them and seemed to be tending one of their group. George's attack must have been a success. Hitch called him on w/t but got no answer. This was no cause for alarm, for in gunfights the w/t aerial was often blown away. They headed for home at moderate speed, expecting George to catch up.

But George did not catch up; he was never seen again.

Hichens had a bad time about losing this Canadian captain with whom he had sailed so often. If only he had carried out the attack himself . . . he should have done . . . it was not good enough to sit off in safety and send your juniors to their death . . . If only . . . It seemed to him that not being killed or captured or at least wounded, he had let his friend down.

He wrote, "George had been straight and simple and brave. So full of life, so keen on his job. Of all people I knew, Conrad's praise of the Anglo-Saxon male seemed most applicable to him. 'A man of courage, initiative and hardihood, yet so little stained by the excesses of many virtues.' "

✳ ✳ ✳

Hitch fought many actions after this. But one dawn after the battle had been broken off and he was steering for home, he was hit by a stray shell.

He had been awarded the Distinguished Service Order with bar, the Distinguished Service Cross with two bars, and had been three times Mentioned in Despatches.

OFFICIAL ADMIRALTY COMMUNIQUE NO. 826

On each of the last two nights, light coastal forces have had short, sharp engagements with enemy patrol craft close to the Dutch coast. As a result of these engagements considerable damage has been caused to the enemy craft and many casualties have been inflicted on their personnel.

During the course of last night's engagement it is regretted that Lieutenant-Commander Robert Peverall Hichens, DSO, DSC, RNVR, was killed. The other casualties sustained during these two nights were two officers and two ratings wounded. The next of kin have been informed.

All our ships returned safely to harbour.

ADMIRALTY, S.W.1.

13th April, 1943

Lieutenant-Commander Peter (now Sir Peter) Scott, MBE, DSC, and Bar RNVR, was the senior officer of two MTB flotillas during the Battle of the Narrow Seas. He said, "I had long hours standing on the bridge peering into the darkness, long hours in which to think of the man I had known in peacetime and whom I had seen last only a few days before, when he had dined and stayed the night at my house in London. A fortnight later I had occasion to broadcast a BBC postscript for St. George's Day. After mention of the Coastal Force battles came the following passage about Hitch:

" 'In this sort of fighting, as I suppose in any kind of specialized fighting, there are men who combine those particular qualities of cool leadership and complete knowledge of the technical side of their job so perfectly that their battles are successful where others fail. Such a one was Lieutenant-Commander Robert Hichens, RNVR, whose loss two weeks ago was the most tragic blow to Coastal Forces and indeed to England. He was a man cut out for the job, because in peacetime his interests, apart from his work as a solicitor, were in motor racing and dinghy sailing. He won the Rudge-Whitworth Cup in the 24-hour Grand Prix at Le Mans with his Aston Martin. I remember seeing that car completely in pieces in a shed at his home at Falmouth five years ago and driving in it again a few months ago at Felixstowe.

" 'In fourteen-foot dinghies he always went best in a strong breeze, and I used to reckon my boat went best in that kind of weather, too. We had some good races in those piping days.

" 'He was known throughout Coastal Forces as Hitch, and most of the tactical theory of motor gunboats was first developed and practised by him. But the chief thing about him was the way he could lead and the confidence he instilled into the officers and men of his flotilla. I remember one of them telling me that his only fear on going into action was that he wouldn't satisfy Hitch. And it wasn't limited to his flotilla, this inspiration. It spread around and developed the spirit which put our Coastal Forces on top whenever they met the enemy, by virtue not of their guns but of their determination . . .' "

# IV  Canadians Flock to the Colours

$M$ost of our young men who fought in the small boats of Coastal Command in the North Sea, the English Channel, the Mediterranean, the Adriatic, and the Aegean in World War Two came to the scene of their battles by a circuitous route.

✻   ✻   ✻

**James R.H. Kirkpatrick**. "Kirk" joined the Royal Military College, Kingston, Ontario, in 1934 as a cadet and suffered through his first year, "although, the interesting thing is, the recruit year is always the one you look back on and have the most laughs about. It's just a tremendous memory because in that year you're welded together as a real team. Friendships are formed that last for the rest of your life." In the summer he and those of his class who were headed for the navy went to Halifax and trained both ashore and in the training schooner *Venture* as midshipmen in the RCNVR. Kirk graduated from RMC in 1938 and went to Osgoode Hall in Toronto to study law. He continued his naval training in the summer at Halifax in the Canadian destroyers *Skeena* and *Saguenay*.

In September, 1939, Kirk was playing golf at his club in Kitchener, Ontario, when his father came out to the second tee with a telegram saying that Kirk was to report "forthwith" to HMCS *York* – the Reserve Naval Division in Toronto. Kirk was appointed to the examination vessel off Saint John, New Brunswick, through the winter of 1939-40 and in the spring was sent to Halifax for a specialized gunnery course, lieutenant (g). At that time Admiralty invited volunteers to go on loan to the RN. He, Tommy Fuller, and Pep Hunter sailed in the *Baltic Rover* for Liverpool and were sent to HMS *King Alfred* in Hove, a wartime school for training RNVR officers – the RN version of the ninety-day wonders the RCN started in 1940 in *Stadacona*, Halifax. The subjects were parade training, seamanship, pilotage, navigation, customs of the service, and anything else that might transmogrify a slack civilian into a taut naval officer. After RMC Kirk found that "*King Alfred* was almost a holiday."

On passing through this British wartime school, Kirkpatrick was appointed to an armed merchant cruiser, HMS *Petropolis*. He had two patrols through the Bay of Biscay to Gibraltar and at the end of the second *Petropolis* was torpedoed. Kirk and some others thought they could get her going again but when two more torpedoes hit they were ordered to abandon ship. Kirk slid into the water, but since he didn't have a lifebelt and the ship stayed afloat he swam back and boarded. He went to the bar to serve himself a drink to get warmed up and back to his cabin to get dry clothes. But soon the ship was listing thirty degrees and down she went. Back into the oggin! How much later he was picked up he doesn't know because he was unconscious. He came to in a destroyer that landed him in Glasgow.

After survivor's leave he went to Dover to motor anti/submarine boat 49, Masby 49, to be in command. Masbys were the ugly ducklings of the small boat fleet and a bad experiment in building boats. Kirk had a crew of one officer and twelve men and in 1941 was employed mostly in air-sea rescue and bobbing along behind minesweepers shooting at the mines when they came to the surface. In the spring of 1942 Kirk was appointed to the flotilla of Lieutenant Peter Howes, RN, in Felixstowe. Kirk was operational.

\* \* \*

**C. Anthony Law**. Tony, seeing the storm clouds gathering in 1937 as Hitler became more aggressive, tried to join the RCNVR in Quebec City, but there were no openings. He had been studying art and now was trying to make a living as an artist, but since war artists were not being mobilized he applied to the army instead and became a Second Lieutenant in the Royal Canadian Ordnance Corps. In July, 1939, he was promoted to Lieutenant and when war broke out he became the Officer Commanding Number 1 Ordnance Depot with the acting rank of Captain. In January, 1940, on a skiing holiday in Lake Beauport he met the commanding officer of the Quebec Naval Division, Commander Fred Price, RCNVR, who asked him if he would like to transfer. Tony did. In March, 1940, he was sent to HMCS *Stadacona* in Halifax for training. Known as the "Mousetraps," these temporary buildings were thrown together as dormitories for officers under training and were the original source of the Canadian ninety-day wonders. (In 1941 they were succeeded by HMCS *Royal Roads* and HMCS *Kings*.)

After *Stadacona*, Law embarked on *Duchess of Athlone* with a group of RCNVRs to go on loan to the Royal Navy. They landed in Liverpool, rode by train to Hove to HMS *King Alfred* and a warm welcome from Captain Pelly, RN. The fiasco of Dunkirk in May, 1940, lent a new urgency to their studies. Upon passing out from *King Alfred* Tony was sent to learn celestial navigation in the ex-Canadian Pacific steamship *Montcalm*, now HMS *Wolf*. *Wolf*, as was the custom at the time, was filled with empty oil drums, which showed a certain pessimism that if they met even their equivalent in the German navy – a merchantman raider – they would be destroyed but the oil drums would keep them afloat. *Wolf* patrolled the Denmark Straits and Law did three patrols in her until he was appointed to HMS *Osprey* in Portland, Dorset, for anti-submarine training.

In March, 1941, he was appointed to the 1st MGB Flotilla, to MGB 53, as First Lieutenant and Navigator. MGB 53 was built by the British Power Boat Company and powered by Merlin Rolls-Royce engines, but she had a gremlin in the gearbox which tended to overheat and cause anxious moments. Law did not see much action in that boat. She could make only twenty-nine knots. Eventually the modified Packards began to arrive and the speed of the "Shorts" rose to forty knots. Law took a command course and was appointed as Captain of MTB 48, his first command. Built by Samuel White at Cowes, Isle of Wight, she had three Hall-Scott engines and a speed of twenty-nine knots. As Tony said, "she was no race horse. But she was *mine*."

He sailed to his operational base at HMS *Beehive* after workups at HMS *Hornet* in Portsmouth. At Felixstowe he joined the flotilla led by Lieutenant Hillary Gamble, DSC, RN. Initially they patrolled to the Dutch and Belgium coast. Then the flotilla was ordered to Dover. It was at Dover that MTB 48 met the enemy for the first time. Law was operational.

**Charles Arthur Burk**. "Bones" joined the navy at HMCS *York* after graduating from the University of Toronto Schools. He and a group of his friends were all members of the Royal Canadian Yacht Club and it seemed the natural thing to do. The winter of 1939-40 they trained in Toronto but in June of 1940 Bones was sent to the Royal Navy as an

Ordinary Seaman (OD) to train at HMS *Raleigh* in Cornwall, just across the river from Devonport.

"Canadians were sent to *Raleigh* in groups of twenty-five because that's what a Nissen hut held. *Raleigh* trained one Nissen hut of Canadian sailors at a time." He was in the second draft of the total of 150 Canadians who went there. He took courses in parade, seamanship, and all the other essentials to the several thousand fighting men there learning the basic trades; one class he remembers was the anchoring arrangement in the battlecruiser HMS *Hood*. In the summer of 1940 after the evacuation of Dunkirk, Hitler's Operation Sea Lion – the invasion of England – was very much in everybody's mind and one day the Captain mustered the ship's company and said the German landings were imminent. When the German invasion fleet was sighted, a warning would be given the populace by the ringing of all the church bells. The professional soldiers would be up in the hills behind the beaches but the sailors (presumably unskilled in land warfare) were trooped down to the quartermaster's stores, each given a piece of lead pipe with a rope at one end to slip over the wrist, and lined up on the beach with their truncheons, waiting for the Germans to land.

"The church bells never rang and with great relief we disbanded."

From there his class went to Devonport barracks, "one of the famous old barracks that dates back to Nelson's days – and the plumbing hasn't been much modified since." Then Bones was drafted back to Halifax to one of the U.S. Navy lend-lease destroyers, HMS *New Market*. Churchill struck a bad bargain when he traded British bases for fifty of these because they were old, rusty, obsolete, and dreadful sea boats, with such a narrow beam they would roll in a heavy dew. But principally they were rusty. On the first occasion of the engineer officer testing steam through he had the screws turning over slowly while alongside in Halifax, and suddenly a full head of steam came on the turbines and *New Market*, dragging two other American destroyers with her, careened into the next jetty and cut a four-foot gash in her bow. Repairs took over Christmas and so it was February, 1941, before they got to St. John's, Newfoundland, where they choked up with rust once more and had to go into a dickey refit. Crossing the Atlantic they were not reassured when they had to stop twice to clean out the boilers again. Stopped! At sea! In U-boat waters! They eventually got to Plymouth. Being an OD, Bones didn't mix much with the aristocracy but he remembers "a peg-leg captain, a pretty tough old bugger. He stayed with her during the refit and eventually when she was sunk he went down with her."

Burk was sent to Portsmouth for an Officer Candidate Board but the night before the Board convened the Germans elected to bomb Portsmouth and so the examining officers declined to come down from London until the fires were out and the unexploded bombs had all been rendered safe. So off he and his mates went for a couple of weeks' leave, he to an aunt who had tennis courts on a nice estate and a sufficient supply of beer. When he returned he was sent to *King Alfred* for training as an acting probationary temporary sub-lieutenant. On passing out from *King Alfred* Burk volunteered for Coastal Forces and was sent to HMS *St. Christopher*, the training base in Loch Linnhe, Fort William, Scotland. After three weeks he was posted to MGB 101, operating out of Lowestoft. Burk was third officer under Lieutenant Allan Seymour-Hayden, RN. For some months 101 did air-sea rescue work and brought in a few flyers who had ditched in the Channel. MGB 14 was being built and Douglas Maitland, RCNVR, was given command of her and Burk was to be Number One. The other boats in the flotilla assembled: Corny Burke had one, Tommy Ladner another. By the middle of 1941 Bones Burk was operational.

**J. Douglas Maitland**. In September, 1939, Doug Maitland was sailing in Cowichan Bay, off Vancouver, British Columbia, when he heard that war had been declared. His crew ceased their race, produced orange juice and gin, toasted the King, and went home by power to Vancouver. Next day he went to HMCS *Discovery*, the Naval Division in Vancouver, and joined the RCNVR. For the next few months he trained five nights a week. In March, 1940, a signal came from Admiralty saying that they required 250 young men between the ages of twenty and thirty, preferably single with boating experience, to be sent over to the U.K. in groups of twenty-five. Maitland, being on duty at the time, was the first to see the signal so he left in the first group in SS *Sinbad* and had his first taste of war when a lone Stuka came by, dropped bombs that missed, and disappeared over the Channel. He disembarked at London and then went down to Hove to *King Alfred*. He had joined as an Acting Probationary Temporary Sub-Lieutenant and now had the "Probationary" removed. He was appointed to the AMC *Cilicia* for astral navigation, patrolled to Iceland and the Denmark Strait, and was near *Rajputana* when she was sunk, then was on a box patrol off the Portuguese coast to Cape Finisterre. In the adjacent patrol was his friend Tommy Ladner in *Forfar*. While Maitland was in *Cilicia* she intercepted three German ships running for home and put prize crews aboard. Maitland was upset because, being so junior, he missed being second officer of the third prize and they never caught a fourth.* *Letitia* and *Forfar* were both sunk while he was on this patrol. Just before Christmas, 1940, when they were heading into the Clyde he was bombed a second time by a Focke-Wulf Condor that flew over them at 200-feet like the Stuka, but it also missed. Maitland was now feeling like a seasoned warrior, particularly when on his last patrol off Cape Finisterre a submarine surfaced – assuming they were a helpless merchant ship – got her deck gun organized, and engaged *Cilicia*. When *Cilicia* answered with a broadside from four 6-inch guns the submarine submerged and made off.

"This was just as well," says Maitland, "because on the second broadside only two guns fired, on the next broadside only one gun fired. These guns, built in the 1890s, were not that reliable."

In January of 1941 he was appointed to training base HMS *St. Christopher*, and in April as First Lieutenant of MTB 69, the flotilla leader's boat, and told to take her around to Lowestoft. He sailed up the west coast of Scotland, through the beautiful Loch Linnhe and through the Great Glen, Inverness. On arriving on a lovely April evening at Inverness, Maitland was ambling up to the village to report to the naval officer in charge when he met a friend from Vancouver, Colonel Edgar P. Burchette, who was in charge of the Canadian Army Forestry Corps logging there for pit props. Maitland persuaded his motor mechanic, Petty Officer Gardiner, that if there was something wrong with engines they would be very well treated in Inverness. Gardiner allowed as how he would like to take two of his engines apart and so they had three pleasant days before putting the boat back together and proceeding with the war. They arrived at Lowestoft in late April when the Germans were first laying acoustic mines off the entrances to Lowestoft and Yarmouth. The Senior Officer, Allan Seymour-Hayden, showed up and they were sent out to explode acoustic mines by going over them at top speed and hoping to be out of the way before they went off. Maitland was operational.

---

*A prize crew is a Royal Navy skeleton crew put on board an enemy ship to take her to a British port. They are armed with revolvers to keep a reduced enemy (in this case, German) crew in line. The captured ship is sold and the sailors of the British ship get the proceeds divided up as prize money. The British captain gets one fourth; the rest of the officers, one fourth; and the crew share one half – all according to rank.

∗ ∗ ∗

**Cornelius Burke**. "Corny" Burke joined the navy at *Discovery* in September, 1939. He trained with Maitland and Ladner, with whom, as it turned out, he spent the rest of the war. He, Budge Bell-Irving, and Tommy Ladner had been at their summer homes on Paisley Island when they heard war was declared. The training that winter was the usual parade ground, at which Corny did not excel. So terrified was he that he would fail his examination that he would arm his bride of thirty days, Wendy (née Bell-Irving), with a broomstick and march her around their bed-sitting room on Robson Street in Vancouver. In March, 1940, he was sent on loan to the RN, made the trip across Canada with his wife, and with the liberal dispensing of bottles of Scotch as bribes, smuggled Wendy aboard the *Duchess of Atholl*. In the next five years we had many war brides coming *from* England but she is the only example of a war bride going *to* England.

Corny joined *King Alfred* but this was the time of the German breakthrough in May, 1940, and he found himself detailed off as a volunteer to go to Le Havre with some demolition specialists and blow up docks and harbour installations. He arrived on a lovely spring day, the Germans were stuck up the Seine sixty miles or so, civilians were walking up and down the esplanade, and all was peaceful. A marked *dolce far niente* attitude prevailed quite at odds with Burke's blow-up-everything dictum. He had a chief petty officer, torpedo gunner's mate, and a hundred ratings and being in command was more or less a question of knowing when to say, "Carry on, chief." The 52nd Highland Division was trapped at St. Valery en Caux and all the ships left to go there and see if they could rescue them, saying to the demolition teams that they would come back and get them if they could. The teams billeted themselves in a warehouse that had a good supply of canned beans and they were living principally on that. But in examining the next warehouse they found it was full of Guinness, so for the next week they lived on beans and Guinness. There was a contingent of Royal Engineers doing the same work in demolition as the navy; social amenities demanded that the army entertain the navy, which they did by serving Black Velvets. Corny had drunk very little champagne in his life, never Guinness until a week ago, and he didn't realize the potency of the mixture.

> I proceeded to get monumentally drunk. About one p.m. a dispatch rider came into the old cobblestone courtyard; it could have been out of some grade B movie. The driver was covered

with dust, leaped off his bike with his wheels still spinning, rushed into the mess, pointed dramatically up the road and said, "Jerries!" At this point I performed the bravest act of my entire naval career. I went weaving out into the courtyard, gazed defiantly down the road, raised my fist in a war-like gesture, and rasped out in a booze-laden voice, "Well, let 'em come."

Before the Germans did come Burke was taken back to the U.K. to finish his course at *King Alfred*, after which he spent three months in the AMC *Chitrel*. He was then appointed to Fowey to MGB 42 under the command of Lieutenant Fitzroy Talbot, RN. Sub-Lieutenant Burke was both First Lieutenant and Navigator, on his foray as Navigator he left Fowey, went around the Lizzard and around Land's End to the Bristol Channel looking for some airmen who had been downed. MGB 42 did not find them, but coming back the Captain wanted to go into Penzance to fuel, went over an acoustic mine that blew the stern of the boat to smithereens, and she had to be beached. No casualties. Corny Burke was operational.

\* \* \*

**Thomas Ellis Ladner**. Tommy Ladner was with Corny Burke and Budge Bell-Irving (in the 1980s a Lieutenant-Governor of British Columbia), sailing off Paisley Island, British Columbia, when war was declared. He had to go back to law school at Osgoode Hall in September but he went to *York* and joined as an Acting Probationary Temporary Sub-Lieutenant, RCNVR. He sailed for the United Kingdom in June, 1940, in HMS *Ettrick* together with a few other Canadian sub-lieutenants and some Newfoundland fishermen who were going over to join the Royal Navy and serve in trawlers. He joined *King Alfred* and after his normal training took celestial navigation. It was at this time that the German air raids were reaching new heights and the number of bomb disposal officers (rendering mines safe) was not enough. The casualty rate was about 80 per cent. One day his class was told by a Royal Navy Commander, "We need five volunteers for bomb disposal. I'll be back in thirty minutes to see which of you volunteer. Preferably the volunteers should *not* be married."

The class discussed this and thought it was ridiculous that they should be asked to volunteer. They should be selected. They should be told what to do. They had joined to do as they were told. When the Commander came back the class leader said. "Sir, we all volunteer. It's up to you to pick out five." Ladner says, "And he did. I, fortunately, was not one of the ones he picked, because three of them were dead within twelve weeks."

After his ninety days at *King Alfred* he joined AMC *Forfar*, an armed merchant cruiser, whose patrol was Scotland to Iceland to the Denmark Strait. On her second patrol she was torpedoed about a 100 miles west of Iceland on 4 December 1940. (Ladner thinks it was Otto Kretchner, "the Tonnage King," who sank them. It might well have been; he sank forty-four merchant ships before he was captured.) Like all the other AMCs she was filled with thousands of empty oil barrels, so she did not sink empty immediately; she broke in two. Ladner's action station was forward but his abandon ship station was aft. He vaulted across the large crack to get to his lifeboat but more torpedoes hit *Forfar* and his lifeboat was blown to pieces. At the same time another torpedo blew oil right up the ventilating systems and he was drenched, which turned out to be a blessing in disguise because oil keeps you warm in the water. He went down a lifeline with his lifebelt over his great coat and swam around. "I ended up with seven others on a carley float, paddled to a lifeboat which was practically empty, and then hauled in others. We finally had about fifty and the next day we were picked up by a 4,000-ton ship coming from Nova Scotia loaded with pit props. She was on fire. What had happened was that her Captain had stopped to pick up survivors of his chummy ship, who had been torpedoed, and had been shelled by the same submarine. The fire was brought under control and five days later we got in to Oban, Scotland. Norman Alexander, who had been with me, was quite badly injured; we were taken by train to Glasgow."

Tommy had a dreadful rash from the oil – he says he's allergic to most things, anyway. He was treated by a friend of his with whom he was staying on survivor's leave, by putting sacks of oatmeal in the bath water he soaked in. While on leave he went down to Fowey where Burke was operating and spent some time with Corny and Wendy. He rather envied Corny dashing about in his boat at high speed setting off acoustic mines. When his survivor's leave was up in January, 1941, he was sent to *St. Christopher* for training.

It was becoming harder and harder to get into Coastal Forces. He had a lot of yachting experience and, of course, had been on *Forfar*, but he had no naval sea time at all apart from his luxury-liner training in *Forfar*. He and a few other Canadians decided they'd better blast their way through the examinations and do better than anybody else. So rather than carousing around with the rest of the class, they studied, gave each other quizzes, and took dog-watch instructions. As a result, Tommy was appointed *in command* of an MGB without having been to sea in one of them. He was appointed Captain of MGB 19. While she was being built he was given a forty-foot air-sea rescue yacht to ferry from Southampton to the Thames estuary. He started off with a motley pickup crew and took her through the Straits of Dover.

It was a pretty hot operation. Large shells were arriving from the German coastal batteries on the other side of the Channel, the boat kept breaking down, the Channel was full of wrecks, going through the Straits at night was a real nightmare. The Straits of Dover, to me, was always a nightmare and I went through it many times. But my first time I was in this yacht and that was an *unbelievable* nightmare. I didn't know damn all about *anything*. I just followed a trawler through. However, I got there, anchored in the Thames estuary, and went back to MGB 19 and took her to *Hornet*.

I was very proud of myself, an Acting Sub-Lieutenant in command. My crew were all permanent-force Royal Navy. All hands very pusser in their white turtleneck sweaters, blue pants, caps sitting square on their heads. I've done quite a few things in my life, had my share of victories. But I'll never forget the day I took my first command to sea.

* * *

**Walter Charron**. Walter was just finishing high school in St. Lamberts, Quebec, when war was declared. He was eighteen, which was old enough to go to HMCS *Donnacona*, the reserve naval division in Montreal, and join as an Ordinary Seaman. In January, 1940, he was sent to *Stadacona* and after basic training was appointed to the AMC *Aurania* escorting convoys out of Halifax, looking for German pocket battleships, and enjoying the feeling of well-being that came when they couldn't find them. The run was Iceland-Bermuda-Halifax. In December, 1940, he was appointed ashore for a leading torpedoman's course but he went before an officer selection board and went as an Acting Probationary Temporary Sub-Lieutenant to *Royal Roads*, Victoria, British Columbia. There he met Captain Grant, who "ran a very tight ship. I think he was probably ideally suited for training young naval officers." Charron passed out of *Royal Roads* in January, 1942, and was sent to the Royal Navy for Combined Operations. His group sailed from Halifax in a troopship to the Clyde and went to Hayling Island in Hampshire for amphibious training in Landing Craft Assault (LCAs). From there they went to Inveraray where they were billeted on the Duke of Argyll's estate. They commenced training an army division a month by loading them on one side of the loch and landing them on the other. Charron was operational.

**Charles Donald Chaffey**. Charles went to school in Vancouver and by the summer of 1940, at age twenty-one, had left his second year in engineering at the University of British Columbia to take a chartered accountant's course. His mother was a widow and money was short. He joined the navy at *Discovery* pretty much on the basis of his yachting time and in October, as an Ordinary Seaman, with a white band on his hat to show he was an officer candidate, he was shipped overseas in *Andes* and ended up in Gourock. A train ride took him to *Raleigh* in Devonport and after training there he was posted to a Hunt-class destroyer, HMS *Pytchley*. She was on the east coast – Edinburgh to London – mostly fighting off E-boat and aircraft attacks. Charles says, "I challenge anybody to know what is going on or see anything when action occurs because everything is lit up with star shells, everyone is making smoke, gunfire is rumbling on, and everything is in a great big mist. You don't really know where the heck you are. I was on the wing of the bridge shooting a little Hotchkiss machine gun, which is supposed to fire fifty rounds, but managed to get only one out before it jammed. Then I had to fiddle with it and get some more rounds off. I was so busy doing this that I didn't see very much, to tell you the truth."

At dusk and dawn the aircraft would attack and on one of these attacks Charles received his first wound. The door of the wheelhouse was blown off, it hit Charles on the head, and he fell unconscious. At Christmas, 1940, Charles was sent to *King Alfred* and the big thing there, he says, "was OLQs, officer-like qualities; that was the big thing!" He passed out of *King Alfred* as an Acting Temporary Sub-Lieutenant, RCNVR, but felt very much in the navy by this time because he had met Admiral of the Fleet King George VI, who had said to him something like "Good show, old chap." In March of 1941 he joined ML 309 under the command of Lieutenant Frank Hellings, RN. They went to *St. Christopher* for training, which Charles remembers chiefly because he had to climb Ben Neves. What that did for his ability as a Coastal Forces Officer he is still not sure. His ML was armed with two 30/30 machine guns on each side, an 1898 12-pounder hand-loader on the fo'c's'le, depth charges, and asdic. By June of 1941 Chaffey was operational.

**Ian Maclachlan Hay**. After graduating from Bishop's University in Lennoxville, Quebec, in the spring of 1941 Ian joined the navy and was sent to train at *Kings*. After this he went to the *Suderoy VI*, a magnetic minesweeper working in the approaches to Halifax harbour. In July, 1942, he joined the corvette *Chambly*, whose Captain was Lieutenant-Commander Tony Pickard, "A gentleman. He really was and just a great guy to work for." Mid-ocean escort from St. John's to Londonderry and back involved twelve crossings in total. "Some people describe sailing as 45 per cent boredom, 45 per cent discomfort, interspersed with 10 per cent sheer terror, and that's how I found the Atlantic convoy world." Hay was in convoy ON-202 when it merged with ONS 18 into one great unmanageable blob. *Group Leuthen* of twenty U-boats was formed into a line awaiting them; their captains watched appreciatively. HMCS *St. Croix* and HMS *Polyanthus* were sunk. HMS *Itchen* picked up survivors from both. The next night she was sunk. "There were only three survivors from the whole of the ships' companies: one from *Itchen*, one from *Polyanthus*, and one from *St. Croix*. (He [the survivor from *St. Croix*] was very odd for a long time. He kept saying,' Why me? Why was I the only one to live?') *Lagan* had her stern blown off, and six merchantmen were sunk. In December of 1943 I was sent to the U.S.A. to pick up a captain's class frigate to deliver to the RN. Having delivered her I got what I had been seeking all along, that is, sent to *St. Christopher* to commission LCI 266.

"All of us in Combined Ops were conditioned to the notion that the losses were likely to be very heavy. I wasn't too fond of this notion, but it was an adventure." LCI 266 was ready for the Normandy invasion of June, 1944.

**Daniel Lang**. Dan Lang was in the cadet corps of Upper Canada College and the COTC at the University of Toronto before he went to Osgoode Hall. He joined the navy in August of 1941 because he had been a small-boat sailor for most of his life. He was sent to *Kings*, age twenty-one, and passed out as an Acting Temporary Sub-Lieutenant, RCNVR. His first job in the navy was most astonishing for a twenty-one year old sub-lieutenant.

The RCN was in a crisis because the number of corvettes (we built a total of 120) coming down the river from the inland shipyards didn't have anywhere near the technical personnel to man them. "So Headquarters sent me on an emergency, really a semi-political mission, to Hamilton, Ontario, to try and recruit electricians from Westinghouse and General Electric, others from the steel mills. Technicians with this background could quickly become naval artificers, engine room stokers and electricians, and so on. So I had some success because those men didn't *have* to join anything; they were in essential war work. It was a question of weening them away, but always, politically, getting the authority from those companies to release them. It was an interesting time and we met with quite a bit of success, I think, because when I left there we had about 800 men with the right qualifications. They were sent to Edmonton, Alberta, for naval training before they joined the fleet."

Lang then joined the corvette *Agassiz* and for the next two years was on the Newfoundland-to-Londonderry run. By the summer of 1942 the U-boats were off the American coast and so a lively time was had on these transatlantic convoy routes. Lang remembers the aces of the RN, Captain Johnny Walker, Commander Douglas Macintyre, and Commander Peter Gretton. These three must have sunk fifty U-boats among them.

After a couple of years of this he met an Admiral Kekewich, RN, who was in St. John's recruiting Canadians for a motor torpedo boat flotilla under construction in the U.K. "Well, that caught our imagination and although we knew little about what an MTB did, it sounded pretty dashing. I think, too, a lot of us were tired of the North Atlantic run. You know you can have just so much of that type of warfare. MTBs seemed like a nice change." He went across in the troopship *Aquitania*, which was packed with so many Canadian and American troops they had to sleep in rotation – four hours in a bunk, then get out and and let somebody else in. They arrived in the Clyde and Lang was sent to the boat of the Senior Officer of the flotilla.

The night he joined they put to sea. Lang, of course, was completely inexperienced, but "the Captain went to get his head down as soon as we left harbour. Fortunately, there was a good helmsman on the wheel and since we were Senior Officer everyone else had to keep station on us. We made it across to Ijmuiden where we got into a scrap immediately. It was just a flurry of gunfire as far as I can recall, it must have been inconclusive. We were up against German armed trawlers. No casualties but it was a hair-raising experience first time out."

Lang had been blooded.

**Malcolm C. Knox**. "Mac" was at school in Montreal when war was declared and went to *Donnacona* to sign up. He couldn't be taken immediately so he joined the COTC at McGill University, as Second Lieutenant in a cavalry regiment. However, horses and he didn't get along very well. Besides, he needed more than one horsepower so he tried out for MTBs and got 4,000 horsepower. In May of 1941 he was sent to *Royal Roads*, twenty years old and in great shape physically; he had been the captain of the junior Canadian water polo championship team two years before and had kept in training. The physical activities were to his liking and he took pride in doing as well as he could. Captain Grant was "an amazing gentleman. He had everybody's respect. He knew just how tough to be and how to get the best out of everybody. We had a great regard for him. It was amazing that in such a short period of time he would build up that kind of rapport with 125 young men."

Mac was appointed to the minesweeper *Chedabucto*, then being constructed in Vancouver. After a shakedown cruise to Prince Rupert she headed for Halifax and arrived on 15 December 1941. Then he was appointed to *Goderich* and moved to St. John's just after the attack on Pearl Harbor. In 1942 the U-boats had moved further west; in the Kreigsmarine they called it "The Happy Time" and also "The American Shooting Season." That winter he spent in *Goderich* his Captain was Lieutenant R.R. Kenney, RCNR. Knox says, "I learned more from him, I think, than anybody else heretofore. I had spent the days of my youth boating in small craft and when I signed on I indicated that I'd be interested in getting into MTBs. Somebody in the dim recesses of Naval Headquarters found this piece of paper and in the autumn of 1942 I was sent to ML 103 as First Lieutenant and the winter was spent patrolling off Halifax and Sydney, Nova Scotia."

In the spring of 1943 he was appointed in command of ML 43 and spent the summer in the Gulf of St. Lawrence based at Gaspé, Quebec. The U-boats had been in the Gulf of St. Lawrence for the previous year but Knox did not see much action.

Then he was sent to Lowestoft to the MTB training flotilla. His first night out was a Z patrol, just to seaward of the convoys. After a few weeks he went to HMS *Excellent* for a couple of weeks' gunnery and aircraft recognition, HMS *Vernon* for torpedo, signals at *Roedean*, and then to New Haven to another British flotilla and more firsthand experience. It was here that Knox was shot at for the first time, in his case by shore batteries. He says, "That became old hat by the time we got finished with it, a nightly experience. You could just about tell the time they'd fire at you after a while. The training was good and it sharpened us up because you don't learn anything about going to sea out of books or in the classroom, but you certainly learn quickly in small craft when you're being fired at. I appreciated the training I got from the Royal Navy."

Mac's first Canadian Captain was Bones Burk, who was "a great character. No matter what he does he puts so much enthusiasm in it that it's contagious. He fires everyone else to do more than they would do otherwise. He's a great leader, no doubt of it."

**David Christopher Wright**. Dave tried to join the Royal Navy as a Boy Seaman when he was fourteen but (a) they wouldn't take him that early and (b) he didn't have the money to go to England anyway. So in September of 1940, when he was seventeen, he joined the RCN as a Boy Seaman (at fifty cents a day). After training in the naval barracks in Esquimalt, HMCS *Naden*, he was drafted to the corvette *Kamloops* in March, 1941. After six months in the barracks where the meals are never that great he "had fish and chips the first night on board. It was a real good meal because it was on board ship – getting away from those barracks meals. It was really a good go."

They sailed to Halifax, where Wright transferred to *Vegreville* in January, 1942. He served mostly on coastal convoys from Halifax to Newfoundland, but there was not much action until they were stationed at Gaspé taking convoys up the St. Lawrence in the spring and summer of 1942. The U-boats had arrived in strength by that time and he saw many sinkings. It was a danger – common with American ships all over the world – that they were trigger happy, and this was the case in the St. Lawrence, too. While under U-boat attack the American merchant ships were shooting at anything that moved. One wounded merchant ship, SS *Essex Lancer*, was saved when she was towed to the beach but seven others were sunk.

In 1943 Dave was a leading seaman and had completed a radar operator's course. The question then was how to get out. "I disliked barracks very much. I went up to the drafting chief petty officer and said, 'Chief, send me back to the west coast or send me overseas.' So the chief volunteered me for MTBs. I didn't volunteer but I was glad to go. I went over in *Mauritania* in January, 1943. I'd collected all kinds of chocolate bars. I must have had a couple of hundred of them, I knew they were short in England. Also a few silk stockings. I thought this might be what the girls wanted, chocolates and silk stockings. Anyway, I has this great big suitcase and I joined HMCS *Niobe* with my duffel bag, my kit bag, my hammock, and my big suitcase full of goodies. *Niobe*, just outside Glasgow, used to be an insane asylum before the war; the rooms had no doorknobs on the inside. I was a good candidate for the insane asylum arriving with all that baggage. Then a bunch of us went up to London and I carried this big case with me, [and] we got lost in the underground. We didn't really know where to stay, didn't know how to meet anybody, certainly no girls, so on the way back from London to Scotland we ate all the chocolate bars ourselves."

Wright was sent to a Royal Navy MTB flotilla at Felixstowe. Several times a week they would be over on the Dutch coast but there was not much doing. He then went to MTB 745 of the 65th Canadian MTB Flotilla on Lieutenant Mabee's boat. Wright was fully operational.

**Robert George Buckingham**. George had a bent toward the navy from Sea Scouts onward and joined in Montreal as an Acting Probationary Sub-Lieutenant, RCVNR, in May, 1940, because "it seemed the navy would be a good service to be in." He and his mates trained on the St. Lawrence – on Lake St. Louis – in a large yacht donated to the navy by a man named Phillip Ross. The autumn of 1940 he went to *Stadacona*, the Mousetraps. He did a three-month training course in Canadian MTB 1, which was brought over from the U.K. to start a Canadian flotilla. This, however, never amounted to anything so he served in an ML out of Weymouth until he could get into Combined Operations.

In January, 1942, he went to the U.K. to join a Royal Navy flotilla and was carried on the books of HMS *Quebec* in Inveraray, Scotland; this was the headquarters for all Combined Operations during the war. He took training in the Landing Craft Assault (LCA), which we used exclusively in the first wave, and the Landing Craft Motor (LCM), which could take a tank or a lorry. Training went on all summer and it was then he met the three most important men in his naval life. The first was Admiral of the Fleet King George VI when he came down to inspect Combined

Ops. "To us he seemed a sailor first and a monarch second; you could tell from the way he talked. With him was Rear-Admiral Lord Louis Mountbatten, a very striking individual. We looked upon him as being quite a spectacular chap. But the one that impressed me more than anybody else was Rear-Admiral T.H. Troubridge, the flag officer for the Central Task Force, Operation Torch. His chief of staff was K.S. MacLachlan, who had been deputy minister in the Department of National Defence in Ottawa but who shifted from the civil service to become a Lieutenant-Commander, RCNVR. The Canadians in Combined Operations regarded MacLachlan as their Great White Father."

In the autumn of 1942 George joined HMS *Otranto* for Operation Torch with his Canadian flotilla. The other Canadian flotilla went to HMS *Ettrick*. A huge convoy sailed from the Clyde. Rear-Admiral Troubridge was in the headquarter ship *Bulolo*, and at one a.m. on 8 November 1942 Operation Torch commenced. They sailed from Britain south down the Atlantic past Gibraltar and into the Mediterranean, landing in North Africa on a point called Sidi Ferruch.

**Harry Edgar Trenholm**. Harry had been going to Bishop's College School and when he was about thirteen the sea stories of the family chauffeur (who had been in the RN in World War I) convinced him that it was a glamorous way to live his life; he tried to join the Royal Navy but could not. But in 1940 he was called by *Donnacona* and asked if he would like to try the RCNVR. He did and was sent to the first class at King's College, Halifax, which had been a theological seminary for the Anglican Church, with lovely old stone buildings, large trees, and green lawns sloping down to the Atlantic. It was commissioned HMCS *Kings*, the white ensign was hoisted, and the principal became chaplain to the mids and sub-lieutenants.

He, like some others, had trouble with his eyes and, like the others, went and learned the chart, came back, and got 20/20. He remembers the tricky line to this day – T-Z-Z-U-A-E-N. He was appointed as a midshipman to HMS *Worchestershire*, patrolling the Halifax-Iceland-Bermuda route. Like most snotties his principal job was bringing cocoa to the officer of the watch and carrying rude messages (diplomatically reworded) from one senior officer to another. After being trained here he was appointed to a Bangor-class minesweeper, HMCS *Swift Current*, and spent six months in his home town standing by her as she was under construction.

Trenholm left *Swift Current* for Combined Operations via *Niobe* and then to Hayling Island in Hampshire to train in LCAs. He was shipped north to Inverness and then to Operation Torch in French Algiers. He and his landing craft were carried to Africa on the deck of an American Liberty Ship, lowered by derrick into the water when they made the rendezvous with the rest of the invasion fleet, embarked his soldiers, and landed them on the beach at Arzeu.

**Robert J. Moyse**. In June, 1939, Bob graduated from United College in Winnipeg; in September he joined the RCN, "because I had always been fascinated by the sea novels of Joseph Conrad and, like a lot of prairie boys, the sea looked to be very romantic. But I really joined because I didn't want to miss the excitement. I don't think it was really out of any great feeling of patriotism but I certainly had been against the Hitler business for some time."

No more commissions were being offered – at least not in Winnipeg – so he joined as an Ordinary Seaman, officer candidate, which gave him a white band around his cap. He went to Halifax for training and then to *Duchess of Bedford* for passage to Liverpool. It was in her he met a group of new entries from Toronto who were headed directly for *King Alfred* because they had been brought in with their commissions. It was a significant feature of *York* during the war that it was a very *social* division; practically all their young officers came from the private schools of Ontario, "the Little Big Four": Ridley, St. Andrew's, Trinity, and Upper Canada College.

When it was time for his interview for a commission the four-ring captain, RN, who was president of the Board, said "I suppose you're from Upper Canada College, too."

"No sir. I went to General Sir Isaac Brock School in Winnipeg."

"And who is General Sir Isaac Brock?"

"Oh, he was the British general who defeated the Americans at the Battle of Queenston Heights in 1812 and pushed them back over the border."

"Bloody good show! Top of the class."

Moyse tried for the Fleet Air Arm (with Hammy Gray, who later got a DSC and a VC) but did not pass his flying instruction because he had no depth perception. He was drafted to HMS *Castleton*, an American lend/lease destroyer. She escorted minelayers up to Iceland and as Moyse commenced his training as an OD in the fo'c's'le, he was subject to the time-immemorial barracking that is the lot of officer candidates serving in the lower deck. Since Admiral Nelson was a cadet, at midday the pipe has been, "Hands to dinner." But when there are ratings on board who are in line for either a commission or a warrant – called commission/warrant candidates, or c/w candidates – the pipe is always, "Hands to dinner – c/w candidates to lunch."

He and Craig Bishop got the usual blasts for the usual things. On one occasion when he was lookout he failed to spot a floating mine and the officer of the watch had to take violent action to avoid it. When he was helmsman he got the usual blast for over-correcting: "The wake looks like the furrow left by a drunken ploughman." And when he had to make a pipe he really didn't know how to handle the bosun's call and just "blew a tune on it the best I could."

In six months he and Bishop went to *St. Christopher* for MTB training and after some time in the training flotilla they were both appointed to Dover. They arrived in bad odour because they had decided nobody would miss them if they stayed over for a few days in London, but when they arrived they found they had *indeed* been expected. They had to report to the Admiral at Dover Castle, who said, "You know, I have a mind to send you to one-man submarines." But, somewhat mollified by their contrite appearance, he merely confined them to the base. There had been big battles between E-boats and MTBs; many of our boats had been shot up and Bishop and Moyes inspected them somberly every morning as they returned.

Bob was appointed to Mark Arnold Forster's boat, made his first trip to the French coast, and was shelled by German shore batteries. He was now a warrior.

**Thomas Osborne Poapst**. Tom joined the navy as an Ordinary Seaman in Edmonton just after his eighteenth birthday in April, 1941, because, "never having seen the ocean, I thought sailing would be a great way to put in a war." He soon found it was not the smooth sailing he had expected because from all over Canada retired chief petty officers of the Royal Navy had come back into the service – into the RCN – as instructors at the naval divisions. The one in Edmonton made Tom's life difficult, which was his job. Poapst says, "It got so that whenever this Chief just *looked* at me I put my rifle over my head and doubled around the parade ground. He voted me the least likely to succeed." Poapst was drafted to *Naden* for new entry training, then to the tug *Standpoint*, an examination vessel. (These were on watch outside every one of our ports during the war, usually near the pilot vessel. When an inbound ship stopped to pick up a pilot, a naval officer would board, inspect her papers, cargo manifest, deck log, and so on; it was to verify that she was indeed one of our side. Jim Kirkpatrick had the job off Saint John in 1940 when the author had it off Halifax.)

In January of 1942 Poapst volunteered for Coastal Forces and was sent to the 80th LCM (Landing Craft Mechanized) Flotilla in the U.K. He did some training with the Lovat Scouts and then went to Inveraray in Loch Fyne where the Canadian 80th and the 81st flotillas were training. Their Admiral was Lord Louis and he would turn up from time to time. Poapst says, "He was a great one for 'at ease men, just gather around me and I'll tell you what's going on. Now you know some of you will not return . . .' "

Like his friends, Poapst was living on the Duke of Argyle's estate in Quonset huts, and a bit more is added to Canadian naval lore by learning that in his flotilla was a "Boxcar" Cuntz from Saskatchewan, a butcher. Thus, with the Duke of Argyle's sheep, the Canadian butcher, and one other skilful hand who could always wangle a barrel of beer, they were living well.

The training had been established to embark troops at one side of the loch, take them across to the other, and land them. There are some techniques for the Captain of a landing craft.

"We started off by dropping a kedge anchor on the way in so you could kedge off if necessary. But another technique developed. I would put my engines astern before I hit the beach, have the pins to the forward ramp out, drop the ramp the moment the ship touched, then with fifty men leaving the boat within a minute the weight was much reduced and I should have sternway on. The reason this was a good technique was that I didn't have enough hands to (a) get the half-ton bow ramp up again and (b) simultaneously man the capstan to kedge off and have the door secured before I turned and headed into the sea. It was my view that when you hit the beach you're already going astern. Because the beach isn't the place to *be*. It's a place to be *from*."

As an able seaman, Poapst was Captain of an LCM – twenty-five tons displacement, fifty feet long, with a speed of twelve knots. She carried either one tank or fifty infantry. Life was pleasant during the training period. The Senior Officer of the 80th flotilla was Lieutenant Jack Koyle, RCNVR, who had been a professional hockey player before the war and so their hockey team often played the Paisley Pirates, another Canadian team. They also had games in Glasgow where the Locarno nightclub on Sauchiehall Street was a favourite with the Canadians: lots of beer, lots of girls, a revolving stage on which two bands played in turn so dancing was constant.

The flotilla was working up for Dieppe but Poapst had smashed his left knee between two boats. He was therefore in hospital in Sherbourne in Dorset when the flotilla went to Dieppe. "I guess I was lucky or unlucky, depending on how you look at it. Andy Wedd, a Sub-Lieutenant, got a DSC. The flotilla lost about seventy-five hands out of the total of 200."

Poapst picked up his hook and as a Leading Seaman was in charge of four of the twelve boats of the 80th flotilla. He also had the job of mailman, which required going into Glasgow every day, and sometimes he would get back later rather than sooner – sometimes much later. On one occasion this enraged Jake Koyle; he told Poapst he was broken in rank from Leading Seaman to Able Seaman and his leave was stopped for thirty days. In two days, however, they were told to sail for Operation Torch. Jake told Poapst to get his four boats going, and Poapst replied he couldn't because he was only an Able Seaman. Koyle said, "Oh, sew the damn hook on again and get cracking."

The flotilla was loaded on a tanker. They sailed south in October, 1942, to Africa and fifteen days later were put in the water four miles off Arzeu, just east of Cape Ferrat.

\* \* \*

**Jack G. McClelland**. Jack joined in the autumn of 1941 at *York* because "I'd always liked the sea, always liked sailing; we had a boat at the Royal Toronto Yacht Club. After graduating from St. Andrew's, I went for engineering and physics at the U of T. After war broke out I was determined to join the navy. I didn't think my interview board went too well. So green was I that it looked to me as though they were all admirals on the other side of the table and I got flustered. At one point the president asked, 'Well now, McClelland, we notice in your application you've had a lot of sailing experience. Have you been sailing all your life?'

" 'No, sir, just since I was about five.'

"I felt like such a bloody fool with that stupid answer, that I'd blown my chance. But I guess they were short and they let me in."

In April of 1942 McClelland went to *Royal Roads* and thought Captain Grant "an extraordinary human being. I loved the naval college, we had a lot of fun. We had a good group and the training was very useful. A great spirit developed there. It was well run and a good part of the navy. First they got us into very, very good physical condition, even though we were not in bad condition when we joined. If you'd ever joined *Royal Roads* in bad physical condition *you're dead in a very short time*."

Upon passing out McClelland was appointed to *Chedabucto* on convoys from Sydney to Quebec. In May, 1942, the first merchant ship was torpedoed in the Gulf of St. Lawrence, south of Anticosti Island. This summer of 1942 the U-boats were well into the Gulf of St. Lawrence and the day after McClelland set sail a ship was torpedoed. The U-boat surfaced, and the merchant ships opened fire. In September the frigate *Charlottetown* was torpedoed and sunk off Cape Chat.

That autumn Jack went to a Fairmile flotilla working out of St. John's. His Senior Officer was "Fog Horn" Davis. The stories about Fog Horn are legion. He said if he was going to be Senior Officer of a flotilla he should *look* like a Senior Officer, and so had the reefer of his sea uniform fitted with gold lace to above the elbows and had the medal-ribbon side of the breast of his jacket decorated with eleven rows of coloured cloth resembling medal ribbons, starting at his shoulder and disappearing into his pocket. He grew a long beard, wore one large gold earring, and had Plimsoll marks tatooed on his stomach.

That flotilla spent a week on patrol in Conception Bay between Wabana on Bell Island and Portugal Cove. From 1942 into January, 1943, U-boats were laying mines off the harbour to the iron ore mine. Jack then went to Toronto to commission a new ML and brought her back to Newfoundland, now in command. He resumed patrols between St. John's and Conception Bay and one night his asdic operator reported a submarine contact. He went to action stations and finally got an echo on radar and fired star shell on that bearing. He reported to St. John's they'd been in contact with the enemy, "but it was clear they didn't believe us." He is certain, however, that it was a minelaying U-boat because a few days later a ship blew up outside the harbour. More mines were raised by our sweepers; George Rundle was their rendering-mines-safe officer (in 1942 he and Denis O'Hagen were two of the few of those originally trained in the U.K. who were still living).

"It was a serious minefield. I learned a lot about that minefield. I was in command but it was really under Rundle's direction because he wanted the mines on the beach to render them safe and towing a mine is not recommended by doctors as being beneficial to your health. But on two occasions the mines would be cut by one of the sweepers and come to the surface rather than explode. We put a line on the mine and then we would *tow the goddamn thing*.

"Down the coast I would find an uninhabited harbour. The hands would get into the boat and pull the mine ashore, then get as far away as possible. Now it was Rundle's job to take the mine apart and find out what the timing device was. He had been doing this for several years. He would always have the mine placed close to a boulder for him to duck behind. He was leading a very dicey life. When we were working with him he rendered seven of them safe. He would lie down on the deck of the boat for maybe ten minutes and try and relax, eyes closed, still. Then he'd get up and go ashore and do the job." His citation in the *London Gazette* said,

> For great courage, coolness and skill in recovering and rendering safe enemy mines under extreme difficulties, experienced as a result of darkness and the nature of the beach.

Jack was Mentioned in Despatches for his part in these operations.

Christmas of 1943 found McClelland on board *Pasteur* sailing for the U.K. to join Kirkpatrick's 65th Canadian Flotilla. In January, 1944, he joined Oliver Mabee's boat as First Lieutenant. They worked out of Brixham and Dover and Jack was soon blooded with an engagement with flak trawlers.

\* \* \*

**Donald C. Harrison**. Don joined the Royal Canadian Navy as a cadet in the summer of 1942 "when *Royal Roads* was changing from a college to train acting sub-lieutenants, RCNVR, to training permanent force cadets, RCN. The Captain was still Stumpy Grant, an inspiring sort of fellow. One time he climbed to the top of the mast on the tower of the castle just to show the cadets he could do it. We thought that quite an extraordinary feat for an old man of forty-five."

Harrison was in *Royal Roads* when the invasion of Normandy in June of 1944 was broadcast, and all the cadets regretted "they had missed the fun." However, in August, 1944, sixteen of his class were divided between the two Canadian aircraft carriers *Puncher* and *Nabob*. In December, Harrison was sent to Great Yarmouth to MTB 745, Oliver Mabee's boat. Lieutenant Bill Counter was the Navigator, Lieutenant George Patterson was the First Lieutenant, and Harrison did everything else. After Counter left the boat Harrison became the Navigator. The day after he joined the flotilla they were sent to the Dutch coast on an offensive sweep. He viewed with alarm those who had returned from a previous offensive sweep with their pumps chugging away keeping the bilges clear the best they could because they had been hit by 4-inch shells. He thought this quite exciting as he left and even more so when shells starting arriving alongside his boat a few hours later.

**Ian W. Robertson**. Ian joined the RCNVR as a midshipman in HMCS *Chippawa* in Winnipeg in 1942, having just completed his third year of university at the age of seventeen. Captain Teddy Orde, RCN, was the commanding officer; he was distinguished by having one glass eye, the first having been lost in the Halifax explosion in 1918 when he was a cadet at the first Naval College of Canada. He has his part in the fables of the RCN by having *three glass eyes*: the normal one for everyday wear; a bloodshoot one to wear the morning after the night before; and one with a white ensign for such occasions as Trafalgar Day and the Glorious 1st of June.

Ian then went to *Kings*. He put in to transfer to the Royal Navy and on arriving in London, England, Ian, who never lacked self-confidence, reported in at the office of the Second Sea Lord at the Admiralty to "a very distinguished gentleman, Commander Deneys, RN." Deneys asked him what he would like to do and said he would get him what he could, except the Fleet Air Arm was full up and so were MTBs.

Ian said, "I'm sorry, sir, but those are the only ones I'm interested in."

"I just told you, you cannot do either. But I can well understand your wishes. Now – I can't promise you anything – but come back and see me next week."

When Ian came back the Commander said, "I can offer you a chance to *compete* to get into MTBs. That means you'll have to take a three-month course with about thirty others and only the top ten will be accepted for Coastal Command."

So off Ian went. He, of course, had never had any trouble with the bookwork and in everything from high-speed pilotage to high-speed communications came near the top of the class and was posted to an RN flotilla.

Roedean Ladies College had been turned into a torpedo school where he did a course. Then he went to *St. Christopher* where he joined the training squadron for navigation, pilotage, gunnery and actual firing of torpedoes at floating targets, high-speed communication, morse, semaphore – all those and others. Robertson said that all the instructional staff had had sea time in MTBs, practically all of them were decorated, and practically all had had command. Ian was posted to the 6th MGB flotilla at Lowestoft; his Captain was Lieutenant Bill Feske, RANVR; they went to Great Yarmouth and then down to Dover. He saw his first action in that flotilla.

"That was fascinating. It was a classic attack – classic MTB-MGB attack developed by Hichens. We got to the coast off Ijmuiden early in the evening; our force consisted of two units, four MTBs and four MGBs. The plan of attack was that the gun boats would come in from one direction to create a diversion by attacking the convoy and what was required of them was a great deal of noise and tracer; setting ships on fire was always considered a plus. We went around the stern of the convoy and up between the columns firing to port and to starboard, hoping that if the convoy fired back they would shoot at each other rather than our craft. The supporting German E-boats were expected to turn inwards in alarm and try and put off these marauding Britishers, at which time the torpedo boats would come in from the bow and launch their torpedoes at a few hundred yards.

"Well, everything was going fine. I was watching the crisscross of the tracer over my head with some interest. All of a sudden there was this awful bump and a cloud of smoke and I thought, 'Oh, gee whiz! My first night and here we go. Either it's the end or it's a swim or it's a prison camp. But this didn't seem to be bothering the skipper at all, who was cursing loudly over the loud-hailer to the next ahead. Apparently what had happened was the boat ahead had suddenly decreased speed without signalling and we had bumped into his smoke machine on his stern and started it going. The whole attack took perhaps ten minutes and then both torpedo and gun boats pulled off into the dark to seaward. But we went at the convoy twice again that night."

They had to leave just before dawn to get out of the range of aircraft by daylight or they would get bounced by the *Luftwaffe*. The First Lieutenant turned to Ian and said, "Okay, that'll be it for tonight. If you'd like to sit down and take a rest there won't be any more action." Ian remembers sitting on the deck and looking out of the charthouse through the open portholes and as he was nodding off to sleep he was suddenly aware of the fact that he was watching the ocean but there were telephone poles and fences on it. He was so tired that he was hallucinating. They had gone to action stations at ten in the evening and by now it was four in the morning. Robertson was well and truly operational and went on to join Bones Burk.

* * *

**Walter Stairs Blandy**. Walter joined in 1943 in Victoria, British Columbia – HMCS *Malahat* – at age nineteen, "because it was the thing to do in those days. All my friends were joining and the navy was where I wanted to be. Nobody mentioned patriotism. It was just a built-in thing. If the King said 'Jump,' you said 'how high?' " He had finished his high school, then two years of Victoria College. On the strength of that and his Royal Victoria Yacht Club connections he had little difficulty passing his selection board at the local naval division. He went to *Kings* and volunteered for MTBs in England but since there were no openings he went to ML 99 in Newfoundland. Between 99 and ML 102 he was on the patrol carried out two years earlier by Jack McClelland, St. John's to Wabana, the iron-ore loading port. They saw no action: by this time the tide of the war had changed in our favour and the U-boats had withdrawn to east of Iceland.

Walter was accepted for MTBs in November of 1944 and went to Oliver Mabee's 726 in Great Yarmouth. Jay Coulter was First Lieutenant and Blandy was Navigator. They were based at Ostend, Flanders, Belgium. Their first job was to go north to the Scheldt estuary. Two of them would secure to a navigation buoy so that their echo would be merged with it and not be evident to the German shore radar. They would be under the direction of a mother ship – usually a frigate – lying further offshore. At that time the E-boats were coming down from the Hook of Holland to lay mines in the Channel and the mother ship would vector our MTBS on. Then there would be a gun battle to try and deter the E-boats from laying mines. "We might drive them off but these E-boat captains were persistent fellows. They would try and sneak back later. Kept us up all night."

* * *

**Leslie Russell Bowerman**. Les had been serving on the hydrographic vessel *William J. Stewart* for four years before he joined the RCN. The transfer from the Canadian Coast Guard to the navy was more or less automatic and Bowerman came in with the rank of Leading Stoker. In January, 1942, he took a mechanical course at *Naden*, was sent to Halifax for more training, and then was drafted to ML 99, being built at Penetanguishene on Lake Erie. They went on patrol in the Gulf of St. Lawrence, based at Gaspé. After a few months of this Bowerman applied for MTB and in December, 1943, went from New York and ended up at

*Niobe*, "the lunatic asylum, where, I knew, I would not have been out of place."

He went to HMS *Attack*, a shore base in Weymouth for motor mechanics. After a couple of months in training he went to the "Shorts," was rated Petty Officer, then went back to *Attack* to do a course on the Rolls-Royce engines, "the *real* Rolls Royce" (they had been trained on the Packard Marlin). Bowerman was then sent to Littlehampton where Lieutenant Kirkpatrick was waiting. Kirk was just commissioning 748 and was interviewing the officers and the chief motor mechanic. Out of all the applicants Kirk chose Bowerman as his chief engineer.

Bowerman had his own engine room for the first time. Recalling it, his eyes shone and his face was animated: "Gee! Looking down at those engines for the first time! Just like Buck Rogers. A mass of four motors, 1,250 horsepower each, twelve-cylinder supercharged engines, a total of 5,000 horsepower. We carried 6,700 gallons of 100 per cent octane fuel in eleven tanks, plus one tank of 'pool' gasoline, four of 87 per cent octane for the generator, two Morse generators, four cylinder, 220 volt."

In February of 1945, MTB 748 went to Brixham and started Z patrols, or rather, they started out to be Z patrols but usually ended up off the enemy coast.

**Gordon Merle Cahill**. In May, 1943, Gordon left high school at age seventeen to join the *Princess Mary*, a ferry running from Powell River to Victoria and Vancouver, in the Canadian Pacific Fleet. He joined as a Wiper but within a month was a Fireman. In December of that year he joined the navy as a Stoker and drafted to *Stadacona*. He volunteered for MTBs and in January, 1944, was sent to *Attack* to take courses on the MTB engines. After this he was sent as an advance party to Brixham, where the flotilla would be based. He was to open a storeroom for the spare parts that would soon arrive. He was there for two months by himself with very little to do except unload the lorries when they came in. The only other one he knew there was the senior RN officer, who had been badly injured early in the war and made it around with two canes and two artificial legs. Their meeting ground was a little pub across the street and their meetings were at noon daily. From noon to two p.m., or three, or four.

Kirkpatrick and flotilla came around. Cahill was still in charge of stores but every night he'd go and watch the boats leave and every morning he'd watch them return to harbour.

"I wanted to get on them. The first time they got into action I wasn't with them. However, after that action I joined the engine room crew under Chief Petty Officer Bowerman. Bowerman interviewed me to see if I was suitable to join the ship. He was very hard to please, as I found out later, very hard to please. Nothing, *nothing* came ahead of the welfare of his engines."

So it was in MTB 748 that Cahill saw his first action off the Channel Islands in May, 1944.

✳   ✳   ✳

**Thomas H. Forrester.** In the spring of 1942 Tom had completed high school at Nanaimo, B.C., and took a job driving a truck in the logging camps and "monkey wrenching"; he wanted to get into the mechanical side of things. But he said, "I'd been around water all my life and I wanted to join the navy, so in November I did. I had two brothers in the navy so I kind of joined the family."

He joined as a motor mechanic. In January, 1943, he was drafted from Esquimalt to Detroit, for upgrading on the motors of landing craft. After his course he picked up an LCI in New York and they sailed for Bermuda.

"An LCI, 250-feet, big buggers. It took four days to get to Bermuda and I was the sickest sailor you've ever seen in your life – for four days!"

After a time in Bermuda they headed east across the Atlantic to Gibraltar – thirteen days. The skipper was a Lieutenant, the second-in-command a Sub-Lieutenant, and about twenty were in the crew. Forrester doesn't remember the names of his captains because they changed around frequently as conditions dictated and no one officer or man really stayed in one particular boat for any length of time.

He was in LCI 273 when they sailed for Operation Torch in October of 1943. They and thirty-six other LCIs ran west to Gibraltar. In these LCIs, which held 250 soldiers, they did not have the same trouble getting off the beach as Poapst did. When 250 men leave the ship, that's over twenty tons; moreover, the kedge they dropped on the way in was connected to an electric capstan so kedging off was no trouble. Closing the ramp doors was no trouble with a crew of twenty. He landed at Arzeu and that was the beginning of Tom's shooting war.

# V   Canadians Join the Battle

*T*he first E-boat attacks on east coast convoys were in September, 1940. Our MTBs of 1940-41 had not done well. They were not reliable and seldom made better than twenty-four knots compared to the forty knots of the German E-boats, which had been designed and built in the late 1930s (when we neglected coastal forces). In an effort to reach parity we appointed a flag officer to co-ordinate future design, alterations and additions, recruiting, training, maintenance, and improvements in general of MTBs, MGBs, and MLs. This was Rear-Admiral Piers Kekewich, RN; his chief-of-staff was Captain A.W.S. Agar, VC, DSO, RN, whose Victoria Cross had been won in a coastal motor boat at Kronstadt in 1919 when he torpedoed the cruiser *Oleg*. The 6th MGB Flotilla formed in December consisted of converted Masbys armed with Lewis, 20mm, and a Boulton & Paul aircraft turret operating four .303 Browning machine guns. The flotilla was under the command of Lieutenant Peter Howes, RN, and was formed at Fowey in Cornwall. Its officers were to become famous in the annals of Coastal Forces: Lieutenants Robert P. Hichens, RNVR; D.G.K. Richards, RN; I.A. Griffiths, RN; A.A. Gotelee, RNVR; L.G.R. Campbell, RNVR; G.E. Bailey, RNVR; George F. Duncan, RCNVR; and Jim Kirkpatrick, RCNVR.

By the spring of 1941 the menace had become serious. Canadians Jim Kirkpatrick, Tony Law, Tom Ladner, Bones Burk, Corny Burke, Charles Chaffey, Alex Joy, and Bob Moyse were seasoned warriors by this time. Experience comes quickly when you are in action a couple of times a week. In August, Lieutenant Howes, under whom Kirkpatrick had been serving, was appointed to a signal's course and Lieutenant Hichens was promoted Acting Lieutenant-Commander and took over as Senior Officer. The night of 8-9 September saw the first successful torpedo attack to be fought on the pattern that later became typical of

MTB warfare in the Battle of the Narrow Seas. Admiral Kekewich had received word two heavily laden merchant ships, with an escort of trawlers and E- and R-boats, were attempting a passage through the Straits of Dover. Lieutenant-Commander E.N. Pumphrey, RN, in MTB 35 was in command of the force of MTBs that intercepted them. His next astern in 218 was Chuck Bonnell, RCNVR; Lieutenant P.E. Danielsen of the Royal Norwegian Navy was in command of 54 but had engine trouble and was left to join up later, at the interception point off Blanc Nez. MGBs 43 (Stewart Gould, RN) and 52 (Barry Leith, RNVR) were at sea and ordered to find the enemy and shadow him. Contact was made at 11:30 p.m. with the two merchant ships of about 3,000 tons, three trawlers, and eight E/R* boats. Pumphrey and Bonnell stole in between the screen at slow speed – barely steerage way – 800 yards. Then they rang on their outboard engines in a crash start. Tracer streamed in green streaks toward them. They fired their torpedoes and disengaged astern. There were no hits, but gun battles went on for twenty minutes.

Kirkpatrick remembers the inconclusive nature of these actions with Scott and Hichens and Pumphrey: "a run in, spurts of fire, and then out." His boat was damaged and although he was sent to Felixstowe to stand by another, he not allowed to remain idle. Another flotilla was working out of Fowey – one boat was French, two Polish, one Dutch, two British – and several times Kirk went out as spare commanding officer. In April, 1942, he was sent to a flotilla in Trinidad. He was supposed to be escorting convoys but mostly he was picking up survivors. At one point (at its worst) he picked up forty-five. He returned to the U.K. in 1943 and went to a flotilla commanded by Lieutenant-Commander H.O.T. Bradford, DSC, RNVR. In July, 1941, Bradford had fought an action with five E-boats in the neighborhood of Brown Ridge that lasted fifty-five minutes and ended in pursuing the enemy to Ijmuiden.

In March, 1941, Tony Law was appointed to MGB 53 as First Lieutenant. In the summer of 1942 he joined a flotilla a steam gun boats (SGBs) at Dover, one of which was commanded by Peter Scott. Tony then got command of MTB 48 in the flotilla led by Hillary Gamble, DSC, RN, on patrols off the Dutch and Belgian coastline. Then they were sent to Dover, called rather dramatically "Hell's Corner." In his first action his motor mechanic was wounded; the victories and the casualties had started.

---

*E/R is a convention for *Schnellboote* and/or *Räumboote*. It is hard to differentiate between these small vessels at night or on a hasty sighting.

The rapid build-up of Coastal Forces had by 1942 got into full swing. By 1945 it was to number 1,500 men and sixty boats; these were engaged in 464 actions in the English Channel and North Sea. A total of 269 enemy ships were sunk for a loss of seventy-six of our own craft. But this was still ahead of them.

*   *   *

Bones Burk got to MTB 101 as Third Officer under Allan Seymour-Hayden. Their job was mostly air-sea rescue. Then he got MGB 14 as First Lieutenant to Doug Maitland. (Corny Burke and Tommy Ladner were in command of two of the other boats.) Bones say Maitland was "an outgoing kind of person. He was always fun. There was always something doing. But also he had a very good understanding of boats. He was another amateur sailor who had spent a great deal of time on the water. He was right at home, a good fellow to work with and a good leader of his crew – who all respected him."

The thing that Bones Burk remembers about Corny Burke is that when Corny was at the base he was regularly receiving fruitcakes from his mother in Vancouver. When he went off to the Mediterranean and Bones remained in Lowestoft, being C. Burk – the same as Corny – the fruitcakes started coming to him. Bones wrote to Corny, thanked him for the cakes, and suggested he write his mother and thank her.

Working out of Lowestoft they had Royal Navy Lieutenant Dyer in command of the flotilla, "who was a much older fellow. He didn't really like the small boats to begin with. He was not at home in that area, it just wasn't his field. Young people are the best for this. He didn't lead the attacks with the dash – and even more important – the *tenacity* of the others which meant coming in for a second and third attack sometimes until the dawn made it necessary to get clear of the coast. One particular night he broke off the action too soon – many thought. They were passing between two of the West Frisian islands off the Dutch coast and an airplane dived on them. They fired back but the Senior Officer returned to the base without having met a convoy at all. This part of the North Sea was known from that night on as 'Dire Straits.'"

Bones then got command of MGB 17, mostly on Z patrols. "You could sit out there night after night and see nothing, then finally they'd come over and we'd try and engage them. They would slip in between us to get at the convoy, fire their torpedoes, and head for home. We'd have a couple of boats on these Z patrols and when E-boats came in we'd try and intercept them; if we could not (and we mostly could not)

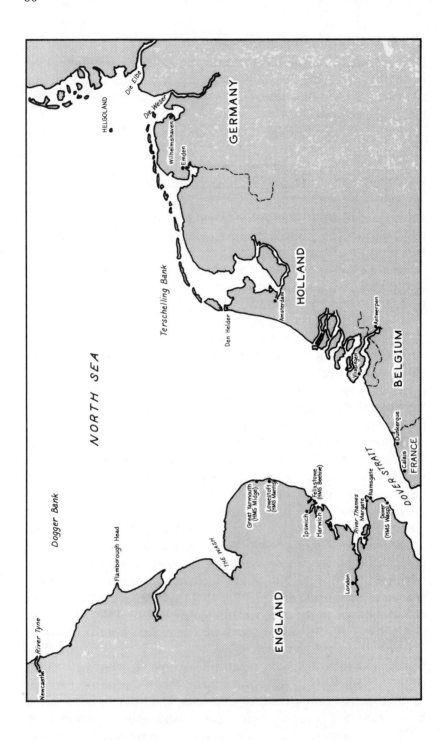

we'd try to intercept them on the way home. This, of course, led to a stern chase and we usually ended up outside enemy bases."

One night Bones was out from Lowestoft and the convoy reported an E-boat attack. Bones tried to intercept but found himself steering a parallel course astern of them, waiting for them to get outside their harbour and slow down preparatory to entering. It was getting late, almost dawn. He found them – right outside the harbour mouth of Ijmuiden. Bones had a group of three boats but Derek Leaf was the leader of another group out that night and Leaf had followed Bones across the North Sea. Leaf was not going to leave all the glory to Bones so, being senior, he ordered Bones to join his group. This made a total of six boats. Leaf was killed and his boat badly damaged, but the First Lieutenant managed to get her back to Lowestoft on one engine. From then on the winter and spring passed in a phantasmagoria of inconclusive actions – streaking tracer, series of gun battles, torpedoes sometimes fired, but never with much effect. Bones was hit several times. On one occasion his First Lieutenant was killed standing behind him. He lost five hands in those few months.

When Derek Leaf was killed Bones took over command of the remains of the flotilla and carried on the battle.

"But it's hard to say or to know if you sank anything or not. You can drill E-boats or R-boats full of holes but it's just like Derek Leaf's boat was full of holes. She was a mess but limped home. I think this is what happened with the E-boats but we certainly put them out of action for a while. And that really was our objective. The Admiralty didn't think much of us sending false signals saying we were in touch all the way across the North Sea because that was not really so. Admiral Kekewich and Captain Agar told us very severely not to do that again. But of course we did."

Burk left MGBs and got command of MTB 442. From her he went to the 461 in the 29th Canadian Flotilla. In talking about Hichens he says, "He was a fearless kind of guy. He was in the MGBs in the early period and was quite a student of the battles. If you were out with Hitch you were out with the best guy in the business. He thought tactics out beforehand, how he was going to handle the attack. And he had ideas. He'd come in very close and then open fire, but with a preconceived battle plan. Many boats end up in a fight and sometimes they don't know what they're doing but he was the best tactical commander, besides, of course, having a tremendous amount of courage."

\* \* \*

Having joined Lieutenant Mark Arnold Forster's boat, Bob Moyse was based in Dover with the usual nightly trips over to the French coast. One of the first things that sticks in his memory is the shelling by the 88mm shore batteries. Sam Gould was part of this group and Moyse says that "he was bloody good and a very brave commander. He used to get us into a lot of trouble. He loved to go at the guard ships in the harbours and shoot them up. I don't know if we ever sank anything but it certainly upset these trawlers."

Another action was when he, with three others, met about seven E-boats just northeast of Calais. The moon, however, was in the wrong half of the sky for them. The E-boats were inshore of them, the moon setting in the west so, with some persuasion, Arnold Forster called off the action.

\* \* \*

In 1942 Dave Wright joined his first MTB flotilla – the "Shorts." They went out four or five nights in the week over to Holland but Dave says, "We never saw too much action in those. When I saw my action was with Lieutenant Mabee in 745 in the Canadian flotilla; he would go *anywhere*. I was his radar operator so I had this little cubbyhole to myself: just me and my radar display. One night the Captain went into a German harbour – I gave him ranges and bearing of the entrance. I suppose captains are supposed to do that sort of thing but he didn't get high marks from me. It's hard down below; you hear the thump-thump-thump of your guns, then the shudder-shudder-shudder as enemy shells arrive inboard. The hull shakes. So did I, scrunched down making myself as small as possible."

\* \* \*

When Douglas Maitland joined Lieutenant Allan Seymour-Hayden on his first operation in MTB 69 as First Lieutenant, they were sent on patrol. But on leaving harbour a mine blew the stern off. Their next astern towed them back in so Maitland "was unemployed again." However, to keep the balance sheet clear, before being hit, 69 had exploded perhaps a dozen mines by running over them at high speed. The instructions always insisted that this be done at maximum speed, but, says Maitland, "They didn't really need to tell us. We cranked on all we could with a right good will, every last revolution we could get out of the propellers." He was then appointed to 71 (a Higgins boat) in Lowestoft and did a half dozen trips across the ninety-mile stretch to the Dutch coast.

But these Higgins boats were not mechanically effective and they were paid off. Admiral Kekewich was often down to visit them on board and all hands were impressed with his grasp of the situation. Maitland says, "He'd greet me with, 'Well, Maitland, and how are you and your crew?' He didn't summon you to his office where you saluted and stood at attention in front of his desk. He was a real man. Super! And one of his right-hand men – who was a Canadian liaison officer, probably the Empire Liaison Officer – was Captain Henry Bell-Irving, one of the Vancouver Bell-Irvings. He had served in World War I in small boats and here he was (the old fool, at sixty!) back again for World War II and just having a ball, a super fellow!"

Then Maitland was put in command of MGB 14, a seventy-foot Scott-Payne design, 1,350 hp Packard/Rolls. His First Lieutenant was Bones Burk. Corny Burke had MGB 17. Tommy Ladner was down at Harwich with MGB 76. In January, 1942, on through that spring and summer they were operating on the usual Z patrols ending up in the middle of the night on the enemy coast. Peter Thompson, from Toronto, in MGB 91 nailed an E-boat one night, captured her. She was one of three E-boats; the other two took off her crew and left her to sink. Thompson was towing her home but after daylight German fighter planes were sent out and sank the E-boat.

On their offensive patrols when they were sent to the enemy coast, a rather macabre rendezvous would be made at about the halfway point. The E-boats, which were heading toward England to attack our convoys, were, perforce, steering the reciprocal course that Maitland's group was steering to attack German convoys off Ijmuiden or Terschelling. Both groups would be cruising at twenty knots giving a forty-knot relative closing speed. They'd see each other, flash by, and disappear; it happened in a blink. There was no radar; it was often foggy or misty and the sound of engines would prevent them hearing each other. Weird, rather.

The first conclusive engagement he had was in MGB 14 and of this he says, "God Bless my First Lieutenant, Bones Burk, because we encountered an armed trawler in the shipping lanes off the Dutch coast, a flak trawler armed with a 4.1-inch gun and several 20mm, vicious things. We spotted her in the mist and I pulled away and went ahead of her and came back on her bow slowly until I was within a couple of hundred feet. Not yards, feet. I had another boat with me and we got the jump on the flak trawler and just smothered her until the point where we only got a small bit of return fire."

MGBs, however, don't sink flak trawlers by gunfire. So Maitland decided to drop a depth charge with a fifty-foot setting. The arrangement he worked out with Bones was, "I'll get alongside and bump her if I have to, but we've *got* to get close to her. When I'm as close as I can be (and you can judge that) just let the depth charge go and tell me. Then I'll give her full throttle." It worked beautifully. The depth charge exploded under the trawler, sprung her plates, started a roaring fire – ammunition was streaking up, steam hissing, a lovely sight! "It came at a time when our fortunes were fairly low and we felt quite good about it. In fact Admiralty felt good about it. I got a commendation."

Another type of patrol had a much quieter start.

"We'd lie in calm water most evenings; the North Sea isn't too pleasant but there are times when it is flat and quiet. We would lie with the engines turned off and listen with our hydrophones. This is a very Harry Tate affair in that it was lowered over the side and turned with a 'swizzle stick.' On one occasion we picked up the thump-thump-thump of the freight vessels and F lighters and then the rapid whirring of two big destroyers ahead of the convoy; it is easy to separate the thump-thump of the reciprocating engine of a merchant ship from the whirr-whirr of a destroyer turbine engine. Anyway, here were two destroyers and we were only gun boats. If we'd had torpedo boats we might have had a go at them. So, discretion being as important in battle as valour, we moved quietly away."

The summer of 1942 was not a good period for Coastal Forces. The British were still short of good boats and equipment and in August of that year when they were at church parade about five Dorniers flew across the harbour, dumped five loads of 500-pound bombs, and one of them took the tail off Maitland's boat.

It seemed a good time to take home leave and so Maitland had Christmas at home in Vancouver. When he returned in January, 1943, he heard that a flotilla of large MGBs – the D-boats, the Dog boats – was being formed to go to the Mediterranean. He volunteered.

＊　＊　＊

After the blowing up of MGB 42, Fitzroy Talbot's boat, Corny Burke was given command of MGB 90, an ELCO boat, Scott-Payne designed and built in the United States by the Electric Boat Company. They operated out of Felixstowe and Dover. There were two of the ELCO boats working together, the other being 92. Both came to an untimely end. Burke said, "Well, I had things nicely wrapped up, crew trained, all the paperwork done, the ship's books were starting to get into shape. I'm rather proud and delighted to have this wonderful boat. Now let's get cracking. My Standing Orders are all properly posted. But one day when we were sitting alongside – I was in my cabin getting the last of the paperwork done – when a rating who was cleaning the Lewis gun somehow got a round in the chamber, pulled the trigger to see if it was working, and fired a .303 into a box of 20mm shells, which immediately exploded. Both boats were in flames with shells blasting all over the bloody place. The whole superstructure was blown to smithereens. Fortunately no one was killed." Burke poured foam into the fuel tanks but it was hopeless. His boat burned to the waterline. There ended his first command.

He got another and operated out of Lowestoft in the 20th MGB Flotilla with Doug Maitland and Tommy Ladner. However, Burke says, "We weren't aggressively led." He marched in to see the Commander of the Base, said he wanted to resign his commission. The wretched Base Commander had to ask, why? Burke said he'd rather not say. The Commander demanded that he say why. So Burke said he wasn't satisfied with his Senior Officer's performance (this is the Senior Officer of Dire Straits). Dyer was sent to the big ships.

Burke started his long career of following Maitland, his next ahead. They had actions against E-boats and convoys off the Dutch coast. Burke says that "one March day three of us led by Maitland did the hundred miles over from Lowestoft to lie off Ijmuiden. We would lie with our engines cut, stay joined together by heaving lines; but nothing happened that night. So just before dawn I said, 'I'll start up. We'd better get out of here.' I started the engines at slow ahead but all I got was a screaming noise.

"The motor mechanic hastened to the bridge and said, 'The clutches aren't working, sir.'

"I started to get very frightened indeed. I didn't want to jump into the North Sea on a blustery March day so I ordered the First Lieutenant to go over the side and have a look. He came up with look of incredulity on his face, 'There aren't any propellers, sir.'

" 'Don't be ridiculous, man, look again. How did we get here?'

"He dived down again, came up spluttering and shivering, 'I've touched the end of all three shafts, sir. There are *no* propellers.'

"What had happened was that I had put the boat up on the ways the afternoon before we left and had three new wheels put on. But a sloppy dockyard matey, tightening up the boss nuts by hand, had not properly tightened them. The thrust of the propellers was such that we got over there all right because they'd stay on by themselves, while turning. But lying stopped all night, slopping back and forth and thumping up and down, the boss nuts simply jiggled on their threads and the propellers came off.

"Doug Maitland had to tow me all the way home. Believe me, it was *not* a labour of love on his part. I can tell you *that* with complete certainty.

"Anyway, we soldiered on with various actions but no great triumphs. Doug Maitland with Bones Burk as First Lieutenant, me with Steve Rendell as First Lieutenant, and Tommy Ladner with an RNVR as First Lieutenant. I was quite jealous of Ladner because he had served with the immortal Hichens."

Burke came due for home leave and spent Christmas of 1942 in Vancouver. When he returned Maitland gave him the good news that the Dog boats needed commanding officers so Burke spent the rest of the war in the Mediterranean.

✳ ✳ ✳

After MGB 19 and his actions with Hichens, Tommy Ladner got MGB 76 and worked with Corny Burke and Douglas Maitland out of Lowestoft. He contributed his bit of information about the Royal Navy senior officer who had joined from the Merchant Navy and didn't really like the small unorthodox boats. "Burke was so infuriated with him because he (Dyer) didn't go in to attack a target, some E-boats off the Dutch coast, that Corny came in and did the classic thing. He went to see the Commander and said that he wished to be relieved of his command. The Commander of necessity had to ask why and Corny said his flotilla commander had refused to engage the enemy. That *really* got things going."

Ladner remembers when he became part of Hichens's flotilla. Hichens took the eight boats to a six-week workup period. These boats were the prototype of a whole class of boats that eventually joined the RN but the engine installations were new; they were the Packard/Rolls Royce marine Merlin engines converted in the United States by the Packard Motor Company into marine engines. There were problems. They were each 1,500 hp and the boats could do forty-four knots with a full load but nobody knew what they did at that kind of speed. So, as the prototype boat, Ladner spent a lot of time testing different types of propellers. It was in late 1942 that he sailed with Hichens, whom he remembers as "really a legendary figure. He was the guy who was the creator of all the tactics which ultimately were used in Coastal Command. First of all he combined the torpedo boat and gun boat groups. He always believed in the slow approach. In other words, when he went in to attack the great thing was to be ahead of the convoy. He used the system whereby he disposed his torpedo boats to the bow and the MGBs would open fire from the opposite side and distract the 'Hated Hun.' "

Ladner had two actions off the Dutch coast, both successful. They were mostly faced with German F-lighters and destroyers bringing provi sions south down the French coast to feed their troops. But Hichens had developed the concept of dropping a depth charge across the bow of a merchant ship because normally MGBs can't sink merchant ships. The big secret of this was to come in so close that the enemy could not depress his guns enough to fire at you. That was another of Hichens's theses – if you're really in trouble you get within a 100 feet.

"He was right. You could then shoot them up. He advocated shooting out the bridge, always shoot out the bridge. He also started to use a very high percentage of incendiary bullets in comparison to high explosive or armour piercing. We used to load our 20mm trays with 50 per cent incendiaries; by the time three boats had plastered all that incendiary over the enemy ship, she was on fire. German alarm and despondency was high."

All in all, Ladner did about six months with Hichens out of Dover, Fowey, Felixstowe, and Dartmouth. That was Hichens's most successful time operating off the French coast and into the Channel Islands.

"One foggy night we crept off Le Havre and sat outside the gates. If you've ever been to Le Havre ... there are huge gates at the entrance to the harbour and we sat there and waited. Then the Germans turned the lights on. Hitch decided that since the lights were on something was going to happen so we crept in. We were four boats and we waited and sure enough the gate opened and out came a *lovely* convoy. At the same time another convoy appeared from seaward entering the harbour; it was foggy, a very foggy night. So we had to make a decision of whether to shoot up the convoy coming in or the convoy coming out. Hitch decided on the convoy coming out. So we shot that up. The great thing to do in these actions is not to shoot each other up so we kept very close formation. When the shooting starts it's very hard to make out what's going on. You have to keep your eye on the target. You have to keep your eye on the boat ahead. If he's hit, then he pulls out. You don't know whether he's pulling out because he's hit or he's pulling out because he's changing his tactic. After we finished shooting them up we sat for about half an hour outside the harbour in the fog while the shore batteries and the incoming convoy actually fought it out with the outgoing convoy. It was one of the great successes of dear old Hitch."

On another occasion operating out of Felixstowe and attacking a convoy on the Dutch side they started the attack but found there were destroyers coming up on either side of the convoy; they were cornered. Ladner was on the inshore side and Fearless and Resolute George Duncan was on the other side of the convoy. Duncan was detached by Hichens to carry out a depth-charge attack. Duncan was hit and swerved around. He started to go at high speed and tried to get through the convoy. He couldn't do it and he disengaged on the shore side and ran aground on a sand bank. He was then plastered with gunfire and his boat destroyed. Everyone was firing at Duncan. Ladner put his throttles hard up and creamed up ahead of the convoy to get out of it. He was hit. He could not get to seaward so he chugged up to a buoy, secured to it in the dark where he couldn't be seen (or a radar echo would just show the buoy).

"When things had quietened down I made my way back to Felix-stowe with a big hole in the bow, badly shaken up. Several wounded, one of whom died later. Because of my reduced speed I ended up after daylight in the shoot-at-sight zone. If you weren't away from the enemy coast by dawn you got clobbered by the Luftwaffe. Anyway, I got home but I ended up in a minefield. The tide was low and these bloody great mines were bobbing all around. I had this boat with her bow down and only two of my three engines going and the pumps thumping like crazy to keep the bow up and all these badly injured people. Finally we got fairly close to the Thames entrance and somebody picked us up, towed us in. But that was the end of MGB 75. It was a terrible night. That was the end of 75 and so it seemed to be a good time to go on leave and I did. I went back to Vancouver and spent Christmas there."

He came home to Canada in convoy in a French freighter in the slowest ship of the slowest convoy. "The only thing that was superlative about that ship were the cockroaches, which were enormous." Arriving in New York was the first time he had seen lights for a long time. "It was really an exciting experience. We went up to the Barbazon Plaza Hotel. God, it was a great moment to arrive there! I remember coming up to the taxi from the dockside and the driver had his radio on and I'd never heard a radio in a taxi before. Coming over the radio was the first time I heard that great song "I'm Dreaming of a White Christmas" sung by Bing Crosby. It was quite a moment. I went up to the Barbazon Plaza and I ordered a quart of milk and two fried eggs and bacon. It was dinnertime in the main dining room but fresh eggs and bacon and milk were all I wanted. A *great* meal! So I was home for Christmas, 1942."

In February, 1942, while waiting to pick up his next boat he had been made temporary captain of a C-class gun boat because the skipper was sick. They were secured alongside and he was told to bring her up to fighting strength the next day. At six a.m. everybody was roused out and told to be ready to go to sea by eight. They ammunitioned and fuelled and took on Confidential Books and put to sea. He didn't know any of the other captains or the senior officers but there were six C-class gun boats going down river when the telegraphist came to the bridge and said he had an enemy report of two battleships, forty destroyers, and eighty E-boats.

"Tell me," said Ladner, "how long have you been a telegraphist?"

"Oh, I've been a telegraphist for two years."

"Are you sure that's an enemy report you're getting?"

"Yes, sir, I'm sure."

"Well, go down and get another one on another wavelength and bring it back to me again."

Of course, it was *Gneisenau, Scharnhorst*, and *Prinz Eugen* going up the Channel.

"So our six boats went blasting over to the Dutch coast in daylight. Air traffic overheard was intense! Aircraft everywhere. German aircraft, British aircraft, all ignoring us. We got about twenty-five miles off the coast and by this time it was dark so the flotilla leaders decided we would circle. We circled and circled and circled all night. We could hear the enemy reports going through – attacks, aircraft reports. We realized what was going on but we were wondering what sort of a burnt offering we were going to be in this whole thing. Finally, about five a.m. the action reports stopped. The Senior Officer called for instructions and found out that operations had forgotten all about us."

That was a real ballzup. They returned to harbour.

In February, 1943, Ladner joined Maitland and Burke in the Dog boats and headed for Gibraltar. The weather was appalling. A huge following sea right through the Bay of Biscay. Ladner was lucky to get his old coxswain, Chief Petty Officer Nichol, Motor Mechanics Booth and Cowley, and two or three gunners from his old boat so he had the nucleus of an experienced crew. He had an RNVR First Lieutenant, Syrett, and a Navigator called Derek (now Sir Derek) Holden-Brown, who was nineteen. Apart from these the rest of the crew of thirty-two were all inexperienced but with the coxswain, the gunners, and the motor mechanics he was able to build up a first-class operation.

\* \* \*

For weeks a convoy of coastal craft gathered along the south coast of England, then moved around the corner to Wales, to the Bristol Channel. They had extra fuel tanks fitted on the upper deck, which pleased *nobody*. The weather was foul; motor torpedo boats and motor gun boats and motor launches act in a most contrary manner at low speed in heavy seas. And the seas got heavier and the wind rose from a fresh breeze to a light gale to a heavy gale; then it abated; then it blew up again. They tried for days on end to form up in the semblance of a convoy. A trawler was to be in the van as anti-submarine escort, radio link with Whitehall, victualling depot, and to fulfil other maternal duties. Once or twice they set out for Gibraltar but the sea conditions forced then to return.

Then the Commander-in-Chief of the Mediterranean Fleet, Admiral Sir Andrew Browne Cunningham, entered the picture and there was the following exchange of signals:

FROM          C-in-C Med Fleet
TO            NOIC Milford Haven
Repeated      Admiralty
WHERE ARE MY BOATS?

FROM          NOIC Milford Haven
TO            C-in-C Med Fleet
Repeated      Admiralty
REGRET WEATHER HAS PREVENTED THEM WORKING UP OR SAILING.

FROM          C-IN-C Med Fleet
TO            NOIC Milford Haven
Repeated      Admiralty
SEND MY BOATS FORTHWITH. I WILL WORK THEM UP.

So off you go. Never mind the weather. Father has sent for you. The convoy was about twenty boats with the big trawler as mother ship. They operated on one engine to preserve fuel but had those tanks on deck to get them as far as Gibraltar. God, how this made them roll! Lurch and corkscrew is closer to describing the motion; the stern lifts up, swings to port, the bow swings to starboard, at low speed the helm has little effect, the bow falls and digs in, the stern rises higher and swings more, then as the sea passes underneath the whole boat moves laterally a few feet, the bow rises and comes back to port, the stern starts to sink, the next wave looms up aft, crest toppling, God we're going to be pooped! No. And it starts again. This huge following sea lasted all through the Bay of Biscay. Most of the time waves were big enough that other boats would disappear from time to time. You would go down into the trough of the wave and climb your way up and then go scooting down the other side, probably at six or seven knots.

They were shadowed by Focke-Wulf Condors that reported their position. The first time Ladner ever saw a Leigh light was when the RAF came out to (a) drive off the Focke-Wulf Condors or (b) keep the U-boats down. Norman Hughes led the 21st MTB Flotilla. It was seven days down to Gibraltar. Maitland was leader of the port column. The trawler sent the convoy's noon positions; at that time of the year there was no way an MTB could have taken a sun-sight or a star-sight off the heaving deck.

Maitland says, "It was blowing. God! It was blowing Force 8. Terrible! And with these deck tanks the boats were unstable. I was frightened. I'd been on water enough to know it was dangerous. I knew what metacentric height and stability meant to a boat and so we spent time trying to get the boats stable enough to make the voyage to Gibraltar. The gale moderated to about Force 6; why we didn't lose any boats nobody really understands to this day."

Maitland bled off some of the deck tanks to reduce top weight. About nine o'clock one morning, abeam of Cape Finisterre on the north of Spain, this four-engine aircraft started circling them. A Focke-Wulf Condor. They signalled the aircraft.

"Why are you here?"

At first he didn't answer. Then the German airman flashed back on his light, "If we knew ourselves we wouldn't tell you!"

But the Condor was homing the U-boats onto the convoy. And by 1943 the U-boat wolfpacks had formed – six or eight submarines usually, but they sometimes had up to twenty.

Unbeknownst to the convoy of MGBs and MLs, two U-boats had been nailed the previous night by the RAF with Leigh lights. One of them was still on the surface, badly wounded. So the Focke-Wulf Condor was also out there to keep an eye on her. That night was blustery, low visibility. Corny Burke was astern of Maitland and Ladner astern of Burke. About midnight Maitland, who had been on his feet for seventeen hours, said, "I'm going to get my head down."

An hour later he heard gunfire. Then he thought, "Damnit, that's one of our own gunners. You know, they were sitting in their hydraulic turrets and they'd fall asleep and my first thought was that one of them had fallen asleep and grabbed the trigger."

Then Maitland saw that the woodwork inside his hut was starting to blow all through his little bunkhouse – holes in the woodwork, the thunk-thunk-thunk of bullets, splinters.

"Well, I can tell you. It doesn't take long to motivate a fellow. I was up on that bridge tcwhoooooosh! There was the helmsman lying on the deck yelling his head off with a hole in his ankle and the port lookout was wounded and there was a fire abaft the bridge. I looked over the side and, Holy God, there was a U-boat, a surfaced submarine alongside of us. As I looked the Germans had their 20mm closed up. I had a drum feed on my 20mm – forty-nine shells. The Germans didn't; they had a clip that held twelve shells. What happened, the first burst had been twelve and just as I looked over they were putting the second clip in. Well, you don't leave your head up at that point so I ducked down and grabbed for the wheel and steered on my knees until the next twelve had hit, right through the bridge."

Maitland counted his twelve again but now had this huge fire to contend with. If the tanks had been full it wouldn't have been so bad but if they're empty the fumes are dangerous. In fact, those gas tanks were more dangerous than the U-boat that was firing at them. The flames were fifty feet in the air by this time and there is not much fire-fighting equipment in an MGB so Maitland had to invent his own. He altered course 180 degrees, increased speed, and ploughed into the heavy sea. A wave swept her from stem to gudgeon, washed all the loose gas off the upper deck, and put the fire out.

What had happened was that one U-boat had come to take off the crew of the disabled U-boat and the two had collided. Tommy Fuller, coming up further astern, suddenly ran through a bunch of German survivors in the water with the little lights on their lifejackets flashing and they yelling to be saved. So he picked up all of them.

Corny Burke had seen the flash of tracer as the U-boat opened fire and thought Maitland's boat would be sunk, a write-off. With admiration and amazement in his voice, he said, "But Doug's a fast thinker. Why look for a fire extinguisher when you can use the whole of the Atlantic. The flames were higher than the mast. I thought they'd all fry. But Doug swung 180 degrees into the sea, and whoooosh, the flames were gone."

That puts Maitland, Burke, Ladner, and Fuller in Gibraltar about to commence the war in the Mediterranean. There we must leave them for a while and return to the United Kingdom.

Charles Chaffey joined the U.K. flotillas in the spring of 1941. He went to MTB 232 under the command of Ian Trewlany in the 21st MTB Flotilla of Lieutenant Peter Dickens, RN. Dickens's and Hichens's flotillas were working in concert all that summer. "This was now autumn and we started out with attempted interceptions on the east coast of England and ending up on the opposite side of the North Sea. We were playing leapfrog all the time from port to port. One night we were in action off the Cherbourg peninsula and in a hail of fire which we weren't really expecting we took a lot of enemy shells inboard and had five casualties. My Captain, Ian Trewlany, was wounded and I had to bring 232 back to Portsmouth on only two engines. This was rather complicated by the fact that three of the engine-room crew got poisoned from carbon monoxide gas and wound up in the hospital as well."

The second Battle of Barfleur was on the 7th of August 1942. Twelve miles off Cape Barfleur at the eastern tip of the Cherbourg peninsula Dickens cut the main engines and engaged the little Ford V8 auxiliary, which only drove him at six knots, but quietly. They were now in the enemy's convoy route and they turned down into it in Baie de la Seine.

They were in historic waters. The first Battle of Barfleur, fought on 19 May 1692 between Admirals Russell and Tourville in the War of the English Succession, was noteworthy for Sir Cloudesley Shovell tacking through a gap in the enemy line, thwarting ex-King James II. This *permanently* discouraged him from returning to England. The second Battle of Barfleur 250 years later we will now examine.

A German force left Cherbourg to escort the sea-going tug *Oceanie* to Le Havre; there were six armed trawlers, five minesweepers (*Minensuchboote*), under the command of Lieutenant zur See Wunderlich. Dickens's group slipped from *Hornet*, a Coastal Force base up Haslar Creek in Gosport, adjacent to Portsmouth harbour. Dickens led in MTB 237. To port of him was 241, commanded by Sub-Lieutenant Jim Mac-Donald, RNZVR (at age twenty the youngest captain in the King's navy), and on the starboard wing was 232, commanded by Ian Trewlany, with Chaffey as First Lieutenant. The night was dark, clear, and windless. The enemy was sighted about a mile to starboard. Dickens ordered a crash start, the boats to separate and attack independently. Six heavily armed

German trawlers and five minesweepers against three British MTBs might seem unfavourable odds, but they weren't. As Dickens later said, "the final profit-and-loss account would not confirm the view that to attack was the thing to do; but then, no business should be controlled by the finance manager." Had they not gone in he had no doubt that a defensive pattern would have been stamped on all their enterprises and an investment could not be made in future profits. The enemy must always be reminded that if he comes in contact with British boats, he will be attacked. Every time! Dickens ran into a curtain of fire and soon had his radio out of action, was on fire, and had his fuel line severed, and a bullet into the wheelhouse put kaput to the steering gear.

Trewlany turned 232 to a westerly course to separate from Dickens and aim for the enemy's rear column. She passed inside the outlying escort and was instantly engaged. Chaffey was navigating in the wheelhouse and Sub-Lieutenant "Gertie" Gill was spare officer and helping him. The heavy tracer ruined his night vision but Trewlany had caught a glimpse of a suitable torpedo target and altered course to fire. As Chaffey arrived on the bridge the Captain fell, riddled by fragments from his right shoulder to his ankle. He tried to remain upright but his Achilles' tendon had been severed and he fell to the deck attempting to keep command from a supine position. Chaffey took charge and noted that 232 was now to the south of the enemy. He tried to take the safety latches off the torpedo triggers but the mechanism was damaged. He turned the wheel to port to close on the enemy but it spun uselessly. Glancing aft he saw the boat to be under control from there and thought he might get a torpedo shot in yet. Just then Gill told him that the starboard engine would only run at half-speed and that the port had failed utterly.

Now, all first lieutenants pray ardently for the day when they will find themselves in command. Mind you, they wish their captains no positive harm in the manner of their leaving this world, but if they must leave it so the first lieutenants can be in command, so be it. When the moment arrives, however, there is a strange aridity of thought, particularly when the ship's company look at the ex-First Lieutenant, now Captain, and say, "Well, and what do you want us to do now?" Chaffey had no option but to take his crippled boat and his wounded crew home. She was on the wrong side of the convoy with engines in a very dicey state, but gritting his teeth and mentally flinching at the gunfire shortly to arrive inboard, Chaffey set off purposely for home at best possible speed.

MTB 241 had been giving a good account of herself on the other flank of the convoy but Dickens's 237 was mortally wounded, the radio cabin and the galley ablaze. He called 241 over to take off his surviving crew. The soul-searing reality of the matter was that on the other side of the bulkhead were 1,500 gallons of high-octane fuel. The motor mechanic had flooded the space with methyl-bromide gas, which at first appeared to subdue the blaze but did not dowse it; extinguishers were borrowed from 241 but to no effect. When the engines were started to return home the added oxygen fanned the fire, which was soon a roaring, hissing inferno. MTB 237 had had it! The survivors stepped over the side, dry-shod, to 241 and returned to *Hornet* just after daylight.

MTB 232 was going to be in refit for a few months and it was only a week or so before Chaffey met Lieutenant-Commander Frank Hellings, RNVR, the Captain of ML 309, in which he had served when he first came over.

"What are you doing here?" asked Hellings.

"My boat has been damaged and I'm going to take a spot of leave."

"The hell you've got leave. I'm going to talk to *Beehive*. I need another officer on my deck to look out for aircraft."

"To look out for aircraft where?"

"Oh, we're going on a raid over to Dieppe."

So, on his leave from the action of the second Battle of Barfleur, Chaffey went to the first Battle of Dieppe. They sailed from Southampton as part of the escort and went across with the convoy. Their main job was supposed to be air-sea rescue and a general sort of screening, but that particular boat only had its 1898 gun on the fo's'c'le and a couple of machine guns – which didn't do very much in clearing the way for our troops going ashore. ML 309 lay two miles offshore and was supposed to go in on the withdrawal, pick up what they could, and try and keep the shore batteries from causing too much trouble, "which was ridiculous, of course, with the equipment we had. If we got within three miles of the shore we were in danger of being sunk and we couldn't even reach halfway there with our guns. After the Canadian troops were repulsed we steamed up and down looking for survivors but between the German shore batteries and the German aircraft which were strafing the troops ashore one got the impression that this was not the greatest of all amphibious landings. The cruisers and the battleships had carried out a pre-landing bombardment but the Germans' heads popped up again as soon as it was over."

Returning in command of MTB 232, Chaffey continued in Peter Dickens's flotilla until January, 1943. Being the only Canadian Captain in the group, Chaffey found it interesting that a lot of the British MTB captains knew a lot of the German E-boat captains from before the war. When they were sent to do an offensive raid off the enemy coast and the E-boats were sent to do an offensive raid off our coast, they were ordered to keep clear of each other. It was not the object of the operation that night for E-boats to engage MTBS or MTBS to engage E-boats; it was to attack each other's convoys. Most of the Brits were racing yachts before the war, as were the Germans and the French; they knew each other. Peter Dickens knew a lot of the E-boat commanders. Hichens had sailed in international races and in addition had entered his racing car in many Grands Prix on the continent; so he, too, knew many of their opponents. This added a courteous eighteenth-century touch to their combat.

In February of 1943 Chaffey returned home for leave and his return trip was in the *Queen Elizabeth*: "A beautiful trip back, royal luxury. That liner was something to be seen and the poker games were no less worthy of attention. We were given the royal treatment. Captain Bell invited us to the bridge and dined us royally. The poker games were ferocious. I've seen eighteen hundred dollars going on the roll of the dice."

In May, 1943, Chaffey was appointed to Greater Yarmouth to a training flotilla and wound up in command of MGB 21 (one of the MGBs in the original flotilla of Hichens). He was there about nine months training new MTB officers and ratings. Occasionally they had the odd patrol line to run. The following spring he joined Tony Law's 29th Canadian MTB Flotilla.

# VI   A Doomed Convoy

*They ventured forth, those small and gallant ships*
*And saw the great ones of the earth in tears*
*Doomed like Odysseus and his labouring ships*
*And proud as Priam, murdered with his peers.*

*B*ehind our small-ship coastal battles in the North Sea and the English Channel is the Merchant Navy. The term "heroic" and "gallant" are much overworked in time of war (all naval officers seem to be gallant, for instance; we seem to have only gallant allies). But these terms are not out of place when we talk of merchant seamen. The overwhelming feature of their service is that they were civilians; they did not *have* to risk the dangers of the enemy or face the discomfort of ocean convoys.

But they did, and over 3,000 merchant ships were sunk, and over 7,000 Merchant Navy seamen followed their ships to a watery grave. In two corvettes, *Moose Jaw* and *Oakville*, and in a fleet destroyer, *Sioux*, I must have seen two score of merchant ships sunk and those ships rescued perhaps a hundred survivors. We in the navy knew the Merchant Navy well. During the 2,060 days of war from 1939 to 1945, there were 25,342 merchant-ship voyages that carried over 181 million tons of cargo to the United Kingdom under Canadian escort. The price of admiralty to us was twenty-four warships sunk and just over 2,000 casualties: not much in the weird and pragmatic bookkeeping of war. There is a lot to be proud of in the way the young men and women of Canada's naval reserve flocked to the colours; there are also some episodes of which we are not so proud, such as this story of the small ships of the Merchant Marine.

In all truth it may be said that Convoy, PQ 17* from Iceland to Russia in June and July of 1942 was not our finest hour. That summer was one of almost total German successes. The Wehrmacht was raging eastward across Russia, Rommel closing in on Alexandria, Tobruk captured with over 30,000 men and all but a fraction of our armour destroyed, Cairo in a panic and the British embassy there burning its files. Admiral Raeder's Kreigsmarine had lost only sixty-six U-Boats, was building more at the rate of thirty a month, and was sinking our ships faster than we could build more – by the end of 1942, 3,067 ships totalling over 12 million tons. Admiral Dönitz had built his U-Boat fleet up from twenty-five in 1939 to over 200 and that year they ranged the world: they were particularly enjoying what they called "The American Shooting Season" as far afield as Halifax, down the coast to Miami, and into the Caribbean and the Gulf of Mexico.

Grossadmiral Raeder had Hitler's approval for his operation "The Knight's Move" against PQ 17. Admiral Schniewind would lead it from his battleship *Tirpitz*: pocket battleships, cruisers, destroyers, submarines, and aircraft formed part of his force. Churchill and the First Sea Lord, Admiral of the Fleet Sir Dudley Pound, were dealing as best they could with a furious Stalin, who besides demanding that a Second Front be opened in the West also demanded more supplies be sent to Murmansk. Admiral Sir John Tovey, Commander-in-Chief of the Home Fleet, did the best he could but *Tirpitz*, poised in a Norwegian fiord, tied up his heavy ships. Tovey wanted to destroy that ship. Raeder wanted PQ 17. Sometimes a random confluence of events leads to great naval battles. It might have been that Tovey could have his Jutland and finish off most of the remaining German heavy units. He had sunk *Bismarck* two years earlier, and she on her maiden voyage.

PQ 17 was the lure. Thirty-four ships, escorted variously by Canadian corvettes, frigates, and destroyers, came from Port of Spain, New York, Boston, Halifax, and St. John's to Iceland. By the summer of 1942 the RCN had escorted the main east-west convoy routes and the tributaries that fed them with thirteen destroyers, sixty-eight corvettes, twenty mine-sweepers, and sixty smaller craft; our strength had risen to 40,000 – 40 per cent of the Allied naval forces in the Atlantic. By the end of that summer, 60 million tons of cargo had been moved. The 10th Canadian Escort Squadron with its red-and-white striped funnels, the Barber Pole

*Convoys to Russia were PQ; from Russia, QP.

Brigade, along with the other Canadian escort groups plied east and west without cease.

> It's away! Outward bound the swinging fo'c's'les heel,
> From the smoking seas white glare upon the strand;
> It's the grey miles that are slipping under keel,
> As we're rolling outward bound from Newfoundland.
> CHORUS (Waving gin glasses aloft)
> From Halifax to Newfiejohn to Derry's clustered towers,
> Through trackless paths where conning towers roll;
> If you know another group in which you'd sooner spend your
>     hours,
> Ye've never sailed beneath the Barber Pole!

This was sung to the tune of "Road to the Isles."

Sedate Englishmen stared in silent wonder. We shared the convoys with the Royal Navy but at that time they alone took the convoys bound for Russia. For those, we got the merchant ships to their point of departure, either Scotland or Iceland.

Of the thirty-four ships in PQ 17, two-thirds of them were American and new to war – Pearl Harbor was only six months in the past. What a prize! Seven hundred million dollars worth of material – 297 aircraft, 594 tanks, 4,246 trucks and gun carriers, and about 156,000 tons of general cargo. In short, it was enough to equip an army of 50,000. The American merchant ships, untrained as most of them were, did not do well. How could it be otherwise? There were mutinies, crews abandoned their ships when the damage inflicted did not warrant it, friendly aircraft were shot at. The escort was professional enough: RN and USN cruisers and destroyers as the covering force. Sir John, with two battleships, a carrier, a cruiser, and a flotilla of destroyers, was poised to the northeast of Jan Mayen Island waiting to cut off Admiral Schniewind. But our warships didn't *do* anything. They were called off before Schniewind's surface attack developed. No surface attack did develop. But of the thirty-four that left Iceland, twenty-three were sunk and only eleven reached Russian ports.

The German battleships and cruisers, moving from harbour to harbour and fiord to fiord along the Norwegian coast, caused much consternation in Admiralty, and at 9:23 p.m. on the 4th of July the convoy was ordered to scatter by Admiralty – by the First Sea Lord, Admiral Sir Dudley Pound, who believed that a surface attack by the German fleet was imminent.

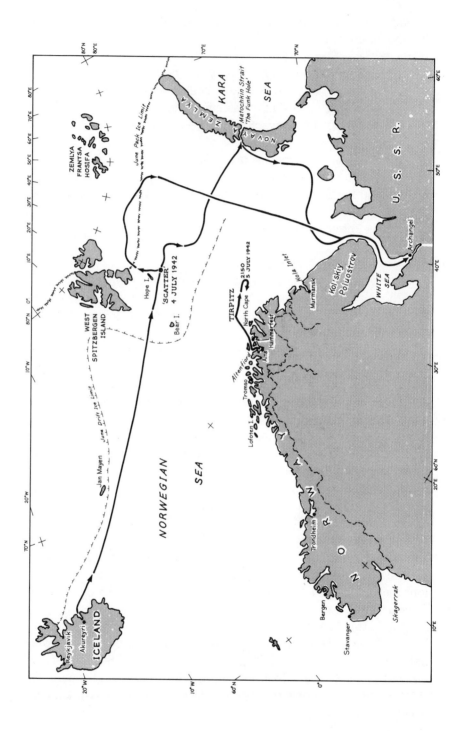

IMMEDIATE

From: Admiralty
To: Escorts of PQ 17
Repeated CS One <Admiral Hamilton>
C-in-C Home Fleet

P/L

Owing to threat from surface ships convoy is to disperse and proceed to Russian ports.

2123B/4

The signal was repeated to twenty-nine information addressees.

This signal was received with shocked incredulity. Whatever the rank of the senior officer of an operation – having been provided with all the information available – *he* should decide what was best to do. The man on the spot traditionally made the decision as to how the battle should be fought, and it was certainly alien to the tradition of the Royal Navy to refuse battle. There was incredulity and a sense of guilt in leaving their charges undefended that has not been mitigated very much by the passing of the years. But since this was the forty-eighth signal received from Admiralty on the conduct of this convoy, and trusting to Admiralty's more comprehensive knowledge of the overall disposition of their own and enemy forces, they reluctantly complied.

Commander Jackie Broome in *Kepple* was senior officer of the close escort. He said later that the First Lord of the Admiralty visited *Kepple* after the debacle and his ship's company mustered hoping to hear *why* PQ 17 had been ordered to scatter. (This was A.V. Alexander, the civilian in Parliament responsible for the navy, the First Lord, not Admiral Pound, the First Sea Lord.) Broome's sailors were addressed like a constituency, not like men who fought. In his cabin afterward Broome asked, "Why was PQ 17 scattered?" All he remembers is that the answer was not an answer, rather a politician's evasions.

Yet *Tirpitz*, *Hipper*, and *Scheer* were in fact still in Altenfiord and did not sail until eleven a.m. on 5 July; they went north up the Norwegian leads, rounded North Cape, and steered a little north of east until 9:50 p.m., when they were ordered back by Admiral Raeder, who believed that an attack on them by Admiral Tovey's Home Fleet was imminent.

So, both the close and distant escort of the convoy had been called off by Admiralty. The convoy was left undefended, told to scatter and make their own way to Archangel at their best speed (they hardly needed to be told that!). Why? Well, hundreds of thousands of words have given "reasons" in books, reports, and inquiries but the *why* does not matter here. Better to get the spirit of the men on both sides, which is really as important as the why – and considerably more cheerful.

Jackie Broome's Rabelaisian cartoons were the talk of the fleet in my day – and still are, I suspect. One showed an admiral (identifiable, I am told, but I didn't know him) in a bathtub with a Wren (identifiable, I am told, but I didn't know her), saying, "And this, my dear, is how a torpedo works." His more circumspect cartoons – funny and always germane – lightened the pages of a tome called "Atlantic Convoy Instructions." One was made into a poster and was conspicuously on the wall at every convoy briefing. It showed a wretched merchantman chugging along miles astern of the convoy. The caption says, "Join The Stragglers Club." At the bottom is, "Subscriptions in Advance Please." His view on deskbound sailors dwelling on matters not falling within their purview is shown in another cartoon of the operations room in Liverpool – from Admiral tactician to Wren plotter, from C-in-C Western Approaches, Sir Percy Noble, to Wren Snodgrass.

Broome commanded *Kepple* and the destroyers, corvettes, mine-sweepers, and anti-submarine trawlers of the close escort. Tucked in astern of the convoy were two of our submarines, P614 and P615. Evidently their precise tactics had not been fully decided before sailing; however that may be, the senior of the two decided that it would be vexing to German surface forces as they came in to attack if they saw two British submarines (who then, presumably, would submerge and cause the hated Hun further discomfort). He therefore made this signal to the Escort Commander.

From: Senior Officer Submarines
To: *Kepple*

In the event of attack by heavy surface forces, I intend to remain on the surface.

Broome replied: "So do I."

By Wednesday, 1 July, PQ 17 had been sighted and U-boats and enemy aircraft closed in. The next day the Blohm & Voss shadower was joined by two Heinkel 115 torpedo aircraft and five more were in the air joining them. A further fifty-two Heinkels were at the ready at Bardufoss and Banak in northern Norway. U-456 was shadowing. The convoy got their barrage balloons airborne. At half past six in the afternoon the two Heinkels bore in to attack. Alarm bells clamoured. By ten to seven there were five more torpedo bombers coming in. A curtain of fire belched from the escorts and convoy. Four Heinkels peeled off and came in from astern firing their cannon. One seemed headed for the Russian tanker *Azerbaijan*. The rescue ships *Rathlin*, *Zaafaran*, and *Zamalek* were in the stern positions and they blazed away with their 4-inch and 40mm. The Heinkels were sturdy aircraft and this one took more punishment than seemed possible. It was piloted by the German squadron commander; he inflicted much damage and took his share as he flew down between two columns of ships. But he faltered out through the van, losing height, and right on through the forward screen. Then he ditched. Their blood properly up by this spirited exchange, the warships closed in; the destroyer *Wilton* was leading. The German airmen could be seen clambering out of their wrecked plane and trying to inflate their yellow rubber dingy. A desperate plight! Two more escorts were perhaps within a mile. That the airmen would have been rescued is certain. It was our custom to do so when conditions permitted. After all, had not Admiral Lütgens stopped to pick up British survivors after HMS *Glowworm* rammed him in *Hipper*. Had not Sir John's *Maori* and *Dorsetshire* picked up *Bismarck* survivors?

But then the picture changed and a rescue commenced that men with a chestful of medals for gallantry and valour still talk about in awe.

Another Heinkel dropped from the low cloud, losing height, heading for her distressed mate and obviously going to land alongside her, right in the path of the destroyers. What to do? After all, one does not shoot at an enemy when he is down. One does not shoot at a sitting game bird; it is simply not done! You must take it on the wing. But if that German crew were picked up they would simply get another aircraft and return to attack again.

"Open fire," said the Captain of *Wilton*. Her main armament bellowed forth and she raced in. The other destroyers opened up. Geysers of water erupted around the damaged aircraft and her helpless crew. Closer and closer the shells exploded. (I said it was not our finest hour.)

The rescuing Heinkel skimmed the waves and, amid the spouts of water and exploding shells, throttled back and gently settled alongside her stricken comrade. The three survivors clambered on board. The pilot gunned the throttle. Amid the water spouts he gained speed, lifted off, and vanished into the clouds. Now *there's* panache!

In the days that followed, the German aircraft did quite as well as their battleships, heavy cruisers, and destroyers would have done had they made contact. Not to dwell too long on a sorry story, for only eleven lonely and battered ships, one by one, made safe haven into Russian ports. But the story does have a few bright spots.

That the Royal Navy and United States Navy felt dreadful about leaving the convoy is a matter of history. And on the 4th of July, Independence Day! But on that morning they were still together. The day dawned windless, foggy, cold – three below zero. In the American ships weather-worn Stars and Stripes were replaced by fresh ensigns.

HMS *Norfolk* greeted USS *Wichita* by signal lamp: "Many happy returns of the day. The United States is the only country with a known birthday."

*Wichita* showed that the USN was just as adept as the RN with an appropriate sentiment. "Thank you. I think England should celebrate Mother's Day."

From his flagship, HMS *London*, Rear-Admiral Freddie Hamilton joined the inter-ship conversation: "On the occasion of your great anniversary, it seems most uncivil to make you station-keep at all, but even today the freedom on the seas can be read two ways. It is a privilege for us to have you with us and I wish you the best of hunting."

In USS *Wichita*, Captain Hill replied that it was a privilege to be with Hamilton, that he was happy to be a portion of his command, but: "Independence Day requires a large fireworks display. I hope you will not disappoint us."

In the light of the way that Independence Day ended, it is all rather sad.

In the days and weeks that followed there were the usual acts of fortitude and cunning, of self-sacrifice and self-serving, of devotion to duty and abnegation of duty. For there are men who are brave and men who are not so brave. Generally, men who are trained and are the inheritors of a fine tradition will act as is expected of them. If they live or die is not really the point. But I have never heard any seaman who has gone through the dangers of the sea and the violence of the enemy talk of cowardice. There are men who are brave and men who are not so brave. And in their efforts to survive there is always an element of whimsy.

Take the case of Lieutenant Leo Gradwell, the Captain of the coal-burning anti-submarine trawler *Ayrshire*. Upon receiving Broome's order to scatter he went to look at his charts. Where to go? Archangel? That seemed silly. To steer southeast would bring him closer to the aircraft bases and into the U-boats that would surely be spread out across their path. So he steered northwest. Choosing the merchantman who was steering the most northerly course as one with whom a meeting of minds was most possible, he ordered him to fall in astern. Thus, *Ayrshire* and *Ironclad* poked off.

A corvette flashed, "Where are you going?"

"To Hell. And the first to come back, we hope."

He was headed for Hope Island and overhauled the Panamanian freighter *Troubadour*, also heading for Hope and making vast quantities of black smoke as she flogged lustily along. A grave danger, you say? The German u-Boats and aircraft would surely see the smoke, would they not? Well, yes, but a coal-burning ship was not entirely unwelcome to a coal-burning trawler short of fuel. As he drew abeam of *Troubadour*, Gradwell hailed her: "Are you a coal-burner?"

"Yes."

"What supplies have you got?"

"Six months."

"Come with me."

And *Troubadour*, suffering from xenophobia and glad of some company, fell happily in astern.

At about seven a.m. of the fifth he overhauled *Silver Sword* and she, too, was pleased to join. As they approached the ice barrier it became evident that his little convoy could not break through to the islands where he had intended to spend a quiet few days until all this beastliness had died down. So he led his flock north into the great fields of ice floes and the masters of the three freighters trustingly followed. It was a daring act: one turn up the wrong channel would have meant being crushed in the shifting ice. In fact, that evening the German Fifth Air Force reported to Naval Staff in Berlin that it would be impossible for ships to get in there.

All that night and the following day they bashed on but then it became evident they could go no further. They stopped their engines, damped down their fires to avoid the tell-tale smoke, and *Ayrshire's* First Lieutenant trudged over to talk to the consorts. As inventive as his Captain, he got those freighters with M-3 tanks as deck cargo to man the guns of the tanks (they broke open the cargo to get ammunition). These army guns added to their own guns might not sink German battleships but they would certainly disconcert them. And, there being nothing like white ice all around to spur the survival instinct, the Master of *Troubadour* remembered that he had a particularly large stock of white paint. Gradwell ordered it shared around and slapped on, starboard side first – the side facing Norway. In a remarkably short time – in *Troubadour*, four hours – all ships were white from truck to waterline, from stem to stern. It worked. An aircraft passing to the south failed to detect them. Two of the ships were painted on one side only. "Rather," said Gradwell later, "like playing Hamlet and Othello with a very small cast."

The wind shifted to south a couple of days later and the ships butted their way out of the ice field, *Ayrshire* coaled and watered from

*Troubadour*, and set course for Novaya Zemla; having no chart of this area he used the *London Times Handy Atlas*, picked up three lifeboats full of survivors from *Fairfield City*, and shaped course for Archangel. It would be good to end the Leo Gradwell saga by having him lead his charges up the River Dvina into Archangel to the cheers of jubilant and grateful Russians, but, alas, it did not turn out thus. In the last few miles of the river he ran out of coal and had to be towed in. "Had we lived, I should have had a tale to tell of the hardihood, endurance, and courage of my companions which would have stirred the heart . . . our dead bodies must tell the tale," said Robert Falcon Scott (1868–1912) at the South Pole.

And we must tell you the tales of the rescue ships that started to sail in our convoys in 1941; their function was to pick up survivors and that was a comfort both to us and to the merchant seamen. Previously we had to leave survivors in the water while we were fighting off attacks by submarines or aircraft.

*Zaafaran*, *Zamalek*, and *Rathlin* sailed in PQ 17. That Admiralty had the shakes about the fate of this Reykjavik-to-Archangel convoy was evident in that these three rescue ships were in a convoy of thirty-four, as were two anti-aircraft ships, *Pozarica* and *Palomares*.

The rescue ships were not all sweetness and light in their mission of mercy. *Zamalek* had stowed on her upper deck an RAF launch with a large blue, white, and red roundel. When the Heinkels attacked this bull's eye was irresistible and she was repeatedly sprayed with bullets. Three of her anti-aircraft gunners were wounded, but they had their revenge and shot down one Heinkel. The next day there were sporadic attacks and icebergs to be dealt with, and at 1:50 of a bright 5 July morning in a sea as smooth as glass *Christopher Newport* was torpedoed. Forty-seven out of fifty were saved. About six in the evening about thirty-five Heinkels attacked and the British *Navarino*, the American *William Hooper*, and the Russian tanker *Azerbaijan* were hit. The three rescue ships scooped up as many as they could. It was many hours later that they caught up with the convoy. They arrived to find that the convoy had been ordered to scatter and were boxing the compass from northwest through north to east-southeast. Captain McGowan of *Zaafaran* was a big man, and he was indignant, and like most merchant seamen he referred to the navy as the "Grey Funnel Line." He sent for his doctor, a naval surgeon: "Look what your shipping firm's done now!"

*Rathlin* headed north to the ice barrier, *Zaafaran* and *Zamalek* steered northeast. Next day a patrolling Focke-Wulf Condor sighted

*Rathlin* and attacked. *Rathlin* shot him down and went in to pick up survivors; all six were dead. All day distress signals were heard from ships and boats. *Zamalek* had been joined by the Admiralty tanker *Aldersdale*, the freighter *Ocean Freedom*, and the minesweeper *Salamder*. They were attacked by four dive-bombers. *Aldersdale* was hit. Because of her better anti-aircraft armament the rescue ship beat off the aircraft and the minesweeper picked up survivors – a seamanlike reversal of roles. About nine miles to the eastward *Zaafaran* was bombed and sunk. While doing these Arctic convoys in *Sioux* we used to wonder how long a man would survive in these frigid waters. "About five minutes," said our doctor. From the doctor of *Zaafaran* we get this beautifully clinical report of a survivor's condition after fifteen minutes in water of thirty-two degrees Fahrenheit: "On boarding the raft, skin anaesthesia was complete to the neck."

*Zaafaran* had been making better speed than *Zamalek* and there had been the usual exchange of good-natured but rude signals on which was faster. Now *Zamalek* tied down the safety valves and sped to the aid of her faster rival. Ninety-seven crew and survivors were picked up. As the sodden Chief Engineer of *Zaafaran* clambered over the side the Chief Engineer of *Zamalek* greeted him with: "Now, which is the better ship?"

*Zamalek* now had over 200 souls on board. Since it is almost impossible to get survivors to stay below it was gravely crowded on deck, but they made it to the Matochkin Strait that separates the two halves of Novaya Zemla. So there were six merchantmen, three minesweepers, three trawlers, a corvette, and her. "Funk Creek," this anchorage was called.

The escorts sallied forth and, through ice, fog, and bombing, picked up survivors from those ships who hadn't made Novaya Zemla. *Zamalek* was full, standing room only. She weaved her way through the bombs, drenched with spray from near misses. One near miss unseated the compass and fractured the main oil-supply pipe. The engines stopped. The pipe was repaired. She sailed on. At four o'clock on the afternoon of the 11th of July she sailed up the Dvina River into Archangel. The anti-aircraft ship *Pozarika* steamed past: she had manned ship and her crew cheered *Zamalek* and their hats sailed into the air. Her Master signalled: "I would greatly appreciate your ensign when you have done with it."

*Zamalek*'s Master thanked *Pozarica* for the protection she had given them, but concluded, " . . . Even so, you're not getting that ensign, it's *mine*."

She went on to sail with a total of sixty-four convoys and save 611 lives. And so did the rest of them go on, either until they were sunk or until the war ended. In any one day during these years there were at least a dozen convoys at sea. Twenty-nine rescue ships were with these convoys. Twenty survived the war. They steamed an estimated 2,250,000 miles in 797 convoys. They saved 4,194 lives and a lot of their crews lost their own.

"Had we lived, I should have had a tale to tell . . . " said Scott. Well, a lot of us did live and so we tell these tales.

So some of the crews of PQ 17 reached safe haven. Haven? Yes, but not a friendly one. As a reprisal against an Allied unwillingness to mount the Second Front, the Russians put armed guards on our gangways, Allied ships' crews were not allowed to visit other ships, mail was withheld – food also. It was certain that they could get no coal. But *Ayrshire* raided the dockyard coal dump one dark night.

So, amidst scenes of desolation and death in the Arctic Ocean, the Barent Sea, and the Kara Sea, the coal-burning, ungainly, unattractive, eleven-knot anti-submarine trawlers had come out of it with some credit. To the thirty-two-knot, sleek, heavily gunned destroyers, the trawlers had always seemed an object of derision, a cross to be carried, a bit of a nuisance, manned by good fellows, of course, and certainly better than nothing. *Ayrshire*'s First Lieutenant (he who readied the army tank guns against the German battleship) had been moved by the muse of poetry:

> Why, we're nothing but a tyro,
> Haven't even got a gyro,
> And as for making smoke, well bugger me!
> We just belch it up to heaven
> As we do our hot eleven, (knots)
> Keeping station on PQ or QP.

> We are given types of gun
> Little use against the Hun,
> And rounds of ammunition – bloody few,
> Then sent out with destroyers
> Whose job is to annoy us,
> As we help escort a QP or PQ.

There were other incongruous scenes among the acts of death. In several cases after a ship was torpedoed the U-boat would surface, take on board a survivor or two, give water and food to those left in the boats, and give them the best course to the nearest land. There were several cases of German aircraft picking up survivors, for example, the torpedoed *Carlton*. Those in the boats were passed by seven Heinkels on their way to attack the remainder of the convoy. They returned with their torpedo-racks empty and one settled down near them. The pilot held up three fingers, and three survivors were picked up. Two hours later a Dornier-24 hospital plane landed and took on ten, three hours after that, ten more. Those left stayed on that patch of ocean so as not to miss the next flight to Norway. Then another Heinkel took on three. One of them asked the pilot if there would be any more. The pilot regretted that there would not. The last plane to Norway had gone.

There were also the gallant examples of defiance: the firing of the ship's guns at approaching torpedoes – and the guns of the army tanks carried as deck cargo – in one case with success. The torpedo exploded a half-mile off. BOOM! And, after a voyage of 300 miles, the seventeen survivors of *Carlton* who could not get on the last plane to Norway made a landfall in the north of Norway. On their ninth day in the boat U-376 had pulled alongside. The Captain gave them biscuits, water, blankets (of U.S. manufacture, salved from the torpedoed SS *Hoosier*), said he regretted he could not take them onboard as he was outward bound, said it was nothing personal, gave them a compass, a course to steer, cigarettes, and then departed – Lieutenant-Commander Friedrich-Karl Marx, a bright picture in a gloomy scene. They landed in Norway, these seventeen, after nineteen days in an open boat, weak indeed, but alive – certainly due to the Heinkels and Dorniers who, by taking their mates, left room for them to come off the rafts into the boat – and certainly due to Lieutenant-Commander Marx of U-376. And he is only one example of the gallantry of German captains.

*Carlton*'s story ends well. They were shipped south to Tromso and those not suffering from frostbite continued down to Oslo. There they embarked in the large troop-transport *Wuri* to cross the Skagerrak to Denmark. Embarked also were a thousand German soldiers. The next morning as *Wuri* drew near the Aalborg channel prisoners and troops handed in their lifejackets. Then, BOOM, they hit a mine. The soldiers, in an alien element and not inured to this kind of warfare, rushed to the ladders to get topside as the ship began to sink. The *Carlton* survivors handed out to them the discarded lifebelts and made the soldiers don them. On deck they began to organize the troops to abandon the ship, which had a twenty-degree list to starboard. Some rafts were by now in the water and *Carlton*'s crew restrained the soldiers from jumping into the water, where the remainder of the rafts were likely to fall on top of them. Some set to work tending the wounded, others gave the soldiers a quick course in how to get away from a sinking ship. The ship heeled a few degrees more. The Germans' hobnailed boots skidded them to the ship's rail. A large wooden platform was likely to slip and crush them. The survivors got them clear. Then they themselves mustered on top of a wooden hatch in the pious hope that it would float clear. Boats were by now putting off from shore and picking up all hands. The men from the *Carlton* were heroes! The Captain fed them schnappes, everyone forced cigarettes upon them. The German officer-in-charge thanked them for saving the lives of hundreds of his troops (only six were lost) and said he would write to the Führer and recommend them for a decoration.

We in the Royal Canadian Navy mid-ocean escorts knew many of these merchant ships, mostly in terms of "Watch *that* bugger; she tends to make smoke." "Watch *her*, she's a chronic straggler." For the next three years we continued to meet the ships who survived.

And so by now what was said by Churchill and Stalin and Roosevelt and Hitler, by Pound and Tovey and Hamilton and Raedar and Goering and Schniewind, has been chronicled to exhaustion. What they did and why they did it is not amenable to easy analysis and still less to a judgement of who was right and who was wrong and to what degree. What they did and why is in the archives. But what will live in the minds and in the hearts of men are those actions by the sailors and soldiers and airmen of which I have told you a few. And *they* certainly do not know why they did them. Men of action are not that much given to mulling over the why. They just did what their instinct and training and tradition had taught them to do. And their spirit reaches out to us over the years.

Roger Hill was commanding *Ledbury* in PQ 17 but I didn't meet him until 1944, when he was driving *Jervis*. He said that when *Kepple* and *Wilton* and *Ledbury* and the rest of the close escort steamed off at high speed he was sure that they were going to death and glory, that *Tirpitz* was just over the horizon. When they realized that there was no enemy, all the crew were despondent about leaving the convoy. After arriving at Scapa Flow the six destroyer captains had a tumultuous session in which they considered resigning, asking for a court of inquiry, defecting to the USN as able seamen. They drank a lot of gin and concluded that Admiralty had made a complete ballzup.

Stalin wondered if the British navy had lost its sense of glory. Church-ill called it the most "melancholy episode" in the history of the navy. But it doesn't really matter much what those men *said*. The acts of selfless courage that the lesser players on the world stage *did* is really more important – to those of us at sea, anyway. We in Canadian escort groups talked to some of the surviving Merchant Navy seamen in the years that followed. When questioned they rather tended to shrug off PQ 17 as one more episode. They had been attacked before that convoy, and since. Most of them, of course, I never met. But I would like some day to meet the Captain and the First Lieutenant of the *Ayrshire*, and the pilot of the Heinkel who plucked his chums out of the sea under the guns of *Wilton*, and the Captain of U-376 . . .

# VII    Battles in the Mediterranean

*"You cannot build a ship in a hurry with a Supplementary Estimate."*

Admiral Jackie Fisher, 1902

*I*n the autumn of 1938 the Admiralty formed plans for fighting both Germany and Italy together, if necessary, and perhaps Japan as well. Although Clausewitz gets credit for the phrase "realpolitik," there has never been any doubt over the centuries that the Admiralty saw things plain and saw things whole, and without sentiment; the fact that Italy and Japan had been our allies from 1914 to 1918 meant nothing. In 1978 James B. Lamb (*The Corvette Navy*, p. 98) wrote:

> It was easy to lose sight of the purpose behind the [Royal Navy's] charm, to regard, as some silly people did, the navy as effete, a Victorian anachronism in a harsh twentieth-century world of air power and total war. But nobody who served with the Royal Navy had any such illusions; they knew from experience that the RN was not merely tough and competent and professional, but ruthless too. What other navy would snuff out a potential threat from a former friend, as the British did at Oran when they attacked the French Fleet, or send a battleship through all the hazards of a narrow fiord to exterminate a nest of German destroyers as the Admiralty did with *Warspite* at Narvik? For all its old world grace and charm, the Royal Navy would cut the throat of its own grandmother if it served its interest, and you'd better believe it!

118

Second only to home waters in importance was the Mediterranean, the route of Persian Gulf oil and raw materials from the Far East. It was accepted that Italy's strategic position and naval and air strength would probably make it necessary to use the long route south around Africa via the Cape of Good Hope. But we might get some convoys through the Mediterranean.

In 1939 at Gibraltar Admiral Sir Dudley North had only two old cruisers, the 13th Destroyer Flotilla, and a few minesweepers. In the eastern Mediterranean was the Commander-in-Chief, Admiral Sir Andrew Browne Cunningham, called, of course, ABC, with the 1st Battle Squadron – *Warspite, Barham*, and *Malaya*; the 1st Cruiser Squadron – *Devonshire, Shropshire*, and *Sussex*; the 3rd Cruiser Squadron – *Penelope, Arethusa*, and *Galatea*; the anti-aircraft cruiser *Coventry*; and the aircraft carrier *Glorious*. Also, he had twenty-six destroyers, ten submarines, and eight minesweepers and escort vessels.

In January, 1939, Admiralty's appreciation of a war in the Mediterranean with both Germany and Italy was sent to Sir Andrew; it turned out to be remarkably prescient. Our putative ally, France, had in the Mediterranean some battleships, a seaplane carrier, cruisers, destroyers, and submarines. Italy had all these and more. Complex corollary factors do not permit a simple comparison but the bald arithmetic of the balance of forces was:

|         | Battleships | Cruisers | Destroyers | Carriers | Submarines |
|---------|-------------|----------|------------|----------|------------|
| Britain | 3           | 7        | 32         | 1        | 10         |
| France  | 3           | 10       | 48         | 1        | 53         |
| Total   | 6           | 17       | 80         | 2        | 63         |
| Italy   | 6           | 19       | 86         |          | 116        |

The awkward truth of the matter was that the combined strength of the British and French fleets was inferior to that of the Italian. Without the French fleet – or worse, their ships surrendering to the German navy – our position was at risk. After France surrendered to Germany, the destruction of the French fleet, by Admiral Somerville's Force H at Mers-el-Kebir and Toulon, was an absolute operational necessity.

The Italians called the Mediterranean *Mare Nostrum*, and at first glance it would appear that they had reason to do so. Taranto was their main base – with three battleships, eight cruisers, twenty destroyers, and scores of smaller vessels – but there were a significant number of Italian ships at Naples, Sicily, Tripoli, Sardinia, Dodecanese, Libya.

Sir Andrew agreed with Jackie Fisher that one couldn't build ships in a hurry. He was to fight battles of desperation and be on the brink of disaster for three years. Only toward the end of 1942 did he have the minimum number of ships he needed.

(It makes one shudder to contemplate the results of the C-in-C of the Kreigsmarine, Admiral Raeder, if he had been allowed to complete his building program before Hitler declared war. He would have had thirteen battleships, thirty-three cruisers, four aircraft carriers, 250 U-boats, and 300 destroyers. To take only one aspect of Germany's building program – that of U-boats – in 1939 Dönitz started the war with twenty-five operational U-boats. In that year they sank 206 of our merchant ships; in 1940 they sank 932; in 1941 they sank 830; in 1942 they were winning the Battle of the Atlantic, sinking merchant ships faster than we could build them: that year, 1,091! What if they had started with, not twenty-five but 250? We can only be grateful that a corporal was dictating Germany's naval policy and directing her naval warfare.)

Germany's invasion of France began on 10 May 1940. The main attack of the German army was from the northwest through Holland into Belgium. General Rommel's panzers came through the Ardennes, across the river Meuse, and swung north to Dunkirk. General Gauderian's panzer group advanced along the Somme River to Abbyville on the English Channel. That they were both ordered to halt there (a blunder) is the only reason that the tragicomedy of Dunkirk was possible: 19,000 soldiers evacuated from Bayonne and St. Jean de Luz; two destroyers from the Mediterranean Fleet crammed 10,000 troops from southern France into themselves and small cargo vessels and took them to Gibraltar; 22,656 from the Channel Islands; from Dunkirk and other beaches, 558,032; another 30,000-40,000 civilians got out in addition. Over 500,000 souls were rescued by the skilful and determined application of maritime power. By the 30th of June, German soldiers controlled Europe. But not the seas around Europe.

In a few weeks the strategic situation had changed beyond recognition; important French vessels to reach England at this time were two old battleships, four destroyers, seven submarines, and six torpedo boats. The main part of France's modern fleet was at the mercy of the Germans and all the assurances of Marshal Pétain and Admiral Darlan that they would not be allowed to be used against Britain were tremulous cries in a gale of German success.

The British cabinet did not hesitate. French ships in English ports were seized; at Alexandria, Admiral Cunningham persuaded Admiral

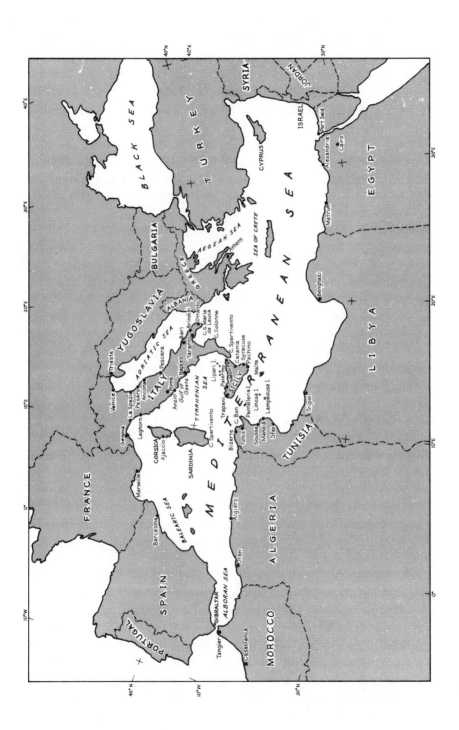

Godfroy to demobilize his ships; the same result could not be achieved with Admiral Gensoul at Oran. At eight in the morning of 3 July Admiral Somerville's emissary, Captain C.S. Holland, asked Admiral Gensoul to see him. The answer was "No." Four choices were sent to him by note: (1) put to sea and join forces with the British; (2) sail with reduced crews to any British port; (3) sail with reduced crews to any French port in the West Indies; or, (4) scuttle the ships within six hours.

Failure to accept any of these alternatives would result in the destruction of the French ships. Offshore Force H waited: *Hood* (wearing the flag of Admiral Somerville), *Valiant, Resolution, Ark Royal*, two small cruisers, *Arethusa* and *Enterprise*, and eleven destroyers.

At 2:39 p.m. Admiral Gensoul at last agreed to see the British delegate; at 4:15 Captain Holland arrived and informed Admiral Gensoul he had until 5:30 to decide. By 5:20 Captain Holland told Somerville that Gensoul would not agree to any of the four alternatives. At 5:35 Captain Holland left; at 5:54 p.m. Force H opened fire.

*Bretagne* was blown apart; *Dunkerque, Provence*, and several smaller ships were seriously damaged. *Strasbourg* and five destroyers won clear of the harbour and reached Toulon. At eight in the morning Captain Holland had begun to try and arrange honourable alternatives for the French fleet – alternatives to being used against us by Germany. Admiral Gensoul could not be accommodated. By six p.m. that day his fleet ceased to exist.

A few days later six torpedo bombers from *Hermes* immobilized *Richelieu* at Dakar. Sir Andrew was left with a situation he could just barely live with. While most of his supplies would have to come the long way around Africa and up the Red Sea to Alexandria, an occasional convoy might still be fought through the Mediterranean. In 1794 Admiral Nelson had said to Sir Gilbert Elliot, "Laurels grow in the Bay of Biscay – I hope a bed of them may be found in the Mediterranean." This didn't seem likely for ABC.

At the beginning of the struggle, Italy had eighty submarines operational in the Mediterranean; this is a great concentration compared to the smaller number of German U-boats in the broad reaches of the Atlantic. Yet they accomplished very little and by the end of 1940 were reduced to ten at either end of the Mediterranean. It became apparent that the struggle would not be waged between U-boats and surface craft but between aircraft and surface craft. Thus, the possession of such island bases as Sicily, Sardinia, Malta, Crete, and many of the smaller islands was mandatory.

In the following years Canadians captured islands whose names you have seldom if ever heard – and neither had those who captured them until they were briefed for their mission. During this time Canadian sailors took part in land operations in a way not possible in the same degree in any other theatre of war, for land bases in this theatre put enemy aircraft as little as ten minutes' flying time from the naval units they attacked. Besides the islands, the airports all along the north coast of Africa could bomb our convoys along a coastline of some 2,000 miles from Alexandria to Gibraltar.

We now see that Benito Mussolini and the Italian Chief of the Naval Staff, Admiral Cavagnari, were forced into a position analogous to that of Hitler and Raeder. Despite their numerical superiority the Italian navy mainly fought a defensive war. Mussolini might as a dramatic actor say the policy for the navy was "the offensive at all points in the Mediterranean and outside," but reality dictated otherwise and, in fact, the Italian offensive was limited to keeping sea communications open to their army in Africa. Admiral Cavagnari knew as well as Admiral Raeder that to put his fleet to sea would ensure a battle with whatever Royal Navy ships could be brought to bear. No doubt this was in his mind, and he, like Raeder, could not afford losses. Further, the weakness of the Italian air force seriously vitiated Cavagnari's chances of success. The Royal Navy offered battle many times in 1940, every time it could. The Italian navy refused, every time.

The main effect the Italian navy had, therefore (even though it seldom left harbour), was to tie down our heavy units to every operation we mounted. It is called the efficacy of a "fleet in being." The German battleship *Tirpitz*, apart from one operational cruise where for the only time she fired her guns in anger (at a weather station), spent her whole war in various Norwegian fiords; but every Russian convoy had to be escorted by battleships and cruisers in case she came out.

If it were not for Admiral Cunningham's fleet, General Wavell's army in Egypt would be fighting the advancing Italian army in the streets of Cairo. *Argus* carried aircraft to Takoradi on the Gold Coast, whence they flew across Africa to Cairo; she herself steamed around the Cape of Good Hope and arrived there on 5 September 1940.

The first brush between the British and Italian fleets occurred on the 9th of July off the Calabrian coast. On paper the British were superior, three battleships to two, but *Malaya* and *Royal Sovereign* were so slow they never came into the action. Torpedo bombers from *Eagle* made an unsuccessful attack; then followed a gun duel. In cruisers and destroyers the Italian were superior, and in battleships as well because two of ours were always puffing up from astern. The battleship *Cesare* suffered a hit and the Italian fleet retired behind smoke. This trend was to continue.

On the 19th of July 1940 a light cruiser, HMAS *Sydney*, together with five destroyers met two Italian cruisers and their destroyers north of Crete. *Bartolomeo Colleoni* was sunk and the remainder fled. The lesson was reinforced: even though our forces are numerically inferior, we will *always* attack.

The safety and supply of Malta caused concern, but on three occasions between October and November that island received reinforcements and stores from Alexandria. In October a new commitment arose with the Italian invasion of the Greek islands; soldiers had to be moved to Crete from Alexandria and then to an advanced base at Suda Bay.

In November, 1940, reinforcements arrived – a battleship, two cruisers, and three destroyers. They and Force H passed unmolested from Gibraltar to Alexandria. Perhaps, it was thought, we need not take the long route around Africa. Winston Churchill was all for this more pugnacious approach and Admiral Cunningham had to point out to him that his (Cunningham's) position differed only in degree from that of Raeder and Cavagnari; we could not squander ships.

From 1940 to 1943 there were many Canadian sailors serving with the Royal Navy in the Mediterranean Fleet (stokers uncounted because they had been lost in the RN records until our Navy Minister, Angus L. Macdonald, demanded their return). It transpired that there were 110 stokers and scores of midshipmen and sub-lieutenants doing their big-ship time; and, most important of all, the radar lieutenants. These were RCNVR officers with degrees in electronics from Canadian universities. The RN had nothing like them. Radar was new to the fleet. Nobody really understood it, certainly not the deck officers, most certainly not the Admiral. They knew how to use it, mind you, but not how to keep it running. The radar officer did; he serviced the radar sets that detected the enemy, directed the guns, and guided the aircraft from the carriers to the target, and then home again. It was in this capacity that they fought against the Italians.

The Italians never really had a *Mare Nostrum*, except perhaps a small one in the eastern Mediterranean for a while and also had a bit in the autumn of 1940 in the Gulf of Taranto. This was sixty miles across from Cap de Colonne northeast to Cap Santa Maria di Leuca, seventy-five miles deep from seaward to the top of the arch of the Italian boot at

Taranto. Here, six Italian battleships were moored in the Mar Grande and nine cruisers and seventeen destroyers in Mar Piccolo. The anti-aircraft guns in this fleet would number over 500 with effective ranges out to five miles. A dozen or so shore batteries flanked the harbour with perhaps 300 more guns. Twenty-two barrage balloons encircled the ships. The battleships were screened by zarebas – anti-torpedo nets.

Sir Andrew had a sense of history. He had studied a plan of attack of Sir David Beatty, who, when frustrated by the German refusal to put to sea after the Battle of Jutland, had proposed a strike by about 200 torpedo bombers against the German fleet as they lay in port. Sir Andrew only had twenty-four but he should be able to do something. He preferred the offensive, although he had been fighting defensive battles these many months to keep Malta supplied. He also believed in Admiral Lord Nelson's dictum that "The best defence is close to the enemy's ports" and had had his eye on Taranto for some time.

Now reconnaissance photos told him the Italians were there, but he had only two carriers, *Illustrious* and *Eagle* (in whom Canadian Sub-Lieutenant B.P. Hunter flew in 824 Squadron). "We'll attack on Trafalgar Day, October 21." This was delayed by a fire in the hangar deck of *Illustrious*. Sir Andrew was furious. He now had to choose November 11 instead, Armistice Day – quite inappropriate to the bellicose actions of his "Stringbags." But then *Eagle*'s near misses of enemy bombs off Calabria made repairs necessary and she could not sail; seven of her aircraft were damaged, also. Well, move the good ones from *Eagle* to *Illustrious*. Now ABC had twenty-one TBRs (torpedo bomber, reconnaissance) – the Fairey Swordfish – the Stringbag.

Although they entered the fleet only four years before, 1936, Stringbags looked like relics of either World War One or a flying circus. They were biplanes, fixed undercarriage, no flaps, top speed of 135 knots officially but this must have been downhill, with a following wind and no load. It would reach about 120 knots straight and level; in a steep dive it wouldn't go above 200. I never flew in a Stringbag until 1944 but she was a stately old lady, bless her dear old heart, wouldn't stall until down to sixty knots and then she would settle down gently, wind strumming on struts, fabric skin rippling.

And Sir Andrew had twenty-one of these to attack the Italian fleet in Taranto, a heavily defended harbour with hundreds and hundreds of guns. It looked as though the operation would end up with Victoria Crosses all around – posthumous, of course – and the Mediterranean fleet without a Stringbag to its name.

The Charge of the Naval Brigade

Cannon to right of them,
Cannon to left of them,
Cannon in front of them,
Volleyed and thundered;
Stormed at by shot and shell,
Boldly they flew and well,
Into the jaws of Death,
Into the mouth of Hell
Flew the Twenty-One.

The twenty-one flew off in two waves, at 8:40 and 9:40 p.m. from 120 miles to the southeast, near Corfu. In the first wave of twelve, six carried torpedoes, six bombs, two of the latter with flares to illuminate the harbour. In the second wave, five had tin fish, the rest bombs and flares. Lieutenant-Commander Keith Williamson piloted the lead plane; Lieutenant Scarlet was his observer. They flew in bright moonlight.

The Italian guns raised a devastating curtain of fire as the Stringbags bumbled in at all of ninety knots. The enemy listening devices had picked them up while they were still offshore and just outside gun range. Lieutenant Scarlet sighted the red twinkling of the anti-aircraft fire.

"That's Taranto," he told Williamson.

"Yes, they seem to be expecting us."

But the Italian gunners had a problem. If the Stringbags came in low, less than fifty feet, the defending guns would be firing at each other, at their own ships, and at Taranto itself if the attacking aircraft came over the harbour. They did come in low – at twenty feet. Three battleships were sunk, and a cruiser and a destroyer were damaged as well as an oil refinery and a sea-plane base. Almost every pilot scored a direct hit, and, even more remarkable, survived an average of 5,000 shells fired at each one.

Two Stringbags were shot down: Williamson and Scarlet lived to spend the rest of the war in chokey, that is, in a prisoner-of-war camp; the other pilot and observer were killed. But twenty-one aircraft and forty-two men changed the balance of naval power in the Mediterranean. In the few minutes over their target they had inflicted more damage on the Italian fleet than the British Grand Fleet had upon the German High Seas Fleet at the Battle of Jutland. (And half a world away this demonstration that the aircraft carrier had succeeded the battleship was observed with some interest by Admiral Yamamoto of the Imperial Japanese Navy – two years before Pearl Harbor.)

If Winnie had not already used the phrase he would have said, "Never were so many ruined so completely and so quickly by so few." Sir Andrew said, "Well done."

\* \* \*

Acting Sub-Lieutenants (Temporary), RCNVR, Terry Burchell and Stu Paddon had joined the RCN in Canada in 1940, the former from the University of Toronto, the latter from the University of Western Ontario. Both were electrical engineers and both were seconded to the RN as radar officers. (Both stayed in the navy and ended up as electrical rear-admirals. Both still argue which was the first to be awarded a Mentioned in Despatches.) Sub-Lieutenant Mack Lynch served in HMS *Orion*. Paddon served first in the light cruiser HMS *Dido* and then *Prince of Wales*. He was in her when she and HMS *Hood* met *Bismarck* and *Prinz Eugen* and *Hood* blew up (and a large part of my heart died with her). He had started in *Prince of Wales* with one radar set; within a year she had a suit of ten radar sets, surface warning, air warning: one to measure range for the main armament, the 14-inch guns, four for the 5.25-inch guns, four to control the anti-aircraft pom-poms; others were added as the war went on.

After the damage inflicted by *Bismarck* was repaired *Prince of Wales* did a Malta convoy. This was the bad year; in one Malta convoy only one merchant ship of the convoy got through, even though as heavily escorted as we could manage. Many warships had been lost, too. This convoy of eighteen merchant ships, besides *Prince of Wales*, the aircraft carrier *Ark Royal*, and the battleship *Nelson*, was screened by six cruisers and twenty destroyers. They were attacked by Italian submarines and *Nelson* was hit in the bow, but one torpedo did not cause this behemoth of 40,000 tons to falter. The air attacks were frequent but not in great numbers. They were told that the Italian fleet was at sea and heading for them. The fleet altered into the wind and the Swordfish flown off and directed on a bearing to intercept. *Prince of Wales* steamed along the same bearing at thirty knots. I've said that Stringbags were not the fastest aircraft in the war. Well, one hour later, Paddon said, "they were still in sight from the bridge of *Prince of Wales* – but gaining." To be fair to the gentle old Stringbags, they *were* flying into a head wind. The Italian fleet never showed up.

\* \* \*

In November, 1940, the battle of Cape Spartivento was the next major engagement. It was the first convoy to be fought through from Gibraltar to Malta and Alexandria and the first aspect of this huge operation is the disparity between goods delivered and protection necessary. A convoy of *three* merchant ships would make the passage, and 1,400 troops embarked in the cruisers *Manchester* (wearing the flag of Vice-Admiral Holland) and *Southampton*. The escort was Force H with Admiral Somerville in *Renown* with *Ark Royal, Sheffield, Despatch*, and nine destroyers. South of Sardinia they would be met by Admiral Cunningham's battleship *Ramilies*, the cruisers *Berwick, Newcastle*, and *Coventry*, and five destroyers. Two battleships, one aircraft carrier, seven cruisers, and fourteen destroyers escorted three merchant ships! And 1,400 soldiers. With a force of that size it meant that there were seven sailors working to get each individual soldier through to General Wavell's army in Egypt.

At 6:30 a.m. on the 27th of November a Sunderland flying boat from Malta sighted a strong enemy force off the southern tip of Sardinia – Cape Spartivento. It turned out to be the battleships *Vittorio Veneto* and *Guilio Cesare*, seven heavy cruisers, and nineteen destroyers. Since Admiral Cunningham's squadron was still some fifty miles to the eastward Admiral Somerville was greatly outnumbered, but he was sure that the best defence of the convoy was a resolute attack. He put his cruisers in the van and turned north. Force H cried "View Hallo" and took off after the Italians at a gallop. At 1:02 p.m. the enemy battle fleet opened fire on our cruisers; they retired under the big guns of *Renown*. But then the Italian squadron turned away to the northeast, and our cruisers turned again and gave chase. Aircraft were launched from *Ark Royal* but scored no hits. Somerville was approaching the enemy coast and in danger of air attack, but after a thirty-knot chase for two hours, the threat to the convoy was now removed and he returned, was bombed on the way back with no damage, and at five p.m. all was peaceful again. The convoy ships reached Malta and Alexandria and 1,400 soldiers joined General Wavell's Army of the Nile.

The opposing aims of Italy and Britain were simple. Italy needed to keep open north-south routes from Europe to Africa to support the Italian army driving toward Egypt. Britain had to keep open the east-west route from Gibraltar to Malta, Alexandria, and the Dodecanese islands. This periodic bashing up of the Italian fleet we have talked of above makes fine reading, makes us proud of our ships, proud of our commanders and men . . . But the sad truth is that we were failing. It sounds just great to say that between June and December of 1940 we sank eighty-nine ships carrying supplies to the Italian army in Africa. But this was only 2 per cent of those that arrived safely in Libya – with 690,000 tons of stores, ammunition, vehicles, and guns.

Worse, our land flanks were not secure. To the west the Atlantic coast was held by Vichy France from opposite Gibraltar south to Casablanca and a thousand miles further south to Dakar. They were not enemies exactly, but not allies either – and dominated by Germany. Operation Menace was mounted to land Allied troops in Dakar. From beginning to end this encompassed the last three weeks in September, 1940. Two cruisers, seven destroyers, two Free French sloops, and three transports carried 4,200 British and 2,700 Free French soldiers. Vice-Admiral John H.D. Cunningham was the senior officer wearing his flag in *Devonshire*. A battle squadron allocated to Cunningham was two battleships, an aircraft carrier, three cruisers, and ten destroyers. Then, still 300 miles northwest of Dakar, Cunningham learned that three French (not Free French) cruisers and three heavy destroyers had passed west through the Straits of Gibraltar and had turned south. Would they oppose the landings? Would they remain neutral? British forces were ordered not to fire the first shot. From here on the whole sorry mess merges into a skein of signals not received, signals misinterpreted, signals that should not have been sent, Somerville's Force H acting under the direct orders from Admiralty and not Admiral North, the Flag Officer at Gibraltar . . . One French cruiser, *Gloire*, was intercepted and went to Casablanca; the others, *Leygues* and *Montcalm*, reached Dakar.

The British fleet lay off Dakar. Emissaries of General De Gaulle entered the port to parley and were fired upon. Fog impeded our bombardment but the French fire was accurate and one cruiser and two destroyers were seriously hit. The garrison commander said, "We confirm that we will oppose all landings." The next day *Barham, Resolution, Australia*, and *Devonshire* resumed the bombardment. One of the ships replying was the French battleship *Richelieu. Barham* was hit four times. *Resolution* was hit by a torpedo. There were Free French landings at Rufisque – the other side of Hanne Bay from Dakar – from 5:30 to 6:30 on the 25th of September. Our troops were driven back into the sea. Cunningham withdrew to the south to consult with General De Gaulle, who wanted to press on regardless. But Admiralty ordered our forces to the nearest British port, Freetown. Our western flank in Africa was still not secure and would not be until the invasion by British and American forces in Operation Torch in May of 1941. So much for the west flank.

The east flank was on the coast of the Red Sea south of Cairo. Italian soldiers had driven us out of British Somaliland and now held that, Italian Somaliland, Abyssinia, and Eritrea. Our convoys from England and around the Cape of Good Hope had to pass these enemy-held land bases to get through the Red Sea and bring men and supplies to Egypt. Our tight blockade of the Red Sea ports ensured we could continue to use this route.

So much for our threatened east and west flank. What about the middle? Italy was moving troops and supplies into Libya at will. The Italians were not doing that well against General Wavell but soon the German Afrika Korps and General Rommel would enter the picture.

Wars cannot be won without command of the sea. But wars are not won *by* sailors. Wars are won *by* soldiers. A survey of the land war, then, will make more clear the policy of Admiral Cunningham. In a very real way in the desert war, General Rommel's opponent was as much Admiral Cunningham as it was Generals Auchinlek, Alexander, and Montgomery. Further, an understanding of the see-saw battles back and forth along the Mediterranean coast will make more clear the narratives of those Canadian sailors who fought on the sea side of the land battles.

The 1st of May to the 1st of June 1941 was a vital period. The last months of 1940 had, on the whole, been encouraging. The build up by the Cape route was proceeding satisfactorily, we were getting occasional convoys through the Mediterranean, a large part of the Italian fleet had been immobilized at Taranto and the French fleet at Oran, and the *Regia Aeronautica*, although its high-level bombing had been uncomfortably accurate and its torpedo bombing of a high standard, had not driven our fleets and squadrons from the central basin. General Wavell had the Italian army in full retreat; we occupied Crete; Malta was surviving.

Then the intervention of the German forces put our plans back two years. Hitler moved Fliegerkorps X of the Luftwaffe to Sicily; this group had been most successful in the Norwegian campaign against our shipping; unlike the RAF attacking *Scharnhorst, Gneisenau*, and *Eugen* in their dash up the Channel, these German flyers were specialists in anti-shipping. By February, 1941, they had fifty-one bombers and dive-bombers, twenty-four twin-engine fighters, and reconnaissance aircraft. The Italian air force had forty-five bombers and seventy-five fighters in Sicily and seventy bombers and twenty-five fighters in Sardinia.

In Malta we had fifteen RAF Hurricanes; eighteen more arrived a month later.

The siege of Malta had started and for a long time supplies would be few. In some instances convoys sailed with fifteen ships and only one got through. On another occasion *all* were lost. Malta was bombed

Admiral of the Fleet Lord Lewin. (*Department of National Defence*)

Admiral Sir Andrew B. Cunningham, Commander-in-Chief, Mediterranean Fleet. (*Ministry of Defence*)

Vice Admiral James Sommerville, Flag Officer, Force H. (*Ministry of Defence*)

Force H. (*Ministry of Defence*)

Commander Lord Louis Mountbatten on the bridge of *HMS Kelly*. (*Ministry of Defence*)

Lieutenant-Commander Robert Hichens, RNVR, the very best of a good Band of Brothers. (*Sir Peter Scott*)

The Canadian 29th MTB Flotilla led by Tony Law, RCNVR. "The Shorts." (*Department of National Defence*)

Sub-Lieutenant Tony Law when
Captain of MTB 48. (*Department of
National Defence*)

Sub-Lieutenant J.G. McClelland.
(*Department of National Defence*)

D class, "Dog Boats,", the "Longs" (as opposed to the "Shorts"), of the Canadian
65th Flotilla, led by Jim Kirkpatrick.) *(Department of National Defence)*

Jim Kirkpatrick and his wife, Winnifred. (*Department of National Defence*)

Leading Writer Kay Barclay, one of Kirkpatrick's shore staff. (*Department of National Defence*)

Lieutenant Malcolm Knox, RCNVR, Captain of MTB 743. (*Department of National Defence*)

A Canadian Tribal Class destroyer, *HMCS Huron*. *(Department of National Defence)*

Lieutenant-Commander Herbie Raynor, Commander Harry DeWolf, Lieutenant-Commander Johnny Stubbs, *(Department of National Defence)*

German E-Boat. *(Ministry of Defence)*

A German U-Boat. *(Ministry of Defence)*

A German dive-bomber. (*Ministry of Defence*)

Royal Navy Swordfish torpedo bomber. (*Ministry of Defence*)

A British battleship firing. (*Ministry of Defence*)

A Canadian corvette. (*Department of National Defence*)

A British battleship, HMCS *Barham*, blows up. (*Ministry of Defence*)

A merchant ship on a Malta convoy. (*Ministry of Defence*)

A huge sea. (*Ministry of Defence*)

The Battle of Sirte. (*Ministry of Defence*)

Stoker Cahill. *(Gordon Cahill)*

Petty Officer Engineroom Artificer
Bowerman. *(Gordon Cahill)*

George Buckingham and Tom Forrester of the landing craft. *(Department of National Defence)*

Leading Seaman Dave Wright, RCN, and his wife, Freda. (*Dave and Freda Wright*)

Lieutenant Gordon Stead, RCNVR, welcoming Winston Churchill on board motor launch at Tripoli, 1943. (*Gordon Stead*)

Landing craft on the 262nd Canadian Landing Craft Flotilla at Normandy. (*Department of National Defence*)

Lieutenant C.A. Burk, RCNVR, and wife Jean.

Signal Lieutenant John Charles, RCN, of HMS *Laforey*. (*John Charles*)

"Either the Admiral routes the
convoy further south or Wren
Snodgrass gets into trousers."
*(Captain Jackie Broome)*

The King visits HMCS *Sioux* just prior to the invasion of Normandy. (*Department of National Defence*)

May, 1945. German E-Boats surrender to British MTBs. *(Department of National Defence)*

Victory Parade up the Mall toward Buckingham Palace. The Royal Canadian Navy contingent salutes. *(Department of National Defence)*

Left to right: Maitland, Ladner and Burke return to Vancouver after Victory in Europe. *(The Vancouver Province)*

Not all lived to see victory. In 1988 Les Bowerman and Gordon Cahill paid their respects again to the shipmate they sailed with forty-five years ago, Ordinary Seaman Calverley, age eighteen. *(Gordon Cahill)*

daily (our submarines in the harbour submerged until the raids were over).

Italian General Bastico (Rommel called him "Bombastico") had 500,000 troops, General Wavell's Army of the Nile 50,000. Nevertheless, Bastico's men were driven back to Tobruk on the 22nd of January in 1941 and to Benghazi on the 30th. The cruisers and destroyers of the Inshore Squadron deployed ahead of them bombarding until the soldiers arrived. Then they brought in supplies. But now troops had to be called away for the defence of Greece and Wavell's forward momentum was stopped at El Agheila – 600 miles beyond Egypt's border with Libya.

By April, 1941, the Afrika Korps had landed and the picture changed. Within two weeks Rommel drove Wavell's troops back into Egypt, with the exception of Tobruk, which was held by British and Australian troops in a state of siege. For many months the only supplies they would receive would be from the navy. Many ships were sunk keeping Tobruk out of Rommel's hands.

Rommel was an ascetic man more at home in his desert tent than the sybaritic atmosphere of Hitler's various "courts." He wrote daily to Lucia Marie, his wife. He demanded much from his men, spared himself never, and was always at the front of the fighting; he did not "lead from the rear." He came to be admired as much by the British Eighth Army – "the Desert Rats" – as he was by his own men. Prisoners were treated with an old-world courtesy by "the Desert Fox."

The Luftwaffe's onslaught on Malta started in January, 1941. Some supplies reached there early in the new year and then four merchant ships got through at the end of March, but two were sunk in the following day's air raid.

Bulgaria joined the Axis on 1 March 1941 and the Germans thrust south into Greece. The Army of the Nile was depleted further and troops were rushed out from England and Australia. (Rushed out? It took two months.) We sent troops and equipment from Alexandria to the Piraeus every three days, for three weeks. Twenty-five ships were sunk but equipment and 58,364 soldiers bolstered our garrisons, particularly the forward one at Suda Bay in Crete. This was never properly developed and so the fleet had to be supplied from Alexandria, 500 miles away. The Italian warships had been timid so far but were bound to attack soon with us practically *in extremis*. Mines were laid at the exit of the Suez Canal and along the convoy routes in the Dodecanese islands, and bombing was constant. We had only sparse air cover; the heavy cruiser *Kent* was lost at Suda by a one-man torpedo boat. Force H bombarded and destroyed shore installations at Genoa, Leghorn, and Spezia, but it didn't help the Crete situation much. It was clear that the Italian battle fleet would soon intervene in Greek waters.

They did, at the Battle of Cape Matapan, the whole action within a fifty-mile radius of Suda Bay.

On 25 March 1941 Admiral Cunningham's intelligence told him that the Italian navy was preparing to sortie. He was anxious to encourage this and so disposed his ships to make it appear he was unprepared. The Italians *must* be encouraged to fight. Vice-Admiral Pridham-Whippel and the light cruisers *Orion, Ajax, Gloucester*, HMAS *Perth*, and nine destroyers were to "lurk" (that was the word used, although it is hard to imagine four cruisers and nine destroyers "lurking"). Anyway, they were to lurk off Gávdos Island – twenty miles south of Crete – by dawn on the 28th of March. ABC would meet them there.

The night of the 26th, the main battle fleet remained in Alexandria giving, so Cunningham hoped, an appearance of tropical somnolence. Shore leave was piped, but the troops were told to filter back early and to stay sober! A reception for local citizens was held on the quarterdeck: demure young girls in décolleté dresses surrounded by attentive junior officers; sturdy matrons attended by the more sedate elders; cigar smoke, the clink of glasses; soft lights under the awnings; the Royal Marine band thumping out its version of light airs from the *Cavalleria Rusticana, Student Prince, Madame Butterfly*, and similar frivolous operettas; much banter and chatter. "There was a sound of revelry by night . . ." Sir Andrew was a marvellous man at a party. Sub-Lieutenant Bill Blakney of Aurora, Ontario, saw him that night moving from group to group, all smiles and light chitchat, "probably hoping that Italian spies would leave early, get on their wireless, and report that soon the Brits would all be sunk in swinish slumber."

On the 27th an RAF flying boat reported three enemy cruisers 320 miles west of Crete steering southeast (toward Pridham-Whippell). That night Cunningham sailed with *Warspite, Barham, Valiant* (Lieutenant Ernie Apps, RCNVR, was her radar officer), *Formidable*, and destroyers of the 10th and 14th flotillas. At dawn on the 28th an air search from *Formidable* found the Italian cruiser force, a little later Pridham-Whippell sighted them, then an enemy battleship was sighted to the north; a torpedo-bomber strike was flown off. Now a third enemy force of three heavy cruisers was sighted. The Italian battleship opened fire on Pridham-Whippell who, while remaining unharmed, noted with considerable gratitude – at 12:30 p.m. – that Admiral Cunningham had hove into view. Both forces now concentrated on the *Vittorio Veneto* (a Littorio-class battleship). But the Italians did it *again*! All three Italian squadrons turned west and headed for home. The prospect of catching them with our ancient ships was slim, unless they were slowed up by torpedo bombers.

Another air strike was flown off. One hit was scored on *Vittorio Veneto* at 3:30 p.m. and this did slow her. The ancient Med Fleet panted in pursuit but, alas, the enemy battleship's speed was restored to nineteen knots by seven p.m., at which time she was fifty miles ahead of Cunningham. He ordered his cruisers to attack and flew off a third air strike.

*Vittorio Veneto* was now steering northwest – toward Italy – with two destroyers ahead, two astern, three cruisers on either beam, and columns of destroyers to port and starboard of all that. Through their hail of shot and shell the ten torpedo bombers attacked at sunset. Only the cruiser *Pola* was hit and stopped but this had important consequences because, later, the heavy cruisers *Zara* and *Fiume*, with a division of destroyers, were sent back to aid her. Darkness was now complete. By dawn the Italian ships would be under their air umbrella. We would have to fight a night action.

The night was dark and cloudy, no moon, visibility three miles. At ten p.m. radar contact, our fleet squadron closed at twenty knots, the fleet in quarter line; at 10:22 the range was four miles; at 10:23 Cunningham sighted the shadows of the enemy, ordered *Formidable* out of the way, and swung the fleet to starboard, which brought them into line ahead again with all guns bearing. At last! Point blank range! A line of 15-inch and 6-inch guns bellowed together. *Zara, Fiume, Pola*, and two destroyers were sunk.

At dawn the sea was empty; the remainder escaped. The Battle of Cape Matapan was ended.

On the 3rd of April 1941 Rommel captured Benghazi, the capital of Libya; three days later the Germans invaded Greece and Yugoslavia and started their drive south; soon they would be on the doorstep of Crete and would greatly outnumber our forces there. We might have frightened off the main units of the Italian fleet but their submarines and mines continued to take their toll. And the Luftwaffe had control of the air. Without air cover our ships could be picked off one by one. And they were. We were about to evacuate from Greece all the soldiers we had brought in with so much travail.

Then the Admiralty said that Cunningham was not doing enough to stop the German reinforcements to Rommel going from France and Italy to Tripoli; he was to use a battleship and a cruiser to block the port even if it meant sacrificing them.

This interference was probably not entirely from Admiralty alone; the war cabinet held strong views and Churchill had always considered himself a naval strategist. Had he not caused the First Sea Lord, Admiral Sir Jackie Fisher, to resign by his interference in the matter of the Dardanelles in 1917 when he was First Lord of the Admiralty. (Another example is seen in Admiralty's shameful meddling in the Russian convoy, PQ 17.) It is better that the commander on the spot decide on what *exactly* is to be done. Cunningham said he could not agree to the certain loss of two ships. He was against using a battleship and a cruiser to block Tripoli without proper air cover. Such an attack would involve a long passage over dangerous waters. But he "would attack with the whole battle fleet." The same day his message was received in London one was sent back to Cunningham from the Prime Minister saying that the navy would be failing in its duty if it did not stop the enemy convoys to Libya. We can imagine the Admiral's emotions at being instructed as to where his duty lay!

But ABC could not ignore this and took his whole fleet to sea. He sailed northwest from Alexandria on the 18th of April, fuelled at Suda Bay, was joined by cruiser forces, slipped a fast merchant ship into Malta to help the logistics (what economy of effort!), and headed toward his target. RAF Wellingtons and naval Swordfish carried out diversionary attacks. At five a.m. on the twenty-first, aircraft from *Formidable* illuminated Tripoli with flares and the whole fleet opened fire. While only one ship was sunk in harbour, dock installations were reduced to rubble. At 6:30 a.m. the fleet withdrew at high speed and reached Alexandria without loss. Upon receiving congratulations from London the Commander-in-Chief sourly remarked that his success was mainly due to the German air force being occupied elsewhere.

The Inshore Squadron continued to supply Tobruk; losses were considerable without air cover but in April 400 tons of supplies were landed *daily*, fresh troops arrived, and battle-weary troops were sent on leave. Tobruk was besieged, Malta besieged. Ship losses mounted. *Ark Royal* ferried off thirty-two more Hurricanes to Malta. This tactic – flying off land planes from the deck of a carrier – greatly expedited matters for the last 200 miles but was regarded with a marked lack of enthusiasm by RAF pilots, who were used to taking off from a mile-long runway: a runway, moreover, that stayed *still*!

On 21 April the withdrawal from Greece was approved by cabinet. Six cruisers, nineteen destroyers, three escort vessels, and eleven transports were used initially. It is interesting to compare this Crete evacuation of April, 1941, to that of Dunkirk of June, 1940. Again we had command of the sea but not the air. But whereas at Dunkirk we had determined and helpful kinfolk twenty miles away, in Greece we were 400 miles from a hostile protectorate, Egypt, most of whose people did not care if we or the Germans occupied Cairo. German air power made daylight operations impossible. At the end of April we evacuated troops for five nights in a row, then evacuated stragglers on two more nights early in May; we took off 50,732 soldiers, 80 per cent of the garrison.

The whole of May was a series of heroic battles, desperate runs in and out of hostile coasts, night boarding of swearing, weary soldiers greeted with a cup of tea, high-speed runs, decks crowded with troops, ships weaving and heeling to avoid bombing and strafing. *Kelly*, captained by Lord Louis Mountbatten, and *Kashmir* were sunk. *Kipling*, with troubles enough of her own, saw this and picked up survivors from both. Italian surface forces could have had a duck shoot had they been there. And with dawn, the bombers, always the bombers, all day. Get to Alex. Refuel and re-ammunition, sail, be off the island after dark, get as far away as possible before first light. Was it worth it? Yes! No matter what the losses? Yes! Admiral Cunningham said, "It takes three years to build a ship. It takes three hundred to build a tradition."

The pongos were in trouble: it was unthinkable we should not strain every nerve to help them. The evacuation of Heraklion by Admiral Rawlings is a typical example: he sailed with *Orion, Ajax, Dido*, and six destroyers, was bombed during the approach, and two ships were damaged. On entering the port the destroyers ferried soldiers out to the cruisers and at 3:20 a.m. of 29 May, Rawlings sailed with the garrison of 4,000 men. The destroyers *Imperial* and *Kimberly* embarked the soldiers' rearguard and set out in pursuit of the rest. But *Imperial's* steering gear – damaged by a near miss the previous day – jammed at 3:45 and she could not continue. *Hotspur* was sent back to take off the soldiers and sink *Imperial*. Dawn was not far off. *Hotspur* now had 900 men on board; day came and so did the Luftwaffe. *Hereward* was fatally hit, left behind, and lost. Other damage reduced the speed of the squadron. Then *Orion* and *Dido* were badly hit and a large number of the troops on deck were wounded or killed. The squadron struggled on southward and arrived at Alexandria on the evening of the 29th, nearly out of fuel and all out of ammunition.

Despite these losses the evacuation continued. On the night of 29-30 May, Admiral King with *Phoebe, Perth, Calcutta*, three destroyers, and the fast transport *Glengyle* lifted 6,000 men from Sphakia with the only damage being that *Perth* was hit; the next night, Captain Arliss with his four destroyers made the trip and got 1,500 more for only two destroyers damaged. That same night Admiral King took off 4,000 more men with the cruiser *Coventry* sunk. King's return to Alexandria on the afternoon of 1 June 1941 marked the end of the Battle of Crete. The navy had fulfilled its task; as many of our soldiers as possible had been sent where they were needed and, when the battle had gone against them, 80 per cent of them had been brought back. We ferried in 63,420 troops and ferried out 50,732. The number of soldiers killed was not small.

A lot of sailors died, too, and a lot of ships. The cruisers *Fiji*, *Calcutta*, *York*, and *Gloucester* were sunk, as were the destroyers *Juno*, *Kelly*, *Kashmir*, *Hereward*, *Imperial*, *Widnes*, *Greyhound*, *Diamond*, and *Wry-neck*. The battleships *Barham* and *Warspite*, the aircraft carrier *Formidable*, the cruisers *Perth*, *Dido*, *Orion*, and *Naiad*, and the destroyers *Isis*, *Ilix*, *Janus*, *Kelvin*, *Nubian*, *Nizam*, and *Napier* were all seriously damaged. Of the merchant ships, forty-four were sunk or damaged.

Buried in official papers in the Admiralty archives are Reports-of-Proceedings of hundreds of individual ships, sailing schedules, operation orders, copies of thousands of signals sent to ships and from ships, and the assorted administrative bumph of war. Here also are private letters. Some of the soldiers taken off the Greek islands wrote of their experiences and left them in the ships that rescued them. From there they found their way into the archives and the official records. In every one is expressed the firm and total faith that if they could reach the sea, everything would be all right. One soldier writes of "the ever-present hope of contacting the Navy," and another says that during the long retreat in Greece "our one thought and hope was the Navy."

From the 1st of June to the end of December, 1941, was the nadir for the Mediterranean Fleet; instead of sweeping from Gibraltar to Alexandria defiantly fighting off foes on the way, it rather skulked at the extreme eastern end of the battle area. Rommel was now receiving supplies in Benghazi as well as Tripoli. Crete was lost; Malta and Cyprus were in even greater danger. Syria and the oil fields of Persia were seen as desirable acquisitions to Germany and the strategic benefits of an occupied Turkey were in sight. The Dardanelles were in the hands of Germany, to whom it soon became evident that Russia was another desirable prize. These were dark days indeed.

Some consolation was the technique developed to supply Tobruk. This was thought to be great fun. The usual practice was for two destroyers to make the run every night, berth in darkness, unload the stores and mail, and be away again before dawn. Fast minelayers – because of their size and speed of forty knots their value far exceeded mere minelaying – would make the trip weekly bringing in new men. Before October the Australian Brigade was taken out and replaced by a mixture of Polish and British: 19,568 men were ferried to Tobruk and 18,865 back to Alexandria. During the whole siege from the 12th of April to the 8th of December 1941 – 242 days – the following were moved: seventy-two tanks and ninety-two guns; 34,000 tons of stores; 32,667 men replaced by 34,112; 7,516 wounded and 7,097 prisoners.

Yes, we had some fun as a relief to the tedium of defeat. The minelayers were valuable maids of all work, and sometimes they laid mines. This class of ship was extraordinary: much smaller than a Tribal class destroyer, they had nearly double the horsepower and made forty knots. On the 17th of August *Manxman* left England. When she passed into the Mediterranean she disguised herself as a French cruiser – with plywood, four-by-fours, canvas, bailing wire and string, put her Jack Tars into matelots' uniforms, hoisted the tricolour, sailed to the enemy coast, laid her mines by night, shaped course back to Gibraltar, and was back in England on the 29th – her sailors in proper rig of the King's Navy and looking her old self, her Frenchified appearance returned to pusser's stores. A nine-day skylark.

\* \* \*

The land war depended entirely on breaking General Rommel's supply route: he could get reinforcements quicker across the Mediterranean than General Wavell could from around Africa. If Hitler could give Rommel the troops he needed, he would win. In the lack of these lay our chance for ultimate victory. Rommel saw clearly that with a suitable force he could drive the Allies out of Egypt; then the whole Middle East was his. Generals Wavell, Alexander, and Montgomery saw this. Hitler did not; he wanted troops for the Russian front. If we could cut Rommel's supply line, the Afrika Korps would be in a trap. Before Christmas of 1941 new u-class submarines joined the fleet at Gibraltar, Malta, and Alexandria, more aircraft were provided for all three bases, and a surface force was again stationed at Malta.

The year ended with a mixture of success and failure. On the whole, our convoys in 1941 had not gone too badly. The first convoy of fourteen merchant ships all got through, screened by four battleships, two aircraft carriers, nine cruisers, twenty-three destroyers, four corvettes, and three submarines. The second, of thirteen merchant ships, got through with two damaged, and was screened by two battleships, one carrier, five cruisers, eighteen destroyers, and eight submarines. The third, of twelve merchant ships, got through with one sunk, screened by three battle-ships, one carrier, five cruisers, eighteen destroyers, and eight subma-rines. In short, the effort expended by the navy was considerable: 121 warships to escort thirty-nine merchant ships.

"The last three months of 1941," said A.V. Alexander, the First Lord of the Admiralty, "were the crisis to our fortunes." Admiral Somerville's Force H had continued success and demonstrated the virtue of a detached squadron; it had even left the Mediterranean to help the Home Fleet sink *Bismarck* off Brest. Now Force K was formed in October under Captain W.G. Agnew in the light cruiser *Aurora* with *Penelope* and a destroyer screen. They arrived in Malta on 21 October and their strikes against Rommel's supply line would be directed by the Vice-Admiral Malta, W.T.R. Ford. On the night of 8-9 November, Force K caught an Africa-bound convoy of seven merchant ships escorted by six destroyers and two heavy cruisers. All the convoy and two destroyers were sunk. The remainder of the Italian warships did not remain to give battle.

The L-class destroyers had been active in the Mediterranean for some time: *Laforey, Lance, Lively, Lookout, Lightning, Legion, Lion*, and *Loyal* (five of them did not survive the war). Captain Armstrong was Captain (D) of the flotilla and the flotilla signal officer was Lieutenant John Charles, RCN (of whom more presently). Now two of them had another bash at the enemy. A convoy of two tankers was bringing fuel from Greece to Benghazi. Captain Agnew in *Aurora*, with *Penelope, Lance*, and *Lively*, sank them, thus making Rommel's fuel supply critical. Rom-mel reported that transport to Africa had nearly stopped; of the 60,000 troops promised him, only 8,093 got through. The number of the Afrika Korps killed by the Army of the Nile has always been a fairly accurate statistic; the number of the Afrika Korps killed by the navy has never been ascertained. But it was not small.

The aircraft carrier *Ark Royal* was sunk twenty-five miles out of Gibraltar returning from an operation. This left Cunningham with no air arm – *Illustrious* and *Formidable* were in the United States having their battle damage repaired and *Indomitable* had not yet worked up. The battleship *Barham* was blown up with a loss of her captain and 860 officers and men. The destroyers *Sikh, Legion, Maori*, and the Dutch *Isaac Sweers* sank the light cruisers *Alberto di Guissano* and *Alberico da Barbiano* off Cape Bon; they were carrying a deck cargo of fuel from Palermo to Tripoli. Hitler ordered a Fliegerkorps back from Russia. Our losses continued but in the last three months of 1941 eighty-one enemy merchant ships were sunk. The trap was beginning to close on the Afrika Korps.

The supplies the navy denied Rommel and those our ships brought to Tobruk swung the balance. Rommel attacked Tobruk twice in 1941 with German and Italian troops and was repelled with heavy losses by the Australian garrison. In any comparison between German and Italian forces, the Italians come off badly. Rommel said their army "was designed for a colonial war against insurgent tribesmen. Its tanks and armoured vehicles were too light. Most of the guns dated from the 1914–1918 war. But its worst feature was . . . non-motorized infantry . . . in the North African desert practically no use against the enemy."

The Army of the Nile was renamed the Eighth Army in September, 1941, and consisted of New Zealand, Australian, South African, and Indian troops as well as British. General Auchinleck relieved General Wavell, who had faced an odd problem. It was not unusual for sailors or soldiers to respect their enemy. But Auchinleck's soldiers spoke of Rommel with an affection sometimes not accorded their own generals. Tommy Atkins's sense of humour has always been a puzzle to foreign officers and an irritation to his own. To suffer a setback by the Germans is bad enough; to have your own troops chortle, "Rommel! That Old Desert Fox has buggered us again," is exasperating in the extreme. All in the Eighth Army were instructed to stop harping on Rommel this and Rommel that, and refer to the Enemy, the Germans, the Hun, the Boche, Fritz, Beer-Guzzling Sausage-Eaters . . . but not Rommel.

The Eighth Army's troubles began again at the Battle of Gazala. A long minefield stretched from the coast into the desert with strong points every few miles. Rommel had 90,000 troops and 560 tanks; Auchinleck 100,000 troops and 850 tanks. Rommel was pushed back but then, as was their custom, the British stopped to consolidate their position. Rommel tried a tactic he had first used in World War One. He stopped retreating and attacked again. On the 20th of June 1942, Tobruk fell; in one day Rommel achieved what he had been unable to do in the previous eight months. Of the garrison, 35,000 surrendered and went into the bag. The Afrika Korps reached the Alamein line on 29 June 1942.

In 1813 the Duke of Wellington said to Rear-Admiral T. Byam Martin, "If anyone wishes to know the history of this war, I will tell them that it is our maritime superiority which gives me the power of maintaining my army, while the enemy are unable to do so." In 1942 the difference was that now we had the war under the sea and war over the sea. War under the sea could be considered only an added weapon, another type of ship. But air power changed war completely. It made the aircraft carrier and not the battleship the main unit of a fleet. It was Sir Andrew's attack on Taranto in November, 1940, that gave Admiral Isoroku Yamamoto the idea for his attack on Pearl Harbor on 7 December 1941. Without air cover we could not supply our land forces; if the soldiers lost airfields – as they did along the African coast – we had no airfields to fly off planes to defend us from enemy planes coming from secure enemy bases in Sicily.

In January, 1942, two enemy battleship convoys had reached Tripoli. With only light cruisers and no air power, we could do nothing to stop them. Admiral Cunningham was going to borrow battleships and aircraft carriers from the Home Fleet and again supply Malta. But in February, 1942, Intelligence told us that *Scharnhorst* and *Gneisenau* were planning to break out from Brest. Not only did this prevent ships of the Home Fleet from going to the Mediterranean, it meant that Force H (now under Rear-Admiral E.N. Syfret) had to be detached to the Clyde.

In December, 1941, Admiral Vian had been covering a convoy from Alexandria to Malta when he ran across Italian battleships escorting their own convoy to Africa. Vian's cruisers charged the Italian battleships and they retreated. Vian returned to his convoy and the Italian battleships returned to theirs. This inconclusive engagement has been called the First Battle of Sirte. In March, 1942, came the second Battle of Sirte – another convoy to Malta from Alexandria. This consisted of four merchant ships escorted by a light cruiser and four destroyers. Vian sailed later with three cruisers and four destroyers as a covering force; six destroyers from Tobruk joined up later; *Cleopatra* and *Legion* sailed from Malta to meet our convoy; and the battleship *Littorio*, two cruisers, and ten destroyers also sailed to meet the convoy. It was probably the first time since the days of sail that it was vital to "hold the weather gauge." From six p.m. until after dark Admiral Vian disposed his forces with his usual consummate skill, and he will ever be honoured for this. The Italian squadron turned away. *Lively* took a 15-inch brick inboard. Like Nelson's tactics at the Battle of Trafalgar, Vian's tactics at the Second Battle of Sirte will be taught for many years. And what was the prize? Four merchant ships. *Four*. The same month on the Atlantic, three convoys were heading east, each comprising about thirty-five ships. Our efforts to hold Malta were generally small, even pathetic. Aircraft arrived in dribs and drabs of ten or twenty at a time; after one resupply of aircraft successfully fought through from Gibraltar and flew off from the carrier and landed in Malta, the whole lot – the whole blooming lot! – were shot down in seven days. The German bombers renewed their attacks at daylight. One merchant ship was sunk; one beached on the south coast of Malta but was then destroyed by bombers; and two merchant ships made Grand Harbour to the cheers of the populace. Of the two that made harbour, both were sunk alongside the next day. Of the 26,000 tons destined for Malta, only 5,000 tons were salved. On the 24th the fleet returned to harbour grievously weakened: fourteen destroyers were damaged, some more, some less seriously. On the 26th *Legion* was sunk.

In April the savage air raids continued. *Penelope* was damaged, *Lance* sunk. The dockyard was laid waste. On the airfields, 126 aircraft were destroyed or damaged. Twenty that got airborne were shot down. It was the virtual extinction of the island's air forces.

At this nadir of the fleet's fortunes, Admiral Cunningham had to leave to be the naval Commander-in-Chief for the invasion of Africa, Operation Torch. He was replaced by Admiral Harwood – he who had sunk the pocket battleship *Graf Spee* at the Battle of the River Plate in December, 1939.

In a June convoy only two ships got through to Malta. An August convoy to Malta had three carriers – *Victorious, Indomitable*, and *Eagle*. The Chief of the Air Staff pointed out to the First Sea Lord that the RAF was down to eighty fighters and losses were seventeen a week; *Furious* was added to ferry thirty-eight more Spitfires. Our Fleet Air Arm was now beginning to look like a proper defending force; these carriers could fly off ninety fighters for the defence of the fleet. This particular covering force was two battleships, seven cruisers, twenty-four destroyers, eight submarines, four corvettes, two fleet oilers, and two deep-sea tugs. The convoy of fourteen included two American merchant ships and the tanker *Ohio*.

Our submarines formed a barrier across the likely approach route of enemy surface forces. The point of maximum danger was always "the Narrows," the strait between Sardinia and Africa – between Cape Spartivento and Cape Bon it was ninety miles and between Sicily and Cape Bon just seventy miles, or fifteen minutes of flying time. German bombers could attack a convoy, return to their home airfield, reload, and be back for another attack within two hours. Some individual German aircraft made as many as four attacks on the same convoy the same day. If the Eighth Army had lost control of nearby airfields, enemy planes would have been only five minutes from us. On the evening of 11 August the convoy was within range of enemy aircraft from Sardinia; thirty-six high-level bombers, dive-bombers, and torpedo bombers came out. None got through our air cover. *Furious* flew off her cargo Spitfires when 550 miles from Malta.

*Eagle* was an old hand at this; she had made nine aircraft-ferry trips to Malta by 1942 and had carried 182 Spitfires. But this was her last voyage – she was torpedoed and sunk. *Wolverine* rammed and sank an Italian submarine. The next morning our fighters kept the enemy bombers at a distance but at noon they came in again, eighty of them. One convoy ship was sunk; another Italian submarine was rammed and sunk by *Ithuriel*. In the evening the third attack came in. One destroyer was sunk. *Victorious* was hit. *Nigeria* and *Cairo* were torpedoed and *Cairo* sunk. *Ohio* was hit but remained with the convoy. The cruiser *Kenya* was hit. Two more merchant ships were sunk. At midnight of the 12th the convoy passed Cape Bon, hugging the Tunisian coast. E-boats now attacked. The cruiser *Manchester* was sunk. Five merchant ships were sunk between 3:15 and 4:30 a.m. *Ohio*, already hit, was crashed into by a plane but was able to carry on. And there was more: a destroyer blew up; a corvette was set on fire; a cruiser was hit and stopped. But at dawn the Spitfires and Beaufighters from Malta were overhead, and by 2:30 that afternoon minesweepers and motor launches from Malta met the convoy. Three merchant ships of the convoy entered Grand Harbour at 4:30. *Ohio* and *Dorset* were straggling astern and both were hit again. *Dorset* sank, while *Ohio* struggled on. At eleven a.m. of the 13th she entered harbour. The fuel she carried enabled air strikes against Rommel to be resumed. Two more merchant ships straggled in.

The total for this convoy, in addition to the merchant ships lost, was: an aircraft carrier, two cruisers, and a destroyer sunk; an aircraft carrier and two cruisers damaged. In those years the cost of fuel and stores in Malta was high.

In August, General Montgomery assumed command of the Eighth Army from General Sir Alan Cunningham, and General Alexander took over from General Auchinleck as Commander-in-Chief (who, you will remember, had taken over from General Wavell).

In September an assault on the German garrison in Tobruk was launched. *Sikh* and *Zulu*, carrying 350 marines, met a cruiser and the 5th Destroyer Flotilla at sea. Eighteen MTBs and three MLs carried 150 more marines who were to land on the north side of Tobruk harbour. Surprise was not achieved and the fire from the shore batteries was devastating. Rommel's tanks churned to the water's edge and added to the carnage. Only two of the twenty-one coastal craft landed their troops, *Sikh* and *Zulu* were sunk, and the cruiser set on fire and abandoned. It had been a rash operation. An assault on a heavily fortified town needs larger forces and air cover; that ships never engage shore batteries had been known since the sixteenth century and, for Canadians particularly, was reaffirmed in the Dieppe raid the previous month. A disaster!

For the British people 1942 marked the fourth year of the war, and in October came the beginning of successes in the land battle when the army launched its offensive at El Alamein. Two naval Albacore squadrons were lent to the RAF in the desert and Air Chief Marshal Tedder thought this "was one of the deciding factors" in our success. Arms and reinforcements continued to arrive in Egypt via the Red Sea, and at Malta for the first time we were consistently fighting off air attacks. (But we had to revert to a couple of submarine and fast minelayer replenishments.) Much to the approval of the populace at home and to the huge delight of the whole fleet, Admiral Cunningham returned to the Mediterranean.

On the 1st of November 1942 Admiral Cunningham hoisted his flag at Gibraltar as the Naval Commander of the Allied invasion of Africa, which was soon to be launched. His theatre was for all of the three landings – at Algiers, at Oran, at Casablanca – and on to the east of Cape Bon, that is, the whole of the western Mediterranean. (Admiral Harwood was responsible for the eastern end.)

There was no doubt that by now, because of his brilliant handling of his small, outnumbered fleet during the dark years when he had not only out-thought and out-fought the German and Italian ships but regained the offensive, Sir Andrew was the most likely candidate for the highest rank of all, that in due course he would become Admiral of the Fleet and First Sea Lord. He was now responsible for the operations of several thousand ships and a million men. Orders of Chivalry had been awarded to him by His Majesty; he had the unqualified approval of the Sea Lords in the Board of Admiralty; civilians and sailors throughout the world sang songs of praise to this great professional seaman. It is delightful therefore to show another facet of this formidable warrior's character. Admiral James Somerville, who had so competently handled Force H in so many battles, had already been made a Knight Commander of the Order of the Bath – which made him Sir James. Now he received the Knight Commander of the Order of the British Empire. Sir Andrew congratulated Sir James: "Fancy, twice a knight. And at your age."

# VIII   The Invasion of Africa

W hy do some men and women enjoy war? For they do. One of the reasons is that war is so *interesting*, and that in the planning of an operation one is sometimes doing what has never been done before. It is also that the stakes are high; the apt expression did not come into use until recently, but "you are playing hardball with the big boys." The admirals and the generals are planning to keep the world free for democracy, for the safety of their country, for a way of life, for loved ones, for promotion. The operational captains and officers plan their smaller battles for the same reasons but with the added pulse-throbbing certainty that if they are wrong they will be killed.

And the *scale* of what was planned in the invasion of Africa – Operation Torch – was *huge*. Sailing from Britain in October, 1942, were a number of advance convoys with tankers, tugs, oilers, freighters, colliers, ammunition ships, and other auxiliary craft that would be needed by the warships. Later in October and early in November would be the four large assault convoys carrying the landing craft and troops for the initial storming of the beaches. On approaching Gibraltar these would break into the sections bound for Algiers and Oran. The American convoys had to start earlier for the long haul across the Atlantic to Casablanca. The immensity and complexity of the greatest invasion in the history of the world to that date can be seen in the tables below. Ships sailing with troops from the United States were met – *on time and at a precise rendezvous* – by landing craft that sailed from the United Kingdom. There were about a million men and a thousand ships involved (514 ships in the first assault), each a cog, each important, from the battleships in which the admirals rode to the heavy troop transports commanded by four-ring captains, to 100-ton landing craft commanded by leading seamen.

### Advance Convoys from United Kingdom

|        | Convoy Size         | Speed (knots) | From            | Sailing Date | Date Due Gibraltar |
|--------|---------------------|---------------|-----------------|--------------|--------------------|
| No. 1  | 7 escort 5 ships    | 7.5           | Clyde           | 2 Oct.       | 14 Oct.            |
| No. 2  | 13 escort 18 ships  | 7             | Clyde           | 18 Oct.      | 31 Oct.            |
| No. 3  | 2 escort 1 ship     | 13            | Clyde           | 19 Oct.      | 27 Oct.            |
| No. 4A | 8 escort 29 ships   | 7.5           | Clyde           | 25 Oct.      | 4 Nov.             |
| No. 4B | 2 escort 8 ships    | 6.5           | Milford Haven   | 25 Oct.      | 3 Nov.             |
| No. 5  | 10 escort 32 ships  | 7             | Clyde           | 30 Oct.      | 10 Nov.            |

### Assault Convoys from United Kingdom

|       | Convoy Size        | Speed (knots) | From  | Sailing Date | Date Due Gibraltar |
|-------|--------------------|---------------|-------|--------------|--------------------|
| No. 1 | 18 escort 47 ships | 8             | Clyde | 22 Oct.      | 5 Nov.             |
| No. 2 | 14 escort 52 ships | 7             | Clyde | 25 Oct.      | 10 Nov.            |
| No. 3 | 12 escort 39 ships | 11.5          | Clyde | 26 Oct.      | 6 Nov              |
| No. 4 | 8 escort 18 ships  | 13            | Clyde | 1 Nov.       | 10 Nov.            |

### Assault Convoys from the United States

|       | Convoy Size        | Speed (knots) | From             | Date Due Casablanca |
|-------|--------------------|---------------|------------------|---------------------|
| No. 1 | 56 escort 38 ships | 14            | Eastern seaboard | 8 Nov.              |

### Backup and Logistics Convoys

|       | Convoy Size        | Speed (knots) | From             | Date Due Casablanca |
|-------|--------------------|---------------|------------------|---------------------|
| No. 1 | 10 escort 24 ships | 13            | eastern seaboard | 18 Nov.             |
| No. 2 | 9 escort 45 ships  | 12            | eastern seaboard | 25 Nov.             |

Note: After the initial assault and supply, reinforcements were sent from the U.S. about every three weeks – the fast convoys (13.5 knots) comprising 15–20 ships, and the slow convoys (9 knots) about 45 ships.

It was a tense few weeks after the last radio frequency had been assigned, the last convoy-composition chart issued, the latest information on minefields distributed, the last item of stores checked . . . If

Admiral Dönitz learned of our plan he could assemble 150 u-boats at Gibraltar, the historic Pillar of Hercules where so many naval battles had been fought for so many centuries. Dönitz could give the world a picture of battle carnage never before envisioned. But he didn't find out. One hundred vessels escorted the 500 merchant ships with only occasional and accidental loss of a ship or so. With all these ships converging on the Straits of Gibraltar the enemy did not guess what was in store. And we are talking here, to consider only the larger warships, of six battleships, eleven carriers, twenty cruisers, and eighty-one destroyers of the Royal Navy and the United States Navy.

Tension mounted as these fleets converged on Gibraltar. The ghost of Sir Francis Drake watched with approval as His Majesty's ships sailed to the place where he had "singed the King of Spain's beard" in 1587. Other English sea warriors had fought here as well: Sir George Rooke captured Gibraltar in 1704; Admiral Lord Howe lifted a three-year siege in 1789; and Admiral Lord Nelson fought his last battle at Cape Trafalgar just to the north.

Since the Dieppe raid we had practised that a special headquarters ship held the naval, army, and air force commanders. They had planned and trained the troops for their special sectors. The headquarters ship and the landing ships infantry (LCIS) would anchor about six miles off and lower the landing craft assault (LCAS). Naval and air bombardment would cover the approach of the soldiers.

Off Algiers ninety-three warships and merchant ships converged at the final rendezvous, then divided and subdivided as they approached the position where they lowered their LCAS. Three submarines marked the release positions. Beachmasters and their staff went ahead to mark the several sectors in each beach – these were analogous to traffic policemen.

Sub-Lieutenant George Buckingham led a section of four LCIS and at one a.m. on the 8th of November found himself steaming in to the North African coast toward Algiers. His particular beach was at Sidi Ferruch. The operation orders were full of detailed instructions as to how to find the beach, but these were rendered unnecessary because the lighthouse was flashing strong and clear. The flotilla leader headed in toward it. They had about a six-foot surf, the roughest Buckingham had ever had. His troops were British Commandos but because of the probable unfriendly reception of men in British uniforms they were dressed in American uniforms. A homey touch was added by each of them carrying a bicycle; their job was to take the Maison Blanche airfield. He got his troops ashore and by daylight commenced five more runs before the Port of Algiers was secured.

At 5:30 a.m. the destroyers *Broke* and *Malcolm* made a frontal attack on the harbour; their job was to prevent the French fleet from scuttling. They came under heavy fire. *Malcolm* was badly hit and withdrew. *Broke*, after charging the boom three times, broke through and landed her American troops. Then she was heavily damaged and withdrew: the next day she sank. At 6:40 a.m. the Maison Blanche airfield was captured and fighters from Gibraltar landed, fuelled, and took off as air cover for our troops. History was made when the airfield near Blida was captured by the Fleet Air Arm fighters from *Victorious*, who landed and captured it around 8:30; when the Commandos arrived it was handed over to them. The shore batteries had been silenced by bombardment and bombing by the afternoon. The headquarters ship and warships steamed into harbour.

Buckingham said, "the troopships steamed in. *Bulolo* was amusing. I'm not sure if Eisenhower was on board but Admiral Troubridge was and, unbeknownst to the officers on the bridge, a near miss from a bomb had damaged the communication between the bridge and the engine room. In heading for their jetty the Captain rang for astern, got no reaction from the engine room (who never received the order), steamed straight ahead into the jetty and, because her bow had been reinforced as an icebreaker, *Bulolo* got about eight feet inland before coming to a grinding halt. She seemed to epitomize the determination of the British to stay. She had not *landed troops on Africa*, she was not *tied up* to Africa, she was *in* Africa."

The Oran landing was similar. The two main convoys met at four p.m. on the 7th of November and divided into seven groups for the three assault areas. By midnight, seventy warships and thirty-two transports glided silently through the dark to the shore. At 5:30 on the morning of the 8th the battleship *Rodney* and three aircraft carriers sat offshore as support in case the Italian fleet or heavy units of the French fleet hove over the horizon: cruisers carried out a close-in bombardment; carrier aircraft bombed and strafed. In the dark, one of our north-south landing forces steamed through an east-west French coastal convoy causing "no little confusion."

Lieutenant Derek Fynn of Vancouver had left the Clyde in a convoy of sixty ships and was due to land American Rangers in the Gulf of Arzeu – to the east of Oran and marked by Cape Ferrat. He was on the eastern section of the landing. In the dawn's early light he embarked the American Rangers. Previous to leaving the U.K. they had had a wedge-shaped keel added so they could ride up over the nets. However, on approaching they found the gate was opened and so had no trouble getting in. They thought the gate might have been left open for the cross-Mediterranean ferry from Marseille. Fynn's section was quiet, with the landings practically unopposed, which was just as well because the First American Ranger Battalion had never seen action before. In any event, they thanked the Vichy authorities because, come daylight, they saw that the net in fact had buoys about six feet in diameter about eight feet apart joined by a big anchor chain with steel spikes about five inches across at the base and about a foot long in a star-type configuration. Had they tried to run over this they would have taken their bottom out. A bombardment from destroyers and a cruiser helped keep the enemies' heads down so that phase went off tickety-boo. For the next forty-eight hours it was continual running of backwards and forwards from the troop transports to the beaches.

Fynn had thought it would be a two-day proposition landing the troops, but because the weather blew up landing craft were getting bashed to pieces against the liners in taking troops and stores off and Fynn's four LCAs were the last ones running. So they kept on for another forty-eight hours. They were told, "just keep running. You've got to go on. Here's something to keep you awake."

What they had to keep them awake was Benzedrine. On the fifth day they were zombies.

Leading Seaman Tom Forrester hit the beaches at Arzeu with his section of six LCIs carrying 1,500 troops in the second wave. Then it was another three days of steady slogging with troops or stores before they were finished with the Algiers landing. He then started moving troops to the east, toward Bone.

Leading Seaman Tom Poapst's section of four LCMs was dropped from the mother ship four miles east of Cape Ferrat in the Gulf of Arzeu. He thought this was a long way to go for a landing and a turn-around, but with a mental shrug Poapst started steaming around the troopers that had come from the United States, collecting soldiers and landing them. As a Leading Seaman he was not expected to know much navigation; he was told to follow his next ahead to the shore. There was a following sea and a northeast wind, which was not good for the chunky landing craft, but that was something that had to be lived with. At dawn he made his touchdown. Poapst was wondering how surprise could ever be achieved on these landings with thirty landing craft on either side of him with their diesel engines going apokata-pokata-pokata. The troops landed, though it wasn't really a "dry landing." He had dropped his kedge on the way in because he had to get out against an onshore wind. Then he ran into a sandbar. The Rangers weren't overly excited by the idea of invading Africa at all at that time of the morning; but this is understandable when we realize that 90 per cent had been civilians three months before.

The landings carried on for two more days with cargo of either troops or Bren gun carriers. (Because of the seas, armoured tanks were not put on board; getting thirty-five tons of tank into a LCM – where it just barely fits – on the leeward side of a freighter in a heavy sea, jockeying your engines back and forth, is not the easiest manoeuvre in the world.) So Poapst's contribution to the invasion of Africa was about 1,000 men and a couple of dozen of vehicles. From there he went to Oran to refuel and then back to Inveraray to train more troops and bring them back to Africa later.

Sub-Lieutenant Harry Trenholm was landed off Arzeu from his American Liberty Ship, loaded with American troops. Because the Brits had blown up the French fleet at Mers-el Kebir, it was thought the local population might feel more charitable toward Americans than Englishmen. He hit a sandbar but didn't recognize it as such. Trenholm hopped out the front to show the troops it was all right to disembark. And it was; he was only up to his knees. But the American lieutenant would not drive his jeep off; he said there was too much water. So Trenholm got in and drove the jeep down the ramp and into the water. He ground ahead onto the sand and then disappeared into a good ten feet of the Mediterranean. This was unfortunate, but it did not deter the troops, who were elements of the 101st Paratrooper Division – being used at Arzeu as infantry. His section of the beach saw some fighting. The French Foreign Legion was defending the area and a couple of their tanks came streaming down the beach to repulse the Allied landing forces. Without any equipment ashore they retreated as best they could. Then a destroyer was called in to engage the tanks, and when the tanks retreated our troops continued their landing. Like the others, Trenholm, was landing stores and troops for forty-eight hours. They were then kept busy a further five days with short periods of rest, but never more than two or three hours at a time.

Sub-Lieutenant Walter Charron makes the point about his landing at Arzeu that your war is really what you make it. At some areas of the beach the troops might have been repulsed by tanks of the French Foreign Legion but at his section "the French were amiable and expecting us, really. Our landing was without incident. As a matter of fact, within an hour of landing, some of the native population had set up stalls on the beach and were selling postcards and souvenirs. You should have seen the American fighting men as they went through the bazaar!

Both the Americans and the natives agreed that free enterprise was a good thing, I guess. One of the pre-war industries of this little town was the supplying of briar roots for pipes. I picked a sizable amount and sold it to a pipemaker in the West End of London, later; he hadn't seen a briar for years. I got a great price."

Charron got his ration of Benzedrine along with the rest, which kept him going until it was time to return to the United Kingdom and regroup before going around the Cape of Good Hope with another convoy of troops going up the Indian Ocean and the Red Sea to Alexandria.

In the western sector at Oran, by noon of the 9th, a secure beachhead was established. By the 11th, 3,000 men, 458 tanks and vehicles, and 1,100 tons of stores had been landed – a well-established bridgehead. In the centre sector all went well except that forty landing craft beached early on an unsuspected sandbar; the vehicles drove off confidently enough, then disappeared into the deep on the other side. In the eastern sector 23,000 men, 2,400 vehicles, and 14,000 tons of stores were landed. In this sector *Walney* and *Hartland* were to charge the defences early; the job of their troops was to prevent the French warships scuttling, seize key points, and prevent sabotage. At three a.m. of the 8th they charged the boom and broke into the harbour. Withering fire demolished them and killed most of their troops. *Walney* sank; *Hartland* blew up. Outside the harbour *Aurora* fought a hot battle with three French destroyers that had emerged from Oran harbour and headed for our transports. As Admiral Cunningham put it, "the *Aurora* polished off her opponents with practised ease."

By nine a.m. the tanks landed. By noon the airfield had fallen to the cycling soldiers Buckingham had landed. The French shore batteries, which had been shelling our troop transports, had been silenced by the nine 16-inch guns of *Rodney*. There were sixty-eight landing craft in the assault wave, seventeen in the second wave. From thirty-four transports 29,000 men were landed, as well as 2,400 vehicles and 14,000 tons of stores. Fighting continued on land and at sea the next day. Dieppe had shown that a frontal assault was not the best way to capture a port. *Broke* and *Malcolm* and *Hartland* and *Walney* were proof of that. They had only been sent into a frontal assault to prevent scuttling and sabotage. They failed, and died.

At noon of 8 November 1942 the French surrendered, fifty-nine hours after the first assault. Since June, 1940, Oran and the French fleet there had been a worry, but Admiral Somerville's Force H had sunk their major units; in October, 1942, *Aurora* finished the job.

One may be permitted to estimate what was in the minds of Vichy Frenchmen during these years while their weak leaders – Admiral Darlan, General Pétain, and the Vichy government generally – put personal bias (Admiral Laborde in Toulon was a violent Anglophobe) and personal preferment ahead of a duty that was easily ascertainable, that is, to resist. They must have known in the mind and felt in the heart that they were fighting the only people who could free their homeland from the yoke of Nazi Germany. How many men died because of this mindset? It can be estimated. What is even more poignant is the optimistic summing up by historians (and I do it, too) of a battle fought to a successful conclusion with "only twenty killed and thirty wounded." When the action is easily identified and the time and date and place are set out, one wonders if the twenty mothers reading the account would view it with the same detachment and optimism. Some men may like war because it is interesting, but there is the other side of the coin.

To turn now to the American landings on the Moroccan coast at Casablanca, Admiral Hewitt's forces sailed from various ports (the air group from Bermuda) and met at 40° North and 60° West on the 26th: sixty warships and forty transports and tankers. They fuelled twice on the way across and on the 7th of November steamed toward a turbulent shore with heavy surf. Hewitt had the power to postpone but decided not to. A battleship, four carriers, two cruisers, and a dozen destroyers split as the huge convoy broke into its component parts for the three assault areas: one to Mehdia, sixty-five miles along the coast to the northeast of Casablanca; one to Fedala, ten miles to the northeast; and Safi, 120 miles to the southwest. At Casablanca itself, guns from French shore batteries and French warships together with bombing and strafing from French aircraft took their toll. But for the other landing points, our troops were practically unopposed; in particular, the southern landing at Safi had achieved success with the astonishing figure of ten killed and seventy-five wounded. At midnight of 10 November Admiral Darlan ordered the French to cease fighting. By the 13th empty merchant ships were on their way home.

Once sufficient troops had been landed at Algiers and Oran, the Allied First Army began its race to Tunis. This port controlled "the Narrows," the Strait of Sicily; from the neighbouring Cape Bon it was only ninety miles to Sicily, less to the halfway island of Pantelleria. The Eighth Army was moving west from Egypt, the First Army east from French Morocco and Oran and Algiers. Rommel was in the middle – but quite a wide middle, of up to a thousand miles – and, so far, he was receiving his supplies from across the Mediterranean. Within a few months he would be squeezed out of Africa at Cape Bon. And that was where the navy came in; Cunningham was the enemy to the north.

The next assault came at Bougie on 11 November 1942. The port and airfield were captured without too much bother, but for want of fuel the ships in harbour had no air cover for three days and one warship and three transports were sunk and several damaged. Bone was 230 miles east of Algiers; it was attacked by Commandos carried there in two destroyers. As soon as fighter protection could be given it was a valuable base but the First Army was still building up and airfields were not all taken quickly. Supplies were reaching Rommel in sufficient quantity that he might well be to the first to Tunis. Enemy bombers ranged east and west along the coast and gave both soldier and sailor a hard time. Sixteen ships were lost from U-boats during the month of the landings; by Christmas nine U-boats had been sent to the bottom.

So ended the African-invasion phase of our battles in the Mediterranean. The planning had proved sound; secrecy had been maintained; and, therefore, surprise was complete. The sailors, soldiers, and airmen worked as one, and the various fleets had shown seamanship worthy of their ancestors. The quiet courage of the Merchant Navy made it all possible. Admiral Cunningham attributed the success to "the spirit of comradeship and understanding . . . exemplified in our Commander-in-Chief, General Eisenhower," but it was the opinion of the fleet that ABC – in whom they lived and moved and had their being – had quite a lot to do with the success. The First Sea Lord, Admiral Pound, wrote his congratulations to Cunningham. We sense the relief he felt:

> I am sure that you had as anxious a time as we did here. I had visions of large convoys waltzing up and down inside as well as outside the Mediterranean, with the weather too bad to land, and the U-boats buzzing around. We really did have remarkable luck.

The first offensive sweep of our forces based at Bone took place on the 1–2 December when they sank an Africa-bound German convoy of four ships and one escort; the next night four more and a destroyer were sunk. Two of our cruisers and several destroyers left Bone each night. Other forces were on the offensive from other bases. From August to September of 1942 we sank 174 enemy merchant ships. The tide was beginning to turn. During December, Malta received 58,500 tons of cargo and 18,000 tons of fuel oil. RAF and Fleet Air Arm planes – scores and scores of them – scoured the seas at will. It seemed a long time ago that we had only the three planes to defend Malta. "Faith," "Hope," and "Charity" had gone to the aircraft's Valhalla but they were not forgotten.

On the 23rd of January of 1943 Tripoli was captured and on the 29th the Eighth Army crossed the Tunisian border, by March they had broken through the German Mareth Line, and Tunis and Bizerte were captured in May. Soon to be mounted would be Admiral Cunningham's Operation Retribution.

MTBs and MGBs and MLs nightly swept east and west close to the coast of the Sicilian channel; destroyer divisions swept further out. In April fourteen ships were sunk while carrying troops and supplies to Rommel, but 18,000 men and 5,000 tons were flown in. On the 10th of April the Eighth Army occupied Sfax; this was the sixth major port to be cleared and opened by the navy, and on each occasion the landing craft had plied continually back and forth, back and forth, bringing in supplies to the soldiers. In the case of Sfax, 20,000 tons were landed in three weeks.

On the 22nd of April the First Army attacked Rommel from the west but it was hard to advance against the seasoned German veterans, who now saw defeat in the offing. The Eighth Army, meanwhile, pushed in from the east. Rommel retreated reluctantly and stubbornly. Three months after his defeat at Alamein, Rommel's 1,200-mile retreat was over. Several times Hitler had told him to hold a position "at all costs" or "to the last man." These hysterics never put the professional soldier in doubt. He once replied, "We either lose the position four days earlier and save the army, or lose both position and army four days later." At the Battle of the Kasserine Pass, Rommel had badly shaken up the untried American troops, but he was not allowed to exploit his success. It was to be his last major effort. On 7 March 1943 he had returned to Europe to try to persuade Hitler to evacuate the remaining troops from Africa back to Europe. Hitler said no. The Germans fought on but it was by now hopeless. Rommel was sent on long-deferred sick leave.

Admiral Cunningham remembered our retreat under enemy fire from Dunkirk, and Norway, and Greece, and Crete. The enemy still had powerful sea and land forces. Europe had still to be won back from Germany by invasion. For that matter, the enemy would soon have to land at Sicily and then Italy, and the Allies would follow. The more German and Italian soldiers who were put out of commission now, the easier the future. These soldiers of the Afrika Korps could not be allowed to reinforce the army in Europe. That would be folly.

Operation Retribution was brought into effect by Cunningham's message, "Sink, burn, and destroy. Let nothing pass." There was to be no Dunkirk for Rommel's troops.

Two enemy merchant vessels were sunk off Skerki Bank on the 9th of May; a number of small craft were also destroyed. About 800 Afrika Korps were captured at sea, but the attempt of the Germans and Italians to return to Europe was half-hearted. On the 13th of May the Axis troops, German and Italian, surrendered. They had been starved into submission by shortage of troops, stores, fuel; mastery of the seas had allowed these to reach our soldiers in larger and larger amounts.

While sweeping the Sicilian channel, the Allies liberated the small island of Galita. Canadian destroyers and MTBs were to take part in many a surrender of such islands. In this case the local inhabitants were delighted to see our "invasion" of their island. The senior officer reported that the surrender ceremonies were "interrupted by the need to salvage the delegates' hats which they kept throwing into the air and the wind blew into the sea, and . . . the mayor who fell overboard." On the 11th of June Pantelleria surrendered, and just a few miles north was our next objective, Sicily, and after that Italy.

\* \* \*

Lieutenant John A. Charles, RCN (now a retired rear-admiral), had been the First Lieutenant of the RCN Signal School in St. Hyacinthe, Quebec, HMCS *St. Hyacinthe*. In April, 1942, he was appointed to the RN Signal School, HMS *Mercury*, for his specialist course, the Long Signal Course. This was at Leydene House, East Meon, near Petersfield – Lady Peel's country house. On passing this he would be a Signal Lieutenant, Lieutenant (S). (With him were Lieutenant Somerville, the Admiral's son, Lieutenant Dreyer, whose father had been a Gunnery Specialist, and Kit James, whose father was C-in-C Portsmouth. In the Royal Navy it seems to run in the family.) A Canadian with him was J.C. "Scruffy" O'Brien, who had been with him at the Royal Military College (and is now a retired vice-admiral). The course ended in October, 1942, and he was appointed as Flotilla Signal Officer to the 19th destroyer flotilla.

These were the L-class destroyers. The leader was *Laforey*; then there were *Lookout, Lightning, Loyal, Legion, Lively, Lion*, and *Lance*. These were beautiful ships: 2,000 tons displacement with a full load of fuel, stores, and ammunition: 354 feet long; beam, thirty-seven feet;

draught, ten feet; twin 4.7-inch high-angle/low-angle guns; a twin 3-inch gun aft; four torpedo tubes. Captain of these destroyers (Captain D) was R.N.J. Hutton; he was the senior D in the Mediterranean. He'd been in destroyers all his life except when he was Commander of a cruiser. Charles said of Captain Hutton that he "didn't have a great sense of humour but he could be a charming host at times. He had very little humour on the bridge, as I was to find out."

Since Charles was the only specialist in the flotilla he had to train and advise all the others who were signal officers of the other destroyers; hence, he frequently travelled in other ships of the flotilla. His problem was complicated because they were constantly getting new ships: the rate of loss of destroyers in the Mediterranean was very high at this period. *Laforey* had air warning radar, of course, and Charles managed to get a Spitfire's very high frequency (VHF) set. With this he was able to contact our fighters visually and send his fighter cover air patrol out to intercept incoming enemy aircraft. He had high frequency/direction finding (HF/DF, called huff duff) and a "headache" set. His headache operator was "a delightful Cockney from the east end of London who spoke German fluently and colloquially. He saved our lives more than once."

They left Portsmouth in November, 1942, to work-up at Scapa Flow. Then they escorted the fifth convoy to go out to the Torch landings in North Africa. They ran into bad weather, about Force 10, and the barometer went down to 9.97 millibars. They did a lot of evasive routing in moving south through the Bay of Biscay and arrived at Gibraltar on December 20, where they fuelled, slipped, and went back to join the convoy. One of the troopships, *Strathallan*, carrying about 4,500 troops and nurses and Eisenhower's secretary, Kay, was torpedoed. *Strathallan* dropped the nurses off in the ship's boats, then lost steam. *Lightning*, *Pathfinder*, and *Panther* went back to escort *Strathallan*. The aim was to get her to Algiers but since she was about 25,000 tons it was not going to be easy to tow her. She had caught fire, so *Lightning* was trying to fight the fire with her own fire mains. Gradually, with *Laforey* towing, she got going about five knots, but she could not be saved. The fire got out of control and it became evident she would have to be abandoned. The rest of the troops boarded the destroyers, which came alongside to take them off, about 1,500 soldiers to each destroyer – quite a bit of top-weight. *Strathallan* sank fifty miles from Algiers.

On 22 December *Laforey* entered Algiers, fuelled, and departed for Mers el Kebir to join Force H. Admiral Somerville's Force H, at this time, consisted of *Rodney*, *KGV*, a carrier, and fourteen destroyers. Since

Captain Hutton was the Senior D in the Med this made John Charles the Senior S in the Med.

His problem was to get all the ships into the right slots on the screen. But to get them in the right slots on the anti-submarine screen or the anti-aircraft screen, he had to know the asdic frequencies, what radar sets they had, who had the huff/duff, and put them all in the right place. This, combined with the fact that they never sailed twice with the same destroyer screen, presented quite a problem to a new signal lieutenant.

Christmas Day of 1942 was spent at sea.

For the next little while they were based at Bone with *Lightning*; this was the only port where the Allies could unload large ships close to the First Army, which had just landed and was striking out to the east. *Laforey* and *Lightning* were part of Force Q, two cruisers and two destroyers. They provided the only air defence in Bone during the day and at night they'd sweep out into the Sicilian Narrows (between Sicily and North Africa) to catch the German traffic between Europe and Africa. *Laforey, Lightning, Loyal*, and *Lookout* and the cruisers *Ajax* and *Aurora* – wearing the flag of CS 12 (Rear-Admiral Harcourt). They would do about a week at Bone then rotate back, either with Force H or into Algiers for a rest period.

On New Year's Day, 1943, were "the worst air raids that I've ever been in. They started with Stukas, JU 87s, who would come screaming down and I swear I could see the pilot in the cockpit. I could have hit him with a baseball. They started their bombing runs and *Ajax* was hit in the first raid. One of the tankers, the *St. Merrill*, was hit, blew up, and spread oil all over the water; this caught fire. *Lightning*, which was berthed stern to the wall (a typical Mediterranean mooring), just went full ahead but still was black all along her side from the *St. Merrill* explosion. One bomb landed off *Laforey*'s quarterdeck and knocked main breakers off the electrical system. The next hit the merchant ship alongside but did not explode. Captain Hutton sang out to the captain of the merchant ship, " 'Are you hit?'

" 'Yes, I think I've got a bomb in my hold.'

" 'What are you carrying?'

" 'Ammunition and 100 per cent octane gasoline.'

"Captain D turned to the torpedo gunner, 'Go and dispose of that bomb.'

There were some Spitfires from an airfield west of Bone but there just weren't enough to deal with the Luftwaffe. This went on for five days, raids every day. And because of the fires in the harbour it was as bright as daylight all night."

Another new weapon, the circling torpedo, made its appearance. These circled in ever decreasing circles and, despite the popular joke, did not disappear* but hit *something*. *Ajax* had been damaged and on 6 January 1943 a tug took her to Philippeville, a little port between Bone and Algiers. *Laforey* escorted her and then came back and got five more days of intermittent raids.

Another operation was to do a sweep into the Straits. This was called a "sink-at-sight" area. In other words, you just shot at what you saw. There was no question of challenge or reply. Airplanes were doing reconnaissance over the Straits and would report back that something was moving; *Laforey* and Captain D would then go out looking for it. On January 11th the idea was to run out into the Straits, intercept shipping, and sink it. The problem was that the water off the North African coast is quite shallow and it was all mined. To get to deep water *Laforey* had to go up fairly close to the coast of Sicily, up off Cape Marettimo, an island off the western coast of Sicily. (The Italians had radar and knew we were there, too.) *Laforey* didn't find anything that night but the headache operator could hear the E-boats talking.

Two Dutch ferries converted to carry LSIS, the *Queen Emma* and the *Princess Beatrix*, were escorted to Algiers by *Laforey* and *Loyal*. On into February and March of 1943 the L-class destroyers moved back and forth between Bone and Cape Bon.

\* \* \*

Ten Canadian corvettes had come into the Mediterranean. The Canadian contribution to the forces there was not inconsiderable: HMCS *Louisburg, Camrose, Regina, Ville de Quebec, Port Arthur, Baddeck, Alberni, Summerside, Moose Jaw*, and *Algoma*. The Senior Officer of the Canadian escort was Lieutenant-Commander W.F. Campbell, RCNVR, in *Louisburg*, and Captain Hutton sent John Charles over to brief him on operations in the Mediterranean. Hutton was to be the Senior Officer of the distant screen of the next convoy. They sailed the next morning, in February of 1943, in a convoy from Gibraltar to Bone, *Louisburg, Camrose*, and eight other Canadian corvettes aided by six British corvettes. At sunset of the second day they were attacked by bombers and torpedo bombers. The bombs came first. There were two near-misses and then the torpe-

---

*For the refined reader who has not had to mix with vulgar sailors, the scornful description of a man who panics easily is: "He'll go round and round in ever decreasing circles until he disappears up his own asshole."

does came. *Louisburg* was hit by a torpedo and sank in about three minutes with a loss of thirty-eight of the ship's company: the depth charges were not set to safe as she went down and exploded around those who had managed to get off into the water. Three merchant ships were hit and *Camrose* went back, sighted the submarine on the surface, and then picked up survivors from the merchant ship.

When they arrived at Bone, Captain D sent a signal to *Camrose* (Lieutenant-Commander Pavillard, "the Mad Spaniard"): "Report on board at 0900 number fives negative sword." Charles scuttled over to *Camrose* to explain what "number fives negative sword" meant.

Captain D gave Pavillard a thorough wigging for stopping to pick up survivors when there was a submarine to be attacked. This rather puzzled Pavillard because the Canadians had seemed to be sinking submarines when nobody else was doing it, about three in a relatively short period of time. *Regina* had got one after a long stern chase during which gunfire was exchanged with gusto. *Ville de Quebec* had also got one, as had *Port Arthur*.

In the spring of 1943 John Charles started running into Canadians in the LCMs, LCTs, and MGBs. One of the LCM captains was Johnny Boak, RCNVR (whose brother, Lieutenant-Commander Boak, RCN, was the Captain of *Sioux* in the North Atlantic and envied his younger brother's war in a more salubrious climate). The other Canadians he ran into were MGB people. When *Laforey* was at Bone, Corny Burke and Tommy Ladner were there. John Charles smiled when he said, "Captain D took a dim view of Canadians. One disadvantage of the MGBs was they didn't make their own water and water was hard to come by in the Med, by golly it was! So Corny came into harbour one day and, vhruuum-vhruuum-vhruuum with this damn boat, he tied up alongside. He didn't ask permission to do anything. He just came on board and said, 'Charles, may I have some water, please?' He didn't even approach D, which would be the normal approach of a commanding officer of an MGB to the commanding officer of a destroyer. D thought Canadians were peculiar. He surely did! We gave Corny his water and I spent a bit of time with him in his boat. He used to anchor outside the harbour. He didn't want anything to do with these air raids. We had met a local French family who had an old Citroen so, in daylight when there were no air raids, it was rather pleasant. Nights were bad, of course."

On 12 March 1943 *Laforey*, *Lightning*, and *Lookout* went out one night to do a sweep up the Straits. *Lightning* was sunk by an E-boat off La Galite Island. The problems of the shortage in naval stores were largely offset by the casualty rate of the ships. Whenever a ship bought it, if she was still afloat – or, if in harbour, she was sitting on the bottom – whalers from sister ships would converge on her and take off whatever gear they could use; sometimes they passed survivors rowing the other way. So John Charles picked up a radar set, at about one in the morning of the 13th, as well as a radio/telephone type 86, a push-button affair to change channels. He could use this for distribution of gunfire, consult the radar plot, and say, "*Tartar* take the one bearing northeast from you, *Lookout* take the one astern of him."

It was all a very impromptu distribution of gunfire but that was the way it was done. Flashless cordite had come in so the enemy never knew what was hitting them. Neither did our destroyers stop to see who they hit. It was usually an Axis ferry between Sicily and Africa, perhaps carrying 1,000 troops – open fire, destroy, and disappear into the night. They had to get back to base before dawn: the Spitfires would come out for about fifty miles and if they didn't get back under them by daylight they'd get clobbered by the Luftwaffe. The rules were made as they went along. Plenty of battles have been lost by using tactics from a previous war, and now the ships and other technology were changing very rapidly. Nothing like this type of war had been seen before. The support of an army short of food and supplies had been common for a couple of hundred years, and bombarding in support of the army had been as well, but engagements at sea were of a type never before seen. Then there was the modern equipment just being fitted, such as radar. The Royal Navy had no radar officers until the RCN loaned thirty-eight lieutenants and sub-lieutenants, RCNVR, to be distributed around the various fleets. Lieutenant Mack Lynch, RCNVR, was radar officer in the *Orion*; Terry Burchell, RCNVR, was in Algiers – there was a Canadian radar officer in *Aurora* and in practically every capital ship in the Med.

One morning when John Charles made contact with the Spitfires the leader came back and said, "Are you Canadian?"

"Yes, I am."

"What's your name?"

"John Charles."

"This is O'Connell."

He had been in Charles's term at RMC. As well, there were two or three RCAF flying Meteors in the pathfinder business. Perhaps we had as many Canadians with the RAF as with the RN.

Then there was this strange contrast between the days and the nights. The night sweeps in the waters around the south of Sicily were tiring. They would sail about five in the afternoon and until about six the following morning they were at action stations. Some nights they fought and some nights they didn't. But over the months they were on this patrol, they sank seven or eight transports. *Laforey* sank three in one night. The Mediterranean at that time of the year is benign. Unless there were air raids they would refuel, embark ammunition, and spend the rest of the day on the beach, mostly sleeping in the sun.

And were we effective? There was no doubt that we were causing Rommel headaches. A post-war analysis of Rommel's progress up and down the coast related to the number of sinkings shows a relationship (with a time-lag of about two months) between the effectiveness of Rommel's supply line being cut by our forces – destroyers, MGBs, MTBs, airplanes, and submarines – and how far Rommel could advance.

The night of the 28th of April *Laforey* and *Tartar* went on patrol and picked up six echoes on radar. Captain D altered straight at them, which gave him three on the starboard bow and three on the port. Charles distributed gunfire: *Tartar* take the ones to port; we'll take the ones to starboard." But, as Charles explained, "while I was down on the radar distributing the fire – down under the canopy of the bridge – there was a hell of a bang and a collision. I thought, God, we've been hit by a torpedo! I popped my head up and torpedoes were going in every direction. You know the water is very fluorescent in the Med. There was a bumping, scraping scream, and this E-boat – or rather, half of it – came bumping down the side. Captain D had cut her in half. We sank three more E-boats, left another on fire, and then got out. But then some Junkers 88s came right over the top of us about 100 feet and we were being bombed in the dark. Most unusual. The chief engineer came up and said we had to reduce speed, that we had broken the stem of *Laforey* and flooded the forepeak and the pressure was building up on the bulkhead of the forward messdecks. So the engineers shored up the bulkhead and *Laforey* proceeded at about eight knots."

Captain D, at about three a.m., told Charles to send a message to *Tartar*, telling him to proceed back to Bone. *Tartar*, however, didn't do anything, just continued to steam around *Laforey*, screening her. They weren't able to get back under the Spitfires by dawn and got bombed pretty heavily by the Luftwaffe but no one got hit. *Tartar* stayed with them and the two of them blazed away with whatever effect they could on the Luftwaffe. When they got back into Bone, out went Captain D's signal again, "Report on board in number fives negative sword," and gave *Tartar* hell for disobeying the message.

In May the army was beginning to move and on Saturday, 8 May, *Laforey* painted ship. Allied aircraft now swept the skies as undisputed masters, so much so that the only damage our ships received from aircraft was from our own, who either did not read our radar-triggered IFF (identification friend or foe) or had failed their ship-recognition courses. Admiral Cunningham ordered all British ships to paint their upperworks red – a good Union Jack bulldog red. The RAF and the RCAF have never been very good at ship-recognition and so Admiral Cunningham made it easy for them. "Twelve destroyers were painted this bloody-awful red. We did it in one day," says Charles.

"The flotilla of twelve was now divided into four teams, three in each team, and we had to cover the First Army, which was nearly at Bizerte; the Eighth Army already had Tripoli. At night there was a lot of air activity, flares and gunfire, everything exploding all over the place. We went in to bombard the shore with *Loyal* just east of Bizerte. There was an 88mm and one of the shells hit *Laforey* and cut the main steampipe between the first and second boiler rooms. Luckily, only three were injured, none dead. But we were stopped in the water with *Loyal* steaming around us making smoke like Billy-be-damned."

On patching up this damage, *Laforey, Tartar*, and *Loyal* found a convoy coming out of Tunis – three radar echoes – at 10:22 p.m. "These night actions are very ghostly affairs. We opened fire at 10,000 yards on a radar range and bearing, worked out a co-ordination between the surface radar and the gunnery radar so we could get the guns to hit on the first salvo. When the echoes disappeared we knew the enemy had been sunk. So proficient did we become in these night actions that the usual star shell were eventually done away with and we would open fire at four to five miles. The night that these three ships mentioned above were sunk Captain D decided to stop and picked up survivors.

"We picked up four. One was the mate of the leading ship and so he knew the approaches to the harbour. Tunis had been terra incognita to *Laforey* up to then. Captain Hutton figured the German mate of this merchantman must know his way in. About three a.m. they were just off Tunis and Captain D said, "I'll give you two minutes to lay off tracks through the minefields." The German knew his life was in jeopardy so he laid off the track. Captain D then put the German right up in the bow of the ship so he would be the first to get it if he laid off the courses incorrectly."

As they went into Tunis the German battery started shooting at them so they had a bit of a duel with this 88mm. When they got in close they found that the French tricolour was still flying in Tunis, but they could see tanks skittering around the streets. At this stage of their entry they got a frantic message from C-in-C saying that the ports of Tunis and

Bizerte were still in enemy hands and the nearest friendly port was Sousse. *Laforey* and *Bichester* made as dignified an exit as they could, running back through the fire of the German 88mm. *Bichester* had been hit by 500-pound bomb and could only steam at slow speed. So she tagged along astern as best she could. The asdic officer, Johnny Kempton, was down pinging off the mines that he could find all over the place. The German mate thought this wasn't part of the deal at all and was jumping up and down in excitement. He had lost his towel and this animated figurehead of the modern man-of-war was grotesque. A prancing naked Italian First Mate!

Some time later, off Cape Bon, they raised a small island called Plane. Low, flat, coral. They headed for that when a man came down from the lighthouse waving a towel. Captain D sent the First Lieutenant and Charles with ten armed seamen, and they landed on the beach. This was an Italian sergeant and he said, "We surrender."

"That's fine, but who are 'we'?"

"I am the senior of thirty-seven Italians on the island. We surrender. But the Germans don't surrender."

"How many Germans are there?"

"About twenty-two."

Some rifle fire started whistling about their ears. Charles shouted that they had better surrender, otherwise the destroyers would pound them to death. Even though the ship was only a half-mile away it was with some difficulty that the Germans were persuaded, but then they agreed to the surrender.

One of the officers was a colonel in the Pay Branch of the Afrika Korps "and he had thousands and thousands of Tunisian francs in the moneybelt around his waist. Only Kempton and I knew this. Actually, we thought that the money was no good but we found out later that it was perfectly legal tender. So we never got anything out of that. What was annoying the Italians was that the Germans were living in the lighthouse. There wasn't room for them all so the Italians had to live out and the only food they had was Cadbury's Milk Chocolate they had captured from the Eighth Army months before. A little bit later in the day there were odd boats coming out, trying to get back to Sicily. I don't know whether they were optimistic or whether they just wanted to be picked up. Anyway, we ran into one, a row boat full of Germans towing a rubber float with seven Italians – and one rifle. The Germans didn't have a rifle so the Italians were aiming the rifle at the Germans, forcing them to tow. It was a funny sort of war; this sort of thing went on for some time. We were picking up odd boats, I don't know how many prisoners we picked up. Anyway, we got back to Bone."

At this stage the North African campaign was over and there was a victory parade in Bone. Admiral Harcourt took the salute and Captain D and John Charles were standing on the dais with him. "It was a most spectacular parade. We had our own troops. They were all in battle dress but there were the Spahis, and the Zouabs and the Goums, these various local French troops – a very colourful parade."

# IX  The Invasion of Sicily

*T*he month of May in 1943 was the turning point of our fortunes in the Mediterranean, the beginning of the successes enjoyed by our small ships. From September, 1939, we had been losing the war, although we never doubted final victory.

After the Operation Torch landings of George Buckingham at Algiers and of Derek Fynn, Tom Forrester, Tom Poapst, and Harry Trenholm at Arzeu, they all moved east along the African coast as the First Army fought its way east toward Rommel in Libya and the Eighth Army was moving west. Tom Forrester's operations were typical. He and about thirty other LCTs would load with infantry and field guns, sail after sunset, and land them *behind* the German lines. They had no escort and did about eighteen knots. "The din was terrific," said Forrester. "Thirty LCTs belting along, apoketa-apoketa-apoketa-apoketa. I'll never know why we weren't followed on shore by German tanks. Anyway, at a set spot – usually about ten miles behind the German front – we'd land our troops. That's 7,000 British soldiers yapping at the Germans' arse; gunfire, mortars, rifle and Bren-gun fire, smoke, flares. All hell would break loose for a few hours, then we would re-embark the soldiers and scatter back behind our own lines."

Rommel was being squeezed into the centre and German evacuation was planned. But Hitler forbade it. Like the Allies, Germany never had doubted final victory; but in the spring of 1943, Germans saw that defeat was possible. In the North Atlantic for the first time in three-and-a-half years of war we had turned the tide on the U-boats. In 1942 they had sunk 1,091 of our merchant ships plus a lot of escorts. The winter of 1942 and 1943 was the nadir of our fortunes. But by the end of 1943 only 309 merchant ships had been sunk by U boats during the year. In our convoys from Iceland and the United Kingdom to Russia, escorts for the first time, were plentiful, and air and U-boat attacks decreased in number and ferocity.

May, 1943, found *Laforey* in Malta having her bow repaired, that is, the cement patch taken out and a new stem fitted. It also saw the Maitland-Burke-Ladner-Fuller quartet approaching Gibraltar in their battered convoy after a fifteen-day trip. Their 1,600-mile voyage was over. The morning after MTB 657's fracas with the U-boat and her resultant fire, Maitland was asked how he was doing. As he was not given to heroics, the laconic reply was, "All now well, damage slight, two casualties only, one petrol tank burned out, and considerable experience gained in fire-fighting."

Toward the evening of 5 May the sky showed blue for the first time, the wind dropped, the sea calmed. Just after midnight course was altered to east-southeast, the last leg of the voyage. The morning of the 6th dawned clear and sunny and they steamed up a glittering golden pathway leading to The Rock. Charles Jerome in 667 and Tom Fuller in 654 – they had been the aftermost ships of the starboard column – had their U-boat survivors on deck waiting to land. Fuller had twenty-six prisoners and only twenty-nine crew, but he found the Germans well trained and obedient; their morale was not high anyway, for they were from two U-boats that had been in collison and sunk each other – the U-437 and U-534. It was not something to make professional sailors proud, so they were docile, subdued.

By the 8th of May all boats had stored, fuelled, and had their extra deck tanks removed. The hands shifted into tropical rig and at last they were guided to their berth in the Coastal Forces base, where there was a chance to relax. They got their first news in weeks from newspaper headlines and it worried them:

BIG RETREAT BEGINS, AFRIKA KORPS PREPARES TO EVACUATE TUNISIA.

Were they going to miss all the fun? Soon all were either ashore or fast asleep, except for the quartermaster.

That evening they avidly exchanged news with their mates from the 19th and the 32nd flotillas, who had arrived in the Mediterranean a month before. All knew the phrase "the price of admiralty," but it struck home particularly hard when they found that this included the death of Lieutenant Stuart Gould, killed when 639 sunk. His successes had been many as an MTB leader at Dover. Apparently he had led two other boats along the North African coast flying German ensigns, in daylight, until he found a suitable target. Then it was down with the German colours, hoist British colours, and open fire. This worked for a few hours but then the Luftwaffe was sent out and he, his First Lieutenant, and his Navigator were killed, as well as most of the hands. The Midshipman brought the boat back to harbour.

On 8 May the Mediterranean Fleet received Admiral Cunningham's "Sink, burn, and destroy" signal. The next few days the Inshore Squadron and Coastal Forces reaped a rich harvest of prisoners escaping from Tunisia in every conceivable small craft available. On the 11th, Maitland, Burke, and Ladner set out for Algiers: a cloudless sky, a sunny day, a sea ruffled by cat's paws. In Algiers they ran into an air raid and were near-missed by bombs; then they sailed for Bone and thus joined the 20th MGB Flotilla. The Canadian MGBs spent the remainder of May in Bone, working up. Corny Burke tells of a harrowing experience.

"We go into the basin at Bone. On the starboard hand are the Coastal Force craft, our base; at the end of the basin are two destroyers; on the far side two cruisers, *Newfoundland* and *Penelope*. Also in the basin are merchant ships from the U.S. loading for the American army ashore. We found we could bribe the guard and get cases of fruit juice; this was very precious and we did very nicely in this trade. But what we didn't know and what the lower deck on one of the Tribals discovered was that there was Scotch whisky. This was exported from Scotland, all the way across the Atlantic to the U.S. – and these convoys were protected by Canadian destroyers, frigates, and corvettes – and then back across the Atlantic for officers' messes of the U.S. Army in Africa. The hands lowered a whaler in the dead of night, and, literally, with muffled oars rowed across the basin and on the outport side of one of these Liberty Ships; they scaled the ship's side and got something like 2,000 bottles, let's say, or 1,000. It doesn't matter.

"Nobody discovered this. They got back on board their destroyer and stashed the bottles away. Not one officer knew and the crew was just electric, sitting on all this booze. They were all sworn to leave it alone. Well, you know the lower deck. Finally, on a make and mend, one rating says to the other, 'Mind you, Bert, just one wouldn't 'urt, now would it?'

"So Bert cracked a bottle. The next thing was that the entire crew was absolutely bombed. Unfortunately the Captain – whose remaining career was inglorious, I think – went strictly by the book. What KR & AI (the King's Regulations and Admiralty Instructions) said was what he did. And KR & AI said was that you mustered the ship's company onto the upper deck and smashed the bottles, one bottle at a time, in front of the entire ship's company. There was an admiral on board *Penelope*;

he heard about this and he heard, to his horror, what the destroyer Captain planned to do. So he went over and saw the skipper, who was a two-and-a-half RN.

"Now look, Old Boy! We're all short in the wardrooms in all these ships. It's just ridiculous. Please cease all this nonsense.'

"The destroyer Captain would have none of it.

"It is in KR & AI, sir. It is regulations and I intend to carry them out.' The whole basin was awash in Scotch whisky. It was a great, great tragedy. But that's what happened to us at Bone."

Bone, of course, was an important supply point, but with the German airfields in Sicily, Sardinia, and Pantelleria the air raids were frequent and ferocious. These raids were made bearable for our gun boats by their taking as chummy ships *Laforey*, *Lookout*, and *Loyal*. In harbour they would snuggle under their guns for the air raids, use their generators to supply power, showers, galley.

Our boats were ordered to Malta, where they arrived in early June, 1943. The yellow bastions glaring in the strong sunlight towered impressively above them as they steamed up into Marsamxett harbour and secured alongside at Sa Maison. The Coastal Forces base at Malta was HMS *Gregale*. Two days later three boats were sent on a patrol off the coast of Sicily and, to their amazement, Cape Passero on the southeast corner was flashing brightly and clearly. Was a convoy about to leave Syracuse? Or arrive? The group stopped, cut engines, and lay quiet, listening, about a mile off. As in the English Channel, just outside the enemy harbour is always a good place to catch a convoy: psychologically they are unprepared for attack, and the crew is wrapped up in the business either of leaving harbour and striking down lines and fenders and securing for sea or of getting secured alongside on return to harbour. But nothing happened that night and before dawn they had to get forty miles from Sicily or they would get the unwelcome attention of ME 109s or JU 88s.

On 10 June was Operation Corkscrew – the invasion of Pantelleria, which the ships had bombarded en route from Bone to Malta. The bombardment now was done by *Aurora* and *Orion* (whose radar officer was Sub-Lieutenant Mack Lynch, RCNVR). *Laforey* and other destroyers were there. For bombardment two artillery captains were required. One, the Bombardment Liaison Officer (BLO), was aboard the ship and was responsible for the safety of our own troops ashore. The other, the Forward Observation Officer (FOO), was ashore and was responsible for zeroing in the gunfire. The tactic was to fire a full broadside so that the FOO could, without doubt, see it land and then, by radio contact with

the ship, move it left, right, up, or down till the fire straddled the enemy position.

The morning of 11 June, Rear-Admiral McGrigor, who had sailed his forces from Sousse and Sfax the previous evening, called in a final bombing attack and called on the island to surrender.

No answer.

The LCAs and the LCIs chugged in and landed troops with little resistance. Malta could not supply enough aircraft and Tunisian airfields were too far away to give continuous air cover to our troops, so Pantelleria would be a handy supply port and airfield for the pending landings in Sicily. Under the bombings and the bombardment this volcanic isle billowed curtains of dust, right up to touchdown. After an hour or so John Charles in *Laforey* received on the 500 KC band (the international distress wave) a signal from the Italian Admiral, saying "Beg to surrender for want of water. Admiral Peress."

The naval gunfire ceased immediately but the bombers were another matter. A chain of them stretched back a couple of hundred miles and this operation could not be aborted. They streamed remorselessly overhead, dropped their loads, and retreated. Eventually the excitement died down and the island was occupied by our troops.

Tom Forrester and his mates were at this landing. They had started from a shore base in Djidjelli, moved east to Bizerte, then to Sousse and Sfax, and finally the assault on Pantelleria. Forrester says: "This was taken by the Brits and the Yanks and then our flotilla moved in. We found that the Germans had all gone so what we had to do was reverse our tactics. We had to take the civilian population *off* so our engineers could build an airfield. The civilians and their livestock. We had the pongos acting as herdsmen. What a sight! A platoon of infantry chasing horses, cows, pigs, goats, chickens, ducks – to our ship. Have you ever tried to chase chickens *up* the ramp of a landing craft?"

A fleet of Noah's Arks sailed south to Africa, each with a full load of livestock all shitting in fright and squawking, braying, bleating, quacking, crowing, whinnying, braying, honking. It was reported by *Camrose* that they could be smelled ten miles to leeward. "So we took them to Africa," said Forrester, "unloaded them, and that's the last we saw of them. Then we scrubbed out for a whole day."

The islands of Linosa and Lampedusa followed in rapid succession, begging to surrender. In Linosa a Fleet Air Arm pilot landed because he ran out of fuel and the Italians surrendered to him. From Lampedusa, the following message was sent to Admiral Cunningham:

To C-in-C Med
From CS 15

Surrender of Lampedusa accepted from Second in Command who fully agreed with terms. Governor not yet contacted. Our soldiers have landed.

All in all it was a great year for *Laforey*. She fired over 5,500 rounds of 4.7-inch ammunition. The events of that summer seemed to happen with a breathless rapidly, which makes chronology difficult forty years later. After the invasion of Africa came the invasion of Sicily, and all these months comprised a succession of battles with the German 88mm batteries (from which the Allies always retreated) firing at moving tanks on shore, troop concentrations, ammunition dumps, crossroads, air-fields. *Laforey*, too, fired at practically everything that summer: E-boats, U-boats, enemy troop transports . . . She wore out the rifling of the guns four times and had to have them replaced. Admiral of the Fleet King George VI inspected them. They had got their own individual signal from ABC:

To *Laforey, Bicester, Aldenham, Jervis*
Repeated Vice-Admiral Malta and CS 12
From C-in-C Med,

Sink, burn and destroy. Let nothing pass.
Time of Origin 08/12/51/A

At the time of Dunkirk the Allies had taken over 350,000 troops from the hostile beaches to the safety of the United Kingdom. General Gauderian had inexplicably halted his advance on our retreating troops and Admiral Raeder with his battleships and cruisers had been unable to halt the evacuation of our soldiers. Admiral Cunningham and General Montgomery would not make the same mistake. Every German soldier who was killed leaving Africa was one less to fight when we advanced on Germany.

The operation orders for the invasion of Sicily were received by *Laforey*. Charles said there were masses of them. They were being amended right up until the last day. *Laforey*'s initial role was to protect the convoys from the U.K. coming down the Straits of Sicily to the southwest of Malta. Other convoys coming from Algiers, Tripoli, and Sousse were to land on the southeast coast of Malta. *Laforey* was based in Malta and had to go out and relieve the destroyers that had brought these convoys in so that they could refuel. This meant that they had to pass the up-to-date orders to the destroyers they relieved. And the bumphf continued to flood in. The names and the numbers and the timings were constantly changed in the light of changing events; Captain D's staff spent a good week getting to know these orders. Moreover, it was extremely uncomfortable in Malta with the smokepots going. Particularly when an atmospheric state of inversion was prevalent, the narrow creeks were filled with this sulphurous smoke. When there was very little wind, it was agony. Malta was full of ships and troops coming in from everywhere.

In March the plan had been approved by the Supreme Commander, General Eisenhower, and the three service commanders-in-chief: Admiral Cunningham, General Alexander, and Air Chief Marshal Tedder. General Montgomery objected; he wanted one additional division, which he got. The time of the Sicilian invasion was set for three hours before dawn on 10 July 1943, and mock-up exercises were started in May in the Red Sea and the Gulf of Aqaba. The work-ups continued until the crews of landing craft had become highly proficient.

Montgomery's British Eighth Army was to land on the southeastern corner of Sicily and concentrate on capturing adjacent airfields for the RAF and the ports of Augusta and Catania for the navy. They also captured Syracuse and landed at beaches stretching around Cape Passero and captured the airfields there. These troops came from Alexandria, Tunisia, Malta, and, in the case of the 1st Canadian Division, from the United Kingdom. General Patton's American Seventh Army landed on the southwestern coast; these came from North African ports and from the United States. The initial job of the Eighth Army was to push north, with the Seventh Army protecting its flank.

The 10th of July 1943: the total available air strength was 113 British and 146 American squadrons – 4,000 aircraft of all types. The total sea strength was 2,500 ships and major landing craft. Vice-Admiral Sir Bertram Ramsay, RN, commanded the British sector and Vice-Admiral H.K. Hewitt, USN, the American sector. Under Ramsay were Rear-Admirals Roderick McGrigor and Philip Vian; under Hewitt were Rear-Admirals A.G. Kirk, J.L. Hall, and R.N. Conolly.

As a result of the Canadian experience from the Dieppe raid, a Senior Naval Officer Landing was in each of the British sectors. Of captain's rank, these had experience in previous landings and had carried out all preliminary and working-up training of their squadrons. They would go in with the first wave of the assault troops and control the inevitable muddle caused by hundreds of craft arriving and departing. Beach masters (traffic policemen) from the navy and the army – colloquially known as "Beach Bricks" – numbered 2,600 in the British Sector. These helped to co-ordinate the close schedule of arriving troops, tanks, trucks, jeeps, stores, and ammunition.

The Italian fleet was still large and dangerous, particularly as the Allies were now invading their homeland. If ever they were going to fight it would be now. Naval strength of the Allies and the Italians in this theatre was:

| Class | British | American | Other* | Italian |
|---|---|---|---|---|
| Battleships | 6 | 6 | | |
| Monitors | 3 | | | |
| Carriers | 2 | | | |
| Cruisers | 14 | 5 | | 7 |
| Destroyers | 71 | 48 | 9 | 32 |
| Escort Vessels | 35 | 1 | | 43 |
| Minesweepers | 34 | 8 | | |
| Landing Ships | 8 | | | |
| Landing Craft | 1,134 | 700 | | 16 |
| Coastal Craft | 160 | 83 | 5 | 115 |
| Submarines | 23 | | 3 | 48 |
| Merchantmen & Troop Transports | 155 | 66 | 16 | |

*Included are 7 Greek, 10 Dutch, 9 Polish, 1 Belgian, and 4 Norwegian smaller craft.

British Empire troops numbered 115,000; the U.S., 66,000. Allied ships totalled 2,590. Among these were the troops of the 1st, 2nd, and 3rd Infantry Brigades of the 1st Canadian Division; the 1st Canadian Army Tank Brigade; Number 40 and 41 Royal Marine Commandos; and the 73rd AA Brigade of the Royal Artillery.

Corny Burke's navigator, Rover Reynolds, tells of another type of work-up for the invasion. The night before sailing Maitland, Burke, Ladner, and most of the other officers of the flotilla met at Monico's, the most popular bar in Malta. The 51st Highland officers were there in full strength and holding the floor with their songs and dances. This could not be tolerated. At one pause Maitland asked the 51st if they knew the secret of getting the best possible aftertaste out of a glass of sherry. No?

Then watch. He ordered a sherry, sipped genteelly until the glass was empty, *then ate the glass.** The whole audience watched intently, we may be sure. Then he passed the stem of the glass to all the 51st: "I have saved the best part for you. Any takers?" This was followed by an army/navy "rugger" match, which deteriorated into a general mêlée. This attracted the attention of the military police – mostly the chairs going into the street through the windows. The one thrown by Burke hit the Provost Marshal on the head, which really was most unfortunate. It was quite a relief to sail a day later to invade Sicily.

Maitland, Burke, Ladner, and the rest of the 20th MGB Flotilla were to patrol as back-up of the Canadians and the Lovat Scouts just south of Syracuse, led by Lieutenant-Colonel Lord Lovat, Royal Marine Commandoes. Before they sailed all captains read to their ships' companies a message from Admiral Cunningham:

> We are about to embark on the most momentous enterprise of the war – striking for the first time at the enemy in his own land.
>
> Success means the opening of the "Second Front" with all that implies, and the first move towards the rapid and decisive defeat of our enemies.
>
> Our object is clear and our primary duty is to place this vast expedition ashore in a minimum of time, and subsequently to maintain our military and air forces as they drive relentlessly forward into enemy territory.
>
> In the light of this duty, great risks must be and are to be accepted. The safety of our own ships and all distracting considerations are to be relegated to second place, or disregarded as the accomplishment of our primary duty may require.
>
> On every commanding officer, officer and rating rests the individual and personal duty of ensuring that no flinching in determination or failure of effort on his part will hamper this great enterprise.

---

*I know of three who can *eat* glass. They only do it when they have a fine crystal. Maitland told me, "I was taught by the Captain of *Icarus* after she returned from the First Battle of Narvik and they were celebrating after about three days without sleep. The secret is in the first bite; if you don't get that right you cut your lips. I've cut mine several times but never cut my gums. You get a flat piece and grind it small, to sand. I've never had any medical problems because of this."

I rest confident in the resolution, skill and endurance of you all to whom this momentous enterprise is entrusted.

Burke read this to his crew. "Well, there it is. Any questions?"

"Captain, sir, please. Will there be any shore leave in Sicily?"

Farley Mowat of the Hastings and Prince Edward Regiment, the "Hasty Pees," was there. They went ashore in the first wave. Present also were Canadian lads from across Canada in all the peacetime militia and permanent force regiments.

The Hasty Pees and the Royal Canadian Regiment and the Seaforths and the Patricias were the first wave; in the back-up were the Edmonton Regiment and the 48th Highlanders of Canada, landing with the pipes skirling their keening regimental march, "The Highland Laddie." Five convoys carried the 1st Canadian Division and their supplies:

| Convoy | From | Date | Speed | Composition |
|--------|------|------|-------|-------------|
| No. 1 | Clyde | 20 June | 8 knots | 8 LSTs, 1 LSG, 1 tanker |
| No. 2 | Clyde | 24 June | 8 knots | 17 MT store ships; 1 LSG, 7 LSTs |
| No. 3 | Clyde | 25 June | 7 knots | 40 MT store ships, 6 LSTs, 5 tankers |
| No. 4 | Clyde | 28 June | 12 knots | 1 HQ ship, 3 LSTs, 8 LSIs |
| No. 5 | Clyde | 1 July | 12 knots | 1 LSI, 13 troop transports |

All these made a rendezvous off the beaches from midnight to noon of 10 July.

In 1947 my wife Alma and I had the singular pleasure of talking about the work-up training of this invasion force. This was during dinner at the Hampshire home – on Hayling Island – of Vice-Admiral Sir Arthur John Power, who was then the Second Sea Lord at the Admiralty. Mock-up exercises were started in May in the Red Sea and the Gulf of Agaba; the work-ups continued until the crews of landing craft had reached a high degree of proficiency. As I say, the conversation was fascinating. Imagine! A lieutenant of only twenty-three talking to the man who had actually *run* the operations! The Admiral's son, Arthur – a course mate of mine at HMS *Excellent* – had heard it all before and so had the Admiral's father. They devoted their full attention to Alma, who was at her most charming that night. On occasion Alma's demure enthusiasm bubbles over and her quiet, inner glow of beauty bursts forth. And with the attention she was getting that night she radiated her unique combination of a dignified hoyden. After a while the Admiral tired of my eager-beaver questions, saw that his son and father were on to a good thing and were stealing a march on him and devoted the rest of *his* evening to Alma. I drank a lot of port and felt rather sulky; at one point I heard Alma describing to Sir Arthur John a rash our newborn son, Ricky, had developed. I wandered over to defend the Sea Lord from such domestic trivialities and it was forcibly implied that I should buzz off, they were doing quite nicely, thank you, on that and many other subjects. Horses was one topic I remember – Alma rode several times a week; she "had a pretty bay mare with a blaze and a stocking on her near fore." And swimming: Alma is still a fast, effortless swimmer. I just wished she would stop calling this Sea Lord "Mr. Power." But he seemed to love it. I fear I digress.

Experience from Dieppe had shown that even a rudimentary knowledge of the craft in which they would go to battle was an advantage to the soldiers. Therefore, in mid-June there was a full-scale exercise for the eastern attack forces with the troops embarked. By the beginning of July the loading of the assault convoys was nearly complete. Admiral Ramsey and his staff moved from Alexandria to Malta. The assembling of the craft for the extra division Montgomery had asked for presented many difficulties that were solved by the staff of Vice-Admiral Sir Arthur John Power, the Admiral Commanding, Malta. They robbed Peter to pay Paul. Not just the boats but the whole of the logistics back-up was involved. As Sir Arthur John recalled a few years later, it "probably had tearful repercussions from many a stock-room clerk in many a factory storeroom from the Mediterranean back through the supply lifeline to England."

Early on the 9th of July, Admiral Ramsay sailed in his Headquarters ship *Antwerp* to witness the meeting of the assault convoys from British and Middle East ports; they then had to rendezvous with the landing craft coming from Malta and North Africa. At noon of that day they met at a spot south of Malta. Then Admiral Ramsay, leading his invasion ships, steered for the coast of Sicily. The assaults in the eastern sectors started with airborne landings just before daylight on the 10th: about 1,600 men of the 1st British Airborne Division embarked in 137 gliders towed by Dakotas and other aircraft; they were to capture strategic points south of Syracuse. Unfortunately, faults in timing combined with a strong headwind caused sixty-nine gliders to be released early. They landed in the sea, and many paratroopers were drowned.

Forrester passed them later. He said, "One of the big problems we had when we got to the final rendezvous – the mustering area, before taking off to the beach – was picking up the paratroopers who were dropped in the water; their tow was slipped too early. Many were in the water but most never got out of their gliders. I guess a lot of men died trapped in a tank or a glider – or an LCI, like us, later." Tom Ladner was there the same morning and said the fault was with the planners. The pilots of the planes towing the gliders – nearly all of them – were green; they had never been exposed to fire before. When the Italian battery opened up with a truly lethal barrage of shot and shell, they slipped their tows and got out. Perhaps remembering *his* first time under fire, Ladner said, "I don't blame them, these pilots. I would have done the same thing."

Forrester landed his troops at Syracuse. From North Africa they had steamed all night with their quotas of 250 soldiers in each landing craft. And the soldiers were squashed in, sitting upright, cramped and uncomfortable. They couldn't stretch out and many of them were seasick and vomiting. What soldier wouldn't welcome an assault on a beach after that!

Forrester describes his landings on Sicily and then on the Italian peninsula. "My ship had what we called a front fo'c's'le and a rear fo'c's'le – abaft the engine room. The engine room was in the centre. We could embark troops from either end. We could take them and put them in either fo'c's'le but they can't transfer from one hold to the other. There are gangways coming down from the both fo'c's'les into the water. You have to go up twelve steps to get up on deck.

"When we gathered and formed up in the flotilla, there were hundreds of us, LCAS, LCIS, LCTS, right up to the big LSTS. They were all ready and we were waiting for the time to land, H-hour. We passed the ships who were bombarding and they they were shooting over the top of us. We could hear the shells whooshing over our heads.

"Now there's a real technique in getting off a beach. It's easy enough to get on a beach. We dropped the kedge anchor on the way in and as we unloaded the troops she was light up forward end and I'd pull her off with the kedge anchor and the motors; there was a power capstan aft so we could power-capstan off. You could go in and put her onto the beach quite heavy and run her right up and she would be high and dry. Then if you run the screws for a little while she would wash the sand out from underneath and back herself out. And two hundred and fifty men left her – over twenty tons. With equipment, they'd weigh two hundred pounds a piece; that's a lot of weight.

"There was opposition on the beach at Syracuse. Tremendous. A lot of soldiers went down. Unload your first cargo of troops, then back to North Africa for more on the first day. But on the second day the big troop carriers would be coming in and now we would be picking troops up from alongside the troop carriers. We'd go alongside the big carriers and the soldiers would come down the scramble nets and we'd head in to the beach. Just running a ferry service until the pongos established a beachhead it was day and night for three days. No sleep. No sleep, never any sleep. When you were on action stations, everybody was busy until action stations were secured. So we never got out of action stations until we were ten miles away from the beachhead.

"There was quite good air cover from Malta. The only time we had any problems from enemy aircraft was at night when our air cover wouldn't come in. The enemy seemed to know when our air cover wasn't going to be there. They just dropped bombs . . . they didn't strafe. They wouldn't come down low enough. There were too many ships, too much firepower to come down. Also, we all had balloons, towed balloons, all the big landing craft; all had the big balloons, blimps, to keep the aircraft up.

"When we finished with Sicily, we had the problem of getting across the Messina Straits. But we went up around there and went across in one day. There was no trouble at all, as it turned out, no trouble at all. The Germans had got out. Civilian ferries could have done it the same way as we did. The rest of the action was more or less running troops up the Toe and up the Italian coastline, up the west coast of Italy, to Naples, up towards Anzio. Naples was a big one.

"So we landed the soldiers. They went across the Straits of Messina to Reggio and fought their way up the west coast of Calabria and then up the west coast of Campania, through Salerno and Naples. When the soldiers were doing all that, LCI 273 was making a diversion on the east coast of Italy. We're on the west coast but it only takes a couple of days to get around to the east coast. So we went around there and we caused problems up and down – raising hell with the Germans around there.

"Again, LCI 273 was picking troops up from behind our lines and bringing them behind German lines. And on the east coast of Italy we always had to take them back off again; we couldn't leave them there because our troops were advancing so slowly; they were having a rough time of it, we heard. We'd take them in, they would create a diversionary action, and we'd bring them back out again. They would be ashore one night until the next night, forty-eight hours at the most. They'd sit under camouflage during the day. A lot of the times we'd head over toward Greece, across the bay, and then come back again. Sometime we'd anchor and camouflage ourselves and wait but not very often, though, the enemy was too close. It's a nasty feeling; we didn't like to do that. But when we got up to Anzio, the beachhead was established but it never grew the way it should have done. We hung around and hung around and that's where one of Jerries' bombs caught up with us and sank my ship, my 273.

"We saved six out of the two hundred and fifty soldiers who were on board. We only saved six of them. The crew was safe on deck; but of all the soldiers, there were none saved but six. The bomb landed right alongside side and it just buckled the deck right up from underneath. Only six. How long did it take her to sink? As long as it took me to go up the gangway from the messdeck up to the top deck – three minutes. She rolled over on her side. We got some of them out of the front fo'c's'le before she turned over. We had the ramps of the 273 but they weren't there after the bomb landed – just disappeared and those poor bloody soldiers were sealed below deck. There are no hatch covers all along that deck that can come off. You have to walk up from the lower deck up a gangway, up a ladder. There were two hundred and fifty of the poor buggers down there. She turned over too quickly. Anybody on deck was saved and anybody below deck was lost. Of the six saved we only got three out from below. One fellow we got out had two broken legs. The other two were still alive. What their injuries were I don't know. I've forgotten the name of the regiment; they were just cargo to us, yes. Get them in and get the hell out of there in a hurry. Mostly infantry, yes.

"Most of your armoured stuff was all in the LCTs and the big LSTs. We used to be the second wave in after the Landing Craft Assault, and ours was the Landing Craft Infantry. We used to go in behind the first assault, as soon as they established a beachhead. What did the LSA have on them? Commandos most of the time, the fighters to get across the beach. Just establish the beachhead. Establish a beachhead, then you establish a bridgehead a few more miles inland. So we were the second wave, the infantry, and then the LCTs astern of the infantry. The LCTs would come in then with their armour. You can see it shaping up. It was quite a sight, some of those big invasions. All the battleships there and cruisers and destroyers. They were all there, all blazing away, the destroyers and the minesweepers. I used to marvel at the minesweepers. They would be right in close to the shore sweeping mines, and the destroyers would be just outside them blowing up anything on the beach that they could find, and the cruisers were out a little bit further. So they were all there. Everybody shooting over everybody else's head. That's right, yes. That's quite an exciting thing for a kid, isn't it? Real cowboys and Indians stuff, isn't it? You always remember the good parts, you know, always the good parts.

"So I lost my ship. I'll tell you how I got to Scotland from Anzio. They gathered all the ship's crew and sent them to a rest camp. I was there but they wouldn't send me. Nobody told me why. So I immediately got on my high-horse and raised hell and got put on skipper's report as a defaulter, captain's report. The naval shore patrol slung me in cells. So I had one quiet night's rest. I came out of cells to be paraded before the Captain.

"He said, 'Have you cooled down?'

" 'Yes, sir. I have.'

"But then I started yelling again and to go after *him*.

"He said, 'You haven't cooled enough. You've got to keep your mouth shut.'

"So I thought I'd better shut, but I told him what was going on.

"He said, 'I realize what's going on. Have you cooled off yet?'

" 'Yes, sir. I'll keep quiet.'

"He said, 'We're going to send you back to Scotland. You've been in the Med for a long time now. You're going back on leave.'

"I had got pretty heated up because I wanted to go to the rest camp. I wanted to be with the rest of the crew. I was browned off with what we were doing all the time. There was never any liberty boat. It was always back and get another bunch of soldiers, take them over and drop them off, and you're back into action again. There were other ships tied up at the jetty in North Africa that never moved. Now the reason they didn't move, I don't know. They probably had no engines or they stole the props off them to keep the other ones going. They were sitting over there doing nothing. And I'd had no rest. Watch on and stop on, day in and day out, week in and week out. I'd been in the Med for a year and a half, going nonstop for a year and a half. I'd *had it*! We were getting browned off about it. Wanting to go home, wanting to get a change of scenery. Wanting to go home, mostly. So that's how I got back to Scotland."

For the first wave of the invasion of Sicily, apart from four medium-sized LSIS (Landing Ships Infantry), the troops were all in landing craft. The leading ships reached the release point, four miles off, at 12:30 a.m. The landing craft started the run in. A hitherto unsuspected reef formed a "false beach." The craft grounded confidently enough, the ramps crashed down, and the jeeps and soldiers charged off in the approved manner. But again they disappeared under water. They rose to the surface, spluttering considerably and cursing "them fuckin' matlots who couldn't even recognize a beach."

The reef was buoyed so that subsequent craft would avoid it, the

Landing Ships Tanks followed, then the guns, and by noon the beach was ours – with only slight casualties. In the afternoon the ships were headed back to reload, for these particular landings were of the shore-to-shore type; that is, soldiers landed on the Sicilian shore from the craft in which they embarked in Malta. Fifty-six LSTs, thirty-six LCTs, and thirty-three LCIs left Malta fully loaded in the following week. (The other type is ship-to-shore landing, where the troops arrive off the beaches in a large transport and are taken off by the smaller landing craft.)

Rear-Admiral Vian was in his headquarters ship and at one a.m. met the convoys from Scotland carrying the 1st Canadian Division. We knew that this beach was far from ideal but had accepted it because it was necessary to capture a nearby airfield at Pachino. The LCTs for this assault had come from Tripoli and adverse winds made them half an hour late. The moon had not yet risen; the swell onshore was uncomfortable; some craft hit the wrong area. Princess Patricia's Canadian Light Infantry (commanded by Lieutenant-Colonel R.A. Linsey) and the Seaforth Highlanders of Canada (commanded by Lieutenant Colonel B.M. Hoffmeister) were detailed for Sugar Beach, and while the heavy surf removed one worry by carrying them over the false beach, it and faulty navigation caused another. Seaforths on the left and Patricias on the right had been the order, but the Seaforths landed on the wrong side of the Patricias. No harm was done, however.

On Roger Beach were due to land the Hastings and Prince Edward Regiment and the Royal Canadian Regiment (commanded by Lieutenant-Colonels B.A. Sutcliffe and R.M. Crowe, both of whom were killed in Sicily). Because of the late arrival of the LCTs, Brigadier Graham in the Headquarter ship *Glengyle* was in a quandary but he chose to load the Hasty Pees into the LCAs; the RCR would be along presently. At 2:26 a.m. the Hasty Pees started their forty-foot descent to the sea. At 3:15 Admiral Vian – never a patient man – signalled his senior naval officer in *Glengyle*, "Will your assault *never* start?"

Brigadier Graham had embarked the Hasty Pees when at 3:35 a.m. a note arrived (in the Admiral's barge; radio silence was in effect) from General Simonds, "You *must* get your assaults away either by LCA or LCT."

At 3:16 a.m. the Hasty Pees in the LCAs had headed for the shore; at 4:01 the RCRs followed. One of the Hastings reserve companies landed 5,000 yards too far to the west but soon joined up with the rest, who had hit their area on the nose. The Hastings touched down at 4:45; at 5:30 they were joined by the RCRs; then they and the Princess Patricias and the Seaforth Highlanders pressed on inland. At 6:45 a.m. General

Simonds reported that the 1st Canadian Division had captured all its objectives.

By this time a slower convoy from Britain had arrived with the groceries and off-loading began. By evening dusk, empty ships were steaming back whence they came. The one shore battery that had opened up had been silenced by the 15-inch shells of *Roberts*.

To summarize events since the North Africa landings in November, 1942, to the Sicily landings in July, 1943: the First Army had been moving east from the landings at Casablanca and Oran toward Algiers. The Eighth Army had fought from the outskirts of Cairo west to Tobruk (which was taken and lost a couple of times), then west to Benghazi. Any evacuation of German troops would be from the vicinity of Tunis, where it was only a short hop from Cape Bon over to Sicily. As events turned out a few German soldiers got out to Sicily. For the moment our headquarters was Algiers and it was there that the 20th MGB Flotilla with Maitland, Burke, and Ladner went. It is worth examining the chart to see how much in the centre of the conflict was Malta, with Germans in Sicily to the north, in Tunisia, Libya, Egypt, along the rim of Africa, and in Crete to the northeast across the Ionian Sea. Germans were heading north to Sicily in any conceivable craft that would take them.

The 20th MGB Flotilla sailed for Algiers, a voyage of 450 miles, in perfect weather with a mill-pond sea, at twenty-four knots, and arrived there in time to experience a heavy air raid and be near-missed by bombs. The inshore squadron had received their "Sink, burn, and destroy. Let nothing pass" signal and for a week or so the destroyers and coastal forces reaped the rich harvest of escaping Germans.

Maitland's boat had been patched up before sailing and the hand who had been wounded in the U-boat attack – with the hole in the ankle – was pronounced fit for sea and rejoined. Luckily, some of the German shells had pierced the rum locker and all four jars had been destroyed. Maitland had told the coxswain to see to it that the hole was repaired.

"Oh no, sir. Let's leave that hole there. That way when we're in action we can get hit in the rum locker everytime. As long as we turn in a broken jar with the seal intact we can get it replaced." That is precisely what happened and they ended up with eighteen jars of rum.

Ladner said that the American thesis for protecting Algiers from air raids was to cover the whole area with smoke. So he had to grope his way into harbour and tie up as best he could. They left Algiers and patrolled off the Cape Bon peninsula, but the end of the German evacuation had not yet come when the 20th MGB Flotilla left Algiers for Malta.

From there they sailed for the invasion of Sicily. The flotilla was to act as an anti-E-boat screen during the landings and patrol off the Straits of Messina at night. All the other Dog boats had arrived from England and so the flotilla now numbered eight; they set off. "The difficulty was," said Maitland, "that there was an electric railroad train running along from Messina down the coast and the Krauts were running hospital trains as troop trains – so our intelligence showed us." So one night he, Burke, Ladner, and a couple of English boats – five of them – went off to Catania to see what they could do about one of these trains. This was about ten days after the initial invasion, and so history must relate that the first victory of the Canadian MTBs in the Mediterranean was against a train, which they duly blew up.

"An unanswered question was, how far into the Straits of Messina should we go? It turned out to be not very far. What happened was, all would be quiet on either bank while you were going in but when you turned to come about the shore batteries you'd already passed opened up from the north and the south. It is perhaps needless to say that in the following weeks the patrolling of the Straits of Messina turned out to be patrolling the *entrance* to the Straits of Messina. Peter Thompson in one of the MGBs went in a bit too far one night and they put a couple of 6-inch bricks right through his engine room and he went into the bag in Germany for the rest of the war. Another British boat got a brick through the bow so that her nose was under water. I set up a smoke screen around him while Ladner towed her out."

On another occasion the flotilla was lying at anchor when they heard the sswisssh and crack of a heavy shell landing nearby. It was very accurate, but where did it come from? As they got under way while more shells arrived, the lookout spotted the flash from a battery on Murro di Porco, five miles away. Fortunately, the *Erebus* was at anchor about three miles further out and she was asked, "May we have some heavy-gun help, please?" She silenced the battery for them. An hour-and-half after that dive-bombers arrived but ignored them and went for the larger ships further out. That evening they were briefed in *Bulolo* by Admiral Troubridge's SOO and while they moved away to find a quiet anchorage before the night patrol they were dive-bombed again. Maitland's 657 disappeared into a great spout of water that seemed to rise from beneath her, but when the water subsided she was still there. Burke closed Maitland to ask him if he was okay. He was making water a bit and four men were injured, but not enough to return to harbour. By this time the flotilla had been running continuously for thirty-six hours and so they fuelled from the *Empire Lass*. In the course of the next three days, the flotilla, although suffering casualties from dive-bombers, shot down three ME 109s. One day later Ladner was ordered into Syracuse harbour, where he really didn't want to go. The land battle between the German and British tanks was still going on. So our sailors had spectator seats for the tank battle on shore and the RAF and Luftwaffe dogfights overhead. There we have 659 and 662 in Syracuse; then 659 (Lieutenant Bob Davidson) succeeded in sticking herself well and truly aground.

Syracuse was still mostly in enemy hands when Corny Burke in 658 crept quietly through the boom and across the harbour to try to pull 659 off the putty. This he failed to do. It was done later by a destroyer, and the position in the harbour where 659 had grounded was thence-forth called "Bob's Patch" after Bob Davidson, her commanding officer. In the afternoon a large white-ensign merchant ship entered the harbour. She was the *Antwerp* and had on board a complete naval party trained especially to take over Augusta harbour when it was captured.

That night the Germans counter-attacked and it appeared likely, for a few hours, that they would retake the city. The NOIC, rather than risk all his port party, withdrew for the night except for the MGBs, which he left behind to bring off any of the last remaining troops. Our Canadians thought this a rather dubious honour. Burke's 658 was left behind to take off the last of the rearguard. The rest of the flotilla left harbour during the evening, some with as many as 125 extra men on board. But with the dawn Syracuse was still in Allied hands and supplies started to pour in at a rate that amazed all of the Coastal Forces. Large LSTs came in with every conceivable type of equipment. At noon an air raid was beaten off and after sunset they sailed again to escort yet another convoy in through the boom. This they achieved just after midnight and then patrolled outside the gate for the rest of the night.

By this time Commander Robert Allan was in command and set up his Mobile Coastal Forces base. Nineteen days after they left Malta they were sent to return for their 300-hour engine overhaul. On entering Marsamxett Harbour they played "Heart of Oak" on the loud-hailer microphone and were given a rousing reception by the boats alongside.

The job of John Charles in *Laforey*, together with the rest of the L-class destroyers, was to provide close support for the Canadian troops in the landing in Sicily. The Eighth Army was landing at Passero on the south coast and the Americans were landing north of Passero on the east coast. The battleships *Nelson* and *Rodney* had been carrying out a bombardment at Catania mostly to divert attention from the main landings. About one o'clock in the morning Charles spotted the little blue flashing light, set for them by the submarine, and started banging bricks into the beach – direct fire, range about a mile. Charles said that that was the first time he had seen the landing craft rockets in action. He's seen them many times but he did not know what they did until he heard the whoooooooosssssssh. The FOOs got ashore and *Laforey* got a call for fire shortly after six in the morning. The Canadian soldiers, you will remember, were heading to capture the airfield at Pachino. For some days *Laforey* patrolled back and forth off the beach answering calls for fire until, on 15 July, she was ordered back to Malta to pick up General Alexander, Admiral Ramsey (the Naval Commander of the British forces), Admiral Hewitt (Commander of the American force), and Air Marshal Coningham, who was in charge of the RAF in North Africa. Charles said, "I was terribly impressed with Alexander. He seemed to know exactly what was going on. I had an opportunity to talk with all these people and Alexander was quiet, calm, cool, collected. Really! A most impressive fellow!"

Charles had an opportunity to show Air Marshal Coningham the difficulty they were having with the IFF, that is, if the aircraft was within striking distance and was not showing IFF then we would open fire at it. These aircraft were all fitted with IFF that would be triggered by our radar, but they did not seem to have their IFF switched on.

Coningham said, "Your radar sets aren't working properly."

So Charles took Coningham down to the radar displays and showed him on the air-warning set the steady stream of bombers that were coming over. He pointed out, "Now there's one showing IFF and there's one that's not." The majority of them were not. We found out later that the USAF and RAF pilots thought the Luftwaffe could home in on our IFF so they just turned their sets off.

*Laforey* went into Syracuse and landed the senior officers for their conference with General Montgomery. It wasn't exactly peaceful. There were fires still burning along the jetty and every so often there would be an explosion. But after five hours or so they took the group back to Malta. *Laforey* was flying Admiral Ramsay's flag and so as they went through Force H, which was patrolling offshore, all the ships were piping, saluting, and sounding the alert on their bugles as Ramsay went through; even in battle good manners are mandatory.

After another five days of bombarding enemy positions along the Sicilian coast, they went south to Malta again to re-ammunition. On the way back they saw the cruiser *Newfoundland* hit by a torpedo, at about sixteen knots, when the lookout reported, "Torpedo to starboard." D turned to starboard to comb the spread – there were two torpedoes coming towards them and he ran right between them. They got contact with the submarine and dropped depth charges. *Eclipse* turned and came across her stern and she got contact and dropped a pattern of depth charges. Up popped the submarine. Captain D turned to the gunnery officer, "Sink that submarine," and both ships opened fire at her. The Italians were just pouring out of the conning tower, it was a flat-calm day and one of the shells from *Eclipse* (on the other side of the submarine) ricocheted off the water and went between *Laforey*'s funnel and mainmast. Captain D said, "Cease fire." They sent away a boarding party but the submarine (it was the *Ascianghi*) sank. They picked up survivors and proceeded to Malta.

On 4 August the Eighth Army captured Catania and then there was a great hassle about the Germans getting out of Sicily back to Italy. Charles thinks this was "a bit of boondoggle". We bombarded here. We bombarded there. But we never attempted to go into the Straits to intercept the Germans going across. It's only about two miles but no ships were sent in. What had in fact happened was that our intelligence people were caught flatfooted and they didn't really know that the Germans were leaving Sicily to cross the Straits of Messina until they were all gone." Messina fell to the Allies on the 17th of August, more than five weeks after the landing in Sicily.

Then *Laforey* bombarded off Catania with Cruiser Squadron 15 (Force K). At night they would move out from shore a bit and steam up and down. Unbeknownst to them, Force H was doing the same thing a few miles further out with the object of bottling up the main Italian fleet. CS 15 was not aware that Force H was out there. A message came:

From C-in-C
To CS 15

Repeated Flag Officer Force H
    If you wish to engage in night action with Force H you should continue to omit him from your night intention signals.

Admiral Cunningham was reminding them that if they didn't tell people who they were and where they were going to be, they were liable to be fired on by all these battlewagons and carriers and cruisers and destroyers of Force H that were steaming by just a few miles further to sea. This was very much a sink-first-and-ask-questions-later operation.

An acerbic little message, that.

\* \* \*

After the invasion the Eighth Army started north. Syracuse and Augusta were taken within seventy-two hours of the landing and supplies were unloaded there. By the 23rd the last ship of the last convoy had departed. The fleet roamed offshore ahead and abreast of the soldiers' advance on land. Some ships caused diversions by landing commandos behind enemy lines, creating din and light for an hour or so, and then taking them off. The monitors *Erebus* and *Roberts* did yeoman service; so did the cruisers and destroyers. In all they answered about 200 calls from the army for supporting fire. At night the MGBs and the MTBs patrolled close inshore.

On 25 July 1943 Benito Mussolini was toppled from power. Marshal Badoglio said Italy would fight on but Germany was not confident that this would be so. General Jodl, the head of operations in Berlin, ordered General Hube, commander of the army in Sicily, to evacuate the three (it must be admitted) first-rate German divisions back to Italy across the Strait of Messina. What Captain Sir William Tennant had been to the British at Dunkirk, Captain von Liebenstein was to the Germans and Italians at Messina. His planning and execution were superb, and, for a variety of reasons – many of them our fault – we didn't know the Germans were gone. Over five nights and six days they were ferried across the strait, mostly at the narrowest point in the north – two miles across. Our destroyers and MTBs tried to penetrate the strait but it was *murder*; on the nine-mile stretch at the northern end, there were no less than twenty-one batteries on the Italian side and seventeen on the Sicilian side; the calibre of these guns varied from 11.2-inch to 6.8-inch to 4- and 3-inch. But from the middle of July the coastal craft were out on offensive sweeps every night; from the 3rd to the 16th of August the following got away:

|            | *Italian* | *German* |
|------------|-----------|----------|
| Men        | 62,000    | 39,369   |
| Vehicles   | 8,111     | 9,605    |
| Tanks      | no record | 47       |
| Guns       | 41        | 94       |

So the war had gone from the 1st of June to the 16th of August. Strategy now took a new turn with a conference in Quebec City. Churchill, Roosevelt, and Mackenzie King met with, among others, the First Sea Lord, Admiral of the Fleet Sir Dudley Pound, RN, and the Chief of Naval Operations, Fleet Admiral Ernest Joseph King, USN. Italy was out of the war. Italians were not "Allies"; the euphemism was "Fellow Belligerents."

In the middle of September the Eighth Army followed the Germans across the Strait of Messina. Flogging north up Italy might be all right for some but our tactic now was to make an end-run and land at Salerno. This was done by British and American troops on the 9th of September 1943. While the hundreds of vessels were converging on the Salerno beaches after midnight – under a bright moon, on a calm sea – a diversion was carried out against islands off Naples and in the Gulf of Gaeta. Afterwards, various small islands were captured – the Isle of Capri was one. This was done by destroyers, MTBs, and MGBs.

Under the terms of the armistice the Italian fleet was to be handed over to Admiral Cunningham. It is hard to change the phlegm of code names for operations; indeed, it is forbidden to wax poetic or philosophical or seek any degree of appropriateness in case intentions are made clear to the enemy. In this case, a sense of poetry and history prevailed. Some staff officer, who had (we presume) learned much from the tome, *Decline and Fall of the Roman Empire,* named the operation to surrender the Italian fleet, Operation "Gibbon."

Vice-Admiral Power was to hoist his flag in the battleship *Howe,* take under his command the battleship *King George V* and four destroyers, and meet units from Force H. Among these were the battleships *Valiant* and *Warspite,* both of which had been present at the surrender of the German fleet in 1918. In all the annals of military history there is perhaps no more final, abject, and degrading symbol of defeat than a line of powerful warships, docile and with guns trained inboard, escorted by the warships of their triumphant enemy with their guns unwaveringly fixed on the defeated. A rendezvous was set off Cape Spartivento, where Admiral Bergamini sailed to meet Admiral Power. On the 11th of September Admiral Cunningham sent a signal:

To Admiralty

From C-in-C Med

Be pleased to inform Their Lordships that the Italian battle fleet now lies at anchor under the guns of the fortress of Malta.

All was not that well at Salerno, however. The landings were contested and the Landing Ships Tank, HMS *Boxer, Thruster,* and *Bruizer* made six shore-to-shore trips between 10 September and 1 October, landing 6,000 men and 1,345 guns and vehicles. These were of the large type; they displaced 5,740 tons loaded as opposed to the 3,770 of the smaller LST; also, they had twice the speed – eighteen knots. After their Salerno duties they sailed for Bombay to take part in the landings planned in Southeast Asia.

While in Canada for the Quebec Conference in August the First Sea Lord, Admiral of the Fleet Sir Dudley Pound, had suffered a stroke and had promptly sent in his resignation. He died on Trafalgar Day, October 21st. The position was first offered to Admiral Sir Bruce Fraser, the Commander-in-Chief of the Home Fleet. He declined with the words that, whereas he had the confidence of his own fleet, "Cunningham has that of the whole Navy."

Andrew Browne Cunningham hauled down his flag as C-in-C Mediterranean Fleet on 17 October 1943 and was succeeded by Admiral Sir John H.D. Cunningham (they were not related). ABC was now First Sea Lord.

＊　＊　＊

To illustrate the stories that follow we must now concentrate on the southern coast of France, where the next large landing took place more or less in conjunction with the Normandy landings of June, 1944, on the islands of Sardinia, Corsica, and Elba on the west coast of Italy, and on the Adriatic and the Aegean.

Captain von Liebenstein of the Kriegsmarine comes to the fore again. He planned and carried to completion an operation that emptied Sardinia of troops he had ferried across to Corsica. Our coastal craft harried them as best they could but German losses were not high. From Corsica it appeared simple to evacuate the whole across to the Italian mainland at Leghorn. At the peak some fifteen passenger ships and 120 barges were used, and some 28,000 Germans were saved to fight another day, which seemed a pity. Also, 1,500 British p.o.w.s were evacuated, which seems strange; one would have thought of them as impediments to the German retreat. It is impossible not to admire such efficiency.

In the Aegean, German garrisons and airfields and harbours had made life hard for our ships for two years. Rhodes possessed a good harbour and two airfields and had been a mortal enemy to many of our brave hearts of oak; Scarpmento was another. Leros came high on the list of undesirables (in German hands, anyway), as did Samos. To island-hop to the Dardanelles would be to open the Sea of Marmara and the Black Sea to free the Russian shipping bottled in there. Such successes would also encourage Turkey to enter the war on our side. With Yugoslavia there was another political consideration: which of the two resistance leaders did we choose to support; Tito or Mihajlović.

In both the Aegean and the Adriatic, German air power was still strong; if far from base during a night operation our craft frequently holed up the next day at remote anchorages under camouflage. Germany was still a power in the Aegean; after the Italian surrender, the 7,000-man German garrison at Rhodes overpowered the far larger Italian garrison. Sir John Cunningham didn't have the forces to mount an offensive against an island defended so well; he decided to try for a number of smaller islands from Casteloriso in the south to Samos in the north.

"Good," said Churchill when he heard of the plan. "This is a time to play high. Improvise and dare."

Part of the improvisation was the commissioning of His Majesty's Belligerent Caiques; these were fishing schooners, now armed and under command of a naval officer. They carried supplies, landed men of the Long Range Desert Group (sort of super-commandos) in cut-and-thrust raids, gathered intelligence, and carried reinforcements to isolated garrisons. Sir John intended to put 4,000 more men into Leros, Samos, and Kos, where the British garrison of 1,300 was encumbered by 4,000 Italians who really had no stomach to continue the war, against us or the Germans. But they did try to improve the airfields, with one tractor and several oxen. The Germans were still firmly entrenched in Crete and Greece. In October a German landing fleet was seen leaving Piraeus; we failed to intercept and our garrison at Kos was overcome. Some of our troops were taken off but 900 went into the bag. Of the 3,000 "collaborating" Italians, the German victors shot ninety of their officers.

Now the German garrison at Kos was built up to attack our small garrison at Leros (1,100). It was a nightly hunt for our destroyers, MTBs, and MGBs to intercept supply- and troop-carrying German vessels. We supplied Leros by submarine, air drop, and caique. On the night of 13 November 1943 the Germans took Leros. We now decided that Samos was at risk and withdrew from there.

The Germans had eighteen divisions in the Balkans and even a

pinprick was important in that it nurtured alarm and despondency in enemy breasts. The hatred of the Yugoslav Partisans was palpable, so that no German walked alone at night; sentries were alert to a high degree, yet many were found with their throats cut by the sergeant mustering the reliefs. Weapons, equipment, and supplies were ferried to the Partisans by caique, and two flotillas of MTBs swept the coast nightly to deny to the enemy the free passage of his supplies by night (exactly as Coastal Forces were doing along the coasts of Belgium and Holland).

The Long Range Desert Group made periodic forays. It was the culmination of a time of violence and piracy unusual even in war. If the Partisans of Tito hated the Chekniks of Mihajlović, the Ustachi hated them more. On one occasion Tom Fuller had captured sixty prisoners and turned them over to the Partisans to guard until he could get them to a p.o.w. camp. When he sent for them, they had all been executed. Apparently one young soldier had a picture of a Partisan girl (with a red star on her cap; they are the Communists, remember), a young girl with her breasts cut off. "He was a foolish boy to carry that around." The Ustachi prisoners all had their throats slit. By this time, Fuller had been in these waters for three years in MGBs, had written off several boats, embarked commandos and boarding ladders to use on enemy ships that would be useful. In one ten-day period he captured or sank twenty-four armed vessels or enemy transports. He took the practical view that this internecine strife had been going on before we came and would continue after we left. He said, "In turning over our prizes to the Partisans, Tito was very nice. On one occasion he gave me a complete barrel of the very finest old Proshak wine, and it was greatly appreciated."*

However, the most important island, Vis, was still in Partisan hands. Nightly we played out from there our deadly game of hide and seek: commando raids; partisan landings-in-force and subsequent retreats; cutting-out expeditions into enemy harbours to fire on ships, spray a shore battery, and run . . .

The first half of 1944 offered the same pattern. Ours had ever been a policy of offence. The philosophy of the depredations of Drake against Spain in the 1600s had been repeated in 1911 by Admiral of the Fleet Lord Jackie Fisher in a letter to Edward A. Goulding, "The vital British policy is that the coasts of the enemy are the frontiers of England."

---

*Lynch, *Salty Dips*, vol. 1, p. 150.

\* \* \*

After the breakout of General Mark Clark's Fifth Army from Salerno and its juncture with Montgomery's Eighth, Naples was captured. To get to Rome it was necessary to do another end-run and land troops north of Salerno, at Anzio. Work-ups and rehearsals were now an accepted policy; much had changed since Dieppe. To take one example, Vice-Admiral Hewitt, USN, was now a veteran of the Operation Torch landings in North Africa, Operation Husky landings at Sicily, and Operation Avalanche landings at Salerno. He, together with our admirals, formulated new premises. Was it, for instance, worth forgoing the obvious advantage of air and sea bombardment to gain surprise? The rehearsals for Anzio – Operation Shingle – were to be in the Gulf of Salerno (now relegated to a practice area since the soldiers had left for Rome). *Boxer*, *Bruizer*, and *Thruster* had just returned from the Indian Ocean. The British rehearsals went well enough but there was some trouble in the American sector with inexperienced landing-craft crews and vessels improperly loaded. But time was short. On 22 January 1944 convoys carrying 50,000 troops and 5,000 vehicles approached the beach at Anzio.

The fiery tail of the projectiles from the rocket craft showed where they were going to land and it became a practice of infantrymen to head that way; opposition there was less likely. Still there was a lot of trouble. A week later the beachhead was only ten miles deep, with 68,886 men, 508 guns, 307 tanks, and 27,000 tons of supplies. The Germans counterattacked with equal numbers and called in their reserves. The fronts of the Fifth and the Eighth Armies were now static; our troops could not break out from Anzio and the navy had the hard job of keeping them supplied. This supply job was always difficult, mainly because of the tenacity and skill of German U-boats. In March there were two in the Tyrrhenian Sea. A trawler, *Mull*, sank U-343 off the south coast of Sardinia, and U-450 was disposed of by destroyers after a ten-hour hunt. Captain H.T. "Beaky" Armstrong had replaced Captain Hutton as the leader of the L-class destroyers. He sank U-223 but not before she torpedoed *Laforey*.

John Charles said, "Yes, and we lost quite a number of ships at Anzio, I think about eleven, mostly warships. There were a few merchant ships but they were mostly warships. So whether it achieved anything or not I don't know. I think we could have achieved a lot more. You can get a great argument as to whether they should have pressed on. I think the American general, Lucas by name, wanted more supplies. Whereas, since they took the Germans completely by surprise I think if they had gone on they might have achieved more.

"At this stage of the game I got a message saying I was to be relieved and returned to Canada. Captain D, Captain Armstrong, sent a message asking if I could stay for an additional period.

"Canada came back and said, 'No.'

"My relief arrived, Lieutenant Addis, RNVR. So I said good-bye to the ship about February 7th and took passage in *Urchin* down to Naples. Then I took *Lancashire* to Algiers; it took *five* days. She was full of returning troops of various kinds and I got involved as the naval-officer-in-charge of the sailors. When I got to Algiers I shifted to the SS *Strathnaver* and arrived in Liverpool on February 20th and had ten days in England.

"I went up to the Signal Division of the Admiralty and they were just preparing the new bombardment plans for the landings in Normandy. I spent quite a number of days going over the procedures with the FOOs and BLOs because I'd had a lot of experience with them. So, I think I contributed a little bit to the success of the Normandy landings. I joined the *Aquitania* on March 2nd, 1944, to go to New York. Boy! Was it loaded with troops! I think there were twelve in a cabin. They were mostly Americans and they played poker all the way. The meals just went around the clock. The troops were stacked in bunks. I'd never seen anything like it before. It was a quick trip. I had a day in New York. And I noticed the difference from before the United States entered the war. Everybody was now so kind to the troops. They really were most helpful. Then I got in a train and reported back to our signal school outside of Montreal, HMCS *St. Hyacinthe*, to Captain Pip Musgrave.

"My shipmates in *Laforey* gave a farewell dinner for me before I left. Oh yes! Those who had been in the ship when I started, the Navigator, Andy McCullock, the Captain's Secretary, Wilson Jones, the Sub, Whitcroft, the Gunner, and, of course, all my signalmen and telegraphists whom I got to know so *very* well. I was really very sad to leave them. I'd like to have stayed and, of course, one of the quirks of fate was that I left the ship, [and] she went down to Naples shortly afterwards and again got into a submarine hunt [chasing U-223]. A torpedo hit the forward magazine and she blew up.

"Of all the officers only Wilson Jones and the Gunner survived. Captain "Beaky" Armstrong had replaced Hutton. The new Gunnery Officer was Bud Boyer, RCNVR. He was killed. It's pretty hard, you know, when you lived with men for eighteen months, always together, there was nowhere else to go. You got to know them pretty well. I don't think

I've had such a close contact in a ship as I had with those in *Laforey*, and particularly Andy McCullock, the Navigator. We had two bunks in the chart house and we literally lived together in that chart house for a year and a half. We were always on our breaks together. I certainly was very sorry to lose them and when Wilson Jones got back he wrote me and gave me the names and the addresses of all the communicators who had been killed. I wrote to the wives and mothers. It is very hard to write such letters; it took quite a while.

"But the life of a destroyer out there was about six months and we had lasted eighteen. A the end of that period, out of the eight L-class destroyers, there were only two left."

\* \* \*

The Allies continued denying to the enemy the support of his soldiers in Italy by sea and to support the Yugoslav irregulars. Vis played an important part and we used it in 1944 in much the same way as the English had from 1812 to 1815 against Napoleon. The changing Balkan politics; the internecine feuds of the various partisan groups whose hatred of each other was only a little below their hatred of the Germans; the uncertainty of the weather; the withdrawal of larger naval and merchant ships for the intended landing in Normandy; the heterogenous nature of the remaining forces, a rag-tag and bobtailed lot consisting of destroyers, submarines, MTBS, MGBS, MLS, schooners, barges, landing craft of various sizes, and caiques: all contributed to a bizarre war and operations more suited to a W.S. Gilbert libretto than to naval history.

The question of which group to support in Yugoslavia, for example, posed a conundrum and several changes of policy. On the one hand was the fact that here was a country with seven frontiers, six republics, five nationalities, four languages, three religions, two alphabets, and one boss. The "boss," Tito, emerged as leader of the Partisans, one of the two resistance movements formed when Germany attacked in 1941, forcing king and government into exile. The Soviet Union, Britain, and the United States had different interests in the two resistance groups despite the fact that they were the "Allies."

International and national rivalries competed with political and military considerations to create a situation of complexity, confusion, and cross-purposes. When young King Peter fled, the British reassessed their position and veered away from the Royalist Chetniks of Mihajlović, who in the early months seemed to be the heroes of the resistance, and moved over to the camp of the Communist Tito (in those days "Communist" did not have the pejorative connotation it has today).

By 1943 our intelligence was supplied by Captain F.W. Deacon and Captain W.F. Stuart, a tough forty-two-year-old Canadian who had spent the greater part of his life in the Balkans. They were parachuted into Montenegro; this group of six included another Canadian of Croatian origin, Corporal Ivan Starcevic. To avoid local clashes was worth our while; more than 100,000 German troops were engaged by 20,000 Partisans who were inflicting heavy losses on the enemy. The Coastal Forces base at Vis was run by Lieutenant-Commander M.C. Giles. Prominent among the commandos at Vis and well known to the Canadians based there was Admiral Sir Walter Cowan, now dressed for operational purposes as a Commander. He was seventy-three. Many years on the retired list and hating every day of it, he had, with boyish enthusiasm, sidled his way back into the service in 1939. He never actually signed up; he just donned a uniform and travelled via the Grey Funnel Line. Forty-odd years earlier he had won the Distinguished Service Order; he got a bar to it in 1944 for Commando service in the Adriatic. He had fought in the western desert first and had been captured by Rommel. Not generally known but true nevertheless, from 1939 to 1945 there were frequent exchanges of prisoners much as there had been when war was a more gentlemanly pursuit. Anyway, because of his rank and age, Sir Walter was exchanged. It was then he joined the Commandos in the Mediterranean.

In Coastal Forces, Commander R.A. Allan, RNVR, was one of the successful commanders of the various *ad hoc* flotillas formed for various nefarious purposes. One night he took to sea his flagship motor torpedo boat, several Landing Craft Gun as his capital ships, MGBs, MTBs, and USN PTs (patrol boats – like our MTBs). By radio and radar he controlled his squadron with the same panache as Admiral Cunningham had used at the Battle of Cape Matapan. Just after midnight he encountered a convoy of three barges and a tug and sank the lot. Three enemy armed barges were attracted to the scene by the din and the glare; two were sunk and the third driven ashore. The night ended with a battle with E-boats – brisk but inconclusive. But by April, 1944, all these semi-autonomous forces were combined into the Anglo-Hellenic schooner flotilla.

By June, 1944, we had inflicted serious losses to the enemy supply line of 249 ships, most of which were smaller than 500 tons. It is a sad story, really, for many of the casualties were impressed civilian crews and barge and tug captains. But those were desperate days. Nonetheless, the Germans still held Crete and Greece and seemed likely to continue to do so as our forces were depleted to be used for the invasion of France over the beaches of Normandy – Operation Neptune.

The invasion in the south of France over the beaches of St. Tropez and Antibes has been named Operation Anvil and opposing views were held by the Allies. The British wanted to keep the thrust toward Rome and enter France over the plains of Lombardy; the Americans insisted that, since their troops would be landing at the Cherbourg end of the Normandy beach, a distraction to the south was necessary. Churchill said that enemy troops were fully employed preventing us from getting out through Lombardy.

Roosevelt said no. Since it would be mainly American troops used in Anvil and since all of the landing craft had been provided by the Arsenal of Democracy, the man who paid the piper called the tune. Operation Anvil was on. Anyway, we owed Admiral Ernest King and General George Marshall a lot for their agreement that the defeat of Germany should come before that of Japan. But Churchill felt his hand had been forced, and because the Anvil code name had reputedly been compromised, it was re-named "Dragoon." A careful reading of Churchill's words on the subject – and those of his advisers – leads one to believe that the new code name was a result of a fit of the sulks and a play on words. In any event, for Vice-Admiral Hewitt, USN, his time as an apprentice admiral to the Royal Navy was over. Sir John Cunningham appointed him in command of the naval forces.

Before Dragoon was mounted the attack on the island of Elba was to take place in mid-May. General Magnum, the commander of the French ground forces in Corsica, was named military commander and a French colonial division of 9,500 troops would be part of the assault. Training and rehearsals did not go well and a delay was imposed until mid-June.

Throughout the war those at sea watched with jaundiced eyes the constant kowtowing to French pride. After all, they had lost their country through what can only be called the "treason" of their political leaders and the ineptitude of their generals, the stupidity of a Maginot Line that need never be assaulted frontally, and the Anglophobia of French admirals that caused us to sink their fleets (when a willing co-operation with RN, RCN, and USN forces would have shortened the war by a year). We were castigated by the French after Dunkirk for taking off only 24,000 of their troops and leaving 25,000 behind. (Some say we "deserted" 40,000 but Admiral Wake-Walker blames the French for not providing berthing parties. The argument still festers today, mostly among academics. Anyway, we *did* take off our own lads first. Who would not?) But the French hero of World War I, Marshal Pétain, became Hitler's pawn in World War II. The French Admiral Darlan came out on the side of the British; he was assassinated in Algiers in December, 1942. The history of the French army is that, while some regiments were magnificent (the Spahis, the Goums, the Foreign Legion), it was a rule of thumb since my father fought in Flanders in World War One that if French were in the line, then there should be good Americans or British or Canadians on their flanks. That is hearsay from my father but I know their ships in World War Two were, in the main, dirty and ineffective and could always find a way to stay in harbour where we would have fixed the defect somehow and got to sea. Winston Churchill said that the cross he had to bear was the Cross of Lorraine.

In June of 1944 thirty-eight landing craft hit the beaches of the south of France and a hotly contested battle followed. Modern technology was again represented by whooshing rocket ships, and again there was the incongruity endemic to war. From some beaches in Camp Bay, Elba, exit is impossible for vehicles. The veteran Rear-Admiral Tom Troubridge was in charge of the naval side and he used a device common to the Napoleonic wars. The LCTs carried 200 mules (in 1806 mules were landed in pulling cutters); these mules carried ammunition to the other beaches, and the mules disembarked as willingly as any soldier.

Vice-Admiral Sir Bertram Ramsay, RN, commanded the British sector and Vice-Admiral Hewitt, the American sector. Under Ramsay were Rear-Admirals Roderick McGrigor and Philip Vian. With these experienced leaders it was easy to feel confident.

# X   The Canadian Flotilla in the Mediterranean

O n the 3rd of September 1943 Montgomery's Eighth Army went across the Strait of Messina, between Scylla and Charybdis (these waters have seen many battles). Maitland, Burke, Ladner and others set up patrols on the south and west coasts of Italy. At the end of September, Commander Bobby Allan, RNVR (later Lord Allan), sailed in convoy with his Coastal Force Mobile Base, mostly LCTs creeping along at six knots and escorted by impatient MGBs. They were headed for La Maddalena on the north coast of Sardinia. Corny Burke, of course, was particularly irritated by this slow crawl. Fortuitously, his First Lieutenant developed severe stomach pains, which might have been a bad piece of fish or might have been appendicitis or dysentery. Never one to take a chance with the welfare of his crew (or go at six knots when he could go faster), Burke sent a signal to Allan; "Sub-Lieutenant Reynolds sick and in pain. Request permission to proceed maximum speed to obtain medical assistance at La Maddalena." This was approved and he shot ahead at thirty knots while the rest of the Dog boats enviously watched him and continued their six-knot crawl.

In March, 1943, the Germans had been corralled on Cape Bon. The job of Maitland and the others was to stop the German evacuation from Africa; they patrolled from Bone to Cape Bon.

They then went to Malta and arrived just after the siege had been lifted. Lieutenant-Commander Gordon Stead, DSC and Bar, RCNVR, commanded the 3rd ML Flotilla in ML 126 and had been there since March, 1942, doing anti-submarine and E-boat patrols and minesweeping. With his ML disguised as whatever he thought the credulity of the enemy would accept, he had steamed the length of the hostile Mediterranean from Gibraltar to Malta when the whole of that sea was dominated by Germans and Italians. For a short-time during the nadir of siege of Malta his flotilla (and some submarines) had been Admiral Cunningham's only warships in that beleagered isle – "A Leaf Upon the Sea," Stead calls Malta.

The MGB flotilla settled down to routine patrols. One night Burke was out, looking for anything, leading a unit of a couple of boats. It was too quiet; he got bored, closed to the land and crept along the shore, and decided that he'd shoot up a lighthouse,. So he did; he let the enemy know he had been there. When he returned it was already known. Burke was summoned to explain exactly what he thought he was doing to further the C-in-C's strategy. The Admiral said, "Burke, in the Royal Navy we leaving the killing of women and civilians to the RAF."

The Canadian captains did not think their flotilla leader was the greatest and again went through an upsetting episode (as they had in the North Sea in Dire Straits). The Senior Officer was an older man, about thirty, and he was not an aggressive fellow. One night he came across an enemy patrol, up-moon, and failed to close to attack. The rest of the commanding officers took a dim view of this. Corny did not throw his usual tantrum only because he wasn't there. The SO was relieved of his command.

Malta was absolutely chock-a-block – from battleships to MTBs, and a fleet of dhaisas was the main means of water transport. All the MGBs got operational orders (enormously thick), so they spent a few days reading what they were supposed to do and how. All personal gear and a lot of confidential books they would not need for this operation were landed. The Short boats, with other coastal forces, were to go right into the Strait of Messina. But the job of the Dog boats was to patrol the approaches.

Ladner said, "I admired the merchant ships and the merchant skippers working under continuous air attack. Our tanker was a small vessel of about 1,500 tons with nothing but 100 per cent octane on board; we fuelled alongside her. While I was fuelling we had to stop three times because of air attack. The idea of having all that open fuel around was frightening. I respected the Scottish skipper of this ship. He had brought her all the way from the U.K. and filled up from tankers in Algiers. We refuelled and went back again and we did one more patrol."

Then they were told to go into Augusta. They steamed in to see British tanks fighting German tanks on this large plain on one side of the harbour; there was an air battle in progress. They were told to go alongside and hang on, which they did. Another group had come in and landed a port party, who were to set up the administration of the port. It was to become the main landing place for all troops; a lot of freight was being unloaded. Alongside their jetty were huge vats of wine, fifteen-feet high and ten-feet wide, enormous things. Of course, the inevitable happened: put a sailor near free booze and you're asking for trouble. British and enemy aircraft looped and droned overhead, anti-aircraft fire bang-bang-banged all round, enemy and friendly tanks rumbled and bashed each other, through it all there were crews, sneaking ashore with brace and bit, boring holes into these vats of wine, and bringing wine back by the buckets. Ladner said, "That had to be the most dangerous thing that could *ever* happen. We might have regretted losing the Scotch whisky in Algiers but [here] we were in the middle of a land, sea, and air battle. So we were very, very tough on these people, dumped all that wine over the side, and put plugs in the vats.

"Anyway, the battle started to go badly. We were ordered to evacuate the town. The Germans were returning. Burke says we'd all withdrawn and left him behind; it wasn't *quite* that way at all. He was left behind, actually, to take off the platoon fighting as rearguard. The rest of us had to take the whole of this shore party back to Syracuse, so I loaded about a hundred people. I was concerned about stability. The weather up to D-Day and $D+1$ and $D+2$ had been appalling, but by $D+3$ it had moderated. So, I had a fellow called Peter Barlow (it wasn't just one flotilla; three flotillas assembled in Augusta) were ordered to take these people back to Syracuse, which we did. But we had so many on board that we could hardly move our guns. Going into Syracuse you go up the canal, which by that time was American territory, and they had covered the whole place with smoke because there was an air raid. You could hardly see your way in. We dumped all those people and came back. By this time it was night but the moon was up and we had the most unusual experience of being attacked for nearly two hours, from the air. I'm sure the Luftwaffe must have thought we were destroyers or cruisers. We had an exciting time, putting up smoke, going around in circles, firing at everything. But you couldn't see the enemy. They were coming from the other side of the moon and we couldn't see them at all. Anyway, we went back to Augusta and that was our base from which we patrolled the Straits of Messina, until we got to about $D+12$.

"Then there were four of us picked to go *through* the Straits of Messina. Admiral Cunningham had decided that in order to establish his victory he had to be able to tell Admiralty he had 'Forced the Straits of Messina.' At that time it was like Broadway, lit up with star shell and searchlights. There was so much star shell overhead – constantly, all night – that there was just no way you could get through. There were about 700 guns on either side of the Strait. That became known as 'Operation Burnt Offering.'

"But as it turned out the operation was cancelled. We stayed on, cruising around. There was not much going on actually after that. The Italians and Germans had withdrawn.

"I went back to Malta to do an engine refit and then we were ordered back to North Africa, to Bizerte and the assault on Sardinia. We three boats were on a little island just off the African coast, which was originally a French naval reserve base, La Galite. We were to take Americans into Sardinia, which was still German-occupied. While we were there, the announcement came that Italy had surrendered. There was a French petty officer in charge of this little island and we invited him and all his hands on board and had a great celebration. Then we went back to Malta and then we moved up to La Maddalena, an island between Corscia and Sardinia. This became our base, [and] by this time we're getting into November, 1943.

"Commander Bobby Allan, a brilliant operator, was in charge of Coastal Forces in that area at that time. Allan complained that the Italians were not co-operating as co-belligerents. The Italian Admiral said, "Well, we've done everything we can. We made our dockyard available to you. We moved out of the officers' mess. The officers' brothel has been available to you but none of you has taken advantage of that.'

"It was the first time we heard of it."

Allied forces could now patrol as far north as the island of Elba. The Vospers of the 7th flotilla joined them. The object of these patrols on the west coast of Italy was exactly the same as the patrols off the coasts of Belgium, Holland, and France, the theatre of war they had left: to harass the enemy and prevent movement of men and materials by sea. This role led to the battle of the Piombino Channel, fought on 14 October 1943 when three boats sailed with Lieutenant-Commander E.T. Greene-Kelly, RNVR, as Senior Officer in 636.

One boat developed engine trouble and had to turn back so 636 and Burke in 658 continued the nine-hour journey to the Piombino Channel. After midnight there was a brief skirmish with a trawler but she turned away. Previously planned tactics were that in such a situation 658 would create diversionary attack and the Senior Officer in 636 would detach and come in again on another bearing. This had no sooner happened when the enemy fired a five-star recognition cartridge, followed without pause by a hail of tracer.

Burke altered toward the trawler but would not open fire. For two minutes he held this course while the tracer whizzed overhead and chopped furrows in the sea around him. As he got closer he challenged with a random letter, hoping it would confuse the enemy. He flashed "Ds." Obediently, the enemy ceased fire. Burke had begun his run-in at 1,500 yards; at 700 yards the enemy opened fire again. All hands watched Burke. Why doesn't he open fire? We'll all be killed before we fire a shot. At the same time, half in envy and half in frustration, everybody admired the Captain's apparent lack of nerves. They ploughed on miraculously unscathed; until the range was down to 250 yards.

"Open fire."

A hail of shot and shell could not miss at that range and the enemy turned away, her fire weakening. Burke relentlessly followed her around and within two minutes she was ablaze from stem to stern. She would appear to have been a flak ship about 130 feet long and armed with a 40mm, several 20mms, and some light machine guns.

Another ship was sighted to port and Burke ordered the challenge (the British challenge). The Navigator flashed the letter "S" continually for about a minute while the range closed and the guns trained on the new target. The unidentified ship was bows-on and so identification by silhouette was impossible. But then Burke's doubts were removed when a stream of tracer shot across the surface toward them.

"Open fire!"

The 6-pounder immediately scored a vital hit and the unidentified ship stopped, with fire spouting midships. The other guns of 658, with the target so clearly marked, were just beginning to concentrate their fire when Burke shouted, "Cease fire for God's sakes – it's 636!"

"Why did they not reply to the challenge?"

"Why did 636 open fire on them?"

"Never mind that," said Burke, "there are a lot of them in the water. Stand by to get them inboard."

As they closed, there was a shout from the gunner of the 6-pounder aft reporting that a ship was approaching. It was not even a case of making a decision. This enemy had to be beaten off before the rescue work could be finished. Burke ordered that the Germans be challenged with their own challenge but the Germans opened fire at once. Burke was nicely situated down-moon and came in at top speed. The enemy fire was heavy, more accurate this time, and thuds and blue flashes amidships told them they were being hit. There were casualties reported from aft. The all-important opening burst of fire – preached by Maitland constantly – was again devastating. As the enemy turned away Burke remorselessly followed every twist and turn, moving closer and closer until all resistance ceased. The second target was now burning brightly and had taken a heavy list to starboard.

Back they went to where 636 was still burning, found a raft with survivors on it, and started to haul them on board. A searchlight from the Italian mainland flashed on and swung around to illuminate both the flaming 636 and the rescuing 658. The range was only three miles and the shore batteries opened up. It was altogether too hot to remain still so Burke took off at high speed, making smoke and dropping flares to simulate fires and distract the shore batteries. Then he altered around and crept back slowly and silently through his own smokescreen. The searchlight lost them. The batteries ceased fire, and they returned to 636 to pick up the remainder of the survivors. The Senior Officer, Greene-Kelly, the First Lieutenant, and seven ratings were missing. The Captain, Freddie Warner, an old friend of Corny's from Lowestoft, had leg wounds. The survivors were stripped, dried off, and made as comfortable as possible in borrowed clothing and covered with blankets. Several had minor wounds but Leading Seaman Chiswell had a shattered shoulder. The only casualty on 658 was Ordinary Seaman Balderson, who had been hit in the stomach; there was little they could do for him except give him morphine and label clearly the size of the injection so that when he eventually got in the hands of the doctors they would know what had been put into him. The motor mechanic from 636 was alive but unconscious and none of their efforts to revive him succeeded; he died about four that morning.

A review of what had happened revealed that 636 *had* seen the challenge but not in time to reply before one of her gunners opened fire, without orders. This resulted in 658's fierce reply.

The next day the body of the motor mechanic, stitched in canvas, was buried at sea. His Captain, Freddie Warner, despite his pain and obviously still suffering from shock, insisted on taking the funeral service: no guard or band, no funeral firing party, no official mourners, just a group of seamen standing bare-headed as the funeral service was read.

"For as much as it hath pleased Almighty God of his great mercy to take unto himself the soul of our dear brother here departed, we therefore commit his body to the sea . . . "

The weighted canvas bundle slipped quietly into the sea.

Burke returned to their new and more northern base in Bastia, Corsica. The wounded were taken to the local hospital, which the Germans had abandoned only a week before. A community of nuns had taken it over and one French surgeon was trying to cope with the wounded from the recent land battle of liberation. Water was scarce, there was a shortage of nurses and medical supplies, and the place was terribly overcrowded. Burke's navigator, Rover Reynolds, said, "As I walked along a corridor filthy with unswept refuse I glanced into one of the wards [and] my heart sank. The scene reminded me of a picture I had seen of a Crimean War hospital before Florence Nightingale got to work. The patients were ill-clad and dirty and there was nothing but shabby blankets on the beds. Everywhere were signs of death and hopelessness. Could we send our men in here?"* In any event, they did; there was nowhere else to send them. Chiswell had his arm amputated and was sent home; Freddie Warner's wounds were treated and he was sent to a shore base with Bobby Allan. The first evening Burke visited his wounded. Balderson seemed to know he was going to die. In spite of his obvious pain, he smiled and whispered to Burke, "Good luck in 658, sir – I was proud to serve in her." He died that night.

MGB 658 had sunk two flak ships unaided; this was undoubtedly a victory and a major engagement in the annals of Coastal Forces. The whole sense of victory, of course, was as ashes in their mouths because of the deaths of their friends in 636. According to the testimony of those shot at it was *not* the fault of Burke. Nevertheless, it was *he* who had ordered "Open fire" – admittedly after he had been fired upon. The loneliness of command consists of many things. This perhaps is the keenest aspect to that loneliness, the death of friends where you have been the cause. There was nothing anyone could do to ease his pain. He was the Captain and the burden was his alone. He would have to live with the memory of it, alone with incommunicable grief.

\* \* \*

In April, 1943, the American PTs (Patrol Torpedo, the Higgins design) unloaded from the oiler *Enoree* at Gibraltar. They were seventy-seven feet long, had a twenty-foot beam, and drew four-feet loaded. The armament was two twin .5-inch machine guns and four torpedoes. Three twelve-cylinder 1,200 hp Packard engines gave them a top speed of forty knots. They displaced sixty tons. But as far as the British gun boats and torpedo boats were concerned, their main armament was their modern radar. This was PT Squadron 15, twelve boats. Their radar changed the whole aspect of coastal warfare in the Aegean and Tyrrhenian. Instead of a radar scan that only gave range and bearing and had to be moved around by hand, they had a radar set that rotated constantly and showed on a screen a clear view of everything around them – the

---

*L.C. Reynolds, *Gunboat 658*.

whole 360 degrees. The PT radar showed a picture of the immediate area (out to ten miles) – the islands, the rocks, and the ships under way – as God sees them, from above, with the PT boat in the middle of the scan. What is around shows in green luminance each time the aerial swings past it ("blips," they are called). Henceforth, our MGB flotillas would always operate with one America PT to act as the "eyes" for our boats.

These USN PTs used to go out but they were never a great success. They had poor torpedoes to begin with, and in the opinion of the Canadian captains they had poor leadership. They were timid, not aggressive. We had been at this since 1940 but they had just come from a school in Miami. Burke says, "The USN flotilla had surface radar which was far superior to ours. So we would take one of them with us; it was invaluable. But it was amazing how *unaggressive* they were. They were picked men; the officers and ratings were all picked men, chosen to serve in USN PT boats. We were getting whatever the manning pool drafted us and by that time, of course, they were scraping the bottom of the barrel. But I wouldn't have traded one British matelot for five Americans. The USN boats would guide us in to the target and that's all they would do. They'd turn away and retire. It was incredible! But we didn't mention it and they didn't choose to bring it up."

Ladner says, "They had four torpedoes on their ELCO boats and twin .5-inch, I think, enough firepower to be of some use. One would have thought, because they had seen very little action, that they would have been just aching to get into these gun actions but they showed no inclination whatsoever. Indeed, the whole of their record in the Mediterranean was not distinguished. I can't remember any, but they had maybe one successful action. Their idea was to fire their torpedoes at maximum range and retire. They didn't show any aggressive wish to get in and mix it up, get close. Or to get into gun actions.*

"One night we were off the Vada Rocks between Leghorn and Elba,

---

*It has not been possible to ascertain if these were the orders given to the flotilla leader by Washington. But between November, 1943, and April, 1945, they fought ten battles on their own and sank only one F-lighter and one E-boat. Cunningham had refused some actions ordered by London because he could not squander ships. Dönitz had his U-boats firing at extreme range until Otto Kretchner in U-99 showed him that getting in the middle of our convoys produced the best result. He would steam down the centre lane, firing to starboard and port. He sank more of our ships than any other U-boat commander, and was called "the Tonnage King." He told us about this in Canada after the war, that to be aggressive was the only way to win.

a good place to find targets . . . We were . . . being told to go where our intelligence *knew* the enemy would be. How our intelligence was always correct was amazing to us. So, we were on patrol and got a signal, 'Suspected enemy movements in Vada Rocks area. You are to proceed immediately to patrol southward from Spezia to Piombino.' They were there, true enough, and we had a brisk fire fight."

Ladner had many actions. "We used to go up to the French and Italian coasts. We went in to La Spezia one night and sank the boom-defence vessel. It was an insulting thing to do and started all the shore defences going. So our boats just withdrew and watched all these *huge* guns being fired; their projectiles were nowhere near us."

Ladner was told off to run the Beach Officer around in the invasion at Anzio. "I had this General plus two RN fellows. My job was just to look after them, take them wherever they wanted to go along the beachhead. It was a very, very dangerous area to be in, actually. At that time the Germans had got the glider bombs going, guided by radio, the "Chase me Charlie." They shot the sterns off a couple of cruisers.

"After Anzio we went to Capri. So we went in [and] 'captured' the Isle of Capri. It was nothing; just a nothing. We sailed into the harbour and all we did was walk ashore. The local populace were there to welcome us, clapping and cheering. Viva, Viva."

Maitland set up his shore base there. "So we 'liberated' the Isle of Capri. The Krauts had left three days ago. Thank God they had! There wasn't any action because the Italian navy had collapsed. There was an Italian petty officer there who was pro-British. I said, 'The first thing we're going to need tomorrow morning is a good car.' There were only nine cars on the island. He brings down this great long Lancia *and* provided a driver. 'The next thing we need is a shore base, an abandoned villa might be suitable.' So he went on a villa-inspection tour of the highest ground in Capri; it was beautiful country. There was a funicular from the port to the top. You could drive up but this was for those walking; it was like an alpine funicular at a ski resort. So we take over Count Chiano's villa – Mussolini's son-in-law. My God! What a place he'd put together there (he was in charge of road construction during some part of the war and had built a highway from Rome to Naples. So he just added a villa – just part of the road contract). It was a magnificent place. I'd never seen anything like it – swimming pools, huge baths. It was the first time I'd ever sat on a toilet with a mink seat-cover. We lived pretty well for a while; we even had our own orchestra.

"We ran a few patrols; there was a lull in the battles; we didn't mind. Then this American destroyer came into port, the USS *Knight*. There was a task force forming up; we were to join under the command of *Knight*. The Captain was a super fellow. *But*, the signal hadn't said that this was a Special Operations vessel and that there was a command force aboard. . . .

"But she steamed in, a lovely ship, a beautiful 2,000 tonner. I reported aboard to the Captain, who apprised me of the situation that they had this force aboard for special duties. I said, 'Well, what do you want us to do, sir?'

" 'I think the best thing – it's up to them – but I think if you report here at ten o'clock tomorrow morning we'll decide.'

"So I reported at ten o'clock the next morning in the wardroom of the *Knight* and there I met this Special Force, comprised of Lieutenant-Commander Douglas Fairbanks, Jr., Lieutenant-Commander Henry North (whose family were the controlling interest in Ringling Brothers Circus), and two famous war correspondents, Joseph Knickerbocker and John Steinbeck. Here were these people in the wardroom and *this* was the Special Force. Fairbanks was in charge. Fairbanks, at ten o'clock in the morning, was lounging on the settee in the wardroom in a dressing gown. He had a steward up there with his suitcase, getting out a couple dozen pairs of silk stockings. It seemed the American Rangers had got life set up for him on the island before *he* got there. Honest to God! It was like a three-ring circus.

"He said, 'Well, we haven't really got any plans yet regarding operations, so we'll just take a day to settle in so will you come back at ten o'clock tomorrow morning, please?'

"So I do and I'm told the same story. 'Come back at ten o'clock tomorrow.' There was not a thing we could do. We were part of this task force and we had to report to this USN Captain. So, we took a bit of time off as well. I had an Italian who got some shotguns out of the lockup in the city hall and we did a little quail shooting at the other end of the island. It was fun and it augmented the food rations. Finally, after the best part of a week they got around to it.

"We were going to capture the island of Ischia. Capri is at the south end of the Bay of Naples, which is like a big half-moon, and at the north end were the islands of Procheda and Ischia. Two beautiful islands, not that Capri wasn't a beautiful place but they were, in my view, far more beautiful with their little built-up harbours and piers. We were going to capture Ischia. So I go down to the wardroom with Tommy Ladner (Corny Burke wasn't there at that time, he was down in Malta), Tommy and the other skippers. I take them all down and we go through the operation orders. What we're going to do is, we're going to head out to sea just at dusk. This is a formidable show, but the *Knight* isn't going to participate in this – the waters are too enclosed and they can't risk the vessel. The operation would be run from my boat. We had five MGBs. A little before dusk, earlier, we'd made a great fuss about leaving harbour and heading out to sea as though we were going somewhere. That was the whole idea, a feint; there might be some Krauts still on the island, or a spy who would send a message that our boats had gone to the north. Good thinking. We were going to alter course after dark and come in on the south side of Ischia, then go up around into the east shore where there is a nice little bay with a long dock. One a.m. was H-hour.

"So we're all strung out and this boat of mine had a fairly spacious bridge for three officers and a couple of lookouts; but now I had these five (Fairbanks and company) and a chief boatswain, USN, a couple of guys with r/t, and ten Rangers on deck aft. Five on each side, with all their arms and ammo. But the funniest part of it all was Knickerbocker. He was up abaft our forward gun. It was a *beautiful* night; dark, thank God! You don't want to be out in the full moon. (Any of these operations, like in the North Sea, or wherever you are, you *don't* operate at night in full moon. You're a sitting duck. At least you try not to; sometimes it's unavoidable.) This was a perfect night. There was no moon, it was still and clear, just a lovely night to go yachting. So we're cruising along and we have a chart table just off the bridge with a little light on it so you can see. I carefully looked at the chart before we left but you don't remember all the small details. By now I had traded some of our rum for an American surface warning radar. They were beautiful things; they'd pick up anything or everything. So we were going along – there was a little tweet on the voice pipe. My radar fellow, Horley, down below, said, " 'Captain, sir, a fairly strong echo about 2,800 yards fine on the port bow.' Horley could tell. If a blip was wooden his echo was a little fuzzy; if it was steel the echo was sharp. He said, 'Sir, I think it looks something like an armed trawler, about a 150-foot trawler. It's a very sharp echo.'

" 'Is it moving?'

" 'It's not moving, sir.'

"We were going very slowly, about eight knots, so we're not closing very quickly. I called the boats astern and told them I had a blip ahead. I wasn't sure what it was. I thought it might be an armed trawler, and that we'd just keep on the present course and when we got a little closer to whatever it is, 'Tom, you and I will detach and take on the trawler;

the rest just continue as planned.' Because they had most of the American troops on board.

"For gunnery control from the bridge, the gunners had earphones, which were not always working satisfactorily as communication with the guns. So we had mounted loud hailers right behind the forward gun and the aftermost gun – plain, ordinary loud hailers . . . when you put it on you go, "phew, phew," to test it. It sort of spits a bit. I went, "phew, phew," and right away the gun's crew know I'm going to pass them a message.

Knickerbocker pops his head up and said, 'Would you do that again, Captain? Would you do that again, please?'

"Here I am, looking for an enemy and wondering what to do and all these people want is news. I'm flabbergasted. Do what sort of thing? So I gave it another 'phew' to test it and then I hear Knickerbocker talking into this machine of his.

" 'And here we are. There's an enemy battleship on our port bow but the Captain has decided to continue and will attack the enemy before . . .' "You see, these fellows, Knickerbocker and Steinbeck, that's the kind of stuff they write. But this was all going to the New York papers – DOUGLAS FAIRBANKS AT SEA.

"But I thought that there was something wrong about this target. It just didn't *feel* right; there was something wrong. Nevertheless, the target was there so I just alerted the gunners and then carried on. As soon as I did that, the loud hailer alerting, again he was taping this.

" 'Here we are facing the enemy who are ahead of us and you can hear the gunfire.'

"What a lot of baloney. Anyway, then Horley called me up and said, 'There's something about that, sir. It's becoming fuzzy.'

"It suddenly dawned on me and I said, 'Hey, Steve, take a look at the chart.' Steve Rendell was my Number One.

" 'Yeah, it's a rock. It's a rock right off the point. It shows on the chart.'

" 'Thank God.'

"We go across this half-moon bay. I took the boats right straight across, then I did a Nine Blue turn. I said, 'The first two boats, Tom, you and I, will put on full speed and go right into the inner end, into the end of the dock, even to the point of grounding. The other boats, you follow in and then the Rangers can jump off the dock.'

"Well, people say nobody gets frightened in action or there isn't such a thing as fear. I can tell you, there is. It's not fear, it's apprehension.

Apprehension and your mouth goes dry. You can hardly talk. That's what apprehension and fear are, in my book. With all these Yanks aboard I wasn't a free agent to do what I wanted. These Rangers depended on us. Anyway, in we go. My God! The landing we did at Capri was nothing in the area of comic opera; in Ischia there were twenty-five hundred people to greet us – at the end of the dock, on the beach, in this lovely open green, all singing, dressed up, wearing flowers. And, in amongst them, were about a dozen U.S. Rangers. They had all the pretty girls, of course. I damn near . . . I was so mad.

"Well, the boats went alongside the jetty and landed the Rangers as planned. We went alongside and did exactly as planned and off jumps Fairbanks and his gang and up they go and they meet the Mayor. This was all pre-arranged; the Mayor surrenders the island to Douglas Fairbanks.

"Then the booze is opened up and it was the damnedest party. I was terrified. The first thing I did was to get the boats all turned around, head to sea. This seemed only prudent in this crazy war.

"There were about fifty U.S. Rangers already there; they didn't need us anyway because *they* knew what we *didn't* know. Their own Rangers were already there. This was just a show. Isn't that terrible? About an hour later the party was getting louder and louder. I turned the boat over to Rendell and went up to Fairbanks.

"Look, I've got five boats and a lot of men and a lot of equipment and the longer we hang around here, the greater the exposure. I'm getting off here and taking my boats *now*. If you want to come, fine. If you don't, that's okay with me.

"Fairbanks was very courteous and apologetic. 'I'm terribly sorry. I didn't appreciate it but you're absolutely right.'

"He was superb, but in the meantime he was having a good time. Oh, hell! He ordered his gang out to the boats and away. Photographers! There certainly were lots of pictures. There were pictures of Fairbanks accepting the surrender from the Mayor. So we get on the boat and we head back and as you can imagine, in disgust. Our wardroom was about twice the size of a table. It was a three-officer wardroom so it didn't have to be very big. But Fairbanks asked me if we had any Scotch or gin or anything on the boat. I said, I had. I had three bottles of Scotch left. I put two bottles out. We were two hours getting back to Capri and we got back about five in the morning; it was light then. While they were sitting down there they were cooking up this news release which was later printed in the papers. They drank up my two bottles of whisky, got off the boat absolutely plastered. My crew were so damn disgusted.

"When they got off, this boatswain from the USS *Knight*, a regular pusser U.S. Navy fellow, came up on the bridge – everybody else of the U.S. forces trooped off. He snapped to attention.

" 'May I have a word with you, please, Captain?'

" 'Certainly.'

" 'Sir, I regret the activities of my officers. There's nothing I can do about it but I tender my own *personal* apology.'

"That was a professional sailor talking."

Ladner thought Fairbanks a fraud. "He was a joke! I gather he got a DSC for that. The fellow was a nothing. Those boats didn't do anything, didn't know how to do anything. I terrified the Yanks once. I was sent out in my boat with two American observers to attract fire from the shore in order to locate the batteries. We had aircraft overhead spotting the shore batteries and this American guy nearly went out of his mind. I would make smoke and then go into the smoke and come out again and all these shore batteries would fire at us. We did that for a couple of hours. It was quite a hair-raising episode. But our observing aircraft did pinpoint all those guns and they they brought in these Mosquito bombers and demolished them. Those Mosquitos were lethal."

Naples fell. It was a shambles; there were fifty-seven ships sunk in the harbour. The old saying is "See Naples and die." John Charles, who was there in *Laforey*, said, "Smell Naples and die."

Ladner was sent with the port party. "I had an Admiral and others but I don't know who they were. It was chaos. We were lying alongside and along came a whole platoon of Americans with rifles at the high port. They were all fussing around, looking under debris and through buildings and verandas. I didn't know what it was all about. I was about to take off again because I thought maybe the port party had been a little too early in getting there. I didn't like entering towns until the enemy had departed. It turned out to be General Mark Clark coming along with outriders and a convoy of jeeps and God knows what. He drove by my boat. I piped him. He didn't respond. He was just seeing what the harbour was like. An hour later along comes one jeep, one jeep with one senior officer and a driver; another jeep was astern of this general. He got out and walked over. It was General Alexander. He asked, 'How is everything? What does it look like to you?' That type of thing. But he was unaccompanied by anybody – just the two jeeps.

"Then we went up to Corsica. Out of Corsica we did the invasion of Elba, which was a very bloody affair. We had been over in Elba a lot. We were landing saboteurs and resistance fighters, at night. The Marine Commandos were very, very big on getting ashore on Elba. Of course, the French had a battalion of Goumier waiting for the invasion. They were a lot of fun. They were there with their tents, their goats, and their wives. They were Berbers – ruthless fighters – and liked the knife more than the gun. Geez, that knife was four-feet long. They usually cut the balls and one leg off an enemy and left him. They were bad for the Germans' morale. The landing was to be on the south coast, dozens of landing craft, destroyers, and a few cruisers. We would stand off and patrol the perimeter of the landing area."

To hold Elba would be an immense advantage and assist the advance toward Florence and Leghorn. The actual landing was preceded by the usual preliminaries. The Canadian flotilla was given its first cloak-and-dagger operation, into which they entered with great enthusiasm (actually, they used the term "False Nose" operation). Anyway, it was stealthy. Three French Agents were to be landed on Elba, led by a French Capitaine de Corvette (Lieutenant-Commander). They loaded the equipment of Burke's 658. It seemed to be much more than could be carried in the dinghy the Frenchmen brought with them, so the dinghy, the packs, sacks, wireless set, and a considerable armoury of guns and knives were taken on board 658. Two miles off the beach they stopped, launched the dinghy, then got under way slowly, towing the dinghy astern. They crept to about a hundred yards from shore and stopped again. The clang of the engine room telegraph seemed louder than usual. All spoke in whispers. It was eleven p.m., time for the party to land. The dinghy was hauled from aft alongside and the four Frenchmen solemnly shook hands with all who were within handshaking distance. The first climbed down.

It is hard enough for a professional seaman to jump into a small bobbing dinghy with a rolling hull alongside it. The first got in, but the second stumbled over the thwart, throwing all his weight to one side of the dinghy and rocking it madly. A flood of French abuse betrayed the anxiety of the man already in the boat clutching wildly at the gunwale. He dropped his pack but fortunately it fell inboard. Before number two had really settled himself, number three arrived hissing a warning. He stretched out a leg and stepped onto the central thwart, transferred his weight, and then found to his horror that the dinghy was sliding away from the ladder. Soon his body was a rigid arc joining the dinghy and the MTB – almost horizontal. He shrieked in fear. A line was tossed to the dinghy and she was hauled in alongside; the three settled down. All now seemed well, so the French officer turned and dropped efficiently into place. Our MTB boys waved and watched them draw away into the dark.

But the dinghy had travelled only a hundred feet when two of the

Agents, heretofore sitting peacefully in the stern, stood up. The naval officer, knowing the meaning of centre of gravity, rested on his oars and ordered them to sit down. They continued to move and the dinghy rocked, but still they did not sit down. In front of the horrified eyes of 658's crew, the larger of the two lost his balance and fell, yelling, into the water. This sudden removal of 180 pounds from one side gave a sharp list to port and water began to pour in. The situation was not yet hopeless but the man in the bow made it so by bending over and trying to pull his extremely frightened friend into the dinghy. The laws of stability had been outraged too often. The dinghy rolled right over. There was a second's silence, then the night was rent with thrashing and shouting. The four made a noise worthy of forty-four. The night rang with cries of the distraught Frenchmen and the hoarse encouragement of the MTBS crew. Two of the Agents were manhandled on board but the other two seemed unable to help themselves and continued to shriek in the upper register. Any Germans nearby would have thought it was a combined operation with the shouting of the French and English, that the Allies were about to land in force. One Frenchman was helped by Able Seaman Smith, who dived in, brought him alongside, and heaved him on board. But they could find no sign of the Capitaine de Corvette, although they could hear him shouting. Once again Smith dived over and realized that the French officer had got himself wedged under the chine near the bows. As the boat lifted in the slight swell, each surge gave the poor fellow a bang on the head, and he was at last dragged aboard.

Burke was becoming anxious by now as a northerly wind had sprung up and they were drifting closer to a point on which there might well be a German battery. But with the last Frenchman embarked, Burke went ahead slowly with his engines and quietly crept away. The French officer decided to send only one Agent ashore in spite of the loss of the radio equipment. So just after midnight they closed the beach again and this time 658's dinghy was used. Able Seaman Smith helped paddle the Agent ashore. They strained their eyes to watch for the dinghy's return. Return it did, and that was the last they knew of that operation.

The invasion of Elba was a major commission for the Free French under a hitherto unknown General Lattre de Tassigny. The plan was that a large force of French infantry would be landed; it had a high proportion of colonial troops, including the fierce Goums.

Burke had been in and out of hospital for the last year with stomach complaints and this was so in June, 1944, before Elba – Operation Brassard. The First Lieutenant, Rover Reynolds, was in command during his absence and one afternoon saw a bevy of beribboned and aiguilletted officers heading toward his boat. Luckily, he had just changed into a clean set of whites and so had the quartermaster. It was General de Tassigne with senior staff officers; apparently he wished to take a tour of the French soldiers in their anchorage. The crew of 658, who had been working a various jobs on the upper deck in their dirty khaki uniforms, disappeared one by one and reappeared in spotless whites as though this was their everyday dress. The General stood on high on the searchlight platform so he could be cheered by his troops and he stopped in the middle of the anchorage and delivered a magnificently vehement and patriotic exhortation over the loud hailer. The gallant troops of Free France were about to move into their first assault, free their great country from the hated Hun to regain their rightful place in Europe. He was landed and the flotilla slipped an hour before sunset for the thirty-mile trip to Elba, zigzagging through mines cut loose by the minesweepers in the van. Three rocket ships followed astern of the minesweepers.

At H-hour a sheath of flame enveloped the hull of each rocket ship as hundreds of missiles soared toward the beach – 4,000 rockets fired in four minutes. But it was apparent that *this* landing was not going to be unopposed. Tracer swung out form the shore and crisscrossed the beaches.

Lieutenant Micky Fynn was in the Elba landings and right in the middle of that rocket firing; it was a bloody business landing his naval Commandos. The French forces had been reconstituted under General Giraud and Admiral Darlan; they had opposed us in North Africa and had now come over to our side. French troops had been demoralized, not knowing which side they were on, and so the Allied High Command decided that they needed to get into action. There were British landing craft supported by some British gun boats, destroyers, and the old China gun boats. (The *Cock Chafer* was one; they were all named after insects. These carried a 4.7-inch and were shallow draught for going up China's rivers, which made them very useful in landing craft support.)

Fynn explains: "This assault force was not landed from landing ships – the 4,000-tonners. We were towed from Bastia by MLS. The soldiers were on board the MLS to give them some comfort crossing. The MLS slipped our tows about five miles out. We went alongside the

MLs, picked up our troops, and went in. We didn't have the range, didn't have the gas to go the whole way under our own power.

"The invasion of Elba had been timed for a certain hour and day and then Intelligence found out that the Germans knew this invasion was coming. So it was decided to sail the whole landing force at the scheduled time and instead of going to Elba head straight for the Italian coast just south of Anzio. We would show ourselves at dusk and during the night just beetle back and let the Germans think their intelligence had been wrong. We left one or two destroyers behind just banging off in the general direction of the land and at night we came back to our base. This was Operation Spam. Anyway, the next day a message came, 'Spam received.' which meant that the Germans had bought our feint. But the whole operation was put back a month. Now, the operation had been based on the intelligence that Elba was held mainly by Italians, whose interest in the war was pretty low; and so the landing should have been fairly soft, easy. But between the feint and when we *did* go in, the Germans had reinforced the whole island with ss troops, crack troops. When the operation took place they were expecting us.

"The south was where the main landings were going to be, the French troops and British landing craft. There was a force of American PTs who were going to carry out a feint off the northern coast. Their job was to go in close to the north coast and play recordings of troops wading ashore. Hard to believe, isn't it? They were commanded by Lieutenant-Commander Douglas Fairbanks, Jr., who was a delightful man. He lived on board our mother ship. Our Admiral for this, and who also lived on board, was Tom Troubridge.

"The landing beach was about three-quarters of a circle and on either side of the pinchers of the circle were gun emplacements which could sweep that beach. They were at the entrance to the harbour on high ground. On the western side of the entrance was a stone mole sticking out and on the inshore side of that mole was where a German flak-lighter lay and, of course, she had 88mm guns which could also control the whole landing beach. Now, this mole had on the seaward side of it an eight-foot-high wall. That F-lighter had to be immobilized. Two LCAs were chosen. I was one.

"We were the last two craft in the port column. About 200 yards from that mole, we two did a forty-five-degree turn to port, which would head us straight for the mole in quarter-line. As we get alongside the mole we now execute a forty-five-degree turn to starboard, northeast. Everything opened up on us. I remember at that time, in bravado if you like, I said, 'Who needs to wear one of these damn tin hats? They're no good anyway.' So I am wearing my cloth cap going in and when everything came at us, 'Where's my tin hat, where's my tin hat?' Bang, we get alongside. Simultaneously, over go the grappling irons.

"But, we're carrying naval commandos. These poor buggers were not *really* commandos, not at all like the Royal Marines. They were beach commandos and they were the poor guys who were usually put ashore with the first wave to set the directing markers, direct traffic and so on. In the planning stage it had called for a proper commando force to do this job of going over the wall and boarding the F-lighter and capturing her. The powers that be said, 'We don't have professional commandos available. You've got commandos. Use your own.' So these poor guys who *really* weren't trained for this sort of thing had to accept this job. The idea was the grappling hooks would go over the wall, shinny up the ropes, over the wall, and board the German vessel. So we got alongside and absolute hell was breaking loose. This was a very short mole with a very steep bluff on the inshore end. In the gun flashes we could see German troops, lobbing grenades at us. The naval commando officer in the lead boat (we were number two astern of him), as he got alongside, was to signal a blue flash to say 'Over grapple hooks.' But a shell hit the armoured door behind which he was crouching, ready to go; as the shell hit the armoured door a steel splinter went through his temple. He was just able to get away his blue flash and he was dead.

"So over they go and here were the Germans lobbing grenades at us. I had one fellow who was less than an arm's length away from me who had one go off directly under him. He had the whole of his buttocks blown away. Now, he is there under the armoured deck, apparently seated there, and all the rest of his people have gone over the side.

" 'Come on, that man, get up; over the side with you.'

" 'I can't, sir.'

" 'What do you mean can't? Get *up*.'

" 'I can't, sir.'

"With that he rolled over and there all his backside was missing. We were issued with little morphine tubes (like a toothpaste tube) onto which you screwed a hypodermic. This fellow was in terrible pain and I gave him one tube of that as we were trying to fire back at these bloody Jerries that we could see still in the gun flashes lobbing grenades . . .

"We had rifles, stens, and strip Lewis and we're firing back. The Senior Officer of our landing was in my boat. His orders had been to radio back when we were alongside. Now, he was unable to establish radio contact. It didn't make any difference; we were alongside. Our job, once the F-lighter was secure, was then to go round the mole and tow her away. Okay, this guy has been unable to establish radio contact, so he said, 'You'll have to take me out to one of the major landing craft where I can make my radio signal.'

"I did and then returned.

"We're running in to the mole again and suddenly there is the most God-awful explosion. The whole of the mole seems to go up. Certainly three-quarters of the mole is missing. I thought, 'Oh, my God! Those poor guys will all be gone. The F-lighter has blown up! I thought it was the ammunition. Eventually it turned out that the Germans had the mole mined and they blew it up themselves. Anyway, there I am, running in. We couldn't see the other landing craft. The damn battle is finished as far as we're concerned. By then the whole of the bay is full of major landing craft. They've all been hit and some are sinking in the bay. Men everywhere, swimming. It looks as if all our operation was at an end – I just went round the bay picking up swimmers. I went over the side half-a-dozen times to help these guys on board. We lowered the ramp. I was pushing them up and the other guys were pulling them in. Everytime I went over the side I took off a little bit more of my clothing. In the end I was standing there in a pair of underpants (in that nice Mediterranean weather) helping get these survivors. We were gradually working our way into the mole just to see who was there. When we get there, there's the remains of the F-lighter, bottom side up. I'm going in to see what I can do with her and just as we get near her (she's just glowing red) I thought, 'Oh my God! She's going to explode. Fires down below, she's just red hot.' Just as I was going to sheer away, I heard a very, very weak cry from the remains of the mole. I look and there are the survivors of our other landing craft, a bedraggled lot. She had been bodily lifted by the explosion and is up on the rock. There are about half-a-dozen of our guys there. I picked them off and then found that we are the *only* vessel moving in the whole harbour. We are the target of all the shore batteries."

Unknown to Fynn at the time but heard by the Canadian MGB flotilla offshore was the chatter between the land forces and the headquarters ship of Admiral Troubridge. Over the r/t, tuned to the invasion wavelength, they heard reports from the Senior Naval Officer Landing (SNOL), Captain Errol Turner, RN.

"Amber Beach impossible . . . Heavy fire from village . . . One craft sank, all others hit. Landed but had to withdraw . . . Suggest we try alternative landing Green Beach . . . Amber and Red Beach both covered by crossfire from batteries." The Canadians were lying three miles off-shore to make sure the invasion went uninterrupted from seaward. All was quiet out there and so they had a grandstand view of the landing. As daylight came the SNOL ordered the next wave of LCIs and LCTs into Green Beach.

In Fynn's area the rest of the landing force got ashore, but they had to withdraw and try again on another beach. They ran the gauntlet of the shore batteries; the F-lighter didn't open up on them because she was being attacked by our people, who were hand-to-hand fighting with the F-lighter crew.

"This was the first occasion on which I saw rocket ships and that was quite an experience. We had to carry radar reflectors so that they could see where we were on their screen and they would fire when we were about 300 yards off the entrance and those five-inch rockets they reckoned that in about ten minutes would get the same amount of high explosive ashore that a six-inch cruiser would get firing all day. They had fired when we were on the way in. We heard this terrible rush over our heads, which was quite awe-inspiring in itself. Then it just seemed the whole beach was lifted. Then the main landing craft went in, got troops ashore, and they went inland. Then the landing craft withdrew. The wave went ashore and inland. The Germans were all hit by the rocket fire. The Senior Naval Landing Officer was "Flash Alf", a Lieutenant-Commander, Acting Commander, acting Captain while holding this appointment. In the wash-up afterwards he said that the shock wave had stunned all the Germans. Those who were not killed were knocked out for about five minutes. They were knocked out and regained con-sciousness when the first wave of our troops was inland. The Germans came up behind them. This meant that the initial wave had Germans in front and Germans behind; they got badly knocked about. Then the follow-up landing craft (major landing craft, the LCIs and LCTs), when *they* came in, were hit by all the guns that the Germans had and these were the guys in the bay, sinking, where I was picking up the survivors. So we were beetling out of there just as fast as we can. We're the only craft moving and they're firing everything at us.

"Then a 20mm gets a line on us and every third one is a tracer. He's got a line on us directly towards our stern and you could see the splashes coming along the water closer and closer. Then they just stopped. They're still coming but we are just out of his range. While we were going out my coxswain turned to me and said, 'You know, sir, we're going right over that shallow anti-landing-craft minefield.'

'I know. We've got a chance this way. That way we're just going to run into the guns.'

"We just cleared. We finally got out of the area and a harbour defence ML, commanded by a young RN sub-lieutenant, took on board all the people I'd pulled out of the water. And he then told us, 'You know, that beach has been abandoned for the last hour.'

"They'd given up the assault when the major landing craft had been hit so badly and the *whole* landing force had been taken round to the secondary beach, called Green Beach, I think.

"We didn't know this. Now, I'm taking on water at a hell of a rate. I've got a hole in my hull from a grenade. That's the one thing about an LCA, beautifully built the original ones were, double-diagonal mahogany with calico between bedded in white lead, beautifully built, strong as can be. But the bottom, of course, is just wood. It was just the sides and the half-decking which were armour-plated. The grenades had made a bloody big hole in the bottom and we're taking in water at a great speed. One of the French colonial troops I had pulled out of the water couldn't swim. What he'd done was he'd got an orange box and tied it to his chest, which kept him afloat. So, we found this orange box, pulled it apart and there were the pieces of wood with the nails sticking out. We had a blanket and so I made a sort of tingle. I put the blanket over the hole and nailed the orange box top over this.

"We were able to cut down the flow of water enough that we could pump with the old hand pump and managed to keep afloat. We found an LCI which was going back to Bastia. I tagged on to her and got towed back. We arrived around midday in this sinking condition. We had to pump all the way. All I had now was the crew and we were taking turns on the pump just to keep afloat and were getting exhausted, quite apart from the fatigue, from the excitement of the whole thing. We were just about dead on our feet. We got right under a crane.

"I said, 'I'll need a lift. The boat is sinking fast.'

"Some petty officer said, 'Oh, can't lift you, sir. Everyone's gone to dinner. You'll have to keep pumping for a while yet.'

" 'Like hell we are, the bloody thing can sink where she is.'

"I told my guys to go ashore. We caught the next boat back to Ajjacio in Corsica, where my mother ship, HMS *Royal Scotsman*, was. God knows what happened to the landing craft. She may have sunk. I don't know. Maybe the petty officer decided he'd better get some troops to leave dinner and get the crane going. I'll never know."

✳  ✳  ✳

While Micky Fynn was solving his problems the destroyers kept up a direct bombardment, but the Canadian flotilla offshore was suddenly jolted out of its security by the whoooooosshh and the crump of a landing shell – they were under fire from a shore battery. One of the Landing Craft Gun – LCG 8 – engaged this battery with her 4.7-inch guns and silenced it. The flotilla then led the empty boats back to their base but on the way ran into a large ship, which they turned to engage.

It was evident that she was large enough to warrant torpedoes. These were fired. They missed. Tommy Ladner was asked for illumination and there was the thump-thump-thump of his pom-poms and then a little group of tiny flares showed up in their ghostly light what their enemy was. It was a destroyer heading toward them at high speed, obviously trying to ram. Every starboard gun poured out its hail of lead as the range closed and Reynolds reports that he had "a vivid picture of this long low craft with the streamlined funnel characteristics of Italian destroyers hurtling across our stern. We could do nothing to prevent him crossing our T in reverse. When he was right astern only our 6-pounder could bear, whereas all his guns were firing on the beam with the maximum broadside. So, for what we are about to receive may the Lord make us truly thankful . . ."

A spout of shells came ripping up the deck. The bridge was filled with noise and light and all hands knocked down. All except Reynolds were wounded and the mast had collapsed and pinned them all. One hand was dead, two badly wounded, the coxswain's legs were peppered with shrapnel, and the signalman's face was bleeding. Able Seaman McEwan had his foot hanging by a slender thread from a shattered ankle. There was no way of dressing the wound so it was cut off and the tourniquet applied to the stump. The foot was wrapped in a towel and thrown over the side. "McEwan was conscious at the time," said Reynolds, "and extremely calm. He saw Mike throw his gruesome parcel overboard and said, 'That was my foot, wasn't it, sir?' "

Two days after the action they held the funeral of the three ratings who had been killed and this time it was from the naval base in Bastia and the formal naval funeral was observed. Almost the whole base embarked in boats of the flotilla, Captain Dickinson and Commander Allan and representatives of each boat. There was a firing party, ship-mates of the dead men, and Commander Allan took the service himself. As the volleys rang out the flag-draped bodies were slipped into the sea and there followed two minutes of silence and return into Bastia at slow speed and ensigns at half-mast.

Elba surrendered on 10 July 1944 and that small skirmish in the arena of total war of the whole Mediterranean was over. But it had been the bloodiest, most bitterly opposed landing so far. The patrols resumed through July and toward the end of the month their keenness was given its highest accolade so far.

Commander Allan submitted a report to the Captain of Coastal Forces summarizing the work of the Coastal Forces at La Maddalena and Bastia for the first six months of 1944. It began,

> Having been in Coastal Forces for four and a half years, I'm inclined to think that the last six months have been in every respect the happiest that have ever been known, not only to me personally, but to Coastal Forces in general.
>
> I attribute this largely to the magnificent spirit in the flotillas attached. The 56th flotilla under its all-Canadian leadership infected us all with the spirit of New World camaraderie and almost embarrassing keenness . . .

Morale is invariably high when the ship has a captain whom the troops trust and who is successful in battle. Still, there are constant attacks on morale. One was that the mail never got through before one or two months; another was that the food was beginning to jade even the most insensitive palate. The Royal Navy has endless supplies of kippers and herring-in-tomato-sauce. They saw no fresh fruit or meat or vegetables for months; the only butter, a rare allocation, was in tins. Bread was scarce, but by foraging in both Bastia and La Maddalena they managed to get a small amount at the base each day from the local bakers. Once, alongside the cruiser *Uganda*, Burke traded gin for bread. MTB 658's cook, Able Seaman Jock Elliot, was self-taught but there was little he could do with the dehydrated potatoes that were their staple. His ingenuity caused him to take the herring-in-tomato-sauce and, when he had bread crumbs, grill them and serve them as "Sicilian lake trout." That had been some months ago; the same dish was now "Sardinian lake trout," and as the flotilla moved north it became "Corsican lake trout." La Maddalena had little to offer in the way of shore-going attractions; it is a rocky, arid island, as barren and featureless as Scapa Flow, with few facilities for games apart from swimming. Most of the hands spent their time on board even when free to go ashore. Burke, fun-loving and always sensitive to the fact that his job, (besides driving his ship) was to entertain the crew, made a raid on a warehouse in the old

Italian base and brought back two tablecloths with napkins to match. He also scrounged heavy silver serving dishes, a beautifully finished chromium sugar bowl with the monogram "R.M." (Reggia Marina), two table lamps, and some silver cutlery. Reynolds tells the story.

"At lunch next day we instituted a new formal ceremony which was observed throughout the rest of the commission and was most impressive to a casual visitor. Our steward was, at this time, a big jovial Able Seaman from Yorkshire named Christon. He was given instructions to set the table carefully and to be smartly dressed in whites when he served the lunch. After several gins, Corny would kick off the ceremony.

" 'Ah, gentlemen, I think we should take lunch. Would you kindly ring for the steward, Mr. Brydon?'

"Tony pressed the buzzer, which sounded three feet away in the galley.

"A knock came at the door and Christon's red face appeared. 'You rang, sir?'

" 'Yes. Would you serve lunch, please, Christon?'

" 'Aye aye, sir.'

"A few seconds later, the meal made its appearance. The meat dish and three hot plates were placed carefully before Corny at the head of the table, and the two vegetable dishes in front of Tony and me. As soon as Christon had shut the door behind him, Corny ordered, 'Vegetable serving party – shun!' Tony and I sat bolt upright. 'Off-lids!' A hand shot out from each side of the table and, synchronizing the movements exactly, we removed the two covers. This was the moment to simulate pleasure and surprise. A forced smile spread over Corny's face as he peered first into the starboard dish and then the other. 'Why! dehydrated potatoes – oh! and dried peas!'

"The corned beef was on the large dish before him. " 'May I induce you to try some beef, Mr. Reynolds? Rare perhaps, but you may prefer this well done. My personal predeliction, I must confess, tends to the medium. Do humour me and try that.'

"And the joint was then carefully served in exactly equal portions on the three plates, and the dishes circulated for individual servings of potatoes and peas.

"All this rigmarole served its purpose at the time, and 658's officers found that to take a meal aboard a boat where a loaded plate was carelessly slapped in front of each officer by a scruffy steward was a real let-down after their own pleasant standards.

"Very occasionally – if, for instance, Corny had received a large food parcel from Canada – he would throw a dinner party with all the trappings. On these occasions Christon was magnificent. He would dress in spotless whites and carry a starched napkin over his arm. He would serve the guests and the officers in exactly the correct order, *and* look as though he was enjoying it, too."

In December, 1943, MTB 658 returned to Malta for refit. NAAFI did a particularly good job that Christmas and they had a twenty-pound turkey, Christmas pudding, fresh vegetables, and four bottles of beer for each of the crew.

On the 4th of January 1944 the following signal was received:

From Commander Coastal Forces

Under a general revision and reconstitution of flotillas the following boats will form the new 56th MGB/MTB flotilla under the command of Lieutenant-Commander J.D. Maitland, DSC, RCNVR: MGBS 657, 658, 663; MTBS 633, 640, and 655.

Lieutenant-Commander T.J. Bligh, RNVR, is appointed in command of the 57th MGB/MTB flotilla. . . .

Doug Maitland, RCNVR, was the Senior Officer. He had been promoted to Acting Lieutenant-Commander. Every boat in the new 56th Flotilla was commanded by a Canadian: Doug Maitland, Corny Burke, Tommy Ladner, Cam MacLachlan, Herb Pickard, and Steve Rendell. Thus, although the crews were British, the Mediterranean Fleet had the Canadian 56th to match the Canadian 29th and 65th in the North Sea and Straits of Dover.

✳ ✳ ✳

We must now move back in this narrative a few months to the landings at Anzio and the Canadians' part in them. To the south, Allied armies were still bogged down between Naples and Rome. It was appallingly slow fighting in bitter weather and Anzio was an attempt to do an end-run some thirty miles south of Rome and cut off German forces from their supply lines. The Canadian flotilla's part in the Anzio landings was to make a feint off the port of Civitavecchia, to the north of Rome.

A lot of the war looked like little boys playing instead of grown men and deadly serious business, and the main method of creating this diversion was to play records of invasion noises over loudspeakers – anchor cables roared out; instructions shouted at landing craft; all the boats carried fireworks to simulate the flashes of big guns. The USN ships were embarrassed by the whole idea, but then, they were strangers to our kind of war. Thunder flashes, Very flares, rockets of a patriotic red, white, and blue were all used.

At sunset, course was set for Civitavecchia with Maitland leading in 657, Burke following in 658, Tommy Ladner in 663, Barlow (on loan from another flotilla) in 659, Rendell in 633, MacLachlan in 640, and Pickard in 655. At midnight they made a rendezvous with the USN PTs, just south of Giglio Island, then moved toward the beach. Stan Barnes was the leader of the American PTs, the "eyes" for our British boats. His r/t call sign was "Stan." Maitland's was "Wimpy." They were a couple of miles off the beach when the r/t loudspeaker bleated.

"Hello Wimpy, this is Stan. I have a target at red four oh, 2,800 yards. Shall I leave it to you and carry on with the main job?"

"Stan, this is Wimpy. How many are there?"

"Looks like one big, two small."

"Sure. We'll take them on."

"They're all yours, Wimpy."

The Canadian flotillas swung away to port. It was a dark night with visibility down to 500 yards so the information the American had given them was invaluable. They knew the range and they knew the course to steer. The range closed, and closed. It was an F-lighter with an E-boat on either beam. The range closed further. Surely they must have been sighted. Yet the F-lighter did not start shooting. From Maitland ahead came the message, "To Dogs from Wimpy. Open fire!"

Streams of converging tracer hit the F-lighter. He replied, desperately, and hit the two lead ships 657 and 658. After the initial pass Maitland swung around for a second attack and this time the E-boats decided to join the action. Both came in at maximum speed firing their forward guns. Maitland, being in the lead, was taking the most punishment but the leading E-boat flashed by, disappearing into the darkness, and was not seen again. The other E-boat soon stopped firing and lay motionless. Both she and the F-lighter were burning fiercely. Two men in 658 were wounded. Ordinary Seaman Brayshaw with several severe wounds about his body and Ordinary Seaman Preston who had been hit in the face with shrapnel. As soon as they entered Bastia the base medical officer took charge of them and whisked them away, but Brayshaw died that day.

Stan Barnes told a meeting of the COs that the diversion had gone smoothly with all sufficient noise and light but that the Maitland action offshore added to the verisimilitude of the whole thing. It was 658's night in harbour and they watched the other half of the flotilla sail at sunset. Then Burke had the unenviable task of writing to Brayshaw's parents.

As the months went by operating in the Bastia, Elba, Leghorn area north into the Ligurian Sea, north of Corsica, these sort of actions continued. A theory they had about the F-lighters was confirmed. With the number of guns they had the F-lighters should have been able to blow our smaller, more lightly armed boats out of the water, but they didn't seem to do so. They carried an 88mm and several 40mms, but their gunners were protected by concrete emplacements and, instead of helping by reducing casualties, this only served to encourage their gunners to keep their heads down in safety instead of firing steadily. Our own gunners had inadequate cover and were never likely to bother sheltering behind it. No, they kept on firing while the enemy had their heads down.

The 56th Canadian Flotilla was off to a flying start. They had met the enemy three times in three nights and come out on top almost unscathed. There were German E-boat flotillas in Leghorn or Piombina and they must have had very different feelings; in three nights, three of their boats had been sunk, two damaged.

I talked to Doug Maitland about these actions in 1987 at the Vancouver Club. We took one of the private rooms and had a pot of coffee sent up and we talked. In quiet, measured tones he told me his history in MTBs from the time he joined the navy in Vancouver. But as we got on to these actions that he led, his demeanour changed. He sat straighter in the chair, then he leaned forward, then he hitched himself to the edge of the chair and put a hand on either knee. He confirmed that he had built on what Hichens had taught and that one of his tactics was to approach at low speed, that being far more effective as the lack of the bow wave and wake gave the enemy less chance of sighting accurately. Secondly, he confirmed the belief that once any action had begun the results achieved depended on the crew, not the officers. All the captain had to do was place his ship as close as possible to the enemy and from that point on the gunners took over. But then his face became animated to a degree I had not seen before in this quiet, elderly Vancouver businessman. His eyes squinted as he said, "But you've got to get in close, as close as possible, a hundred yards, fifty, less. And slow speed. You must go slowly, preferably on the same course as the target so you can stay alongside her. If you're close enough she can't depress her guns sufficiently to hit you. *That's* the way you get them. Fire tracer. Set them on fire. Rake them fore and aft, fore and aft. Again and again. *That's* the way you get them."

✳ ✳ ✳

Captain Stevens had now been appointed as Captain, Coastal Forces Mediterranean (CCF) in July, 1943, and he and Commander Bobby Allan had devised a new form of attack. The first trial was "Operation Gun" and consisted of a patrol in force, commanded by Allan himself aboard a PT (because of the good radar), as many MTBS and MGBS as he could put to sea, and, most significant of all, three LCGS. These had the same hull as the small LCIS but had two 4.7-inch guns on them manned by Royal Marines.

Three units were sent north to scout various areas and report to "Admiral Bobby" if they got a target. Everything went as though the Italian forces were co-operating – a convoy of six lighters were sunk. After star shell had been fired to illuminate them it was just a question of target practice. The gunnery of the Royal Marines had been bang-on, sometimes hitting with their first shell. Further, the LCGS were using flashless cordite and could not be seen. Like John Charles in *Laforey* where they also used flashless cordite, the enemy forces never saw the ships who sank them.

In April, 1944, the 56th carried the Senior Officer of Inshore Squadron, Captain Dickinson, and Commander Allan to the north but a severe line of squalls forced them to shelter in the little harbour of Calvi. They could hardly have been closer to naval history. It was here that Admiral Nelson – who at the time bore the same title, Senior Officer of Inshore Squadron – had lost an eye in a landing party.

In late May the Honours and Awards list came out in the *Gazette*. "The King has been graciously pleased to approve awards to Officers and Men in the Mediterranean Station as shown below . . ." Maitland and Burke each received a Distinguished Service Cross and Ladner got a Mentioned in Despatches. This upset Maitland and Burke no end, as Ladner, who had been in Coastal Forces a long time and had sailed with Hichens in the Channel, was quite as entitled to a gong as anybody else. He has been described as keeping his boat 663 maintained with "relentless efficiency" and probably had the best record for reliability in the flotilla. She always seemed ready for operations and had not missed a patrol or action since the flotilla was formed. "I always felt safer with Tom there," said Maitland. "He could always be relied on. Ask him to do something and you could forget it; you could consider it done. He *never* failed."

On 5 June the invasion of Normandy was announced. By the end of June the Eighth Army had passed Rome and was speeding north. At the end of June the Canadian MTBS left for the Adriatic.

As the flotilla left La Maddalena, the Captain Coastal Forces sent a signal to the Senior Officer of the 56th – to Maitland.

From: CCF
To: SO 56

The Canadian flotilla is so essentially a part of us all here that we lose much of ourselves in your departure. Good luck, and may the spirit you have shown bring continued success in your work in the new area.

On the 3rd of July the flotilla returned to Malta for refit. Social life in Malta had changed for the better with the coming of the Wrens and, while the days were filled with arduous labour, the end of the day's work saw cocktail parties, picnics, and moonlight swimming. The armament was added to, and the gun power was now impressive: a 6-pounder forward and aft, and from forward and aft they could pour out shells from a 2-pounder pom-pom, four 20mm, and two Vickers .303s.

As we said earlier, after the Germans advanced into the Balkans, the British had difficulty in finding out what was happening inside Yugoslavia; they had to choose between Colonel Mihajlović's Chetniks or Tito and his Partisans. Brigadier Fitzroy Maclean was parachuted in to form a conduit of information and organize the locals; supplies began to trickle in mainly from Vis, a tiny island about twenty-five miles offshore. Most of the Dalmatian Islands had been taken by the Partisans but as time went on the Germans realized that they must occupy these islands because the overland routes of supply were threatened continuously by bands of Partisan guerillas. Sometimes, instead of returning to Vis, our boats would hide, camouflaging in creeks by day and patrolling by night. Now they were joined by Royal Marine Commandos, Royal Artillery, and a squadron of RAF Hurricanes. The situation in July, 1944, was that Vis was a fortress containing 4,000 Allied servicemen and 9,000 Partisans but surrounded on all but the seaward side by islands held by the Germans.

The flotilla departed Malta and fuelled at Augusta, now a backwater in the war, then sailed to Brindisi. Here the base-ship for Coastal Forces was the Italian seaplane-tender *Miraglia*. Her administration was surely the strangest compromise the navy could produce. Her Captain was Italian and had an Italian skeleton crew on board, but as a base she was run by British officers and men. Lieutenant-Commander Freddie Warner, whom we last saw in hospital after 636 was sunk, was the Captain of the British half and gave them a warm welcome. Tommy Fuller had been operating in this area for over a year and in a series of successful operations against the caiques and schooners of the enemy had triumphantly towed prize after prize back into harbour, all of them full of valuable supplies. The Germans could not allow this state of affairs to continue and more destroyers, F-lighters, and E-boats began to appear on the Dalmatian coast.

On the 30th of July 1944 the Canadian flotilla entered Comiza harbour at Vis. Ten miles to the eastward were German garrisons on the islands of Brac, Hvar, Korcula, and Lagosta. Burke had to go to hospital; the doctors suspected pleurisy. Reynolds assumed command. After arrival they met the Senior Naval Officer, Lieutenant-Commander Morgan Giles. He briefed the MTB captains on an operation coming up, a "False Nose" job. They would be out three nights in a row. Because Reynolds was the junior – he was still a Sub-Lieutenant – he was tail-arse Charlie. The first night their job was to cover a landing in Korcula (forty miles east of Vis), FOOs who were to play a vital role in the big operation planned for the third night. They were back at Vis at seven a.m. to fuel and sailed again as escort for a force of landing craft to a point on the southeastern tip of Korcula. They landed a Partisan company and eight 25-pounders with their Royal Artillery crews. At dawn, these guns would fire over the island and bombard the twin towns on each side of the narrow strait that separated the island from the mainland of the Peljesac peninsula. The war continued to provide the contrapuntal themes of comedy and tragedy; two Royal Artillery officers had carried out a reconnaissance of the enemy positions in Orebid and Korcula dressed as peasant girls, moving about with as much feminine grace as they could muster and artlessly picking grapes in the vineyard, then crouching behind the vines to draw maps of the gun implacements.

The 56th escorted landing craft to a halfway house, a cove on an island between Vis and Korcula; this reduced the passage-time for the invasion the next night. At dawn they returned to Vis to pass on additional intelligence provided at the last minute by one of the small parties of those gallant men (the FOOs) who remained for days at a time on the scantily protected hillsides of the occupied islands, to spot and report the passage of enemy ships. They sailed at sunset.

The landings were made with complete surprise before dawn on the 2nd of August. When enemy fire did open up it was directed at a decoy ship designed for that very purpose. A landing craft had a canvas funnel rigged and two large canvas gun turrets. When the bombardment

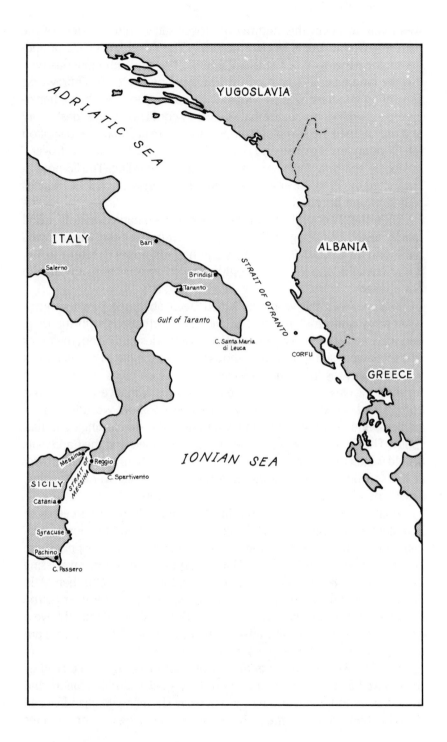

was ready to begin this dummy destroyer sailed into full view of the battery at Orebic, but at its extreme range. The Royal Artillery 25-pounders on the other side of the island opened fire, and simultaneous with this the landing craft (the dummy destroyer) began to let off fireworks simulating gun-flashes from behind each turret. Soon the Orebic batteries replied with vigour, but at that range they could not hit the "destroyer" and only helped the FOO plot their position more accurately and spot on the 25-pounders. For half an hour the batteries shelled the "destroyer," obviously believing that she was doing the bombarding. The 25-pounders shifted target to the enemy anti-aircraft batteries and RAF Hurricanes roared in and bombed.

Then the 25-pounders and the infantry re-embarked and all sailed quietly away. The sea-going side of the operation felt that the planners had done a first-class job. But they still had fifty miles to return to Vis, it was daylight, and they could only make six knots. The Luftwaffe did not appear.

In Yugoslavia the womenfolk had been absorbed into the army, wore army uniforms, marched in the same formations with the men, and were included in every combat unit. Grenades hung from their hips and rifles were slung over their shoulders, and the packs on their back were the same as those the men carried. In the evenings as they set out for a raid it was a scene from a particularly imaginative operetta as a company of Partisans – men and women – well-trained, well-disciplined, ruthless, and aggressive, would swing down the streets singing in harmony. They would embark in one of their schooners and the Canadians would watch the graceful craft slide out of the harbour under the power of the soft putt-putt-putt of the motor, hardly audible over the singing. They faded into the dark on their deadly mission.

Then came the battle of the Mljet Channel. Burke returned from hospital having practically discharged himself as fit and the next significant operation was that Royal Marine Commandos had to be put ashore on the northwest end of Mljet Island as spotters to report on passing enemy ships. Maitland put them into the right position and then Maitland, Burke, and Ladner moved into the Mljet Channel for their patrol. Over the r/t from Maitland came: "Hello Dogs, this is Wimpy. I have a possible target. Four small ships moving fast up the Mljet Channel. I am steering to intercept, speed twenty-two knots. Out."

Even at twenty-two knots they could not close the range so they must have been E-boats. After an hour they sulkily admitted failure and turned away to lie quiet under the Yugoslav shoreline. Maitland closed the other two and over a megaphone told them that he had three targets at a range of three miles. He told them to go quietly to action stations, get into cruising line to port, and follow him. They began their slow approach. Six knots, no bow wave, no luminescence aft. The targets appeared to be three large ships surrounded by several smaller ones. They steamed slowly on; the range got less and less. Night glasses scanned the horizon ahead and then, there they were – three in sight, dead ahead. Still Maitland carried on his slow approach. All forward guns were now bearing and dim shapes were crossing ahead of them slowly. At last Maitland signalled: "Here we go, Dogs. Speed eight knots attacking on the port bow. Tommy, light please. Range is 500 yards."

From Ladner came the pom-pom-pom and the veil of night was lifted by his star shells. There lay the convoy, range 300 yards. All ships opened fire. The hits flashed and sparkled on what looked like an F-lighter. The remainder of the convoy, two large schooners, received the full attention of the after guns of the two lead ships and all of Ladner's guns except the pom-pom, which was doing the illuminating.

For twenty seconds fire continued unopposed and then multi-coloured tracer sailed toward our force. Although our boats were only crawling along at eight knots they had soon passed the convoy and came upon a straggler; she paid the penalty common to stragglers. Streams of 6-pounder, pom-pom, and 20mm transformed her into an inferno. Burke's boat was hit and three of the engines were out of commission. The chief engineer got one engine working and the three Canadian boats moved in for a second attack. This time they illuminated an E-boat and two landing craft, which opened ineffective fire against them. Again Maitland went in, and in, and in, at slow speed; at 200 yards he ordered, "Open Fire." All three of the enemy were left as burning hulks. Ahead of this group were three large schooners and they opened fire when the Canadian flotilla was 600 yards away. Fire was returned. MTB 658's forward 6-pounder crashed shell after shell into a schooner's hull, then switched target for the high poop deck. Always go for the bridge – in this case the poop deck, aft. There was an explosion, followed by a display of fireworks; they had hit an ammunition locker.

Maitland now pulled ahead of the schooners for his next attack. This gave all hands time to get extra ammunition up from below and get squared away from the damage that had been inflicted on them. One of the large schooners had stopped, the other two continued on their previous course. Our incendiaries had set fire to brush on shore and this was burning briskly and would nicely silhouette any targets sailing by it. Maitland reversed course and started back at eight knots when the leading enemy ship challenged. At 400 yards the challenge was replied to by twenty guns pouring a continuous hail of fire. She swung away toward the shore and her gunfire stopped. Fire was shifted to the second schooner and she, now silhouetted against the fire ashore, was set aflame. Maitland had been keeping track of the third schooner, the stopped schooner, now some miles astern, still visible on the radar screen but not to the eye. Maitland informed the other two, "We just saw that one disintegrating on the sunflower (radar screen)."

Two of the convoy were left holding to their original course. Again the Canadian flotilla pulled ahead in the dark and waited. Maitland's radar screen now showed only stationary echoes. He therefore moved back to mop up. One schooner had disappeared and could not be found, even with the help of star shell and more burning shrubs. Eventually she was spotted, beached at the foot of the cliff. All guns opened fire and left her burning. They continued along the Channel to the next stationary target, which turned out to be an abandoned oil tanker. She was sunk. They had now been in action continually for five hours. The Mljet Channel showed no echoes; it had been swept clear of enemy ships. The victory was complete. They returned home. Maitland and Burke had been hit many times. Ladner had emerged unscathed. There was not a single casualty.

Later the Partisans brought in fourteen prisoners. The schooners, they said, were about 300 tons each, one carrying ammunition and the other food. They had just completed a refit and therefore had been sunk on their first voyage. They had sailed from Korcula and were bound for Dubrovnik. In forwarding Maitland's report to the Commander-in-Chief, the Captain Coastal Forces said,

> This action may well be regarded as a peak performance of the 56th MGB/MTB flotilla, with all its RCNVR Commanding Officers under the magnificent leadership of Lieutenant-Commander J.D. Maitland, DSC. That he was faultlessly followed and supported by Lieutenant C. Burke, DSC, and Lieutenant T.E. Ladner is clear from the action report, and to one who knows them is almost to state the obvious. As the Senior Officer stated in his report, "This was team work of the highest order . . ." In the light of the reports from Intelligence it is thought that this action may be described as the shrewdest blow that the enemy has suffered on the Dalmatian Coast and may well have speeded the evacuation of the islands.

The boats returned to Italy for refit. By now Alllied armies had moved so far up Italy that the port of Ancona was available to them. On the mainland this would put Venice and even Trieste within striking distance of their patrols. They were just behind the front line. Canadian soldiers were fighting at Rimini just fifty miles up the coast and the big push involving the Canadians and the Eighth Army was just starting. They met their old friend *Laforey*, who was moving up the coast each night and bombarding enemy flanks. Minesweepers were keeping a channel clear for them. Montgomery was preceding his advance with his famous artillery barrages and it was fascinating for the Canadians on their nightly patrols to have a view of that tremendous barrage. Huge flashes rent the darkness and small red balls of tracer trundled slowly across the gap, looking so harmless at that distance.

On one of these night patrols 657 had her stern blown off and 633 (Steve Rendell) was towing her back. Burke in 658 was sent out to help. They had lost one boat of the Canadian flotilla. The losses were to continue.

Tommy Ladner had by now been fighting at sea in MTB and MGB battles for four years, and whoever looks after the welfare of gun boat officers decided it was time he came ashore. Despite exhaustion he was not sleeping too well, and his weight was down to 135 pounds. He left 663 to become Staff Officer Operations for the Captain of Coastal Forces at Malta. Seven days after Tommy left her, 663 hit a mine and sank.

Doug Maitland, who had fought in gun boats and torpedo boats in the North Sea and the English Channel since 1941 and who had led them for a year of eventful action in the Mediterranean, was also approaching his limit of endurance (although he did not mention it). But the welfare of their members is one of the prime qualities of the Royal Navy. He and Ladner had been watched over and cared for by their senior officers and now Maitland also was appointed ashore. He became Staff Officer Operations to the Senior Naval Officer Northern Adriatic – his old friend, Captain Dickinson. Burke was now appointed as Senior Officer in Command of the 56th MGB-MTB Flotilla and promoted to Acting Lieutenant-Commander. He and Reynolds went back to Ancona to be fitted with American radar.

War provides startling contrasts. Reynolds, sitting in the magnificence of the opera house seeing a production of *Tosca*, could not imagine his other world of darkness and flame. For everything there is a season: a season for work, a season for play; a season for fighting and a season for resting. But it would appear that Burke played as hard ashore as he fought afloat. He still has an enviable exuberance forty-seven years later, which I saw last when in 1988 he led the Battle of Atlantic parade in Vancouver.

Doug Maitland, Tommy Ladner, Corny Burke, Lou Stead, Budge Belle-Irving, Steve Reynolds, and twenty others had lunch together at the Vancouver Club a short while ago to listen to a talk by the Naval Historian, Commander Alec Douglas. Corny dominated here. He has to, and everybody enjoys it. But in the past hundred pages you will have noticed how he has been in and out of hospital. Maitland and Ladner have been moved to shore billets. But Burke, who had gone through all they had, forced on regardless. Besides, he was now Senior Officer of a flotilla of which a man could be proud. Their performance had not gone unnoticed by Admiral Cunningham. A signal was received:

From: C-in-C, Med.
To: Captain Coastal Forces, Med.

I have observed with pleasure the conduct of the Light Coastal Forces operating from Bastia and in the Adriatic during recent months. The constant harassing of the enemy sea routes has had a direct bearing on the success of the armies fighting in southern France and Italy, and highest praise is due to the officers and men whose uniform vigilance, daring and skill have been responsible for the destruction of many tons of enemy shipping and escort vessels, as well as to base personnel who have maintained our craft in fighting conditions.

It is requested that you convey my appreciation and congratulations to all concerned.

# XI   The Invasion of France

Our Tribal class destroyers in 1944 were HMCS *Haida, Huron, Iroquois, Athabaskan*; these displaced 2,000 tons loaded, were 355-feet six-inches long with a beam of thirty-six-feet six-inches, and carried a ship's company of 200. Their armament was six 4.7-inch guns, two 4-inch guns, several 40mm and 20mm, and four 21-inch torpedo tubes. They had a speed of thirty-six knots, driven by geared turbine engines with 44,000 shaft horsepower. Compared to our 70- to 110-foot boats of the Coastal Forces with their 6-pounder and smaller guns, these destroyers sound like large ships, but they are truly small ships compared to the 40,000-ton battleships with their 15- and 16-inch guns and the cruisers of 10,000 tons with their 8- and 6-inch guns. Yes, destroyers are small ships.

We have seen how transitory were battles in MTBs. Their night actions were visual contact only and sometimes an engagement could last as little as three minutes before they flashed outside each other's ken; some battles lasted perhaps half an hour. But in destroyers with their six radar sets and their comprehensive operations rooms, which could keep track of all ships in the area up to five miles away with devastating accuracy, the actions went on for several hours because contact was never lost. But despite knowing the courses of our own and enemy ships, and despite the information passed by other ships over the r/t, and despite the overall view kept on the whole of the Channel area by a benevolent C-in-C in Dover Castle whose Wrens could call you up if you were getting into trouble – despite all this, a night action still deteriorated into a mêlée.

One such night action took place between the Channel Islands of Guernsey and Jersey and Cherbourg, across the Gulf of St. Malo. Four enemy ships were reported steering northeast from Brest heading up to

Cherbourg, probably Narvik or Seetier class. Their hulls were slightly larger than our Tribals; the ship's company was slightly more but it was in armament they outdid us; the early-built carried four 5-inch guns with eight 37mm and some smaller, the later class carried 5.9-inch guns and eight 21-inch torpedo tubes. They were opponents not to be taken lightly.

At sea that night we had *Haida* and *Huron* in company with HMS *Tartar* and *Ashanti*. They were steering on an interception course along the "tramline" the route along which German coastal convoys must pass. The Polish destroyers *Blyskawica* and *Piorun* were two miles to seaward with *Eskimo* and *Javelin*. At 1:17 a.m. radar contact was made and the flotilla altered formation from line ahead to line abreast, throwing a barrier four miles wide across the intended path of the enemy, range 20,000 yards. The enemy destroyers fired torpedoes but since we were pointing at them to "comb the spread" they passed through our ships to port, to starboard, and, with many a gusty sigh of relief by us, disappeared astern.

Our ships opened fire; the German T 24 and Z 24 returned the fire and turned southwest; *Haida* and *Huron* went after them at full speed. Z 32 turned north and ran into the two Poles; she was soon hit but disappeared from the scene in the smoke and the dark at least temporarily. ZH 1 turned west and was engaged by *Tartar* and *Ashanti*. She slowed and disappeared so *Tartar* and *Ashanti* went to the help of *Haida*, who was taking on T 24; she fled but not before *Tartar* was damaged. Four German shell burst on her superstructure, cutting communication with the guns and torpedo tubes. A fire blazed forward, and abaft the bridge the mast crashed down carrying all the radar and wireless aerials with it. Several men were killed, more wounded. Splinters from the German fire had pierced the boilers and scalding steam was rushing skyward. In general, *Tartar* was not in a very bellicose mood for perhaps an hour while she got things under control; nevertheless, she kept her guns firing in local control and with *Ashanti* went after ZH 1, which blew up. *Haida* and *Huron* were in hot pursuit of Z 24 and T 24, scoring hits on the retreating enemy, who was soon out of range.

One must picture the sorting of all this information from the comparative quiet of the plot where radar ranges and bearings of all targets are chanted to the plot officer, who marks them on his paper plot (about four feet wide by five feet long). His own ship's position is shown by a light shining upward from beneath the glass top and everything relative to him can be easily comprehended. It is a perfectly balanced team with an ad-lib script. But so often had they worked together, so many thousands of hours, that the voices seldom go above a murmur and

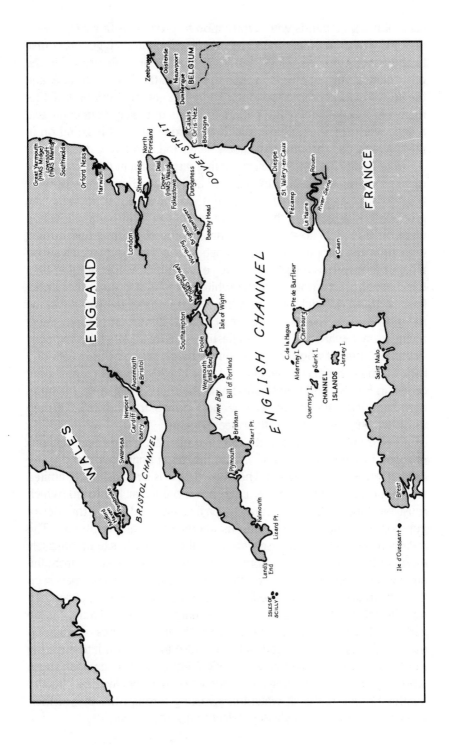

each of the nine hands with information to provide instinctively awaits his turn. The plot officer then gives a summary or a suggested course to the captain on the bridge, who hasn't as clear a picture up in the gusty dark, spray over the bow, rain in his face, the flash of gunfire, and the verbal reports of four lookouts. There is a general hubbub but after many night actions there is a pattern to it: it is not really distracting, and a destroyer captain can have a fairly clear idea of what is going on in the howling dark around him much better than an MTB captain.

*Haida* and *Huron* lost their retreating targets and in returning to the main group ran across the missing z 32 and chased her to the eastward. z 32 twisted and turned to the south, to the west, all in vain. She grounded on a rock and that was the end of her. This particular action went on from 1:17 to 4:10 a.m. – three hours of twisting and turning with guns and torpedoes firing, damage received and damage given, on a dark night with low visibility – twelve warships manoeuvring in tight turns at thirty-six knots with the white glare of star shell, the amber flashes of our 4.7-inch guns and the 5-inch guns of the Germans, the red glow of hits, the flickering fires burning, 20mm and 40mm tracer arcing lazily toward one and then flashing overhead. All of this happens within an area of about sixteen square miles, just off the shoals of a rock-bound coast and minefields. Add the crackle of voices rapping out orders in English and German and hear the roars of big guns, the bam-bam-bam of the 40mm and the pow-pow-pow of the 20mm: 2,000 men in twelve ships playing out their deadly game.

Over 2,000 men, a minute number of the millions and millions engaged in the global theatre of war, this night confront death by fire, by shell and shrapnel, by sea. Their world now is circumscribed, limited to the moment and the place. Each has a particular job to do, which must be done faithfully, accurately, paying no heed to the thunder of guns or the shudder of the ship as enemy shells arrive inboard. The radar strobe has to be precisely *there*, or the pointer has to be precisely *there*, or they must pick out from the medley of voices flashing from the airwaves the one that concerns the safety of their ship. IFF may keep them from firing at friends, but if a friend's aerials are shot away then he will not be able to identify himself that way. Voice signals can be garbled. Radar sets can develop those eerie little creatures – which no man ever sees – who sporadically feed false information into even the most scrupulously maintained technical equipment. Gremlins. Those who have been maintaining the hundreds of miles of electrical circuitry for this precise battle sit watchful, sweating through the trial of their work and ready to remedy any defect that might occur.

These are the Laws of the Navy
Unwritten and varied they be
And he that is wise will observe them
Going down in his ship to the Sea.

On the strength of one's link of the cable
Dependeth the might of the chain
Who knows when thou mayest be tested
So live that thou bearest the strain.

The "headache" operator's radio receiver is tuned to German frequencies. When approaching the enemy, the operations officer periodically glances over with an interrogatory look on his face. The operator nods in return. He is listening to find out when the enemy will release his torpedoes. The moment can be pretty well predicted from the plot by putting oneself in the enemy's position. "If I was him I would fire about now." The ops officer glances over to the headache operator.

"The enemy is altering course."

Almost at the same time the headache operator translates what he has heard in his earphones: "Altering course to starboard to fire torpedoes . . . still altering . . . still altering . . ."

The plot officer lays off his ruler and runs it on the compass rose and thus knows from whence the torpedoes will arrive. He calls the bridge. "Captain, sir, the enemy is altering course to fire torpedoes now. They'll come from Green two oh. I'll give you the German's executive signal."

"Starboard 10, coxswain," says the Captain. Steer, 070."

The plot officer gets the signal from the headache operator, "Captain, sir, they've launched their torpedoes. They should be arriving in about twenty-five seconds."

And they do. The ship's narrow beam is presented to them. They pass one to port and one to starboard, and the next move is now considered.

The phrase "the fog of battle" has been used since the days of the ships of the line when the fog was truly a fog of smoke with battleships hammering it out with a hundred guns at ranges of a 1,000 or 500 yards or even alongside each other. The term persists today – the fog of battle. Those who have not experienced it can perhaps understand the rapidity of the changing situation and the calamity of a mistake with a dozen or more ships of 2,000 tons travelling in excess of thirty knots, gun mounts belching flame. And those who have experienced it will remember.

$*$  $*$  $*$

Since the autumn of 1943 our Tribals had been attached to the Plymouth command as part of the 10th Destroyer Flotilla under the command of Captain Basil Jones, DSO and bar DSC. Basil Jones had served in the gunnery school in Portsmouth, Hampshire, HMS *Excellent*. He had first gone there for his sub-lieutenant's course in 1921. He remembered a certain Lieutenant (G) on staff who had harried his class with vigour, Lieutenant Arthur John Power. Not fazed by this, Jones returned to Whale Island (as *Excellent* is also called) in 1928 to qualify Lieutenant (G) himself. In 1934 he was appointed back as First-Lieutenant; the Commanding Officer then was Captain Arthur John Power.

I didn't meet Basil Jones until I was doing my Gunnery Lieutenant's course at *Excellent* in 1946. Saint Barbara is the patron saint of gunners; her feast day is celebrated in November at HMS *Excellent* with rugger games and a mess dinner. A busload of officers from the Royal Artillery arrived, as well as some Swedish gun merchants and retired gunnery officers from all over the United Kingdom. One of these last was Basil Jones; we found we had much in common. Sir Arthur John Power was now the Second Sea Lord and my neighbour on Hayling Island. Also, Jones and I discovered that we had a past captain in common. Commander Hugh J. Woodward (a cousin to the Duke of Norfolk) had been Jones's Captain in the destroyer *Tumult* in 1919. I said that when I was a Midshipman Hugh Woodward was my Captain in HMS *Alaunia*. Jones remembers Woodward with startling clarity, "He was rather a Winstonian character, quick and clever and impatient."

"Yes, and by the time I met him in 1940, after he had retired from the service but had come back in for the war, he was even more impatient than you would have remembered him. I was eighteen and didn't know much but should have known to keep out of the way of the Captain when he was on the bridge; albeit bridges are crowded, midshipmen are supposed to be invisible and certainly not stumbling across the Captain's path.

" 'Snotty,' he said, after I had done this a second time, "in future when I arrive on the bridge go up in the crow's nest and stay there until I leave the bridge.' "

In 1942 Basil Jones had commanded a destroyer in the Mediterranean, HMS *Isis*, and after that had gone as Captain D of the 12th Destroyer Flotilla in *Pakenham*. He was based on Malta and the Vice-Admiral there was Arthur John Power. *Pakenham* and *Paladin* took on two Italian destroyers and, while the Italians had been sunk, *Pakenham* had gone to the bottom, too. Jones was then appointed as Captain D of 10th, he in *Tartar* with *Nubian*, *Eskimo*, *Ashanti*, and *Javelin* in the 1st Division and HMCS *Haida*, *Huron*, *Iroquois*, *Athabaskan*, *Blyskawica*, and *Piorun* in the 2nd Division.

On the night of the 29th of April *Haida* and *Athabaskan* had been sent on an operation with minelayers to the enemy coast and by three a.m. the minelayers had finished their work and the force was on its way home. It was, however, a perfect night with good radar conditions and *Haida* and *Athabaskan* received a signal from Plymouth; the gentle modulated voice of a Wren telegraphist filtered into the operations room. "Maple Leaf, Maple Leaf. This is Sister Three. We have some hunting for you. Steer southwest at good speed. Over."

"This is Maple Leaf, Wilco Out."

At 3:13 a.m. the soft voice called again, slightly more forcibly: "Maple Leaf, Maple Leaf. This is Sister Three. Your target will pass ten miles north of Ile de Bas in fifteen minutes. Over."

"This is Maple Leaf. Roger Out."

By 4:13 a.m. the range was rapidly decreasing and the Wren gave her last vector. "Maple Leaf, Maple Leaf. This is Sister Three. Your echoes are merging. Heads up. Heads up. Over."

"Maple Leaf. Thank you. Out."

*Haida* gave the order "Ignite" and *Athabaskan* fired star shells. *Haida* and *Athabaskan* opened fire and as they did so turned bows on to the enemy to comb the spread of enemy torpedoes. But just at the end of the turn *Athabaskan* was hit and large fires broke out above and below decks. The Captain, Lieutenant-Commander Johnny Stubbs, ordered, "Stand by to abandon ship," and the boats were made ready but not lowered. The damage control parties worked feverishly, but with a second explosion *Athabaskan* listed to port and "hands abandon ship" was ordered. *Haida* had her priorities and so she swung across the bow of *Athabaskan* to lay a protective smokescreen and they altered away at full speed to resume her pursuit of the Elbing destroyers. When these were demolished *Haida* returned to *Athabaskan*, picked up what survivors she could, and, being told that MTBs were on the way to pick up the remainder, dropped her boats and life rafts in the water and left after fifteen minutes, during which time thirty-eight men were taken aboard.

Pale dawn etched the land. Commander Harry DeWolf in *Haida* had lost one ship; he could not risk losing another, and soon the Luftwaffe would be out to bomb him. He could see Johnny Stubbs swimming around his men encouraging them to sing, shout, move their arms, move their legs, and Stubbs gave his last order when he said, "We'll be all right, *Haida*. We'll be all right. Get out of it."

John Stubbs had been about all a man could ask for in a friend and a Captain. From the naval college at age eighteen he had developed a high degree of professional competence. Apart from unyielding insistance in making his ship effective, he was amiable, a lot of fun to go ashore with. All these young pre-war RCN officers were as good as any you'd find in any navy in the world; but with surprising differences, each was his idiosyncratic self.

Harry DeWolf had a quiet sense of humour but it was not much evident during the months we are considering; with him as with all the captains, the welfare of the ship and the men came first. God help the officer who transgressed against either; it was certain that nobody else could help him. DeWolf was searing in his condemnation, and loud. When in action he always used full helm, hard-a-starboard, hard-a-port. His troops called him "Hard Over Harry."

Lieutenant-Commanders Herbert Rayner on *Huron* and Jimmy Hibbard on *Iroquois* also had their quirks. Herbert Sharples Rayner was known as a "Holy Joe" by his men, but not in a pejorative sense. His faith in God and his adherence to the form of the Anglican Church were clear and serious. He was not a barrel of fun. Sober and sedate, he smiled seldom in this vale of tears, and when displeased his light blue eyes became glacial. Yet when creaming along at night with his guns blazing at a willing foe his voice would be raised in song – between helm orders – a strong voice and true throwing out sea chanties or hymns.

Jimmy Hibbard was know to his crew as "Jumping Jimmy." He was intense, excitable and would stamp up and down with his feet going slap, slap, slap. Yet when the thunder of the guns spoke and the acrid bite of cordite filled the air, a calm would descend upon him. For millennia a captain's place when his ship is at hazard is on the bridge, where he can see around all points of the compass. Even on dark rainy nights, even in fog, the captain's place is on the bridge. With a moral courage I have not often seen duplicated, Jimmy Hibbard broke with tradition. He was probably the first captain in history to fight his ship from the operations room. One night, such was his obvious grasp of the tactical situation by suggestions he made to the Senior Officer in the cruiser that the SO rather petulantly passed control to *Iroquois*.

D 10's job was to keep the English Channel clear of enemy surface ships so that the Allied invasion of the continent could proceed unmolested. Jones did. In four months the flotilla sank two Elbings, two

Narviks, six M-class minesweepers, nine armed trawlers, six merchant-men, and one AMC, two flak ships, three motor vessels, one tanker, one Sperrbrecker, and one coaster. Damaged were three Elbings, two Narviks, six minesweepers, four armed landing craft, and five transports. In addition, *Haida* sank a U-boat. That made a total of thirty-four surface ships, one submarine sunk, and twenty surface ships damaged.

Night after night during those four months they put to sea, fought their battles, returned at dawn, landed their dead and wounded, made good the battle damage, refuelled, re-ammunitioned, and the hands got their heads down for a few hours in the afternoon. Periodically they'd have a night in harbour – much more rarely two nights in harbour. Morning after morning units of Basil Jones's ships arrived home to Plymouth, whence Vice-Admiral Drake had sailed in 1588 to wreak havoc on the Spanish Armada. Plymouth, had been a naval town since 1311;* the dockyard's artisans had been tending the wounds of English ships for over 600 years and took pride in *their* ships; the citizens loved *their* sailors. Among the Wrens in Plymouth barracks and in the signal stations the crew had found some gentle moments with walks in the Devon countryside on sunny summer evenings when they had a stand-down. Perhaps, to get out of the bombed ruins of Plymouth, they took a bus to Ivybridge for tea; the green fields and flowering hedgerows and birdsong contrasted poignantly with the violence of the night before.

Admiralty had conveyed congratulations to the flotilla for the "spirited action which has caused a potential threat to the main operation [the landing of our soldiers] to be removed." This formal recognition by their Lordships was appreciated, but not quite as much as that composed and sent to them by the Wrens in the signal station who had waved good-bye and hello to them so many times.

### The Fighting Tenth

> There are specks on the horizon
> As familiar as can be,
> D 10 with his flotilla
> Proceeding in from sea,
>
> Battle ensigns at all mastheads,
> An impressive sight to see,

---

*In 1946 I was leaving a hotel in Plymouth in mess dress for a Trafalgar Day dinner at the RN barracks, "What's on tonight sir?" asked the hall porter. I told him Trafalgar, 1805, Admiral Nelson, etc. He sniffed disdainfully, "Oh yes. The new boy."

The Tartar and the Tenth DF
Come in triumphantly.

The pendants now come visible,
Four-three, Five-one, Two-four,
Tartar, Ashanti, Huron,
Soon there will be more.

Blyskawica, Haida, Javelin,
Piorun, Eskimo,
Buntings on their Signal Bridge,
Stokers down below.

Passing through the gate at last
They move more cautiously,
The same old signal flying,
"Act Independently."

We hope we'll always see you thus
With ensigns flying free
For the Fighting Tenth's a lovely sight,
When coming in from sea.

Since 1939 Canadians had been serving in Royal Navy aircraft carriers, battleships, cruisers, destroyers, submarines, particularly as radar specialists. Canadians served in the Mediterranean and the Pacific, in the Arctic on Murmansk convoys, in the Indian Ocean. The contributions of Canadian junior officers to winning the war are not much mentioned in the four volumes of *The War at Sea* by Captain S.W. Roskill, RN, or in the fifteen volumes of *History of United States Naval Operations in World War II* by Admiral S.E. Morison, USN. They may get a line or two in *The Royal Canadian Naval Operations: 1939-1945* by Dr. W.A.B. Douglas, an official history soon to be published.

Midshipman (later Rear-Admiral) Dick Leir had the distinction of being sunk by Japanese aircraft in *Prince of Wales* when she and *Repulse* went down off the coast of Malaya in December, 1941; he went to *Exeter* and was sunk again in the Battle of the Java Sea. The Canadians' sense of humour perturbed their captains. But it was the truth when Leir told Captain Leach of *Prince of Wales* that as a boy he had caught a salmon in British Columbia that weighed more than he did; the Captain was outraged and prevented Leir from repeating the story to President Roosevelt (who would have known that an English salmon runs to about eight pounds, while some B.C. salmon run to a hundred).

There there was Signal Lieutenant (later Rear-Admiral) Bobby Murdoch. He was serving with Captain Hillary Worthington-Biggs as Flotilla (S). In 1945 they were bombarding Japanese in Burma from Rangoon south on the Malay peninsula. But this involved passing a stretch of the coast of Siam and Canada had not declared war on Siam. When they reached the Siam coast, Murdoch would report to his Captain ("who'd had three destroyers sunk under him in the Mediterranean and was living on black coffee, cigarettes, and finger nails"). He would tell his Captain that he must leave the bridge now; Canada wasn't at war with these people. When out of Siamese waters he would return to the bridge. "My Captain was irritated that one of his officers would remove himself from the war and then come back in."

Then there was Midshipman (later Commodore) Willie Hayes, who was torpedoed in HMS *Liverpool*, then went to *York*, and the night before the Battle of Matapan was torpedoed in Suda Bay by an Italian one-man submarine. He joined the destroyer *Isis* but left her when she went into refit after being hit with a bomb. He then went to *Valiant*, which was sunk by a limpet mine. He lost his kit repeatedly in these disasters and would ask his father – a lawyer in Swift Current, Saskatchewan – for financial help. When news of *Liverpool* being torpedoed appeared in the newspapers Willie knew his dear old dad would be worried so he sent a telegram: "Safe. Please send ten pounds." After *York* he sent, "Safe again. Please send ten pounds." And similar telegrams went home after the bombing of *Isis* and the sinking of *Valiant*.

When his father received the *Valiant* telegram he passed, it without comment, to his partner. His partner said, "You'd think Admiralty could save them cheaper than that. Are you sure you can afford this war?"

Twenty-three Canadian officers were attached to the Channel Anti-Aircraft Guard when it was first formed in September, 1940. The English Channel and the Straits of Dover were always an ordeal: bombarded by shore batteries from the French coast; attacked by aircraft of a bewildering variety; harassed by E-boats, submarines, flak ships. All conspired to make the merchant seaman feel uncertain, so twenty-three Canadian officers were attached to the Anti-Aircraft Guard. They carried their own guns with them when they boarded the merchant ships, fired at whatever they could on the way through the Channel, and when they got to harbour transferred to another convoy going the opposite way. In addition to these there were Canadians in the Balloon Brigade. Merchant ships towed a barrage balloon astern, which irritated the dive-bombers no end. In addition to these, 1,500 Canadian ratings were serving in defensively equipped merchant ships; they manned the 4-inch gun aft.

Hundreds of Canadian officers had graduated from *King Alfred* by this point and had found their niche in the Fairmile launches and the MTBs and MGBs. The *Iroquois* (Commander W.B.L. Holmes in the first commission), the first of the Canadian Tribals, had arrived at Scapa Flow for work-up in December, 1942. Since then all the Tribals had escorted convoys to north Russia and were joined in 1943 by HMCS *Algonquin* (Lieutenant-Commander Debby Piers) and *Sioux* (Lieutenant-Commander Eric Boak). By 1943 the harrying of the Germans extended through the whole of the Bay of Biscay to Gibraltar and in the Channel and North Sea. No German convoy was safe. Captain Harold Grant (later Vice-Admiral and Chief of the Naval Staff) was given command of the British cruiser *Enterprise* and with *Glasgow* on 28 December 1943 engaged eleven German destroyers, three of which were sunk; the remainder retired back to France.

Admiral Grant spoke of this engagement a few years later. "This action was a gunnery officer's dream. We engaged the Germans at 20,000 yards and the eleven of them really outweighed us in firepower. And they made a fight of it. They threw out smoke-floats, made smoke from their apparatus aft, came straight at us, and were soon straddling and hitting. We were punishing them but the heavy smoke made it difficult to assess the damage. Also, German planes had arrived overhead with glider bombs and conventional bombs. I received a hit from a German shell and a glider-bomb set up a huge explosion just a hundred yards off. So there you have it, the 6-inch guns firing at the eleven destroyers and the 4-inch guns and 40mm firing at the attacking aircraft. Glorious!"

Ships with a red Maple Leaf on their funnels became an increasingly familiar sight in U.K. waters. A Canadian minesweeping flotilla had been formed under Lieutenant-Commander (later Rear-Admiral) Tony Storrs: *Caraquet, Fort William, Wasaga, Blairmore, Malpeque, Cowichan, Minas, Milltown, Bayfield,* and *Mulgrave.* HMCS *Canso, Thunder, Georgian, Vegreville, Guysborough,* and *Kenora* were distributed among the British flotillas. In addition to these were the corvettes; *Prescott, Calgary, Mimico, Alberni, Woodstock, Regina, Baddeck, Camrose, Lunenburg, Drumheller, Mayflower, Louisburg, Rimouski, Trentonian, Moose Jaw, Port Arthur, Lindsay, Kitchener,* and *Summerside.*

Two Canadian landing ships, *Prince Henry* and *Prince David*, were joined by their flotillas of assault landing craft. *Henry* was to carry the 528th and *David* the 529th. In addition, there were three Canadian flotillas of the larger infantry landing craft to make the cross-channel voyage under their own power; the 260th, the 262nd, and the 264th – thirty craft in total.

Based in Londonderry were Canadian frigates: *Waskesiu, Outremont, Cape Breton, Grou, Teme, Matane, Swansea, Stormont, Port Colborne, St. John,* and *Meon.* The River-class destroyers *Ottawa, Kootenay, Chaudiere, St. Laurent, Gatineau, Qu'Appelle, Saskatchewan, Skeena,* and *Restigouche* were en route to Plymouth by the end of May, 1944.

Despite the depredations of our destroyers the enemy still had a formidable force, certainly enough to disrupt the close-packed columns of the Normandy invasion fleet of over 7,000 ships. Germany still had sixteen destroyers, fifty E-boats, and sixty R-boats. But the nightmare of all was the U-boat. If Admiral Dönitz was on the ball he could have over 100 U-boats in the Channel area within a week. It is interesting to speculate about the intentions of the German Chief of Intelligence of the Wehrmacht – the Abwehr – Admiral Wilhlem Canaris. For a long time he had been anti-Hitler and seeking "an honourable peace." By 1944 he and many generals knew the war was lost and had hatched the abortive plot to assassinate Hitler. It is hard to see how thousands of ships could sail from the United Kingdom and the United States, arrive in intense concentration at the entrance to the Mediterranean in Operation Torch, and not be met by a 100 U-boats. But the U-boats were not off Gibraltar in November, 1942, when the Allies arrived; neither did they come later. Neither were U-boats gathered in June, 1944, in Operation Neptune across the English Channel. And the Cordon Sanitaire of ships we threw around the invasion area ensured that none got in.

In early 1944 on both sides of the Channel, Coastal Forces grouped. Plymouth looked across to the E-boats and R-boats moving into Cherbourg and the Channel Island ports. Portsmouth forces were strengthened; they faced new German concentrations at Le Havre. Dover added to its flotillas to meet the German threat in the eastern Channel area and five additional flotillas were assigned to sail with the invasion convoys and patrol the assault anchorages.

Among those forces had now come two all-Canadian flotillas – the 65th, under the command of Lieutenant-Commander Jim Kirkpatrick, and the 29th, under Lieutenant-Commander Tony Law. These flotillas had been organized in March, 1944, and most of their officers and men had had lively experiences with British Coastal Forces in the Channel and the North Sea, Law and Kirkpatrick since 1940.

Across the Channel was the *Bundesmarine* – fast attack craft, E-boats – whose Commander in an evaluation in *Seekriegsleitung* noted that "in grand strategy, Germany has gone from being the hammer to being the anvil. . . . (Now) the task of Germany's armed forces is to defend the European Theatre of War long enough for our leadership to bend the enemy to our political will."

There was no shortage of targets. Every week 400 ships entered or departed the Thames estuary. In 1942 the Führer der Schnellboote (Fds) had five flotillas of eight boats each. In the summer season of short nights he concentrated on the Channel area where the distances to targets were short. In the long winter nights he moved a lot of *Schnellboote* to the North Sea. We had destroyers and aircraft to use in concert with our torpedo boats and gun boats. Fds did not. Our boats were radar equipped; few of those of the Fds were. He developed tactics with energy and skill. One was the concept of *Stichansatz*.* This was to cross intervening waters in formation, disperse at our detection limit, attack at high speed while firing, and then retreat and regroup for the trip home.

But despite the depredations of our Coastal Forces, Fds had developed boats and tactics quite appropriate to their role. And their boats were well handled. It was not their job to engage our torpedo boats and gun boats; it was their job to sink merchant ships and return. Analysis and contrast of their tactics (fire and retreat) and our tactics (engage anybody if you can't find merchant ships) may show them to be wiser. It is certain that they had their Hichenses, Dickenses, Scotts, Ladners, Kirkpatricks, Laws, Maitlands, Burks, and Burkes.

We grouped our forces to meet the pre-invasion threat. In 1940 Tony Law had commissioned MGB 53 as First Lieutenant. In February, 1944, he commissioned the 29th Canadian MTB Flotilla at Hythe, the same place he had commissioned MTB 53 four years before. The 29th consisted of 71-1/2-foot hard-chine craft built by the British Power Boat Company. They had a speed of forty-one knots, were powered by three American Packard-built Rolls-Royce Merlin engines with a total of 4,500 horsepower, and carried an armament of two 18-inch torpedoes, one power-

---

*This word translates literally to "random" or "probing" attack, hit-and-run affair. In these the Germans used for communication a one-time code called *Schnepfentafel*, which translates literally to "snipe table," which seems inappropriate. But in the slang of the day a "Schnepfe" was a "tart," "lady of easy virtue", or worse. Surely it is imaginative to associate the hit-and-run and the concept of a fleeting liaison, a one-time job, a surreptitious affair.

mounted 2-pounder pom pom, a 6-pounder power-driven gun forward, two twin 20 mm. The ship's company was two officers and fifteen ratings but the Senior Officer's vessel carried an extra officer and signalman. The 65th MTB flotilla under Kirkpatrick had Dog-class Fairmiles: 110 feet, thirty knots, two 6-pounder guns, a pom-pom, two twin 20mm, and a couple of .303s artistically arranged according to the gunnery officer's taste. Our gunboats were as nasty pieces of work as any the enemy might meet – shag-nasty flak ships. These larger Dog boats were also known as the "Longs" (as opposed to Law's "Shorts"). Kirk's boats carried a captain, a first lieutenant, a navigator, and twenty-six men.

In early March, 1944 – three months before Operation Neptune – Law sailed to work-up at HMS *Bee*. There he met his old friend Lieutenant-Commander Peter (now Sir Peter) Scott, and, in MTB 748, his own officers and men, and the other Canadian flotilla leader, Kirkpatrick – known variously as "Kirk" or "The Brain." The other boats joined: Bob Moyse in 463, Craig Bishop in 464, Charlie "Chuff-Chuff" Chaffey in 465, Glen Creba in 462, and Barney Marshall in 466. Admiral Percy W. Nelles, the Chief of the Naval Staff from Ottawa, visited the two Canadian flotillas, inspected them, had lunch, and was taken to sea to get an idea of the sea-going qualities of the boats. As they sped into the outer-harbour they found themselves in very rough waters but Nelles, having salt spray cover his face for the first time in years, twinkling eyes turned to Law and said, "Go faster, faster." On return to harbour he left wishing them sadly "the best of luck and good actions to you all. I wish I were going with you."

All was not work. In a Ramsgate hotel the naval mess sometimes reached frenetic peaks of activity; when they had a stand-down the tiny bar resounded with laughter and song. Above the fireplace hung a captured German ensign and a painting of an MTB flotilla; also, there was a painting showing Ramsgate harbour in the early 1900s, with yachts and paddlewheel steamers, bright-blazered men with straw hats and walking sticks, and white-gloved, white-gowned ladies with parasols.

The flotilla was moved to Dover and senior officers were summoned by the flag officer, Admiral Pridham-Whippell; they puffed up the steep hill to the castle, crossed the moat, and passed through the ancient portals and long tunnels toward the operations room. The Chief of Staff and Staff Officer Operations were waiting and they were briefed about a convoy that was expected to pass through their parish the following evening. This was estimated to consist of four German LCTs; these might have originally been designed as landing craft but now the Germans, more or less with desperate improvisation, were using them as flak ships with 88mm, 37mm, and 20mm guns. Besides these there would be E- or R-boats; they would pass off Berk Buoy between eleven and midnight. The Admiral chatted with them briefly and sent them on their way.

Law and a British flotilla sailed in two columns approximately 200 yards apart at a speed of twenty knots. At eleven p.m. the familiar German star shell, greenish in colour and brilliant, was sighted ahead. Then, there they were: radar echo bearing ten degrees on the starboard bow at 3,000 yards; four of them. The MTBs roared forward and our red mingled with the enemy's green tracers blazing away: the battle was on. This night the Germans were accurate and their shots skittered over the water, hitting with a sharp resounding ssputt-ssputt-ssputt and creeping closer. Bishop's bridge was hit before he got into 300 yards. The spirited exchange ended and Germans and Canadians parted.

In order to re-engage, Law altered to a parallel course approximating that which the German convoy must be steering. Then he had what was known in Coastal Forces as "Ionized MacGoffoneys"; these were first cousins to Gremlins. He got contact again on radar at 2,000 yards, altered course toward the radar sighting, and the echo altered course as well. Law increased speed, but the echo kept the same distance away, and when he dropped speed, it dropped speed. Star shells disclosed nothing, and since they were getting into the RAF bombing zone where MTBs were forbidden to enter, they headed for home. The 29th MTB Flotilla received a commendation to Admiralty from Admiral Pridham-Whippell:

> The quick and accurate appreciation of the Senior Officer, Group Baker, enabled him to engage the close escort of the convoy in a spirited five minute action at short range, causing damage to the enemy and materially assisting the withdrawal of Group Able.
>
> This is the first occasion on which a unit of the 29th Flotilla has had an opportunity of taking part in offensive operations in this command and it is regretted that their departure on the 27th May precluded further experience of their keen spirit.

- Charles Chaffey had spent from December, 1941, into 1942 in the flotilla of Peter Dickens. His flotilla and Hichens's flotilla were at Lowe-stoft and very often worked together, Chaffey in MTB 252. In action one night off the Cherbourg peninsula they were badly shot up and the Captain, Ian Trelawny, was wounded. Chaffey brought her home. Three of the hands were wounded and three engine-room crew got poisoned from carbon monoxide gas on the way back. They limped home on two engines.

While she was in for repairs he met Lieutenant-Commander Frank Hellings, Captain of 309.

"And what are you up to, Charlie?"

"This weather's good. My boat is in refit so I'm taking a spot of leave."

"Oh no. I'm going on a special operation and I need another officer. You come with me."

"Where are you going?"

"Dieppe."

Chaffey was delighted to go. They didn't actually see the Canadian soldiers landing. They were patrolling offshore and were supposed to go in afterwards to pick up what they could and try to keep the shore batteries from causing too much trouble – which, of course, was ridiculous with the equipment they had. If they had got within three miles of the shore they would have been sunk. There was no air cover and the fiasco and loss of Canadian life at Dieppe has been chronicled elsewhere. Chaffey was not a casualty; after the raid he fitted a little leave in and then went back to his boat. Under the leadership of Peter Dickens he went on offensive patrols up and down the French and Dutch coasts and confirms that a lot of British captains and crews personally knew the E-boat captains and crews from peacetime. It was certain that Peter Dickens knew a lot of them, he and Hitch. Odd things he remembers. It was nice for example, to get home in the morning because when you had been at sea you got an egg for breakfast, scarce at that time and quite a treat.

In February, 1943, Chaffey got home to Canada for leave and returned in *Queen Elizabeth*. He then went in command at Yarmouth in MGB 21, an ancient boat of the original Hichens flotilla.

In December, 1943, he joined Tony Law's 29th. He was active through the Normandy invasion, driving first 486, then 465. He found Law "a leader to be respected; he knew his job. He'd studied and talked to other flotilla leaders about tactics and most of his operations were textbook. He knew what he was doing; we knew what we were doing. It doesn't matter what a captain does as long as he's bloody competent. Tony was."

But all were concerned (and they were not the only ones to be thus concerned about their leader) that once in a while Law *might* get a little bit excitable to the extent that he *might* do something that was a bit too rash.

"You see, in my estimation he was always trying to prove himself. It's hard when you grow up with guys like Hichens and Dickens, hell-bent for leather, let's go get 'em types. Tony is not naturally that way; he's an artist. But when he had to go in to attack he'd make sure he did a good job of it. At one time he was going in to have a go at a couple of German destroyers off Le Havre. Now their night gunnery is good; their shells started blasting close by; these 5-inch shells were whizzing through our mast. We had to wind Tony down, 'Take it easy. We're not going to take on these people.' It was always Tony's idea to get in so close they couldn't depress their guns enough to fire at you. But it was probable with these destroyers that we would be blown out of the water before we could get that close."

The kaleidoscopic memories. They stole a dockyard locomotive for a joy ride; they tied a barrage balloon to the base captain's barge and sent it sailing across the harbour; unfortunately, it smashed into a jetty and the irate captain was not easy to deal with. Dave Killam and a couple of other friends got killed off the Normandy beaches in MTB 460, when they hit an oyster mine. He was 150 yards ahead of Chaffey; there was an explosion, spume and spray mounted fifty feet, and that was the end of 460. Chaffey picked up about fourteen of the crew but the rest were killed or drowned. Glen Creba was killed, also.

The 29th arrived at Ramsgate in the middle of May and was sent on a mine-gathering expedition to the coast of France. Word had been received of a new German beach mine and the Royal Engineers wanted to have a look at one. So Law was sent to steal a couple off the enemy beaches. MTBs 462, 464, 460, and 465 sailed. It was a calm night and the phosphorescent sea made them feel unpleasantly conspicuous. The engineers were landed. Law remembers "after we finished work-ups at Ramsgate one of our first operations was collecting these mines for the army. So, I leading my flotilla and Willie de Looze leading his Dutch flotilla, we set the army ashore under the great guns of Cape Griz Nez. There we were, silent. Everything very peaceful. We didn't *dare* make any noise. Willie, in a muted voice, called across to me, 'Tony, don't look now but there is a convoy going by.' This German convoy had all its guns pointed out to sea. What German would expect British torpedo boats to landward of them? They steamed slowly by beautifully silhouet-ted and I couldn't do a damn thing about it; we missed a great chance. Can you imagine being on the enemy's beach with an enemy convoy with her guns facing to seaward and not being able to *do* anything? However, we got our mines and went home at forty-two knots."*

---

*Law, "White Plumes Astern."

On the night of 22 May boats 459, 464, 465, and 466 left Ramsgate in company with four British boats to intercept a heavily escorted German convoy moving between Dieppe and Boulogne. It was a dark night, a choppy sea, a strong northwesterly wind, and they moved to a north-south patrol line twenty-four miles off Boulogne. After about an hour the Brits detached to the southward and a few minutes later the Canadian boats obtained radar contact with the enemy convoy. Law's flotilla turned toward them, fired star shell, and opened fire. Then gun flashes from shore indicated that the coastal batteries were going to illuminate; they ran into the glare of the bursting star shells. Ian Robertson, who was serving as navigator to Bones Burk, told me, "these frays were called '*Invitation to the Dance*'; the brilliant and copious star shell from the coastal batteries resembled the chandeliers of a ballroom and the MTBS and E-boats waltzed around at high speed exchanging pleasantries." The simile had struck the E-boat captains as well. Kapitanleutnant Klose, the commander of a German group, was engaged by our destroyers on a raid the night of 5-6 November 1943 and said in his war diary that he was subject to "Star shell from two destroyers with full orchestra following."

Law led his boats out of the ballroom into the relative obscurity of a dark foyer. His Brit counterparts were retiring under cover of darkness. The German force was four heavily armed flak ships with accompanying E-boats and R-boats now thoroughly roused and vigilant. As Law ran in the Germans swung their guns away from the retiring British craft and turned their full fire on the 29th. The battle went on five minutes, both sides blazing away. At the end of the line of German ships the 29th swung out to sea. They had scored hits in this slashing action fought under the blaze of star shell; there was no time to assess enemy damage.

Kirkpatrick had commissioned his 65th flotilla with care. He personally selected of all his captains (he tried to persuade Bones Burk to come to him but Bones preferred the Shorts), interviewed all his crew himself, worked the flotilla up with remorseless energy, and applied the principles of leadership he had learned at RMC to build a good fighting unit. On the same night Law had accepted the "Invitation to the Dance," waltzing in the ballroom with a German convoy between Dieppe and Boulogne, the 65th had its first action to the west of him. From Brixham, boats 735, 726, 745, and 727 sailed into the waters of the Channel Islands to ferret out E-boats. At three a.m. they were eight miles northeast of Jersey, made contact with a convoy at 6,600 yards, disposed themselves in broad quarterline formation, and ran in on the convoy's beam. There were two escort ships to the seaward side of the convoy. The two lead boats, 735 and 726, closed them; the skirmish lasted but a few minutes but 2,500 rounds of shells were pumped at the enemy. The other two boats, 745 and 727, passed the escorts and headed for the convoy, but, being blinded by star shell and tracer, they fired their torpedoes by radar. Now closing the range to less than 100 yards they ran the length of the enemy convoy with their gunfire MTB 726, mistaking 745 for an enemy E-boat, opened fire on her. Jack McClelland says, "She was coming out of a smoke bank and as soon as I saw her I opened fire. Then stopped two seconds later when I recognized her." This action ended in the usual nebulous way. Undoubtedly enemy ships had been damaged, though probably none sunk; firing torpedoes by radar is not a good tactic.

Kirk said that "by the time the two flotillas were well worked up. I was extremely proud of my flotilla. I thought they were really well trained and well disciplined and a good bunch, too, a good bunch. I would say the same would apply to Tony Law's flotilla. We had to get rid of one or two of the ship's company and they were very happy to go. We didn't *make* them happy to go but they just weren't for MTBs. Those who remained were fine. But I had a couple of problems and, of course, the way you get rid of a man who is not too good is you promote him out of the flotilla. Give him a rank that isn't in the establishment of the flotilla. There is always room ashore. Both flotillas had a spare crew ashore, and engineer officer, repair mechanics, a paymaster lieutenant to handle the administrative problems, and Wren writers to help with the book work. So if we had a hand who did not fit in, who was backsliding or anything like that, we put him in the spare crew and then he was on tap for any other boat who needed a replacement for the night. It doesn't sound like it but this was really a severe punishment. No man likes to be just filling in here and there. He likes to be *in* the boat and *with* the crew. Those who remained were a very happy bunch. We didn't exactly like the funeral parades. Aside from the deaths we were a very happy bunch."

Kirk's engineer was Petty Officer Les Bowerman. He tells the story of one night off Jersey when they were shelled by shore batteries and had thirty-five shrapnel holes; on another occasion 745 counted seventy-six shrapnel holes. One night they were sitting with motor stopped off Brest and Bowerman, Petty Officer Cahill, and Stokers Kelly and Reid were talking on deck. With a rooooossssh! the shells started arriving. Kirk rang for full ahead and it seemed to Bowerman that the motors were a little slow starting – at least he thought so. As it turned out, a heavy calibre shell landed just ahead of them. If they had started earlier they would have been hit. But the gas tanks were now leaking. Bowerman said to Kirk, "You'd better put a rope on me because I'll have to go over the top of the tanks and the fumes are very strong." The two tanks, in fact, were holed and they were lucky they didn't blow up. They had many casualties during that time but only one fatality, a young Able Seaman from Nanaimo – Calverley, age eighteen.

Bowerman and the rest of 745's crew were in a rest camp in England the night of the invasion, a stand-down after five nights running. So Kirkpatrick moved himself over to Ollie Mabee's boat and led the other division over to the Cherbourg peninsula. "He would drive himself like that," Bowerman said. "I thought an awful lot of Kirk. I don't think I would have wanted to have sailed in a ship like that with anyone else. I think he felt the same about us. We got along well together. I felt safe with him on the bridge, he knew what he was doing as far as skippering goes. I think we did a pretty good job in the engine room, myself and my crew. I don't think Kirk could have had better people. We seemed to do the job and he was happy about it. And another thing, my engines were never out of commission for an engine failure. The only time they were not running was when disabled in action. Apart from that the engines were always ready to go. But after I had the engines running at full speed and turning over prettily, when the guns started firing there was only one place for the engine-room crew, flat on our stomachs between the engines. We never, never broke down at sea or had to be towed back. The reason things went so well for us, Kirk looked after his end of it and we looked after our end of it."

Stoker Petty Officer Gordon Cahill was also in 745 with Kirk and was sorry that when the bullets started flying toward him, he couldn't lie down between the engines because his action station was on the upper deck. He was in charge of the smoke-making apparatus. What was worse, he really had little to do until smoke was ordered and then all he had to do was turn a spigot. He wished passionately that the Captain would cease and desist from steaming the flotilla through the Channel Islands in daylight hours.

All along the coast after D-Day it was evident that the end of the German garrisions was approaching, and the Germans were doing their best to get rid of all their ammunitions. Cahill says "and Kirk was either the best Captain or the worst Captain, depending on which way you looked at it. He was the best Captain in that he knew how to look after his ship and his men and we all had confidence in him. But he was the worst Captain because he would insist on going through the Channel Islands in daylight. But maybe he didn't have a choice. The Germans never hit us because we were going pretty fast and zigzagging but Kirk always thought this was great sport. He'd have his hat off and his head sticking above the dodger into the breeze, laughing as he weaved the flotilla back and forth between the shell splashes. He thought it was great sport. I never did."

Even when Cahill would make smoke it was particularly galling knowing that some shore batteries had radar and his smoke wasn't hiding them anyway. And their routine was not easy; their schedule, by this time, was two nights out and one night in. After several months they were getting tired.

Leading Seaman Dave Wright joined Lieutenant Mabee's boat in May, 1944, in time to do trials and have a brush with flak trawlers. Wright was the only radar operator, at least to start with; another joined later. All of the hands could sleep at their station until action was joined but the engine room and the radar shack had to be constantly alert.

There were many things about radar sets that Wright did not like. One was that when they were being shelled from the Channel Islands he could pick up the projectiles on their way in, "so easily that I could give the Captain a bearing and enable him to see the origin of the shell. I didn't *want* to see 11-inch shells arriving. Then the drill was that the air force would go over the next day and bomb the battery."

The actions continued with flak ships and E-boats; on one occasion one hand was killed and several wounded and there were many holes in the ship. That time the engines were damaged and they had to creep back at six knots. Their return from this particular landing was filmed by a National Film Board crew, who were in the U.K. taking pictures of the Canadian forces. Another night four were killed, and they were buried in St. Mary's churchyard in Brixham.

Wright was talking to a couple of ladies there and they said they'd look after the graves and see that there were flowers on them. He never gave this much thought until in 1965 he got back to Brixham, went to St. Mary's churchyard, and, sure enough, the graves were well tended and with fresh flowers. When he got back to Canada he wrote to the secretary of the church, who replied, giving him the name of Miss Phyllis Jackman. She was the one Wright had been talking to the day of the funeral. He started a correspondence with her because he wanted to thank her and the other lady who had been looking after the graves. The other lady had died but in 1968 when he went back to the U.K. again he met Miss Jackman, by then age sixty-eight. He and his wife, Freda, told Miss Jackman that they would be delighted to see her if she could possibly get over to Canada. Two years later she did. They showed her a lot of British Columbia and took her on a trip to Alaska on the

*Prince George*; she came back in 1972 for another trip. Wright said it seemed little enough to do for her; she had looked after his dead shipmates' graves for twenty-seven years.

Mabee was second in command of the 65th – that is, he operated four boats and Kirk had four – and Wright's principle reaction to him was, "Mabee scared the hell out of me. He could get in all kinds of trouble. If we were in the patrol area close to the Channel Islands, around one of the ports, he would probably stick his bow in just to nose around a bit. To him there was nothing more interesting than that. I was in the radar cabin but the fellows on deck said they could see the sentry on the cliff sitting by his little fire keeping warm, and there we'd be fooling around below the sentry to see if there were any ships to shoot up. The radar cabin was only big enough for me to sit in. I couldn't even turn around in it. I had this great big life jacket and my tin helmet on and I was trying to make myself as small as possible knowing that I'd be the first to see any enemy ships. I was a radar operator and I was *supposed* to pick echoes up but I was always afraid I was going to. These were my thoughts all the time. It seemed to me to be crazy to be getting shot at. The fellows at the guns could stay asleep. The only ones awake were the engine room and me. I spent most of my watch hoping I would have nothing to report. But Mabee would go in anywhere to stir things up. It seems that that was what he was supposed to do – take these blooming chances, like going into an enemy harbour. Whether it was part of the game I don't know, but it never impressed me."*

Malcolm Knox arrived in the 65th Flotilla in January, 1943, and got boat 743. In one of the early actions when he was Tail-End Charlie an E-boat was sunk and he was told to pick up survivors. He got about nine of the crew after circling around for some time. But the Germans seemed strangely reluctant to get on board. It transpired later that the Germans had spotted his boat as being Canadian both from "HMC MTB" painted on the side and from the Maple Leaf on the funnel. This was just after the time of the Battle of the Bulge and one of the French-Canadian regiments – Régiment de la Chaudière, he thought – had found some of their troops murdered, shot in the head with their hands tied behind their backs; so the next time this regiment was on the offensive they

---

*In the three years I have known Dave Wright I have learned something of the nature of courage from him. Dave is slight of body and mild of manner, anxious to do what he can to help, unobtrusive, asking nothing for himself. And he was *always* afraid, from the time his boat left harbour until she got home again. Yet he *always* mastered his fear and did his duty. I admire him.

took no prisoners. This had become quite well known at that time and, to make matter worse, the Canadian cook was on the upper deck with knife in his hands to cut away the wet clothes of the survivors. One of the Germans, while in the water before being picked up, was still belligerent and had a revolver and took a pot shot at the Canadians on deck, but he missed. A guilty conscience maketh cowards of us all. They stripped the prisoners, took them below, wrapped them in blankets, gave them a hot drink, and treated them as best they could.

Knox talks about his training period with Bones Burk before he got command. "Bill is a great character. No matter what he does he puts so much enthusiasm into it that it's contagious. He fires everybody up to do more than they would do otherwise. He's a great leader, no doubt of it."

Burk married in the U.K. and later on Knox went to the christening of his daughter. His wife was a frequent visitor in the ship and, like Mrs. Kirkpatrick, drank tea in the wardroom.*

Although it isn't mentioned much in these chronicles there was some difficulty in getting men who were *suited* for MTB warfare even though they had *volunteered*. This was the case with the two first lieutenants who came to Knox originally. One was sent back into general service and the other transferred to Beach Master. There there were some who could not stand the constant battles. But I have never heard a man in the navy called "coward." There are men who are afraid and men who are not afraid; there are men who are afraid only in certain circumstances and not in others; there are men who are brave and men who are not brave. But if they don't fit where they are they may well fit somewhere else. Courage is just being able to handle fear under a particular set of circumstances. It is mostly the ability to push fear to the back of your mind. But everybody I know has always lived with it, albeit at the back of his mind. There are men, too, like Dave Wright, who always felt fear and always mastered it and did their duty. And that is an admirable trait.

In March, 1944, Knox had 743 in Brixham operating with Kirk around the Channel Islands. At this point the Beaufighters were making a sweep down the coast at sunset passing information back and the flotilla would get any specific indication from which ports German convoys were leaving. They would head to intercept. The Channel is a treacherous

---

*Bones Burk married an English nurse, Jean. She continued to work until it was time for their first child to be born, then she moved to wherever Bones was based, saw his boat off in the evening, and welcomed him home in the morning.

place, tides and rocks and shoals and swirling irregular currents. The shore batteries, of course, were a menace as always. Sometimes they had a visitor out for the night and on one occasion it was a padre. They were coasting along and wandered inside range of the shore batteries. There was a clap like thunder and spouts of water all around and this gentleman of the cloth was down on his knees with his prayer beads in his hand. "It wasn't exactly setting the best example for the fighting part of the crew so he wasn't invited again. The fellow who came most often was Gib Milne, a naval photographer from Toronto, the one who produced that marvellous book of naval war photographs titled, *H.M.C.S.*" The exchange of call signs between Knox and Kirk was always a source of some wan humour. Knox was very proud of his call sign "Night Hawk" and always thought that Kirk's call sign "Little Child" was so inappropriate. He mentioned this one day and Kirk said, "Your theological knowledge is sadly lacking, have you never heard? 'A little child shall lead them?'" However, he seldom called up using his proper call sign. Everyone knew that Kirk was on the air when they heard over the r/t, "Calling all cars, calling all cars."

Knox says, "Kirk was very courageous and certainly had a lot of experience in the North Sea as an MTB skipper. Being Senior Officer of a group like that, eight ships and the shore people, I guess he had about 400 bodies to look after. Even in those days he was a master at handling people and when defaulters came along he certainly had novel ways of getting the truth and applying punishment to them. He managed to keep the admiration of the men and maintain discipline, [and] this is not an easy combination. I can't put my finger on it but he had a way of getting at the truth and he carried it on into later life because he became a chief magistrate in Kitchener. But he was daring – one morning the hands in 743 thought he was daring to a fault. This particular morning he led them into St. Peter Port, the harbour of Guernsey, and they were all sure that the shore batteries were going to do them in – at point blank range they were going to do them in. It was just that Kirk wanted to see what was in there. When he saw that there was nothing in there worth doing he high-tailed it out at a rate of knots."

The kaleidoscope of war: a Lancaster bomber coming back from a raid on Europe and apparently with some bombs left, found the group lying off St. Malo and thought, "What the hell", dropped his bombs, and luckily missed. On another occasion a Liberator (an anti-submarine bomber) came in quietly with his propellers feathered until he was above them, switched on his Leigh light (a million candlepower), and caused everyone to have to change his underwear.

\* \* \*

In January, 1944, Jack McClelland joined Oliver Mabee's boat and became operational out of Brixham, operating primarily in the Channel Islands. In those months and in that part of the Channel they were working alongside the flotilla of Commander Buckley, USN. They were the stars of the movie *They Were Expendable*. They had made the movie (from the book of the same name) where they sank a great many Japanese battleships. But the thing that struck the RN most about the USN was how they could never stop running off at the mouth on the r/t, constant chatter, mostly inane idle chatter. The RCN didn't think much of these representatives of the USN.

One night Mabee's boat drifted off station, which is a *very* dangerous thing to do. *Blyskawica* and *Piorun* swept by and shot them up. A couple of the hands were wounded and it was a great sight to see these great destroyers bearing down belching flame, but not so good to realize they were at the receiving end. They made smoke, fired Very lights, and roared on the r/t "Cut it out, cut it out. We're Canadian." Ollie Mabee went to see the captain of the *Blyskawica* the next time they were in port and presented him with a big shell splinter he had taken off his own deck. There was a lot of misidentification and, with the best will in the world, if you weren't where you were supposed to be you were going to get bashed.

Daniel Lang picked up 727 under construction up a little creek near Dartmouth. A ship-builder there, who built yachts during peacetime, now constructed torpedo boats. Les McLernon from Montreal was the Captain, Lang was Number One, and Monk Davidson was Navigator. They worked up in Holyhead, then joined the other Canadian boats. The other commanding officers were "Sea Time Charlie" (Bert Morrow was so named because he was always bragging about the amount of sea time he had), Owen Greening, Oliver Mabee, and John Collins.

Their first operation was to the Channel Islands in company with Royal Navy craft out of Dartmouth, to give them experience in tracking enemy shipping. "But our main enemy seemed to be shore batteries on Jersey, Guernsey, and Sark; we learned a lot about shore batteries; we didn't learn much about attacking enemy shipping. They got close to us, the shore batteries, indeed they did, but never did hit us. We were lucky. They would never fire on you as long as you were moving closer to them, but as soon as you would start to move away, that was when the shooting would start. So just as soon as they did, we *knew* we were moving away from them and we would immediately start zigzagging and laying smoke. But you'd have bright moonlight nights when it was almost as bright as day; smoke was good. Even so they got close enough that you got spray on board, from shell splashes. On yes! There would be these great big geysers coming up all around. And we were steaming right through these shell splashes. Well, we were trying not to. They were big guns, too – 4-inch, 6-inch."

The first fierce action was off the Channel Islands when they caught a heavily escorted convoy – one very large merchant ship in the middle. That was the convoy – one ship with ten escorts. They never had much luck with torpedo attacks; the mechanism for firing a torpedo was an amateur's little gadget. To push the little model boat back and forward in the dark and do your aim-off was difficult compared with what the E-boats had, sophisticated binoculars and speed-and-inclination finders. We had nothing like that. Ours was a little thing you'd buy in Woolworth's. Lang knew the chance of hitting anything with a torpedo was slight. So when they saw this convoy with this big ship in the middle, they decided to penetrate the screen and do a gun attack. Dan Lang's 727 did.

"Boy! It must have had explosives or petrol on board because it went up like the sun. In the meantime, we got into dogfights separately with various members of the escort. Our gun power was superior, we were right in, close. We went in line abreast and I can remember when we turned, a simultaneous turning . . . into line ahead. Then we had a broadside onto them. You couldn't miss. Two hundred yards, then one hundred."

As time went on they fired lots of torpedoes, and missed, and always got told how expensive they were to replace, "so we stopped firing them. That's crazy! To criticize us for firing torpedoes because they were expensive to lose. Well, we were really gun boats with torpedoes.

"Prior to D-day, we were patrolling the Carentan peninsula (Cherbourg is the tip of it) and we would go up the inside of that passage between the Channel Islands and the mainland. We had dust-ups in there all the time, you couldn't characterize them as major engagements by any means.

"Immediately before D-Day they carried out Operation Lion, a landing in Tor Bay, by mostly American landing craft. It was a rehearsal, really, of D-Day, with a tremendous number of ships involved. MTBs were to be the outside screen. The Wrens in the Commander-in Chief's ops room kept a maternal eye on their radar scoopes – watching the children out at play. Our Wren controller told us that E-boats had moved out of Cherbourg, heading our way; she gave us the enemy position every few minutes.

"But somehow the E-boats got past us. We didn't see them on our radar; they got past the destroyer screen; they got inside amongst the landing craft and created havoc. Ships were blowing up all over. As the Germans were retiring back to Cherbourg, our Wren controller on the shore radar vectored us on the them. It was rough and dark and this girlish voice was vectoring us. We were up at full speed.

" 'Canada Seven, this is Little Sister. Steer one-seven-oh. Over.'

" 'Little Sister, this is Canada Seven. Wilco. Out.'

" 'Canada Seven, this is Little Sister. Alter to one-seven-five; range two thousand; closing. Over.'

" 'This is Canada Seven. Wilco. Thank you Little Sister. Out.'

" 'Canada Seven, this is Little Sister. Your bearing is steady, closing, range, one thousand. Watch it, watch it. Over.'

" 'Canada seven. Roger. Out.'

" 'Canada Seven, Canada Seven. Heads up! Heads up! You're merged.'

"That meant our blips had come together. I'll be damned if I could see anything and then all of a sudden there was an E-boat – right alongside. I could have jumped on board. He saw us at the same time. He was so close in, we couldn't even get our guns on him and he went out of there like a rabbit. I've never seen anything like it. She moved away from us so fast, both away from us and forward of us. Can you believe it? That flotilla of E-boats got back to Cherbourg scot-free.

"The Captain of that E-boat flotilla was famous. I think he was a son of one of the German generals on the Normandy front. He had some worthy exploits. He was a magnificent person in the way he conducted them. The funny part is we got to know what those men were like from some of the British sailors who had been captured by them. [Our sailors] always got back to England in about three weeks. As long as they were captured by the Kreigsmarine they were fine. Not so if they got into the hands of the Gestapo. We'd get to know the names of these men – in the E-boats – and a sort of sketch of their personalities. I gather they had quite accurate information on us.

"The German captains would pick up our survivors and release them in France or Holland, just let our men go and they'd work down from a chain in the underground, through France, into Spain. Golly! That was well known. As long as there was no Gestapo involved. I know that with our Coastal Forces people in MTBs or MGBs, as long as they fell into the hands of their opposite numbers in the E-boats, they were home free. But if an intelligence officer or Gestapo officer got to them, it was a different story. But they were protected from them as much as could be by the E-boat crews particularly; they were let go into that escape route. Now I don't know, but the escape route was pretty well established then. They were handed from group to group until they got to Spain. This was extraordinary because the Kreigsmarine must have known where to start them. Oh yes. They certainly did.

"I know I've heard stories about meetings which are fabulous. Norm Garriock, who was and still is, I believe, a senior official in the CBC, head of the English-language production network, he was going out to open a CBC station in Winnipeg (this must be fifteen years ago) and on the plane was a CBC technician and Garriock fell into conversation with him and found out that he was an E-boat captain and had been shooting at Garriock's boat in the Scheldt estuary, when Garriock's boat sank the E-boat. When the MTB of the CBC's head of English production sank the E-boat of the CBC's technician. Interesting for them both."

＊　＊　＊

The 26th Destroyer Flotilla had spent from December, 1943, to June, 1944, in escorting the fleet and convoys to Russia, five times up to Altenfiord to try and persuade the German battleship *Tirpitz* to come out and play, and strikes at enemy coastal shipping in the Norwegian leads. Captain D was in HMS *Myngs*. The rest comprised HMS *Vigilant*, *Verulam*, *Venus*, *Virago*, and *Volage*, and HMCS *Algonquin* (formerly *Valentine*) and *Sioux* (formerly *Vixen*).

Before we left Scapa Flow to come south, *Sioux* had been inspected by the King. His Majesty loved to get back to the fleet. The monarchy always has had a distinct naval trend. His father, King George V, had been sent at age twelve to the naval college at Osborne. He then was promoted in the ordinary way – he commanded a gun boat on the North American and West Indies stations – to the command of the cruiser *Crescent* as a post captain. George VI had also gone through the naval college, done his sub-lieutenant's courses in the usual way, and served in the fleet at the Battle of Jutland. He had been awarded a Mentioned-in-Despatches for that battle.

He bounded on board *Sioux* looking fit and affable, inspected the ship's company, and stopped to talk here and there. He spotted the oak leaf of my Mentioned-in-Despatches.

"What did you get that for?"

"A u-boat sinking, sir,"

"And the DSC?"

"Another u-boat, sir."

"Have you picked up the medal yet?"

"No, sir."

"You should do that."

"Aye, aye, sir."

What an absolutely marvellous idea! That could be taken as an order to spend time in London to attend an investiture at Buckingham Palace. I would not forget to remind the Captain of this when my jaded spirits needed reviving.

We sailed from Scapa Flow for Cowes in the Isle of Wight and anchored in the Roads. As far as the eye could see The Solent was jammed with shipping. At every jetty landing craft or motor torpedo boats would be twenty to thirty deep, everything from the landing ships of 16,000 tons to assault craft of two tons.

The invasion of Europe was known as Operation Overlord; the naval side of it – the landing of our troops on the beaches of Normandy – was Operation Neptune. It was with great enthusiasm that we saw the minesweepers get under way in the middle of the afternoon; this would allow them to form up before dusk to sweep the Channel during the night. These were the spearhead of 4,126 ships and landing craft to be thrown on the assault beaches and used during the follow-up. These assault ships were protected by 1,213 warships, served by 736 auxiliary craft, and supplied by 864 merchant ships. Just under 7,000 vessels, 79 per cent of them British.

It is an interesting commentary on the course of the war to note that 90 per cent of these soldiers would be going into action for the first time while 90 per cent of the sailors were veterans of several years' fighting. After the navy rescued our soldiers from Dunkirk there came a long period known as the "Phoney War." Our soldiers could not get back to the continent; the Germans were consolidating their positions. But the day war was declared, 3 September 1939, ss *Athenia* was sunk by Leutnant Lemp in u-30. By Christmas of that year 206 ships had followed her, and, through 1943, 3,376 Allied ships had gone to the bottom. No, there was no Phoney War for the navy.

From 1940 our Canadian soldiers had seen little action apart from those who attacked Dieppe. They saw more in the invasion of Sicily and Italy. But the invasion of Normandy was the big effort that was to win the war. In effect, most of our soldiers had been training for three years. By contrast, most sailors I knew had been fighting for four years. (Counting a cruiser and two corvettes I had served in before going to *Sioux*, I had put in a total of four years, five months of sea time. All the ship's company in *Sioux* were old hands in battle. We never thought of ourselves as battle-hardened veterans though; we thought veterans were men of sixty from the last war.)

Matelots like to point this out to pongos from time to time. A sailor and a soldier who had been school friends in Toronto in 1938 met again in 1944 in London, England. Said the sailor to the soldier, "Well, Harry, and where have you been since you joined?"

"My regiment was landed in Norway in April, 1940; but so were the Germans and one of your cruisers had to take us out of there."

"Then what?"

"We went to France. But in June we had to get out of there. Dunkirk."

"Then what?"

"We practised in Salisbury Plain for three years, then went to build up the garrison at Crete. But . . ."

"Yeah, we took you out there. Where are you on leave from now?"

"We're with Monty in the desert."

"How do you like that?"

"Not much. Too far from the Navy."

We heaved in anchors, formed astern of Captain D, and set off across the Channel. I had my supper at six p.m. and got my head down till midnight, when we went to action stations. Then I was in the gunnery director, which controls the main armament, the four 4.7-inch guns. On the principle that it's impossible to get too much to eat or too much sleep, I chewed a corned beef sandwich, cushioned my head in my arms, and dozed again in the director for four hours. From four a.m. on we heard the constant drone of aircraft carrying paratroopers who were to secure vital bridges and crossroads behind the assault area. Somewhere in the sky above *Sioux* was the First Canadian Parachute Battalion. By about five a.m. of the 6th of June we could see the coast, a flat featureless blur except for the church spire at Bernières-sur-mer. We were heading for Juno Beach, which would be stormed by General Crerar's First Canadian Army. By 5:30 a.m. the drone of aircraft rose to a constant roar and up and down the shoreline, east and west as far as we could see, were the flashing, oscillating lights of saturation bombing. The rumble and boom was constant in the dawn, the whole coast flickering like sheet lightning. We were all well and truly awake having had a quick cup of cocoa as a pick-me-up. The wind was light from the west at twenty-five knots, a choppy sea, a flooding tide, sunrise 5:58, H-Hour at 6:30. Captain D moved the flotilla to line abreast and the curtain of night lifted on the greatest naval stage ever seen.

Our flotilla was eight of the ninety-four destroyers spread out across Sword Beach to the port of us to Gold Beach to starboard; they stretched away to the west to the American sector. Astern were *Warspite*, *Ramillies*, and *Roberts* with their 15-inch guns. The cruisers *Scylla*, *Danae*, *Dragon*, *Frobisher*, *Arethusa*, and *Mauritius* were to the east and *Ajax*, *Argonaut*, *Emerald*, *Orion*, *Flores*, *Belfast*, and *Diadem* to the west. The large landing craft were chugging in and astern of them the large liners were anchoring and lowering their smaller landing craft. Overhead Spitfires and Mustangs banked in two-mile circles.

In the summer of 1940, 260,000 British and 70,000 French troops had been evacuated from the beaches of Dunkirk after Germany had conquered Poland, Belgium, Denmark, Norway, Holland, and France and broken through to the sea. At that time Winston Churchill had said, "Britain will fight on . . . if necessary for years . . . if necessary alone . . . We shall go back." At dawn of the 6th of June 1944, we did.

For months before this landing, submarines had been creeping inshore and taking pictures of the coastline through their periscopes. Aircraft had been swooping in and out doing the same thing. The result was a composite of the coastline of Normandy from Cherbourg to Le Havre. Our section on Juno Beach was what we were looking for and yes, there it was! *That* was the right silhouette. That was the street; that the building. To look from the photograph to the shoreline was to see a replica. Captain D gave the order to open fire and up and down the coast the guns spoke. Over a thousand of them. It was six a.m. Sand spouted as our broadside landed a little to the left. Small corrections were made between broadsides, the shots were now in line, and concrete and brick debris were flying instead of sand. Over our heads we heard the whoooosh of the cruiser's 6-inch shells and above that the russssh of the 15-inch shells. The ceasefire bells clamoured. I took my eyes out of the director binoculars and looked around. It was 6:30; the dear old pongos were hitting the beaches: the Queen's Own Rifles, the North Shore (New Brunswick) Regiment, the Regina Rifles, the Royal Winnipeg Rifles. They waved as they passed.

For Operation Neptune the 29th Flotilla was divided into two striking forces. Law was Senior Officer of one of these in 459, Dave Killam was astern in 460, Charlie Chaffey in 465, and Tail End Charlie, Barney Marshall, in 466. The other force was led by the divisional leader Bones Burk in 461. Astern of him were Bobby Moyse in 462, Craig Bishop in 464, and Glen Creba in 463. Burk left for the Normandy beaches on the night of the 5th. They were stationed on the eastern flank of the invasion fleet to bottle up the German ships in Le Havre. It was evident that the planning had gone down to some fairly minute details. Off Juno Beach they passed a typical old Trinity House, red, lightship with white markings on her side, JUNO BEACH; further on they passed a floating kitchen. The mother ship for the 29th was the British cruiser *Scylla*.

The next day Law took over the patrol, about twelve miles off Cape Le Havre. The night was filled with alarms and excursions as star shell and tracer soared skyward, now in one direction, now in another, none near them. About two a.m. Law spotted six silhouettes, which his radar set confirmed; they were R-boats. At 700 yards Law's division closed the range and opened fire at 150 yards; Law's boat was hit several times. One hand on the pom-pom, although seriously wounded, continued to feed his gun. In 466 two gunners had also been wounded. All four boats suffered damage or casualties but one R-boat was blown up and another set on fire. With the dawn they returned to Mother *Scylla* to land their wounded.

*Scylla*'s sick bay, however, was already filled and the doctor directed them to a hospital ship lying inshore of *Scylla*; they reached her only to find that she, too, was full. They wandered around the anchorage looking for another hospital ship. A destroyer's doctor came on board to do what he could for them, but with no operating equipment his aid was limited. However, an hour later he found them a hospital ship with space and the wounded were comfortable at last.

Law got his head down for a couple of hours. A signal arrived from *Scylla*, "Come alongside." The four captains made their way to *Scylla*'s bridge where Admiral Vian was standing rigged out in blue battle dress with his steel helmet at a jaunty angle. Their introduction to him was interrupted by a cheeky German tank that broke through the army lines, rolled to the edge of the beach, and imprudently started to fire at the flagship. Vian remarked, "What an insolent fellow. I admire his courage." *Scylla* did not deign to reply with her 6-inch guns. Two of our tanks closed in and took the German tank prisoner.

The next week passed this way, with *Scylla* vectoring the 29th on to likely targets. One morning Law's signalman spotted *Algonquin* entering the anchorage and flashed her, "Hello Big Canada, this is Little Canada." In reply he got, "Hello Little Canada, this is Admiral Nelles. Will be visiting you at 0800." The crew pulled themselves together from the night patrol, tossed down some food, squared away the mess decks, and the Admiral jumped nimbly on board despite the heavy sea that was heaving them up and down. MTB 459 remained in the assault area that afternoon made fast alongside *Algonquin*. It was Debby Piers's birthday and he invited all the crew on board to dine, with a movie afterwards.

During these first days the 65th had some fairly extensive actions in the Channel Islands – off St. Helier, for instance – and suffered and inflicted casualties. On the morning of D-Day they were on the western flank off the Cherbourg peninsula and so they did not see that much of the landing – just the fireworks in the sky that night and the following night.

# XII   Europe Set Free

On the night of the 5th of June 1944 and the morning of the 6th, Canadian River-class destroyers, frigates, and corvettes patrolled to the north and south of the invasion waters; the Tribals patrolled back and forth to the south of Brest. The 65th Canadian MGB Flotilla patrolled off the Cherbourg peninsula under Kirkpatrick. The 29th Canadian MTB Flotilla patrolled off Le Havre under Bones Burk. The Canadian Army approached Juno Beach with *Algonquin* and *Sioux* and Canadian minesweepers ahead of them. At dawn the Canadian destroyers and the rest of the flotilla bombarded from one mile offshore. The check-fire bells stopped our bombardment and the Canadian troops landed. That day, across five beaches from Le Havre to Cherbourg, 130,000 men went ashore; by the end of June, 875,000. As our soldiers got inland the Canadian Army swung to the north through France, to Belgium, to Holland. Our torpedo boats and our gun boats followed them.

Tony Law of the 29th was now in 459; he had Bones Burk (called "Daddy Bones" by Tony) in 461, Killam in 460, Moyse in 462, Creba in 463, Joe Adams (later Craig Bishop) driving 464, Chaffey in 465, and Barney Marshall in 466. Night skirmishes went on. One night *Scylla* vectored them to two targets – two Möwe-class destroyers as it turned out. The range closed to 1,000 yards. There seemed to be much more flak than usual coming from the targets, and bigger, and accurate; the targets must have radar. Then *Scylla* came up on the r/t: "Hello Slattery. This is Bibble. We put you on to two German destroyers. We cannot help, sorry. Over."

"Hello Bibble. You said it! Out."

Law made smoke; everybody made smoke. They all increased to maximum speed and retreated into the gloom.

By the 15th of June the invasion anchorage had become a neighbour-hood where one had good friends, friends, and acquaintances. One of the 29th's acquaintances was the 40,000-ton battleship *Nelson*. One day 466 hailed her. The Commander stuck his head over the side and was asked, "May we have some water, please?"

"Don't you realize, youngster, that we have to make our own water on board this ship?"

"Please, sir, we have none. May we have just a little."

"Well, all right then, but I can only let you have 800 gallons."

"Thank you, sir. But our tank can only take forty-five."

Having scored this minor victory the MTBs put the touch on *Nelson* for fresh bread.

The Germans thought we would not land on the Normandy coast; there was no harbour there. We brought our own. We in *Sioux* had seen the harbour built. "Gooseberry" was a breakwater of old merchant ships towed over and scuttled head to stern. "Mulberries" were massive floating piers towed over and then scuttled to the bottom. Above water they looked like normal jetties. Ships berthed inside, protected from the wind and sea. They needed to be. A gale drove them all into the Mulberry harbour, and glad they were to be there; it blew up to hurricane force.

On the 2nd of July, Law was told that Captain McLaughlin, Captain Coastal Force, wished to see him.

"Hello Law. I have some very bad news for you. We have just received a signal that MTB 460 has struck a mine and blown up. There are only six survivors. Both officers as well as nine ratings are missing and two bodies have been picked up. We can't tell you how sorry we are about this terrible disaster. My staff and I offer our sincere sympathy to you and your flotilla." Thus it was that Dave Killam and nine of this crew left that gallant band.

The war wended its dreary course with skirmishes with E-boats, R-boats, flak ships, destroyers, shore batteries. Sometimes it was quiet for a week on end and then would come an hour of frantic skirmishes. By the end of July the Canadian Army was moving up toward Holland and Canadian MTBs followed.

On the night of 15-16 July, Law in 459 was once again on patrol off Le Havre with 464 and 466. About 11:30 p.m. they were shelled by Trouville's shore batteries on the south bank of Seine Bay. They were vectored to a small buoy, steaming close to Le Havre, near the shoreline toward D'Antifer: as they moved to attack German aircraft dropped flares. Expecting to be bombed, Law stopped the boats dead so their wakes would not show. The shore batteries spotted this and opened up. A salvo of shells crashed around them. In the second salvo a shell hit Law's boat in the engine room with a loud and devastating explosion. The coxswain and Law were pinned down on the bridge by a piece of the engine-room deck and 459 began settling rapidly by the stern. Law called Barney Marshall to come alongside and Joe Adams to lay a smokescreen between the stricken boat and the shore. Star shell came ahead from an inquiring enemy. The whole after-end of the ship was now awash and it was impossible to get out the bodies of his engineers. Law stayed with his ship till he was up to his waist in water; two electric pumps were brought alongside to get her pumped out. But the hole in her side was fourteen-feet long, the whole height of her from the gunwale to down below the waterline. By morning 459 was being towed slowly down the swept channel. Salvage operations began. There was nothing left of the engine that had taken the 88mm shell and the final indignity came when a floating crane latched on to her and hauled her aloft. That was the last that was seen of her.

The burials took place near the Trinity light vessel *Juno* on the outer area of the anchorage. Boats 464 and 466 tied up alongside each other and on their decks gathered their crewmen and those survivors of 459. The sun shone brilliantly, the sea was calm, and the simple service followed its dignified pattern.

In August the new MTB 486 was commissioned and, leading 485, 461, 462, 464, 465, and 466, Law headed back to Ramsgate. The replacements for the dead were motor mechanic Petty Officer Jim MacKay and Leading Stoker Brown. Stoker Roberts was the surviving member of the previous crew. Their paymaster, Hal Ritchie, had finally won his battle with the Great White Father of the Royal Navy Paymaster Corps and managed to get them on Canadian rations. In round numbers this was about three times as good as the RN ration in variety and quantity. Engineer Lieutenant Berlin – called, of course, "Irving" – got those boats in for refit past their 300 engine-hours and by the end of August, 1944, they were fighting fit again. By this time the Canadian troops were moving quickly along the coast toward the heavy guns of Calais and Cape Griz Nez, doodlebugs were spluttering overhead, and MTBs attacking between Boulogne and Calais were controlled by radar from Dover Castle. It was a synchronized effort with bombers and fighters patrolling the coast reporting enemy shipping movements. Off Cap Griz Nez one day they were told to stop and the Dover batteries opened up on a German coastal convoy. When this bombardment came to an end Law's flotilla was sent in to fire their torpedoes and – one of the few times during the war – an enemy ship blew up.

* * *

As divisional leader, Bones Burk had four of the flotilla out while Law's four had their night in and thus he was in command of many of the actions similar to those described above. After the usual brouhahas off the invasion coast they moved north to the Ostend area. He, in 461, had more successes than perhaps any of the other captains. It is perhaps wrong to quantify an officer's performance, but he did seem to have the mark of a true mariner, that is, a sea sense. And he had the good fortune to be wherever the trouble was. Captain Basil Jones said the same thing of Harry De Wolf, "There is no doubt that he – 'Hard Over Harry' as he was known to his friends – was an outstanding officer, not only in his skill but in aggressive spirit. Furthermore, he had the priceless gift of fortune of there always being a target for him to fight in whatever area he was told to operate." Burk was the same.

Ian Robertson was appointed as Burk's navigator and thinks "it was one of the luckiest days of my life. The second division almost always operated by itself under his command. So here I was, Number Three on the Senior Officer's ship, where I could learn from Bones Burk, who was a superb MTB officer with an unbeatable record; the RN would be the first to agree. Keith Scobie was the First Lieutenant. Bones was a natural leader in the best sense of the word and of a kind I've met very few of in my life. There was no side to him, no swank. He just somehow managed to get on with everyone who worked around him. All the hands would do anything for him. He didn't seem to try for this, he was extremely natural. There was no bluster about him. He had an infinite patience and on top of that he was an *ace* in the full sense of the word as he proved in engagement after engagement. He led a quiet life in harbour. He had married an English girl, Jean – Mrs. Burk to us. She would visit us in the ship."

Robertson joined him in May, 1944, during the working-up period so he was with him all through the invasion of Normandy and moving up the coast toward Ostend as far as the Canadian Army moved north. By that time the E-boats were husbanding their resources and were not bellicose; they fought a defensive war by laying mines. But Narvik, Elbing, Seetier, and Möwe-class destroyers, if they did not abound, were plentiful enough to cause one's heart to go pit-a-pat when a radar echo looked big enough and moved fast enough to be a destroyer. They had worked out of Aramanches and moved to Ostend but the rigours of the past four years had taken their toll and Burk came down with jaundice and was sent to a hospital in Belgium.

Robertson was starting his long trek on the road to Coastal Forces expertise and his first major victory was overcoming seasickness. On the way over to the invasion until they got under the lee of the Cherbourg peninsula he was feeling distinctly uneasy and not at all like invading the continent of Europe. But he had learned an important lesson, that he could time when he was going to be sick. He could still do his job plotting the ship's course and providing whatever information the Captain asked for, and when he knew he was going to be sick he would plot ahead a few minutes, tell the skipper what he was doing, nip out of the chart house, vomit, get back to his work, stuff a few dry biscuits into himself, and keep going. That night of the invasion he was sick about once every half-hour, two minutes at a time.

Before the flotilla moved north Robertson had been based at Dover and they had quarters ashore (you couldn't sleep aboard the Shorts). They worked in the ship in the day while in harbour and retired to their apartment in the evening. One warm summer evening, very late, they had all the lights out and the windows open. It was a nice evening, a beautiful view, something like Arnold's "Dover Beach." The shore batteries at Calais were now bombarding sporadically but steadily around the clock to anything within range – which, of course, Dover was. After midnight the shelling started but by this time all our hands were getting pretty blasé. You can develop the knack of knowing from the sound of the enemy shore battery if the gun is pointed at you or not, that is, if it's a dull rumble or a sharp crack. This night they weren't sure whether it was a rumble or a crack or a combination, but down came all the chandeliers and the stucco off the wall, and the shutters in the window were blown in. It was a *very* close miss. Soon they moved north to Felixstowe, set in lush and lovely countryside where they could exchange the smell of engine-room oil and wet clothes for clover and new-mown hay. The Felix Hotel still had its squash court, which they could use, and they were often fortunate to berth right in front of it.

The flotilla was well worked-up and battle-hardened by November of 1944 when Walter Blandy joined Ollie Mabee's 726 as Navigator. They were based in Ostend doing the run north of the Scheldt estuary at night, two in a team tying up to navigational buoys (tied to a lamppost, as they used to say). Destroyers further out to sea with good radar acted as their direction ships and when they saw an E-boat coming down the Hook of Holland they vectored them on. Our MTBs were kept busy discouraging the E-boats from laying mines. The gun battles were the usual flare-up and then darkness again, but, says Blandy, "They were persistent, very persistent. We'd drive them off but they would come back later and lay their mines. You could also say they were very brave when at that point of the war it was murder for them to come out.

"Besides the navigation of the boat my principal duty was to administer morphine to any of our hands who were injured. This, of course, is a normal humane measure to deaden pain but a more important part of my job was to make sure they had a big tag on them saying what dosage they had already had so that the medics ashore would not overdose them."

MTB 726 was due for refit so they had Christmas in Poole, at the yard of the British Power Boat Company. Like the other boats – indeed, like all the fishermen in the area – they replenished their stores from torpedoed merchantmen. On one occasion there were so many fish boats alongside a sunken freighter that they had a job getting on board. And when they did, they found she had been stripped clean.

"Kirk was the tops! He had a wonderful personality. He was aloof and he was the boss. He had married an English girl and so spent most of his time in harbour at home. But Mrs. Kirkpatrick would visit us in harbour."*

Blandy continues: "The war was now going into its sixth year and a code of ethics had built up, if it is not an oxymoron to talk about ethics and war in the same sentence. But as seaman versus seaman there was mutual respect between the Germans and the Allies. I'm fighting you, I think I'm better than you, I think I'm going to win the war, but on the other hand I give you credit for having the same thoughts yourself. May the best man come out on top. There was never any hate. With us in the navy in general and Coastal Forces in particular it was a gentleman's game and we played it according to certain rules – may the best be the victor. For instance, if you sink your enemy you do everything possible *not* to leave him. Pick him up; he's not an enemy anymore, he's a survivor. If I can't pick him up because of the circumstances at the time, I'd mark the spot so that I can come back later or send somebody else.

---

*I met Winnifred Kirkpatrick when I visited Judge Kirkpatrick in Kitchener, Ontario, two years ago. A wife's view of a flotilla commander is very different from his admiring officers. She said, "I would be down at the jetty every morning to watch them come in. One morning as the boats got closer I saw that Jim had a bandage around his throat. I thought, 'Oh, good heavens, he's been hit in the neck.' But then I saw his wide smile as he saw me and I wondered. My heart was going faster. As the boat got closer I saw that what I thought was a bandage was only a white towel he had wrapped around his neck to keep spray and rain out. I was so *cross* with him."

"Leave was getting more frequent; it was apparent the war was drawing to a successful conclusion. Leave in Ostend was more than passable; it is not a terribly active city but there was a place called Cercle Inter Allée – in pre-war days it was a gambling casino. It was mainly drinking and dancing. It had a copy of the Mannikin Pee (as in pissoir). This was in commemoration of a small boy in one of the Belgian towns in the sixteenth century who, when the town was besieged by the enemy, went up to the wall and pissed all over them. That so encouraged the citizens they hung on for another four days and the siege was lifted. So there was a statue of the Mannikin Pee in the fountain of Cercle Inter Allée. In this club this small statue stood in the corner; the plumbing was arranged that if you sat your friend in a special chair, then excused yourself and went to the heads and turned on the tap, your friend got it full in the face. Things like that used to amuse us. I bought a little brass one to take home for my mother.

"I met some nice girls but none who made bells ring. There were quite a few girls around but the way it transpired for us was that we never really got over being tired from the last trip and we were going out again tomorrow. So it was a question of just going to the casino and drinking and watching the dancing and perhaps having a dance yourself. But we didn't want to get tied up with any of the local belles. There were the usual ladies of the evening but paying for it was always thought to be slightly ridiculous to sailors.

"On the English side of the Channel we had the usual quota of Wren girlfriends who were valued as much for the work they did on board as for their company ashore. You would wake up refreshed from an afternoon zizz just about time they'd be finishing their day's work. Then you'd be in in shape for the evening ahead.

"By this time, the squadron was a bit of precision machinery: it was a pleasure to watch work. All were competent in their field, all the crews trusted their officers and the whole lot of them trusted the Captain, and all the captains followed Kirk as the unquestioned leader. No bums. That was the really good thing about it. Kirk had managed in the early days to remove any bad hats, any slackers, any irritants. Those left were cohesive, vital, effective."

When the fighting moved up the Dutch coast, Dave Wright was based first at Yarmouth and then at Ostend. Occasionally they would get five days leave in London but it didn't do Wright much good because he never had more than twenty-five dollars in his pocket the whole time he was in the navy: he was helping support his mother at home; his father had died when he was thirteen. However, he went down to London with a little money and stayed at the YMCA, but he was always looking for a job to pay for an evening's fun. He worked at a brewery for a few days, pushing bottles around. When that was finished he got a job as a movie extra. The movie was *A Way to the Stars* and it was about the integration of the RAF and the USAAF. He and his shipmates had to dress as U.S. Army Air Force officers and stand around in a pub drinking beer. Wright saw himself in the final version of the film – about five seconds worth.

In Ostend the hazards were of rather a different sort. It was perhaps more dangerous ashore than it was afloat. The countryside was heavily mined and on one occasion the truck that carried supplies for the flotilla was bringing them back from Bruges, ran over a land mine, blew up, and killed several.

In the matter of looting stations Wright was fortunate. Once after Walcheren Island they came across a recently torpedoed ship, now abandoned, superstructure still out of the water, and he got a good brown suit off her: good material, a nice fit, too. He stayed at Ostend pretty well until the end of the war and after some time, as local inhabitants, they got a thriving black market going. Their telegraphist used to bring the ship's stores from NAAFI and do the cooking; he always managed to get more stores than he needed and he'd drop some off at one of the local burghers and then go back and get more for the ship's company. As long as they were fed well they didn't mind. The army, of course, was in a better position to run a black market by being ashore. Wright knew one Canadian soldier in the quartermaster stores who, according to him, sold the same jeep three times. "What he would do was that he would sell it to a local farmer who would hide it under a haystack. Then the quartermaster would get his chums to search the farm, commandeer the jeep, frighten the life out of the farmer because it was illegal for him to have military equipment, and then sell it again somewhere else. Rumour has it that he made so much money that, not being able to get it out, he bought a small farm in Belgium before he went home to Canada."

In the winter of 1945 Wright was able to get down to London to meet his girlfriend in the Auxiliary Territorial Service. The girls were in the barracks up on Mill Hill in London, so he and his chums would go under the barrack fence and into the girls' quarters and there they would sit, "quiet as mice, because their sergeant would have given a lot of trouble. We could have been shot or something. We'd sit there by the little fire and make toast and whatever else we could get and talk very quietly so no one could hear us. Sometimes we'd bring a bottle of beer in but most of the time we were drinking tea. When we were down in London I was living in the YMCA and sometimes I could take Freda to a show."

After D-Day, when C-in-C felt the western flank was not exposed to serious attack, except perhaps from submarines, he moved Knox and his chums to Falmouth. Knox remembered "SOO started us on long-distance hauls. This is the first time they'd ever done this with boats like ours, right down into the estuary at Brest. That's a long, long haul from Falmouth; we'd leave about noon to get there by dusk. Our main concern was never to run on our outside fuel tanks but going that distance we had to go on outside tanks. Fortunately we'd be heading back by that time, but it *did* give us a lot of concern. We lived, always, with this fear, the fear of explosion from the high-octane gas. No RN boats ever tried to go this distance. The Canadians tried it out first, to see if it worked. Then we'd go there and stay overnight and then hole up during the daytime, hide under a tree in an inlet. Actually that wasn't too dangerous then because the Allies had pretty well got control of the skies.

"We were watching for submarines trying to sneak out of Brest. We never did see any, mainly we came across fishing boats. Finally SOO decided to try to put us overnight in a wee village, L'Aberbach, on the Normandy coast, which SOO said had been liberated by Patton's advancing armies. Well, I don't know whether that was correct or not. The first night we got in I remember waking up and wondering why the boat was on such a damn funny angle. Of course, we were on the bottom. Vulnerable. The tide came in and I felt better. It wasn't pleasant, waiting. We got in there and the French were *scared*, and they were scared for us. I can remember some funny things in that little town, though. We went into the local pub and they gave us a great time.

"We spent maybe two or three hours with them; lots of wine, no booze. I don't think they were afraid for us because of the proximity of German troops, but I think they were afraid of collaborators amongst their own people. This was just off Ile D'Ouessant, Ushant Island, off Brest. We were there for two or three days, waiting because we expected the German garrison to be evacuated; when they were we were supposed to clobber them. They didn't evacuate them so we left.

"I remember one beautiful afternoon there. I saw the soldiers attacking Brest. I could see shelling and smoke and I saw an American jeep go racing through the flak, through the village. All in the jeep had their heads down, going about as fast as a jeep could go. Then, right in the midst of the battle, a canoe comes out from the shore, a double-paddle canoe, with a young lady in a bikini sitting in the bow and a man in his bathing suit paddling. They came out with some chickens to trade for coffee and soap. A peculiar war. Even a good war.

"We had these unusual contrasts. I often remarked, at the time, that our life was such a contrast. At night we were in the terror of darkness and gunfire and noise and smoke and flame and death. The next morning we'd be back in that beautiful countryside: green fields, warm summer sun, the smell of clover and flowers and the sound of children laughing at play. The contrast was almost undesirable. In other words, you'd rather stay with the horrors while you were at it, than to keep breaking back and forth. We had various actions after that, I forget . . .

"We got in a terrible foo-fa-rah one night there, one night with the Polish destroyers *Blyskawica* and *Piorun*. Aw! They were sure shooting the hell out of us. Jack McClelland got shot at. 'Jake' he was called. He was in the 65th. He talks about *Blyskawica* and *Piorun* shooting at them one night. I can remember because I was the first one to really raise the alarm, because I knew we had drifted across the parallel, out of our area. Yes, it was the same night. I remember – I rang the action bells before anyone on the other bridges was awake. It was a beautiful calm night. You could see everywhere and I could see these darn shapes. I think the radar must have gone asleep, too. Then the Poles just opened up on us. I remember trying to get out of there. We got away first. We didn't wait for any orders. They were firing right at us. I remember Les McLernon was *good*. He'd wait for the first fall of shot and then he'd go hard over in the opposite direction. Then he count, one, two, three – then hard over the other way and the shot would come right down where we had left.

"But we were saved by an RN frigate. She heard us yelling over the r/t, 'For Christ sake, lay off. We're Canadians! We're friendly forces!' But that didn't stop them. So our RN group commander in the directing frigate – our Senior Officer for a whole area and several units of MTBs – came up on the voice intercom with the proper voice procedure and the identification code, a calm, unhurried voice with a rather vexed tone.

" 'Unknown destroyers, unknown destroyers, this is Father Abraham, Father Abraham. You are firing at my flock. Cease and desist. He sees the sparrow fall; he sees the sparrow fall. I repeat, unknown destroyer . . . '

"They stopped. I think we lost one or two men from shrapnel. So we had a lot of foo-ra-rahs.

"Kirk as a flotilla leader was daring, oh yes, a very daring leader and very much admired by the flotilla. He was a competent seaman and navigator. His rule was 'Follow me.' That is really what it was, when you went into action. The British often made him shut up. He used to call over the r/t, 'Calling all cars, calling all cars . . . ' which was something out of a cop movie or radio show. They'd hear that ashore and they didn't like that too much; they'd tell him to use proper r/t voice procedure. They always had trouble with the colonial's way of doing things, didn't they? But Kirk knew E-boat warfare. He knew the overall picture. Most of the captains, like McLernon of 727, had been in many fire fights in Coastal Forces. Those like McLernon and Kirk and Mabee were all experienced fighters.

"I know that the navy establishment, the RN establishment, was never enamoured about pouring money into Coastal Forces, the permanent force RN was not enamoured as to the effectiveness of these forces. I think that was a built-in bias rather than based on actual fact. But we *did* cost a lot of money, for small craft we were high-priced help. The boat was expensive. Yes, and the gasoline. I remember it's equivalent in Canadian dollars was about three dollars a gallon (in 1944!) and we carried fifteen thousand gallons. Jack McClelland, who has handled a lot of money in his life, is still a bit awed by the amount of money he spent by moving his boat out of the dockyard (where Wrens couldn't come aboard for parties) to some other jetty where they could. He said, 'I bet those parties cost, in gasoline, a hundred dollars, just to move the boat half a mile.'

"We did a good harassing operation, the 65th Flotilla. German coastal shipping could never move by day because of our air superiority. They could only move at night and without us harassing them they would have got more men and supplies back and forth. Eventually, coast shipping almost completely stopped.

"I remember meeting Robert Hichens, oh yes, he was very famous . . . I met him at Lowestoft. He was a revered idol, by *everyone*. And there were other men, too, not quite to the extent of Hichens, but very close. They were extraordinary men! All volunteers, they weren't all permanent force: Peter Scott and Peter Dickens and Sam Gould . . . Hichens was undoubtedly the star and a modest man. I mean, all bedecked with these medal ribbons, you wouldn't think he'd done anything and yet his record was absolutely outstanding.

"As the breakthrough came in Normandy and the troops started to move up the coast to Calais, the last thing we did was go down to St. Malo again. SOO thought there was going to be a ship moving there and by golly there was! There was a big ship coming out of the Channel Islands; this was just about dawn. We didn't need radar it was getting so bright. We said, 'Golly! Here's the chance of a lifetime.' We couldn't see an escort *anywhere*. Of course, we primed up everything, including the torpedo tubes, which we generally didn't, and started racing in – and my gosh! It was a hospital ship. It had the Red Cross on the side. And we respected that. Well, we couldn't take a chance. No, we couldn't. It could have been a disaster. I don't suppose the E-boats would have sunk a hospital ship either, from what we knew about them. Oh no, they wouldn't ever. Even if they knew we were moving troops they wouldn't take a chance; they wouldn't do it. They were not that type. Latterly, when they had Gestapo men on board, sitting on the bridge with a pistol in his holster, I don't know what might have happened then. This was a development which really ruined the morale of those E-boat crews.

"One morning, though, when we went out of there, we were wondering what was going to happen to this Isle Ushant which had this great big battery on it and the Germans were trying to hold all these batteries that were offshore. It was manned, I remember, by a German commander with Italian troops. It had fired on us quite a bit when we'd be in that area. That day, what a sight coming over the horizon from the west. It was *Warspite*; so, we sat back as she bombarded the battery. That did it! That did them in, finally.

Midshipman Don Harrison joined Oliver Mabee's boat in September, 1944. The Captain did his job, the First Lieutenant did his job, the Navigator did his job, and Harrison did everything else. Being a stranger to warfare he was of two minds about seeing his first action. But it happened on his first time on the coast of France when 745 was shot at by 88mm shore batteries. He was relieved to note that the Captain did not stay to debate the issue with these large guns.

About two months later he was moved to MTB 736 as Navigator – promotion came rapidly in those days. Archie Byers was his Captain (he had been a timber cruiser in British Columbia before the war). In the autumn of 1944 the flotilla was based mostly at Yarmouth doing Z patrols and sometimes on on offensive sweep over to the other coast.

At this time of the war there was not a lot of enemy coastal traffic moving up and down the Dutch coast. The Germans were trying to supply the isolated garrisons that had held out as the Canadian troops by-passed them. Once they did move in on one or two merchant ships that were heavily escorted by flak trawlers, R-boats, E-boats, perhaps six or seven escorts to each ship. The MTBs didn't mind taking risk, but this was not really worth it.

Harrison only saw Kirkpatrick socially in harbour. One of his classmates – another midshipman from *Royal Roads* – had gone to Kirk's boat so Harrison got invited over. Midshipman Ian Davidson had been known as "Flossy" Davidson all through naval college because he was considered rather too artsy-fartsy for sailoring. But when Mrs. Kirkpatrick, Winnifred Kirkpatrick, would come down to the boat to pour tea on an afternoon in harbour Harrison would be invited over, meet the great man, and marvel at how Flossy would chat socially with Mrs. Kirkpatrick about the arts and crafts and classical music. It certainly was not a typical picture of an MTB wardroom on an afternoon in harbour.

After the Canadian Army by-passed Dunkirk and took the port of Ostend and after it was cleared, four MTB flotillas were based there, living on their boats. The 65th spent the winter alternating back and forth between Holland and Britain. Ostend harbour was full of wrecks – the Germans had sunk a lot of small ships and demolished everything they could. The object was to open a convoy route into Antwerp. The Germans were quite heavily encamped on the south shore of the Scheldt estuary at Breskens and also further down the coast at Zeebrugge. These shore batteries controlled the approaches to Antwerp.

"We mounted an invasion of Royal Marines in LCAs with covering cruisers and destroyers. The 65th was standing offshore to screen them against attempts by E-boats to harass the landing forces and, although the MTB hands did not see that much of the close-in fighting, they saw the results when they got into harbour afterwards. A Fairmile came into Ostend which had taken a shell through the bridge – in the starboard side, out the port side – killing the captain, the coxswain, and the first lieutenant, who had been all standing in a row. There was blood just pouring down the scuppers, just like a pirate story. A terrible sight! I had heard of the scuppers running red with blood but that's the only time I've seen it. I hope I never see it again.

"One must feel a certain admiration for the German garrisons who were hanging out. We had to hand it to them. They were tough, dedicated people. Every night E-boats would come down, lay mines in the swept channel, and we would chase them away. They came down from their base at Ijmuiden and our flotilla would sail, rendezvous with our mother frigate who would vector us on. Our boats leave about sunset, do a night's work, and come in about eight a.m. So, a few hours' sleep, later in the day sightseeing around town, then out to sea again at sunset. We patrolled two nights out of three. The Belgians ashore were friendly and, of course, glad to see us. It was rather fun because there were good shops, restaurants, good wine; sometimes we would just doze peaceably in the park." Harrison remembers in the spring of 1945 saying, "Isn't it marvellous. I don't have to write any final examinations."

The war was now entering its sixth year, and the world of coastal craft had developed a culture with its own folkways and mores. Idiosyncrasies abounded. One flotilla was practically exclusively officered by the permanent force; they made a point of wearing long scarves done up in their school colours, and all wore their hair much longer than was usual. After all, there was no need to lower one's sartorial standards just because one is in a small boat and not a pukka man-of-war.

The routine was to leave Ostend at sunset, do a patrol, and in the morning go on to Flushing – the harbour of Walcheren Island – and stay over during the day. There was a nice lake in the middle of the island; by now they carried a twelve-foot dinghy and they'd go sailing. They would be alongside *Thames Queen*, an old paddlewheeler that used to carry trippers from London to Ramsgate. In her they could have a shower and better meals than could be provided by their own galley. The V-1 flying bombs were chugging their way over, mostly to the U.K. but some were aimed at Flushing. Stores were always difficult to come by but now it was a science; when passing a sunken, abandoned merchantman they would go to looting stations. The water off the Dutch coast is shallow and the superstructure is still dry. On the Watch and Quarter Bill each hand had his cruising station for normal watchkeeping, his defence station when half the ship's company was closed up, his action station, his station for entering harbour, and his looting station. On one occasion they got half a dozen 20mm gun barrels from a sunken American ship.

Cahill found that after the action moved north to Ostend the life became almost pleasant. They would go into Flushing in the morning, spend the day there, then do another patrol back to Ostend. While there, the ship's company made friends with a group of United States Army Air Force and three airmen came down one evening and did a night patrol with them. "We got on quite well and when we had shore leave we would spend it with the USAAF. But like all ratings we talked too much and talked too loudly and there is not much privacy in an MTB.

Our friends in the USAAF had said that on our next long leave they could take us home to New York because they were going to do a ferry run. We had this long leave coming, or we thought we did, but Kirk fooled us. He gave us our long leave six days at a time. So we couldn't get home. He had worked a crew up at considerable trouble and expense and he wanted to keep it in England.

"Les Bowerman was a nice enough fellow but he wasn't easy to work for. Anything that stood in the way of the welfare of his engines caused the engine-room crew to have a hard time. One evening – talking about the relationship between Kirkpatrick and the engine-room crew and his confidence in them – Bowerman had one generator stripped for maintenance and Kirkpatrick wanted to go to sea. He said to Bowerman, 'Can you get that generator going?' Bowerman, much to the disgust of all the rest, who wanted a night in harbour, said, 'Yes, I can get it going.' He worked all night in that engine-room and made his hands work, too, putting that generator back together. We went to sea. It might have endeared him to the Captain but his stokers didn't think much of it."

Toward the end the pace heated up and the usual routine was to sail about three p.m., return about seven a.m., land wounded, re-ammunition, re-store, take on fresh water, and refuel. They would finish by 11:30, have a tot of rum, sleep for three hours, and sail again. Though nothing was happening, Cahill couldn't sleep at sea. He could make himself comfortable somewhere, but he was expecting action to be joined at any minute, the adrenalin was flowing, and he just lay there all tensed up waiting for something to start.

The rates of pay have always been notoriously low in the RCN, particularly in those years, and when on one of their five-day leaves in London they ran out of money, along with David Wright, the hands took a job working in a brewery. They got twelve shillings a day and all the beer they could put in their burberries when they left each day. This gave them good flying speed for the evening's adventures. Then it was back to their boats for a different kind of adventure.

"One night the 6-pounder gunner was adrift, didn't sail with us. That night we ran into a fleet of E-boats between Ostend and Flushing, fired star shell and closed in, within 300 yards, then within 200 yards, and if our regular gunner had been on board they would all have been dead. He was a first-rate shot, he never missed. We lost a good opportunity at enemy ships that night because of one hand's slackness. But it was a good sign of the sort of Captain Kirk was. He could have sent him to chokey. He could have sent him away for ninety days or longer. He could certainly have drafted him off the ship. But he was not going to lose a crack gunner. Anyway, this gunner didn't get any leave at all for a long, long time – like the rest of the war. I don't think Kirk ever completely forgave him but he still had a crack gunner."

*  *  *

As the war moved to its climax and as our troops got deeper into France and Holland and eventually into the German homeland, day-to-day life assumed a more festive air. One much appreciated visit they had was from Bishop Wells, accompanied by Padre Ernie Foote; these two Canadian clergymen officiated at Sunday divisions and church service. Bishop Wells was a stately clergyman, and while chaplains in the navy wear no rank, they have a monkey jacket with brass buttons and a cross on the sleeve. This and their "Come-to-Jesus" collar denote their function. In the Bishop's case he carried a bit more authority because he had medal ribbons from the Boer War and World War One as well as this war.

The festive air was enhanced by the Dutch flotillas paying off so that they could return to their liberated country. They threw an elaborate dinner party at Dover, called a *Rijsttafel* – a rice table. By November the fighting moved up to the Hook of Holland and Ijmuiden and they were doing patrols similar to those described for the 65th, based mostly in Ostend and running up and down the coast. Trips to Buckingham Palace were becoming more frequent as the gongs were handed out. His Majesty dished them out at a great rate to some of the longest queues in London. By this time Bones Burk had received two bars to his DSC and had two Mentioned in Despatches.

Canadian Army nurses by this time were numerous and Glen Creba became engaged to one. In Ostend the officers in the Shorts were now living ashore at the Queen Mary Hotel, which had been the E-boat officers' mess. Joseph, the owner/manager, greeted them and showed them to their handsome rooms with the same aplomb, no doubt, as he had greeted the E-boat officers. Law's group also went to Cercle Inter Allée. A palatial staircase was flanked by potted palms, and at the top was a large room beautifully decorated with paintings by contemporary Belgian artists. In the centre was a large chandelier beneath which was a circular dance floor. When the orchestra wasn't playing, the pianist, Charlie, tinkled away. The main liquid was apples steeped in alcohol. One bite was quite enough for ten minutes. The Coastal Forces, soldiers of all nationalities, nursing sisters of several different armies, and females of local talent jammed the room and formed a merry throng. Every so often a newcomer would be sprinkled by the Mannikin Pee to hilarious laughter.

One day, in February, 1945, there was a terrible holocaust in Ostend when most of Law's 29th and a lot of other torpedo boats and gun boats caught fire and blew up. There had been a lot of high-octane gasoline in the harbour and it ignited. The blast was felt for miles as torpedoes and depth charges exploded. The explosions continued for seven minutes and the concussion was felt on the shores of England and across the North Sea. Seven British and five Canadian MTBs were destroyed. Sixty lives were lost, twenty-six from the 29th. Canada's Minister of the Navy, the Honourable Angus L. Macdonald, telegraphed to Law:

> I have been thinking much about you in the last few days and should like to express my great personal sympathy over what has happened. I know how you must feel about a matter of this kind, but you may be sure that what you have accomplished is, in itself, sufficient to justify you and your officers and men for all time.

Tony Law talked it over with Bones Burk. The war was coming to an end. Victory was only a few months off. It was pointless to start again. They both came home.

Thus, the saga of Tony Law's 29th Canadian MTB Flotilla and Jim Kirkpatrick's 65th MGB Flotilla draws to a close. Their battles were in the highest tradition of the Royal Canadian Navy. They never refused action when success was even remotely possible. Many died, but those who still live will remember with pride. It had been a good war, well fought.

Just before D Day Knox's 743 got a large hole in her and went to refit. So Knox was in front of Buckingham Palace watching the King and the Queen and the young princesses waving when the news of our return to the continent was announced. Although they had been holed many times and had several wounded (including Knox, who was hit once in the neck), no one was killed and so he found his war eminently satisfactory. It is satisfying to end it outside Buckingham Palace waving to your Monarch.

On V-E Day there was an intriguing signal from the Kreigsmarine:

> The Commander of the Bundesmarine [the admiral commanding E-boats], refuses to surrender to anybody but MTBs. Representatives of every MTB flotilla are to greet these E-boats off the Hook of Holland and escort them to home waters. The port of

surrender will be signaled separately, referring to this signal.
Proceed with all despatch.

It was rather like the Grand Fleet meeting the High Seas Fleet in 1918.
At least twelve MTBs steamed across to the other side of the Channel in
two columns and the Führer der Schnellboote put to sea in an E-boat
(and leading others). With his Admiral's flag flying he steamed southwest between our two columns. The two columns turned blue 18 so
we were now steaming in the same direction and we brought them
back to England.

And what of the Canadian 56th MGB-MTB Flotilla of Lieutenant-Commander Corny Burke in the Mediterranean? They went on to more
battles and more victories. They had a good war, too. Corny had arrived
at that state of bliss where he never again had any trouble with the
Senior Officer. He *was* the SO.

Toward the end of the war after Maitland and Ladner had left, Burke
was reading KR&AI and discovered that if one wrote to Buckingham
Palace one could receive autographed photographs of Their Majesties
for the wardroom. Of course, he had seen these in other ships but it
never occurred to anybody that little boats were entitled to such things.
So he duly wrote and in the fulness of time there arrived two signed
photographs, of which he was very proud, particularly because they
were the only small boat to have them.

On paying off they were to be returned to Buckingham Palace. It
was very clearly set forth. Burke said, "I had no intention of doing that.
So, I was leaving before the ship was paid off and the war was still going
on and Reynolds by this time was in command, gone from an eighteen-
year-old midshipman, then a twenty-year-old sub-lieutenant in command. 'Now look, Reynolds, I'm going to write these off, destroyed by
enemy action. I'll leave them up in the wardroom but after you pay off,
you mail them off to me, you understand? You can have the ship's bell,'
says I kindly. So it was agreed and I got my pictures. In writing them off
I just picked a date. I didn't even bother to check a date. I just picked
any date. I said they were destroyed by enemy action. I was summoned
by Captain Stevens.

" 'Do you know who Rear-Admiral Berry is?'

" 'No, sir.'

" 'He is the assistant to the Second Sea Lord. And do you know what he does? He makes appointments for captains and when I saw an envelope on my desk this morning from the naval assistant to the Second Sea Lord, I said, 'Thank God! My appointment has come. I'm going to be promoted. I opened the letter and it's all about Mr. Corny Bloody Burke.'

" 'Oh, indeed, sir,'

" 'And the letter pointed out that Rear-Admiral Berry (how he got into it, I don't know) but he found out (and how such a thing could have crossed his desk is forever a mystery to me) and he had checked, or had someone check (because it was unusual for boats to be writing off pictures of Their Majesties), he'd had this matter checked and found out that the 658 wasn't in action in the night in question.'

"I asked if he would care to come aboard and discuss the matter. I rushed back to the boat and got clean handkerchiefs and draped the photographs. Captain Stevens came in and sat down and gave no indication whatsoever that he'd even seen the photographs.

"He said, 'Burke, I'll tell you what I'll do. I'll write to Admiral Berry and I'll say that the boat was actually in action to the best of my knowledge but the date was wrong for some reason, the boat had been frequently in action, and it was one of those times.'

"Well, when I got to London on the way home, my father-in-law, Commander Henry Bell-Irving, was in London and was a temporary member of White's Club in St. James. As you know, there is no stuffier, more exclusive men's club in the entire world. But due to the exigencies of the war, he was a member and he decided he'd invite us around. White's Club on that night, because the war was won, was full of very, very senior types indeed. I found one Rear-Admiral who was deep in drink, leaning up against the bar, and I chatted with him on equal terms because we were both into the Scotch. He was telling me what he told Monty and he was dropping names all over the place. Well, I said, 'I haven't done much, sir. But I'm one of the first to write off pictures of their Majesties since Nelson's time and get away with it. All of a sudden from being drunk he was very sober indeed, and with steely Rear-Admiral's eyes, said,

" 'So *you* wrote that lettah!'

"And who was I talking to but Rear-Admiral Berry. What bad luck! But he forgave me. At that point he was in a forgiving mood. We got back to Canada in May of '45. Peace was declared just as we were getting back. Maitland, Ladner, and I all crossed in a troopship. London, then New York, and our wives – two wives, Tom wasn't married then – came east from Vancouver on the train and met us in Montreal.

"We got to Ottawa and Douglas Abbott had just been made Naval Minister, succeeding Angus L. Macdonald. He'd only been in the job about two weeks and he instituted the policy that any officers returning from overseas were to report to him. So Maitland and Ladner and I troop up to Abbott's office and around his office were photographs of major Canadian vessels of war. One of the biggest pictures was the *Quebec* (formerly the *Uganda*) where I had traded gin for bread. Maitland immediately recognized the *Uganda* and said, 'Oh, look! There's the old *Uganda*, now the *Quebec*.' And Abbott gave an enormous sigh of relief, 'Oh, that's the *Quebec*,' said he. 'I've been wondering. I knew she was an important ship but I didn't like to ask.'

"We were very fortunate to have been three close friends fighting as much of the war together as we did. We supported each other on all occasions. I always felt safe with Tommy Ladner as my next astern. His boat was *always* where it was needed. Doug Maitland was a great leader. He was a fine, fine leader in every respect and people were prepared to follow him with the utmost confidence; he was highly successful. We had a good war following Doug."

# Epilogue

It is fifty years since the guns started firing in World War Two and Canadians went to sea in landing craft, motor launches, gun boats, torpedo boats, and destroyers. Canadians fought a limited action in Korea from 1950 to 1954, in ships you have met in these pages – *Haida*, *Huron*, *Athabaskan* (the second), *Iroquois*, *Algonquin*, *Sioux* . . . But there has been peace for a longer period these past forty years than ever before in history, probably due to our alliance in NATO. Our enemy then is an ally now – West German destroyers sail with ours in a NATO squadron. Our ally then, Russia, has been an enemy for forty years but may soon be, if not an ally, at least more amiable. We have *retired* admirals today who have never heard a shot fired in anger.

These yarns I have chronicled are mainly to satisfy men's desire to know what went before them; there is no didactic intent, although the lessons learned are there. Mostly they are tales of the adventures of young men and women. It was a hard school, and like all hard schools it prepared its students for a life where nothing again caused them too much worry. There could be no deep despair after what they had been through, and no decisions in the rest of their lives seemed difficult after those they had to make in combat. Tom Ladner is a successful lawyer; he and Maitland and Burke have all done well in Vancouver business circles. Some became better known than others – Dan Lang as Senator Lang; Jim Kirkpatrick as a judge in Kitchener, Ontario; Gordon Stead as the senior mandarin in the federal civil service; Tony Law as painter-in-residence at Saint Mary's University in Halifax . . . but they all did well in civilian life. We are mostly about seventy years old now, some eighty. Time has thinned our ranks – Charles Chaffey died a few months ago, a gallant officer was he.

There have been reunions in England to which our lads have gone and talked to Peter Scott, Peter Dickens, and scores of others; they still admit the professional sovereignty of Hichens. In the Royal York Hotel in Toronto this October about 200 of our Coastal Forces sailors and their wives will gather to remember. In June this year Alma and I made the pilgrimage to Normandy on the forty-fifth anniversary of D-Day; there were ceremonies at both the Canadian and the German cemeteries. In England afterwards we went to the MTB bases and saw some of the Canadian graves there. And remembered.

The yarns of these maritime warriors of so long ago are all told lightly and they remember the good times, the incongruities, the ballzups. War may be immoral, stupid, and a waste of money and lives, but it is admirable, inspiring, to see well-trained men selflessly giving themselves to a cause they think just. Maitland, Burke, Ladner, Stead, Budge Bell-Irving, and a dozen others gathered at the Vancouver Club a year ago to talk to the Military Historian from National Defence Headquarters, Alec Douglas, CD, Ph.D. Whatever the pecking order now is in civilian life, there is a different one here. At one point four of us were trying to decide what might be best to do. I had no view since I was a guest. Corny Burke said it would be best if we did this. Tommy Ladner said it would be best if we did that. There was a silence; both looked at Maitland.

Last year when I was in Pointe Claire I had dinner with Bob Moyse, his wife Caryl, and Bones Burk (Jean was in England visiting relatives and friends). Bob gets wound up, exhilarated, emotional, and he talked a lot before and during dinner. Story after story. I noticed Caryl keeping a maternal eye on him; Bones, I thought, was looking at him with compassion. With the desert and a glass of port there was a silence. Bob was musing; nobody interrupted his thoughts. Then he said, "You know, Hal, we tell you all these stories, and laugh and joke about what we did. We don't tell you about limping home in the early dawn, exhausted now the adrenalin has stopped flowing, soaking wet, the boat full of holes, perhaps some dead, and the wounded crying out in pain that the morphine injection cannot completely stop."

There are no good wars.

# Appendix A: Honours and Awards

In the fifteenth century "The Gazette" published news and gossip of interest to the court – both the Royal Family and the Courtiers. By the reign of Queen Elizabeth I it expanded to include formal announcements of matters of interest to the administration of the realm and of the Empire. This became the official organ of H.M. Government, *The London Gazette*. One hears such expressions as "He has been gazetted three times for gallantry." The Preamble is always: "His Majesty the King has been graciously pleased to award to . . . (name)."

**Harry G. Dewolf**
1 January 1941: Mention in Despatches (MID)
  Citation: The London Gazette does not provide any details of the MID, listing his name only – Commander Harry George DeWolf, Royal Canadian Navy.
1 January 1943: Mention in Despatches (MID)
  Citation: For valuable services in command of HMC destroyers in the early months of the war in convoy escort duty in the Western Atlantic, and overseas during the evacuation of France.
9 May 1944: Distinguished Service Order (DSO)
  Citation: For gallant and distinguished services as Senior Officer of Destroyers in successful night actions in the English Channel on the 26th and 29th April, 1944.
29 August 1944: Distinguished Service Cross (DSC)
  Citation: For outstanding courage, skill and devotion to duty in HM Canadian Ship *Haida* in action with German destroyers.
10 October 1944: Mention In Despatches (MID)
  Citation: For bravery, skill and devotion to duty in HM Canadian Ship *Haida* in anti U-Boat operations.

14 November 1944: Mention In Despatches (MID)

Citation: For courage and determination in HM Canadian Ship *Haida* in a series of successful attacks on enemy escorted convoys off the coast of France.

1 January 1946: Commander of the Most Excellent Order of the British Empire (CBE)

Citation: Commodore DeWolf has held various administrative appointments including that of Director of Plans at Naval Service Headquarters at a time of rapid expansion of the Royal Canadian Navy. As Commanding Officer of one of HM Canadian Tribal Class Destroyers he served at sea with unparalleled success during the invasion of the continent. On being re-appointed ashore, he holds the position of Assistant Chief of the Naval Staff, which appointment is being filled with perspicacity and ability.

6 May 1946: Legion of Merit, Degree of Officer

Citation: For exceptionally meritorious conduct in the performance of outstanding service while serving as Chief Staff Officer to Rear Admiral G.C. Jones, Royal Canadian Navy. He frequently conferred with Commander Task Force TWENTY-FOUR and his staff in connection with planning and the operational control of the surface forces under Commander Task Force TWENTY-FOUR. His excellent professional grasp of strategic and tactical situations, together with his intelligent and cooperative attitude, contributed materially to the success of operations conducted by Commander Task Force TWENTY-FOUR.

December, 1948: King Haakon VII's Cross of Liberation

### James Calcutt Hibbard

1 January 1943: Distinguished Service Cross (DSC)

Citation: For gallantry and distinguished services before the enemy. Acting Commander Hibbard has served over a considerable period of time in command of HMCS *Skeena* and as Senior Officer of a Convoy Escort Group. He has consistently shown himself capable of carrying responsibility and of setting an inspiring example to those about him. He has carried out his duties with the utmost zeal and efficiency, particularly when he was Senior Officer of a Group escorting one of the first convoys to be heavily attacked by a U-boat wolf pack in mid-Atlantic. On this occasion the convoy was under attack for sixty-six hours.

14 November 1944: Bar to Distinguished Service Cross (DSC and Bar)

Citation: For good service in destruction of a submarine.

## Herbert Sharples Rayner

11 March 1941: Distinguished Service Cross (DSC)
Citation: For courage and enterprise in action against enemy submarines.

11 July 1944: Mention in Despatches (MID)
Citation: For leadership, resolution and skill in HM Canadian Ship *Huron* in a successful action with enemy destroyers in the English Channel.

29 August 1944: Bar to Distinguished Service Cross (DSC and Bar)
Citation: For outstanding courage, skill and devotion to duty in HM Canadian Ship *Huron* in action with German destroyers.

10 October 1944: Mention In Despatches (MID)
Citation: For bravery, skill and devotion to duty in HM Canadian Ship *Huron* in anti U-Boat operations.

15 September 1947: Croix de Guerre (avec Palme)

## John Hamilton Stubbs

3 December 1942: Distinguished Service Order (DSO)
Citation: For services in action with enemy submarines while serving in HM Canadian Ships.

11 July 1944: Distinguished Service Cross (DSC)
Citation: For leadership, resolution and skill in HM Canadian Ship *Athabaskan* in a successful action with enemy destroyers in the English Channel.

(Note: Lt.-Commander Stubbs was lost with his command, HMCS *Athabaskan*, on 29 April 1944. This award appears to be related to earlier actions and, although approved before his death, was only gazetted in July.)

## John Douglas Maitland

30 May 1944: Distinguished Service Cross (DSC)
Citation: For outstanding courage, leadership and skill in Light Coastal Craft in many daring attacks on enemy shipping in enemy waters.

12 September 1944: Mention in Despatches (MID)
Citation: For courage, determination and skill in Light Forces in successful actions with enemy coastal forces off the west coast of Italy.

11 January 1945: Croix de Guerre (avec Palme)
Citation: For exceptional services in co-operation with the French Forces during operations on the Island of Elba.

26 January 1945: Bar to Distinguished Service Cross (DSC and Bar)
Citation: For outstanding courage, skill and determination in operations in the Mediterranean in Light Coastal Craft.

## Cornelius Burke

30 May 1944: Distinguished Service Cross (DSC)
 Citation: For outstanding leadership and skill in Light Coastal Craft in
 many daring attacks on enemy shipping in enemy waters.
11 July 1944: Mention in Despatches (MID)
 Citation: For outstanding leadership, courage and skill in Light Coastal
 Craft in a successful engagement with the enemy in the Adriatic.
23 January 1945: Bar to Distinguished Service Cross (DSC and Bar)
 Citation: For outstanding courage, skill and determination in opera-
 tions in the Mediterranean in Light Coastal Craft.
24 April 1945: Second Bar to Distinguished Service Cross (DSC and Two
Bars)
 Citation: For courage, outstanding leadership and devotion to duty
 whilst serving in Light Coastal Forces in an attack on the Island of
 Lussino.

## Thomas Ellis Ladner

10 September 1942: Mention in Despatches (MID)
 Citation: The London Gazette does not provide any details of the MID,
 listing his name only.
10 November 1942: Mention in Despatches (MID)
 Citation: For skill and bravery in an attack on an enemy Convoy while
 serving HM Motor Gun Boats.
30 May 1944: Mention in Despatches (MID)
 Citation: For outstanding courage, leadership and skill in Light Coastal
 Craft in many daring attacks on enemy shipping in enemy waters.
1 January 1945: Distinguished Service Cross (DSC)
 Citation: For gallantry or outstanding service in the face of the enemy,
 or for zeal, patience and cheerfulness in dangerous waters and for
 setting an example of wholehearted devotion to duty, upholding the
 highest traditions of the Royal Canadian Navy.
26 January 1945: Bar to Distinguished Service Cross (DSC and Bar)
 Citation: For outstanding courage, skill and determination in operations in the Mediterranean in Light Coastal Craft.
20 February 1945: Mention in Despatches (MID)
 Citation: For services in action in the Mediterranean in August, 1944,
 in Light Coastal Forces.

## James Ralph Hilborn Kirkpatrick

3 March 1944: Distinguished Service Cross (DSC)
 Citation: For outstanding courage and skill in action with the enemy
 in Light Coastal Craft.

3 October 1944: Mention in Despatches (MID)
Citation: For undaunted courage, resolution and skill during a series of actions against enemy forces while serving in Light Coastal Craft.

## Malcolm Campbell Knox

12 June 1945: Distinguished Service Cross (DSC)
Citation: For bravery, skill and great devotion to duty in damaging attacks against enemy shipping off the Coast of France.

## Charles Anthony Francis Law

31 March 1942: Mention in Despatches (MID)
Citation: For daring and resolution while serving in HM Destroyers, Motor Torpedo Boats, and Motor Gun Boats in daylight attacks at close range and against odds upon the German Battle-Cruisers *Scharnhorst* and *Gneisenau* and the cruiser *Prinz Eugen*.
30 May 1944: Mention in Despatches (MID)
Citation: For outstanding courage, leadership and skill in Light Coastal Craft in many daring attacks on enemy shipping in enemy waters.
29 August 1944: Distinguished Service Cross (DSC)
Citation: For gallantry, skill, determination and undaunted devotion to duty during the initial landings of Allied Forces on the coast of Normandy.

## Charles Arthur Burk

4 May 1943: Mention in Despatches (MID)
Citation: For bravery, skill and dash while serving in HM Light Coastal Craft in action against the enemy in the Channel.
2 May 1944: Distinguished Service Cross (DSC)
Citation: For gallant and distinguished services in Light Coastal Craft in successful engagements with the enemy.
14 November 1944: Bar to Distinguished Service Cross (DSC and Bar)
Citation: For courage, leadership and determination in close action with the enemy while serving in Light Coastal Craft.
26 December 1944: Second Bar to Distinguished Service Cross (DSC and Two Bars)
Citation: For gallantry, skill and determination and undaunted devotion to duty during the landing of Allied Forces on the coast of Normandy.
30 January 1945: Mention in Despatches (MID)
Citation: For courage and determination in an attack on an enemy convoy while serving in Light Coastal Craft.

### Charles Donald Chaffey
26 December 1944: Mention in Despatches (MID)
Citation: For gallantry, skill, determination and undaunted devotion to duty during the landing of Allied Forces on the coast of Normandy.

### Desmond William Piers
2 June 1943: Distinguished Service Cross (DSC)
Citation: This officer has served continuously in His Majesty's Canadian destroyers since the commencement of hostilities. As Senior Officer of a Convoy Escort Group in the North Atlantic, he has, by his vigorous leadership and aggressive attack, been an inspiration to those serving under his command.

### Eric Everesley Garrat Boak
19 June 1945: Distinguished Service Cross (DSC)
Citation: For outstanding courage, determination and skill while serving in HMCS *Sioux*, in escorting a convoy to and from North Russia under continuous and fierce attacks by the enemy and in exceptionally hard weather conditions.
30 May 1946: Knight (First Class) of the Order of Saint Olaf
Citation: In recognition of assistance given at the evacuation of the Norwegian population of Sorova, West Finmark, Norway, in March, 1945.

### Patrick David Budge
18 February 1941: Mention in Despatches (MID)
Citation: For good services in an attack on an enemy U-boat.
29 September 1944: Distinguished Service Cross (DSC)
Citation: For outstanding courage, skill and devotion to duty in HM Canadian Ship *Huron* in action with German destroyers.

### John Alexander Charles
2 January 1945: Mention in Despatches (MID)
Citation: For good services during the landing of Allied Forces at Anzio.

### Frederick John Boyer
23 May 1944: Mention in Despatches (MID)
Citation: For outstanding courage, resolution, leadership skill and devotion to duty in operations which led to successful landings on the Italian mainland and at Salerno.

21 December 1944: mention in Despatches (MID) (Posthumous)
Citation: For good services during the landing of Allied Forces at Anzio.

### Thomas Huston Forrester

20 June 1944: Distinguished Service Medal (DSM)
Citation: For great courage and leadership when a landing craft was sunk off Anzio.

### Thomas George Fuller

14 July 1942: Distinguished Service Cross (DSC)
Citation: For skill, bravery and resolution while serving in HM Motor Torpedo Boats and Motor Gun Boats in an attack on an Enemy Convoy near the French Coast.

4 April 1944: Bar to Distinguished Service Cross (DSC and Bar)
Citation: For undaunted courage, determination and endurance . . . in light Coastal Forces in many sweeps against enemy shipping in the Aegean under fierce and constant attack from the air, and in maintaining supplies to the Islands of Kos and Lemos until they fell to superior enemy forces.

5 September 1944: Second Bar to Distinguished Service Cross (DSC and Two Bars)
Citation: For great courage, determination and skill in operations in Light Coastal Craft.

5 December 1944: Mention in Despatches (MID)
Citation: For great skill and daring while serving in Light Coastal Craft in a series of sharp and successful encounters with enemy forces in the Adriatic and Aegean.

### Gordon Wilson Stead

29 September 1942: Distinguished Service Cross (DSC)
Citation: For bravery and sustained devotion to duty in keeping the approaches to the Harbours of Malta clear of mines.

23 May 1944: Bar to Distinguished Service Cross (DSC and Bar)
Citation: For outstanding courage, resolution, leadership, skill and devotion to duty in HM Ships . . . in operations which led to successful landings on the Italian mainland and at Salerno.

### William Prine Hayes

14 November 1944: Mention in Despatches (MID)
Citation: For courage and determination in HM Canadian Ship *Iroquois* in a series of successful attacks on enemy escorted convoys off the coast of France.

10 July 1945: Mention in Despatches (MID)

Citation: For resolution, zeal and skill whilst serving in HM Canadian Ship *Iroquois* in an attack on enemy shipping off Norway.

### Harold Ernest Thomas Lawrence

19 May 1942: Mention in Despatches (MID)

Citation: For good service in HMCS *Moose Jaw* in action against enemy submarines and in rescuing survivors from a sunken Merchantman.

16 December 1942: Distinguished Service Cross (DSC)

Citation: For gallant services in action with enemy submarines while serving in HMCS *Oakville*. Lieutenant Lawrence was in charge of a boarding party of two men from HMCS *Oakville* which attempted to prevent the scuttling of a U-boat. With complete disregard for his own safety, this Officer, accompanied by a Petty Officer, boarded the U-boat, and having subdued the enemy crew, he took action in an endeavour to prevent the scuttling of the U-boat, notwithstanding the fact that it was then sinking. His spirited and determined conduct was worthy of the highest traditions of the Royal Canadian Navy.

### John Gordon McClelland

14 June 1945: Mention in Despatches (MID)

Citation: This Officer exhibited a high degree of seamanship and courage in command of one of His Majesty's Canadian Motor Launches engaged in dangerous duties whilst assisting in the recovery of enemy mines.

### Louis Raymond Pavillard

1 January 1944: Mention in Despatches (MID)

Citation: This Officer displayed outstanding gallantry and undaunted devotion to duty in an action with an enemy U-boat in the Mediterranean.

19 December 1944: Distinguished Service Cross (DSC)

Citation: For gallantry and skill in anti U-boat operations in HMCS *Camrose*.

### John Parmeter Robarts

23 May 1944: Mention in Despatches (MID)

Citation: For outstanding courage, resolution, leadership, skill and devotion to duty in HM Ships . . . in operations which led to successful landings on the Italian mainland and at Salerno.

## Anthony Hubert Gleadow Storrs

14 September 1944: Legion of Merit (U.S.A.)

Citation: Acting Commander Storrs was in command of the 31st Minesweeping Flotilla of the Sweeper Group which swept the various channels necessary to ensure the safe approach of the main Assault Force to its pre-determined position off the cost of France. A/Commander Storrs swept and marked these channels in enemy-mined waters, under cover of darkness, in a cross tide and during adverse conditions of weather. His courage, skill and sound judgement displayed in the execution of this complex and difficult operation signalled his resourcefulness and outstanding ability, and contributed materially to the success of the operation.

1 January 1945: Distinguished Service Cross (DSC)

Citation: For gallantry or outstanding service in the face of the enemy, or for zeal, patience and cheerfulness in dangerous waters and for setting an example of wholehearted devotion to duty, upholding the highest traditions of the Royal Canadian Navy.

13 February 1945: Bar to Distinguished Service Cross (DSC and Bar)

Citation: For outstanding courage and skill in minesweeping operations during the landing of Allied Forces in Normandy.

# Appendix B: Canadian Flotillas and Their Captains

|  |  | Dates in Command |
|---|---|---|
| **MTB 459** | | |
| LT | C.A. Law, RCNVR (Senior Officer of the 29th Flotilla) | 26/1/44–11/9/44 |
| LT | J.H. Shand, RCNVR | 12/9/44–14/2/45 |
| **MTB 460** | | |
| LT | D. Killam, DSC, RCNVR | 25/2/44–1/7/44 |
| **MTB 461** | | |
| LT | C.A. Burk, DSC, RCNVR | 28/2/44–17/9/44 |
| LT | T.K. Scobie, RCNVR | 18/9/44–3/2/45 |
| LT | J.R. Cunningham, RCNVR | 4/2/45–9/2/45 |
| LT | C.V. Barlow, RCNVR | 10/2/45–14/2/45 |
| **MTB 462** | | |
| LT | R.J. Moyse RCNVR | 1/3/44–28/8/44 |
| LT | J.H. Shand, RCNVR | 29/8/44–11/9/44 |
| LT | R. Paddon, RCNVR | 24/1/45–14/2/45 |
| **MTB 463** | | |
| LT | D.G. Creba, RCNVR | 16/3/44–7/7/44 |
| **MTB 464** | | |
| LT | L.C. Bishop, DSC, RCNVR | 26/3/44–24/2/45 |
| LT | C.V. Barlow, RCNVR | 25/2/45–6/3/45 |
| LT | L.C. Bishop, DSC, RCNVR | 7/3/45–9/4/45 |
| **MTB 465** | | |
| LT | C.D. Chaffey, RCNVR | 27/3/44–14/2/45 |
| **MTB 466** | | |
| LT | S.B Marshall, RCNVR | 29/3/44–27/7/44 |
| LT | T.K. Scobie, RCNVR | 28/7/44–17/9/44 |

| LT | S.B. Marshall RCNVR | 18/9/44–7/1/45 |
| LT | J.M. Adams, RCNVR | 8/1/45–14/2/45 |
| **MTB 485** | | |
| LT | D.G. Creba, RCNVR | 31/7/44–10/3/45 |
| **MTB 486** | | |
| LCDR | C.A. Law, RCNVR | 5/8/44–24/2/45 |
| LT | C.D. Chaffey, RCNVR | 25/2/45–3/3/45 |
| LT | T.K. Scobie, RCNVR | 4/3/45–8/3/45 |
| **MTB 491** | | |
| LT | C.A. Burk, DSC, RCNVR | 4/10/44–26/1/45 |
| LT | R.J. Moyse, RCNVR | 27/1/45–10/3/45 |

---

| **MTB 748** | | |
| LT | J.R.H. Kirkpatrick, RCNVR (Senior Officer of the 65th Flotilla) | 19/2/44–23/5/45 |
| **MTB 726** | | |
| LT | A.P. Morrow, RCNVR | 1/2/44–22/5/45 |
| **MTB 727** | | |
| LT | L.R. McLernon, DSC, RCNVR | 7/1/44–4/4/45 |
| LT | G.D. Pattison, RCNVR | 5/4/45–21/5/45 |
| **MTB 735** | | |
| LT | J.W. Collins, RCNVR | 14/2/44–2/10/44 |
| LT | J.R. Culley, RCNVR | 3/10/44–21/6/45 |
| **MTB 736** | | |
| LT | S.O. Greening, RCNVR | 29/3/44–10/12/44 |
| **MTB 743** | | |
| LT | M.C. Knox, RCNVR | 15/5/44–31/5/45 |
| **MTB 744** | | |
| LT | G.M. Moors, RCNVR | 14/2/44–22/10/44 |
| **MTB 745** | | |
| LT | O.B. Mabee, RCNVR | 15/1/44–19/5/45 |
| **MTB 746** | | |
| LT | G.D. Pattison, RCNVR | 11/12/44–15/1/45 |
| LT | J.W. Collins, RCNVR | 16/1/45–18/5/45 |
| **MTB 797** | | |
| LT | R.C. Smith, RCNVR | 30/12/44–12/4/45 |
| LT | R.C. Smith, RCNVR | 20/5/45–21/5/45 |

# Bibliography

Blore, Trevor. *Commissioned Bargees: The Story of the Landing Craft*. London: Hutchinson & Co., 1946.

Broome, Jack. *Convoy is to Scatter: The story of PQ 17*. London: Futura Publications, 1977.

Burrow, Len, and Emile Beaudoin. *Unlucky Lady: The Life and Death of HMCS Athabaskan*. Toronto: McClelland and Stewart, 1987.

Butcher, Alan D. *I Remember Haida*. Hantsport, Nova Scotia: Lancelot Press, 1985.

Dickens, Peter. *Night Action: MTB Flotilla at War*. London: Peter Davies, 1974.

Farley, Edward I. *PT Patrol*. New York: Exposition Press, 1957.

Harris, John. *The Sea Shall Not Have Them: Air-Sea Rescue in World War II*. London: Hurst & Blackett, 1953.

Hichens, Robert. *We Fought Them in Gunboats*. London: Michael Joseph, 1944.

Irving, David. *The Destruction of Convoy PQ 17*. London: Granada Publishing, 1985.

Jane, Fred T. *Jane's Fighting Ships*. London: Sampson Low, Marston & Co., 1945.

Jones, Basil. *And So To Battle*. Hastings: Sparkes Printers, 1969; privately printed.

Lamb, James B. *The Corvette Navy*. Toronto: Macmillan of Canada, 1978.

———. *On The Triangle Run*. Toronto: Macmillan of Canada, 1986.

Law, Anthony. *White Plumes Astern*. Halifax: Nimbus Publishers, 1989.

Lawrence, Hal.  *A Bloody War*, Toronto: Macmillan of Canada, 1979.

———.  *Tales of the North Atlantic*. Toronto: McClelland and Stewart, 1985.

Lynch, Mack.  *Salty Dips*, 3 volumes. Ottawa: The Naval Officers' Association, 1983, 1985, 1988.

———.  "HMS *Orion*." Unpublished manuscript, 1989.

Macpherson, Ken, and John Burgess.  *The Ships of Canada's Naval forces 1910-1981*. Toronto: Collins, 1981.

Morison, S.E.  *History of United States Naval Operations World War II*. Oxford: Oxford University Press, 1948.

Milner, Marc.  *North Atlantic Run: The Royal Canadian Navy and the Battle for the Convoys*. Toronto: University of Toronto Press, 1985.

Pope, Dudley.  *Flag 4: The Battle of the Coastal Forces in the Mediterranean*. London: William Kimber & Co., 1954.

Reynolds, L.C.  *Gunboat 658: Attack in Enemy Waters*. London: William Kimber & Co., 1955.

Rogers, W.L.  *Greek and Roman Naval Warfare*. Annapolis: United States Naval Institute Press, 1964.

Roskill, S.W.  *The War at Sea: 1939-1945*. 3 volumes. London: Her Majesty's Stationery Office, 1954–61.

Roy, Reginald H.  *1944: The Canadians in Normandy*. Toronto: Macmillan of Canada in collaboration with the Canadian War Museum, the National Museum of Man and National Museums of Canada.

Schull, Joseph.  *The Far Distant Ships: An Official Account of Canadian Naval Operations in the Second World War*. Ottawa: The Queen's Printer, 1952.

Sclater, William.  *Haida*. Toronto: Oxford University Press, 1946.

Scott, Peter.  *The Battle of the Narrow Seas: A History of the Light Coastal Forces in the Channel and the North Sea, 1939-1945*. London: Country Life, 1945.

Stead, Gordon.  *A Leaf Upon the Sea: A Small Ship in the Mediterranean, 1941-1943*. Vancouver: University of British Columbia Press, 1988.

Vian, Phillip.  *Action This Day*. London: Frederick Muller, 1960.

Wade, Frank.  "A Midshipman's War: The Story of a Young Man in the Mediterranean War 1941 to 1943." Vancouver, unpublished manuscript, 1989.

# Index